SEXUAL PREDATORS

Convicted sex offenders released from custody at the end of their criminal sentences pose a risk for re-offense. In many U.S. states, sexually violent predator (SVP) laws have been enacted that allow for the post-prison preventive detention of high-risk sex offenders. SVP laws require the courts to make dispositions that protect the public from harm while respecting the civil rights of the offender. This book describes these SVP laws, their constitutionality, and aspects of their operation. Courts hear expert risk testimony based heavily on the results of actuarial risk assessment. Problems associated with this testimony include the lack of a theory of recidivism risk, bias due to human decision-making, and the insularity of scholarship and practice along developmental lines. The authors propose changes in legal standards, as well as a unified developmental model that treats sexual violence as an "evolving" condition, with roots traceable to childhood and paths that extend into adolescence and adulthood.

Robert A. Prentky is Professor of Psychology and Director of Forensic Training at Fairleigh Dickinson University. He has been engaged in research and writing on sexual offenders for 35 years, evaluated or supervised the evaluation of 2,000+ sexual offenders, and has served as an expert witness for 20+ years. He is a Fellow of the American Psychological Association (2003) and the Association for Psychological Science (2006).

Howard E. Barbaree is a psychologist and Professor of Psychiatry at the University of Toronto and Vice President, Research and Academics, at Waypoint Centre for Mental Health Care. He received the 2001 Significant Achievement Award from the Association for the Treatment of Sexual Abusers and the 2011 Don Andrews Career Contribution Award from the Canadian Psychological Association. He was Editor-in-Chief of *Sexual Abuse: A Journal of Research and Treatment* from 2004 to 2010.

Eric S. Janus served as President and Dean of William Mitchell College of Law, St. Paul, MN. He is the author of *Failure to Protect: America's Sexual Predator Laws and the Rise of the Preventive State* (Cornell University, 2006). He served as co-counsel in extended litigation challenging the constitutionality of Minnesota's Sexually Dangerous Persons Act, and provided invited media commentary on sex offender policy both nationally and regionally.

This is a scholarly, thoughtful, and provocative piece of work, rich in facts and history. I had planned a quick skim, but became rapidly engrossed. Though written from a North American perspective, its arguments and messages are far from parochial, and challenge those who carry out risk assessments in legal settings as well as those who use them. It shines a spotlight on the floor where law and science attempt to dance, clearly depicting how each sways to its own music, but noting that the tune really comes from the orchestra of politics, the media, and public opinion. While the aim is "not to question the risk assessment enterprise, but ... to improve it as a tool of the law", it would be an obtuse reader who did not begin to question their own practice, their reliance on a science that is young and uncertain, and their belief that they can "get it right" (or can even be sure of what "getting it right" means). In their preface the authors say, "We appreciate that there are those who will take marked exception to our perspective, and we look forward to constructive dialogue." So do I.

Don Grubin MD FRCPsych
Professor of Forensic Psychiatry,
Newcastle University, Newcastle upon Tyne, England
(Hon) Consultant Forensic Psychiatrist, Northumberland
Tyne and Wear NHS Found Trust

Prentky, Barbaree and Janus provide a unique, comprehensive, data-driven and compelling, yet remarkably even-handed, treatise on the history, public policy, and implementation of sex offender laws. They also offer a clear, rational and ethical roadmap for the future of sex offender evaluations and their use in the legal system. An invaluable tool for forensic evaluators, this extraordinary book should also be required reading for judges, lawyers, legislators, policymakers and anyone else concerned about the prevention of sexual offending.

Charles Patrick Ewing, JD, PhD
SUNY Distinguished Service Professor Past President,
American Board of Forensic Psychology Editor,
Behavioral Sciences and the Law

Robert Prentky, Howard Barbaree, and Eric Janus offer an essential analysis of the tangled morass of research dedicated to the difficult subject of sex offender recidivism. Against an environment of social panic, *Sexual Predators: Society, Risk, and the Law* constitutes a sober, interdisciplinary resource for any audience that provides needed perspective on appropriately assessing risk without succumbing to fear.

Corey Rayburn Yung, JD
Professor of Law
University of Kansas School of Law

Sexual Predators: Society, Risk, and the Law is an in-depth, scholarly and pedagogic textbook about the complex relationships between SVP legislation for the preventive detention of high-risk sexual offenders and mental health experts' testimony and risk assessments.

Written by three outstanding and experienced academics, the book patiently explains North American SVP laws and thoroughly reviews theoretical and empirical work on human decision-making and the theory and practice of recidivism risk assessment. One chapter specifically addresses the heuristics and biases related to assessing risk under uncertain conditions.

The authors cautiously and convincingly build their cases for changes in legal standards, theory-driven risk assessment, and a developmental model of sexual violence as a problem evolving throughout life.

Together with practical examples from productive professional careers and illustrative analogies, this is a rich and thought-inspiring text with theoretically and empirically well-grounded advice for clinical practice.

The book should be greatly interesting and generally useful to advanced students and active professionals in forensic mental health, criminal justice and policy making.

Niklas Långström, MD, PhD
Psychiatrist and Professor of Psychiatric Epidemiology, Karolinska Institutet, Sweden and National Scientific Advisor, Swedish Prison and Probation Administration

In *Sexual Predators* the authors, three of the top individuals in this field, paint a nuanced, comprehensive picture of the sex offender assessment field. Although their primary focus is on sexually violent predator cases, they explore issues relevant to all sex offender evaluations. The authors provide clear explanations for what could otherwise be daunting topics—for example, the social and legal context of specialized sex offender statutes, the history and current status of sex offender assessment instruments, the role of cognitive heuristics in shaping our decisions, and the mathematical underpinnings of prediction. They propose sensible recommendations for both evaluators and legislators. The reader will be rewarded with an increased depth of understanding of the major controversies in sex offender assessment and management.

Philip H. Witt, PhD, ABPP
Past President – American Academy of Forensic Psychology

Prentky, Barbaree and Janus's book represents the most comprehensive text to date on sexually violent predators. The authors integrate research findings, case law, statistics and clinical expertise through a lens that draws on parallels from a wide range of scientific and historical domains. This unique perspective brings clarity to the most challenging aspects of sexual offender risk assessment, such as the interpretation of test data and clinical decision-making. It's a must-have text for anyone working in the field of sex offender risk assessment.

Barry Rosenfeld, PhD Professor, Department of Psychology and School of Law Fordham University

The preventive detention of sex offenders is premised on risk of re-offense. This ambitious book explains how this risk is presently assessed, identifies systematic limitations, and offers well-supported directions for improvement. The book will prove invaluable for researchers, policy-makers, and participants in sex offender civil commitment and violence prediction generally.

Fredrick Vars, JD
Associate Professor of Law
The University of Alabama School of Law

INTERNATIONAL PERSPECTIVES ON FORENSIC MENTAL HEALTH

A Routledge Book Series

Edited by Ronald Roesch and Stephen Hart
Simon Fraser University

The goal of this series is to improve the quality of health care services in forensic settings by providing a forum for discussing issues related to policy, administration, clinical practice, and research. The series will cover topics such as mental health law; the organization and administration of forensic services for people with mental disorders; the development, implementation, and evaluation of treatment programs for mental disorders in civil and criminal justice settings; the assessment and management of violence risk, including risk for sexual violence and family violence; and staff selection, training, and development in forensic systems. The book series will consider proposals for both monographs and edited works on these and similar topics, with special consideration given to proposals that promote best practice and are relevant to international audiences.

Published Titles

Learning Forensic Assessment
Rebecca Jackson

Handbook of Violence Risk Assessment
Randy K. Otto & Kevin S. Douglas

Dangerous People: Policy, Prediction, and Practice
Bernadette McSherry & Patrick Keyzer

Risk Markers for Sexual Victimization and Predation in Prison
Janet I. Warren & Shelly L. Jackson

How to Work With Sex Offenders: A Handbook for Criminal Justice, Human Service, and Mental Health Professionals, Second Edition
Rudy Flora & Michael L. Keohane

Managing Fear: The Law and Ethics of Preventive Detention and Risk Assessment
Bernadette McSherry

Case Studies in Sexual Deviance: Toward Evidence Based Practice
William T. O'Donohue

Forensic Psychological Assessment in Practice: Case Studies
Corine De Ruiter & Nancy Kaser-Boyd

Sexual Predators: Society, Risk, and the Law
Robert A. Prentky, Howard E. Barbaree & Eric S. Janus

Forthcoming Titles

Handbook of Forensic Social Work with Children
Viola Vaughan-Eden

SEXUAL PREDATORS

Society, Risk, and the Law

Robert A. Prentky
Howard E. Barbaree
Eric S. Janus

Routledge
Taylor & Francis Group
NEW YORK AND LONDON

First published 2015
by Routledge
605 Third Avenue, New York, NY 10017

and by Routledge
2 Park Square, Milton Park, Abingdon, OX14 4RN

Routledge is an imprint of the Taylor & Francis Group, an informa business

Library of Congress Cataloging-in-Publication Data
Prentky, R. A., author.
Sexual predators : society, risk and the law / by Robert A. Prentky, Howard E. Barbaree, and Eric S. Janus.
p. ; cm. — (International perspectives on forensic mental health)
Includes bibliographical references and index.
I. Barbaree, H. E. author. II. Janus, Eric S., author. III. Title.
IV. Series: International perspectives on forensic mental health.
[DNLM: 1. Sex Offenses—legislation & jurisprudence—United States. 2. Legislation as Topic—United States. 3. Risk Assessment—methods—United States. W 32.5 AA1]
HV6556
364.15′3—dc23
2014047704

ISBN: 978-0-415-87044-3 (hbk)
ISBN: 978-0-415-87045-0 (pbk)
ISBN: 978-0-203-79624-5 (ebk)

Typeset in Sabon
by Swales & Willis Ltd, Exeter, Devon, UK

To a dear friend, Dr. Doug Kirby, a kindred
spirit who took calculated risks under
conditions of uncertainty and left his heart in
his beloved mountains—a passion we shared.

RAP

To my wife Lynn, who has supported my
academic career for 40 years, by expanding
my vision, challenging my intellect, and forgiving
my distraction and absences associated
with projects like this book.

HEB

CONTENTS

SERIES FOREWORD

The International Association of Forensic Mental Health Services (IAFMHS) is an interdisciplinary professional society representing forensic professionals engaged in research and practice in forensic mental health. Its membership includes psychologists, psychiatrists, social workers, nurses, and lawyers representing over 22 countries worldwide. Its goals are to promote education, training, and research in forensic mental health and to enhance the standards of forensic mental health services in the international community. IAFMHS holds an annual conference and publishes a journal (*International Journal of Forensic Mental Health*) and a book series (International Perspectives on Forensic Mental Health).

The goal of the book series is to improve the quality of health care services in forensic settings by providing a forum for discussing issues related to policy, administration, clinical practice, and research. The series covers topics such as mental health law; the organization and administration of forensic services for people with mental disorders; the development, implementation, and evaluation of treatment programs for mental disorders in civil and criminal justice settings; the assessment and management of violence risk, including risk for sexual violence and family violence; and staff selection, training, and development in forensic mental health systems.

Sexual Predators: Society, Risk, and the Law, by Robert Prentky, Howard Barbaree, and Eric Janus, is the latest book in the series. This book serves a number of purposes. It provides an analysis of sexual predator laws, which in the United States date back to the 1930s. The authors review the legislation and legal procedures as they have evolved since that time, and note that despite many challenges to these laws, provisions for the indeterminate confinement of sexual offenders found dangerous continue to be a major focus of society's response to managing sexual predators. They then turn to the role that risk assessment plays in determining which offenders should be committed under these laws. The authors acknowledge that the demand for risk assessments of sex offenders is high and likely to continue for the foreseeable future, and one goal of the book is to ensure that best practices are used to provide empirically grounded opinions about the risk of future offending. They note that sex offender risk assessment has been largely atheoretical, and make the convincing case that the field will not progress without a clear theoretical framework. Their book provides such a framework, presenting a model for both practitioners and the courts to follow as a guide to risk assessments and how they are used in court. Their model relies on a foundation that assesses risk from multiple domains. They provide forensic evaluators with a critique of actuarial risk assessment instruments and their strengths and limitations as they are applied in sexual predator evaluations. Readers should find particularly valuable their discussion of how the broader research on the neuroscience of risky decision-making can be instructive in understanding the challenges to objectivity inherent in forensic risk assessments.

An impressive feature of this book is that it goes well beyond simply improving the current approach that favors the indeterminate confinement of sex offenders. The final chapters shift the focus away from assessment to an analysis of policy and practice. It is in these chapters that the book may have a substantive impact on the future of sexual predator assessment and treatment. They make the case that the problems associated with attempts to reduce the likelihood of re-offending "can only be addressed through policy changes that re-structure and re-prioritize demonstrated effectiveness of our interventions, be they treatment in prison or registration/notification in the community." They argue that policies emphasizing treatment of known sex offenders will not be effective in reducing sexual violence in our society. They point to research showing that the majority of sexual offenses are committed not by recidivists but by new offenders. As a consequence, placing the bulk of our resources into confining and treating sex offenders will have a limited impact on the incidence of sexual assaults. They advocate a primary prevention approach that would require a comprehensive public health plan to address the factors that promote expressions of unwanted sexual behavior. They comment, "Thus far, we appear to be quite content to focus only on the few bad actors that are caught. We seem remarkably resistant to primary prevention strategies that alter the calculus of sexually violent behavior *before* it occurs." It is the authors' hope that their book will serve as a catalyst for improvements in our current approaches to sex offenders as well as providing a blueprint for the future that will serve to markedly reduce sexual violence.

Ron Roesch
International Perspectives on Forensic
Mental Health Series Editor

PREFACE

For the past 75 years we have trodden a narrow path between protecting society from *dangerous* sexual offenders and guarding the due process rights of sexual offenders. Although there are of course those who would argue rather vociferously that we have strayed off the path too far in one direction or the other, a principal vehicle for managing *dangerous* sex offenders since the late 1930s has been a form of civil commitment. In the first incarnation of these laws, often designated "sexual psychopath laws," the civil commitment decision was often viewed as a diversion from the normal criminal process, applied to offenders who were viewed as "too sick" to punish. Some form of treatment was provided. During just one decade, roughly 1975–1985, widespread disapproval was successful in challenging and repealing many of these sexual psychopath laws. In the more recent incarnation of these laws (post-1990), sexual offenders found *dangerous* have been civilly committed at the expiration of their criminal sentence. These laws, generally referred to as sexually violent predator (SVP) laws, are based on the premise that some offenders are too dangerous to release from prison. Although aggressively challenged in court, these laws have been deemed constitutionally valid in the US. Although these SVP laws are found only in 20 states, they appear, at least for now, to be a solid fixture in the legal landscape for managing sex offenders.

This unusual "psycho-legal" management scheme has created a considerable cottage industry of practitioners tasked with servicing all facets of the laws, from adjudication (requiring attorneys possessing a unique knowledge and skill set required for these special commitment hearings) and forensic experts (more often psychologists, occasionally psychiatrists, who offer opinions about dangerousness) to therapists (typically Masters-level psychologists who provide treatment) and custodial staff who provide security for a clientele that technically are no longer "prisoners." This book was conceived primarily for forensic psychologists and psychiatrists who provide expert evaluations and expert testimony, and for the judges and lawyers whose roles require advocacy and judgment about the validity, relevance, credibility and weight of expert testimony.

Although our book is clearly focused on sex offenders, we trust that we have something to offer for the larger domain of violence risk assessment. We begin, in Chapters 1 to 3, by setting up the problem addressed by civil commitment legislation, and discussing briefly the background of these governing laws. The following four chapters form the corpus of the book, the core of our analysis, a critical examination of the state of the art with respect to risk assessment. Chapter 4 provides a brief historical context for the development of actuarial assessment and a conceptual framework within which to understand the empirical basis for actuarial prediction. Chapter 5 describes (1) the development of an actuarial instrument, (2) the evaluation of the quality of actuarial prediction, (3) the most commonly used actuarial instruments, and (4) the published literature containing independent cross-validation studies. Chapter 6 reviews the problems experienced in estimating the likelihood of recidivism with sex offenders and takes a critical look at attempts that have been made to solve these problems. Chapter 7 steps back to take a broader look at actuarial science, as practiced with sex offenders, and the important role of theory in a science of sex offender risk.

We acknowledge that the field has come a long way since the halcyon days in the 1950s when pronouncements were based on clinical instinct. We argue, however, that science is an evolutionary process, that *normal* science assumes that the scientific community knows (or thinks it knows) what the world is like, and that when a bolder vision changes the assumptions about the world, scientific paradigms may shift. We maintain that there have been no bolder visions, that the field of sex offender risk assessment remains atheoretical and *preparadigmatic*, and that a coherent, theoretical framework, when it comes, will presage the next generation of risk assessment.

One observation deriving from this basic assumption of *normal* science is apropos. With rare exception, there is a disconnect between the scientific community of investigators developing and validating risk assessment scales for sex offenders and the *relevant* world—the court system. The science of risk assessment is *practiced* in the courtroom under the watchful eye of a judge and jury and in accordance with the rules of prevailing law—not the rules of science. For science to more effectively enrich the legal system, there must be "common ground" (Petrila, 2009). Attorney Petrila's (2009) second "thought on the state of the field" was that "One of the most salutary developments in the field has been the creation of research-based assessment tools. However, even the best instrument does not automatically convert bad practice into good" (p. 391).

The symbiosis between good science and good practice must recognize, as an example, the inescapable reality of the "n of 1" in the courtroom. This familiar conundrum—the application of group-based data to one individual—is addressed in Chapter 10 (and much more eloquently by

Professor Slobogin (2007) in *Proving the Unprovable*). Common ground recognizes the distinctive needs of both law and science and proposes a mutually acceptable solution. The tool box that contains only a life table may be good science in some quarters but is bad practice in court. Common ground demands that the science that gets filtered into the courtroom must acclimate to the prevailing evidentiary rules and turbulence of cross-examination. Contorting the science to accommodate admissibility or survive cross-examination benefits neither the grace of science nor the sanctity of law. We appreciate that there are those who will take marked exception to our perspective, and we look forward to constructive dialogue.

Chapter 8 approaches the assessment of *dangerousness* (or risk) from a different perspective by infusing forensic practice with lessons learned from the seminal science on risky decision-making under conditions of uncertainty. These remarkable contributions from neurocognitive scientists have much to tell us about the error of our forensic ways. By focusing on the heuristics and biases that undermine objectivity, we hopefully offer broader insights for the practice of forensic assessment. We hope that this is one of the contributions we can make to the greater arena of forensic assessment of violence. In Chapter 9 we look at the nexus of public opinion, public policy, and enactment of legislation, posing a pivotal question: Are the costs of our preventive interventions justified by the benefits derived, and, in particular, do the benefits derived from SVP laws justify the cost of involuntary confinement, and the diversion of scarce resources from other forms of prevention? We conclude in Chapter 10 with wide-ranging recommendations for the use of science within the forensic arena, including risk judgments and communication, probabilistic vs. categorical expressions of risk, the challenges of innumeracy, unpacking risk, and suggestions for the next generation of risk assessment scales.

Our overall perspective is that the next generation of risk assessment will break loose from its atheoretical mooring and embrace a theory-driven model that takes a lifespan perspective on risk. The net result hopefully will be the first *paradigm* for violence risk assessment with sexual offenders.

R. A. Prentky
H. E. Barbaree
E. S. Janus

ACKNOWLEDGMENTS

Both as a forensic practitioner and as a researcher, I owe a deep debt of gratitude to the pioneers of the neurocognitive science of decision-making—Robyn Dawes, Baruch Fischhoff, Reid Hastie, Daniel Kahneman, Paul Meehl, Scott Plous, Paul Slovic, Amos Tversky and many others—from whom I have learned so much about my own field. I am further very much indebted to my many colleagues, chief among them Kirk Heilbrun, Charles Patrick Ewing, Neil Malamuth, John Monahan, Doug Mossman, and Phil Witt, for the remarkable clarity of thought and judgment that defines their scholarship.

I have been blessed with wonderful graduate students over the past several years who have been the backbone of my research, many of whom contributed, in their own inimitable fashion, to what has gone into this book—most notably, Dr. Anna Coward, Dr. Adeena Gabriel, and my postdoc who has been "stalking" me for seven years—Dr. Raina Lamade.

Robert A. Prentky

The data set we used to illustrate the points in Chapters 5 to 7 was the result of the work of a number of individuals. The data set represented information coded from clinical files and records from the Warkworth Sexual Behavior Clinic (WSBC), a treatment program for sex offenders at Warkworth Institution, a Canadian Federal Penitentiary at Warkworth, Ontario. These clinical records were compiled over the period from 1989 to 1996. Many thanks to Dr. Ed Peacock and other staff at the WSBC for their careful and detailed documentation of demographic information, developmental histories, treatment progress, criminal histories, and other critical information concerning the participants in the treatment program.

Many thanks to the participants in the treatment program who agreed to allow us to use their information for research purposes.

Calvin Langton conducted and supervised the coding of the data from the information in the clinical files, including the scoring of the actuarial risk assessment instruments and the recidivism data. At the time, Calvin was a PhD candidate at the University of Toronto and an employee of the Centre for Addiction and Mental Health. Calvin used these data to complete his PhD dissertation under the supervision of one of the authors of this book (HB) and this data set has been the basis of numerous publications on issues relating to the issue of risk assessment. Articles listed in the References with an asterisk are empirical studies that used the WSBC data set. Many thanks, Calvin, for your work on this data set. Karl Hanson and Leslie Helmus were extremely helpful in providing advice and information concerning the use of Bayes' Theorem and Logistic Regression in actuarial prediction.

Many thanks also to Sonja Dey for assisting us with organizing the References.

Howard E. Barbaree

I want to acknowledge with gratitude the work of the research assistants, all students at William Mitchell College of Law, who assisted me in this project: Randall Cohn, Rachel Mowry, Nic Puechner, and Jacob Elrich.

Portions of my materials are based on previously published materials.

Eric S. Janus

1

HUMAN DANGEROUSNESS AND THE LEGACY OF FEAR MANAGEMENT

> Dr. Elizabeth Sinskey, Dan Brown's fictional Director-General of the World Health Organization in *Inferno*, observes that, "Only one form of contagion travels faster than a virus and that's fear."

Sexual violence is a national scourge. Indeed, for a country that champions human rights, it is a disgrace. The National Violence against Women Survey reported that close to one-fifth of all women report that they have been the victim of an attempted or completed rape at some point in their lives. More than half of that group reported that the sexual violence had occurred before age 18 (Patricia Tjaden and Nancy Thoennes, Full Report of the Prevalence, Incidence, and Consequences of Violence Against Women: Findings from the National Violence against Women Survey). These estimates do not begin to reflect the untold number of unreported and thus "unknown" child and adult victims of sexual violence.

In commenting on the unalienable rights set forth in our Constitution, the Honorable Charles Gill (2005) observed that:

> The truths, the rights, justice and the blessings of liberty were not extended to all people by our fundamental documents. Slaves, children, and, to a large degree, women were excluded. They were property, mere chattel, in varying degrees. Slaves had no rights, since they were property, and the child-citizens, similarly, had no rights except to someday succeed to the rights of their fathers.
>
> (p. 4)

Like the original Constitution, our country's laws have historically failed to extend their writ to the protection of women and children, especially from sexual violence. In this and the following two chapters, we address the laws and policies that have been adopted over the last two decades to remedy this historic failure. We return at the end of the book to a discussion of the efficacy of those laws and policies. Our ultimate goal is to enable the power of good law uniformly and consistently applied to mitigate sexual violence in all sectors of society. Primary prevention is instrumental, and law lies at the heart of primary prevention. Law itself, however, can be the victim of fear. When legitimate fear about sexual violence is magnified through the media, resulting laws and policies all too often lack the sober judgment and empirical grounding necessary for a comprehensive and systematic program of sexual violence prevention.

In this chapter, we seek to illuminate the way in which fear, often whipped up by the media, can distort public policy and sabotage the most constructive laws. We turn to historical examples of such "moral panics" to illustrate the power of fear and its potentially treacherous effects. But we caution our readers not to misinterpret this historical discussion. We do *not* equate sex offenders with the innocent victims of many prior fear-inspired waves of legislation. Nor do we mean to demean or minimize the fear that sexual violence engenders. That fear is real and legitimate. Rather, our point is that fear, especially when magnified by the political process, can hamper our efforts to make good public policy. When fear trumps science, when it silences good faith discussion of policy, it is prevention that suffers, in the present case, prevention of sexual violence.

Unfortunately, the law has *not* guided the development of comprehensive and systematic approaches to the prevention of sexual violence. Instead of identifying root causes and best-practice responses, our public policy has been reactive, driven by fear and the political exploitation of fear. Instead of encouraging robust accountability for effectiveness of our laws, all too often policy-makers ridicule or ignore science, resulting in countless resources allocated to reactive legislation that is rarely held to account for its effectiveness in preventing sexual violence.

It is time to conform our prevention policies to the reality of sexual violence, not the tabloid version. Policy-makers need the more accurate facts from the best science on the root causes of sexual violence, what perpetuates it, and what can mitigate it; to the point, policy-makers must be apprised of the most effective tools for combating rape and sexual assault. Good science must drive good public policy. Only in that way can we achieve the maximum prevention, not merely the maximum votes.

Though the science and law are admittedly an odd couple with occasional strains in their marriage, our primary point in the first three chapters is simple. Science and law must partner to markedly reduce sexual violence. But the partnership requires vigilance. Fear, politics, and the heuristics of the imperfect human brain can readily undermine this goal. Insisting on empiricism and illuminating the role of fear do not diminish the importance of prevention, they advance it.

Like all other physical assaults, rape is a battery offense. Unlike most other *non*sexual battery offenses, rape is uniquely and profoundly violative (Moor, Ben-Meir, Golan-Shapira, & Farchi, 2013; Perilloux, Duntley, & Buss, 2012). It is at once both frightening—as all assault would be—*and* humiliating and demeaning. Almost 40 years ago, John Gunn (1976) noted that "rape is frequently a humiliating, terrifying, dangerous, and painful business for the victim" (p. 58). Moor and her colleagues referred to "a trauma of paralyzing dehumanization" (p. 1051), noting that "dehumanization and humiliation [are] highly prevalent and almost invariably predictive of a freeze response in rape" (p. 1051). The sequelae of nonsexual assault—cuts, bruises, black eye, bloody nose, broken bones, perhaps a concussion—heal with time and generally leave the victim with few serious long-term physical or emotional scars. By contrast, rape frequently leaves its victims with interminable emotional scars that are resistive to time and treatment. Moreover, although all crime instills, in varying degrees, feelings of vulnerability, there is no other crime that creates so profound a sense of vulnerability as rape. Rape crosses all boundaries of civil human interaction, ceding safety, undermining trust, and crippling future intimacy. It is in this way that rape is a very different "kind" of crime.

Rape is different in one other respect. It targets two segments of the population—women and children. Although, yes, there are adult male victims of rape (Turchik & Edwards, 2012), the overwhelming majority of adult victims are women. Controlling legislation, enacted predominantly by men, has been precipitated, with minor exceptions, by heinous sexual crimes against children, *not* women. Although our assertion may appear cynical, the essential point is that the threat of sexual violence sweeps across the entire population, frightening women, parents, and those who care for and about women and children. There is no other crime that casts so long and pervasive a shadow over society. In response, we have devised a variety of mechanisms for countering the perceived threat posed by sex offenders. All of these mechanisms require a determination of the "amount of threat" posed by individual sex offenders. This determination is, in essence, the subject of this book.

It is for this reason—to place sex offender legislation and risk analysis in context—we begin first by highlighting three historical instances in which fear precipitated untold injustice and irrational laws. We follow with an overview of the horrific sex crimes that precipitated the first wave of sex offender civil commitment legislation (Sexually Dangerous Person laws) beginning in the late 1930s, and conclude with a discussion of the "cycle" of events, beginning with a widely publicized crime, typically a sexual homicide, and the ensuing fear that leads to a legislative response. This cycle, first articulated by Donald Sutherland in 1950, appears very much in evidence today.

A Laconic Historical Perspective of Social Fear

Some 2,500 years ago Sophocles wrote three plays dealing with Acrisius, the mythical king of Argos. Very little remains of these plays, save a few fragments. One such fragment is widely quoted as: "To him who is in fear, everything rustles." Fear is a deeply ingrained, hard-wired protective response to mortal threats when the earliest hominids lived in trees or caves and had ample to fear. Our preservation instinct remains alive and well. Indeed, our fascination with psychopathy may be attributable, in part, to the relative absence of this intrinsic feature of the human condition. Civilized human history, certainly since the time of Sophocles, is littered with the remnants of *fear gone awry*. Although fear may go awry by peculiar and uncertain biogenetic circumstance (e.g., psychopathy), the most frequent and far-reaching cause is humans, intentionally manipulating fear, typically for some social, political, or religious gain, occasionally resulting in witch hunts, vigilantism, and punitive statutory or ecclesiastic regulation of the feared objects.

"Witches" in Puritan New England

17th-century Puritan New England brings to mind images of pillories, stocks, and the infamous witch trials. In its report on *Psychiatry and Sex Psychopath Legislation: The 30s to the 80s*, the Group for the Advancement of Psychiatry (GAP) (1977) observed:

> Colonial Massachusetts during the 17th century can be taken as a prototype for illustration. . . . In early colonial days and continuing up to the late 18th century, Puritan criminal law was heavily infused with Mosaic law. Sin and crime tended to be equated, and hence the sinner was a criminal. Criminal law was the worldly application of the law of God. No separate ecclesiastical courts were required because religious notions involving sex were incorporated into the application of the civil law. In a broad sense, the primary goal of criminal law was the enforcement of the morals and religion of the people . . . .
>
> Whippings administered to secure reform were not paltry affairs. These punishments were carried out in the stern conviction that they were being administered with the ultimate goal of reforming wayward persons. By way of excluding sadistic elements, specific directions were given to set limits on the selection

> of those administering such punishments. Hence, no one who was "cruel or barbarous" would be permitted to do the whipping, and the number of lashes to be "laid on" was specified—usually 15 or 20. Even a "detestable offense" did not get more than the Biblical, 39, citing the authority of Paul's "second letter to the Corinthians." Whipping was also the chosen punishment for adulterers and for girls who delivered illegitimate children. . . . Old Testament language is still used, as witnessed in the current statutory definition of sodomy in Massachusetts as "the abominable and detestable crime against nature either with mankind or with a beast."
>
> (p. 847–849)

Offenses of a sexual nature continued to be punished by whipping well into the late 18th century. From 1692 until 1780, the crime of adultery was punished with 40 lashes and sitting in the gallows for one hour with a rope around one's neck as a reminder that the offense was "deadly serious" (GAP, 1977). Although initially the Puritans were reluctant to impose capital punishment without "scriptural authority" (GAP, 1977), by 1648 rape became a capital crime. In fact, rape was the only capital offense without Biblical justification (GAP, 1977). Adultery involving a married woman was a capital crime for both parties, but sexual relations between a married man and a single woman was mere fornication (GAP, 1977).

The crime for which Puritan New England, and Massachusetts in particular, was far more readily known—witchcraft—extended over a very brief period, about 14 months (February 1692–April 1693). During this period of a little over one year, roughly 160 people were accused of witchcraft and about 100 were imprisoned. Of that number, 20 were executed in 1692 by hanging (not by burning at the stake). Those accused of witchcraft were often social outcasts (e.g., Tituba was a slave, Sarah Good was a homeless beggar, and Sarah Osborne was a sickly, elderly woman). The Puritans feared Satan and believed that witchcraft was endemic. Prevailing wisdom was that Satan relied on the "weakest" among us—children, women, and the "insane"—to achieve his evil end. The sign of Satan was witchcraft, and the community, frightened by the dire warnings issuing from the theology of the "purified" (Puritan) Church of England, responded with hysteria. To be fair, European belief in witchcraft was centuries old. At its height, witches were actively "hunted" for a period of about 100 years, coinciding with the Reformation (1560–1660). Accused witches were treated equally (often torture) by the Protestant and Catholic Churches. Protestant beliefs (and solutions) on these matters are clearly articulated in *Malleus Maleficarum*, a treatise on witchcraft and the prosecution of witches, written in 1486 by a German Catholic clergyman (Heinrich Kramer). What occurred in New England was a predictable response to the strict code of Puritan doctrine, the intense fear of Satan (or the Devil) and his servants on Earth, and the "ways" and powers of Satan, all reinforced by the elders and ministers of the Church.

Slavery

Slavery in the United States, on a vastly larger scale than the brief episode of witchcraft, defined an entire class of humans as sub-human solely by virtue of skin color. In characterizing slavery as "The Negro Holocaust," Gibson (1979) stated,

> Immediately following the end of Reconstruction (1865–1877), the Federal Government of the United States restored White supremacist control to the South and adopted a laissez-faire policy in regard to the Negro. The Negro was betrayed by his country. This policy resulted in Negro disfranchisement, social, educational and employment discrimination, and peonage. Deprived of their civil and human rights, Blacks were reduced to a status of quasi-slavery or second-class citizenship. A tense atmosphere of racial hatred, ignorance and fear bred lawless mass violence, murder and lynching.

Slavery effectively lasted in the United States for almost 250 years, from 1619 until the Thirteenth Amendment formally outlawed the institution of slavery in 1865. One year later, in 1866, the Ku Klux Klan was founded, and two years later (1868) the Opelousas Massacre or Opelousas Riot took place when African Americans sought to join a political group of the Democratic Party in the neighboring town of Washington (Louisiana); a local unit of the White supremacist group Knights of the White Camellia went to Washington to insure that that didn't happen. *Lynchings took place in the United States for another 100 years after the passage of the Thirteenth Amendment.*

Gibson (1979) stated,

> Most of the lynchings were by hanging or shooting, or both. However, many were of a more hideous nature, burning at the stake, maiming, dismemberment, castration, and other brutal methods of physical torture. Lynching therefore was a cruel combination of racism and sadism, which was utilized primarily to sustain the caste system in the South. Many White people believed that Negroes could only be controlled by fear. To them, lynching was seen as the most effective means of control.

Gibson described lynchings as an institutionalized method of terrorizing Blacks to maintain White supremacy, fueled by "deep-seated and all-pervading hatred and fear of the Negro." For 60 years, from 1880 to 1940, lynchings were a primary means of social control.

The root of terrorism according to Gibson was fear of Black social and economic advancement. Gibson quoted W. E. B. DuBois as saying in 1915 that "There was one thing that the White South feared more than Negro dishonesty, ignorance and incompetency, and that was Negro honesty, knowledge, and efficiency" (White, 1929, p. 97; cf. DuBois, 2008). As with the mythology that drove witchcraft hysteria, so too a deeply entrenched narrative enforced slavery and its violence (e.g., all Black men want to rape White women, Blacks, primarily Black men, are indolent, deficient in mentality, or criminals by nature). The narrative has been so reinforced over so many generations that it remains an endemic feature of American society. The same shrill racist narrative exists today; today, however, it is likely to be condemned as, if nothing else, politically incorrect. The *original* driving force, however, as articulated by W. E. B. DuBois and the many scholars that followed him, was *fear* of competition in the social and economic marketplace. Parenthetically, a very similar narrative was heard in Nazi Germany regarding the Jews. Although condemned as inferior, the fear reportedly stemmed from the dominance of Jews in systems of commerce and the news media.

McCarthyism and the McCarthy Era

The "Attorney General's List of Subversive Organizations" was a centerpiece of President Truman's "loyalty program," initiated in 1947, well before the "rise" of Senator McCarthy. The chief architects of McCarthyism were Senator Joseph McCarthy (Republican, Wisconsin), first elected in 1947, and J. Edgar Hoover, Director of the FBI. Senator McCarthy came to prominence in 1950 when he publicly asserted during a speech that he held a list of 205 card-carrying Communists in the U.S. State Department. He further claimed that Communists had infiltrated the U.S. Army and President Truman's Administration.

The House Committee on Un-American Activities (HUAC) was formed originally in 1938, turning from its original mission of investigating German-American Nazis during World War II to concentrating on Communists (e.g., the Federal Theater Project of 1938). HUAC's first high-profile case involved charges of espionage against Alger Hiss 1948. Hiss was ultimately convicted of perjury. HUAC's most notorious investigations involved those in the Hollywood film industry, beginning in 1947. At least 300 members of the film industry were "blacklisted" and denied work. Between 1949 and 1954, HUAC, along with the Senate Internal Security Subcommittee and the Senate Permanent Subcommittee on Investigations conducted 109 investigations. The so-called "Hollywood Ten" refused to testify, were held in Contempt of Congress and were sent to prison for periods of six months to a year. The infamous Red Channels, along with other newsletters, published lengthy lists of individuals considered "leftist." Anti-Communist committees, panels, and "loyalty review boards" were established all over the country, at the state and local level as well as private agencies, all looking for Communists hiding in the workforce. Although the workforce, including the Armed Services, was the primary focus of "Communist hunts," McCarthyism was also concerned with a variety of public health services, including vaccinations, mental health care, and fluoridation, all of which were considered plots by Communists to poison or brainwash the American people. Ultimately, many thousands lost their jobs, including several thousand members of the Armed Services and longshoremen.

Many laws were passed by Congress to protect the United States, mostly from Communists. The Alien Registration Act of 1940 (referred to as the Smith Act) made it a criminal offense to "knowingly or willfully advocate, abet, advise or teach" activities advocating the overthrow of the Government of the United States. Under the Smith Act, hundreds of Communists and others were prosecuted between 1941 and 1957. The McCarran Act established the Subversive Activities Control Board, which had the mission of identifying organizations that were "fronts" for Communists. The Immigration and Nationality Act (McCarran-Walter Act) of 1952 required the government to deport immigrants or naturalized citizens engaged in subversive activities. Arthur Miller's play *The Crucible* in 1952 used the Salem Witch Trials as a metaphor for the McCarthyism of the time. In 1952, at the Republican National Convention, McCarthy proclaimed, "Our job as Americans and as Republicans is to dislodge the traitors from every place where they've been sent to do their traitorous work." The last piece of legislation, the Communist Control Act of 1954, was effectively an extension of the Internal Security Act of 1950.

On December 2, 1954 the United States Senate voted 65 to 22 to condemn Joseph McCarthy for "conduct that tends to bring the Senate into dishonor and disrepute." Senator McCarthy remained in office until his death in 1957, at age 48, from hepatitis, alleged to be related to alcoholism. The era of Senator Joseph McCarthy, although profoundly scarring on the national psyche, lasted a brief time, roughly from 1950 to 1955. The term "McCarthyism," coined originally by Herbert Block in a *Washington Post* political cartoon (dated March 29, 1950), has come to refer to wanton accusations of disloyalty, subversion, and treason, typically without regard for legitimate evidence. McCarthyism has come to represent in America the very worst of what can happen when blind dogma drives irrational fear to the brink of panic and becomes the catalyst for radical solutions to assuage fear.

Sexual Violence and Sexual Panic: 1930s–1940s

In America, "witches," African Americans, and Communists all came to represent sources of fear and repugnance so profound that panic ensued, draconian laws were instituted, and vigilantism became a scourge on civil society. For a variety of reasons, any comparison with sex offenders is obviously flawed, indeed warped. Unlike "witches," African Americans, and Communists, sex offenders are criminals, not victims. Sex offenders constitute an extraordinarily heterogeneous group with only one "class" being the predominant target (child molesters), and the "relationship" of society to the loathed group is complex, with mixed messages regarding the sexuality of children common in the media and advertising. Nonetheless, the historical pattern repeatedly observed non-offending targeted groups holds true for sex offenders—fear driving rapid enactment of (often) ill-conceived, uninformed laws, and occasional vigilantism.

The focus of this book is on yet another source of fear and loathing—sex offenders.

A wave of gruesome murders, many "serial," occurred around the US during the 1930s and 1940s. With a few exceptions, most of the crimes included sexual assault, and many victimized children. Importantly, these crimes precipitated the first generation of sexual offender laws, to be discussed shortly in detail.

Perhaps the most infamous was the serial killer of children, Albert Fish. Fish, referred to in the press as the Gray Man, the Werewolf of Wysteria, the Brooklyn Vampire, the Moon Maniac, and the Boogey Man, claimed that he had victims in every state and estimated the number at 100. Fish's paraphilias and preferred sexual acts were said to include fetishes, cunnilingus, fellatio, anilingus (oral stimulation of the anus), sadism, flagellation (flogging, whipping, beating), coprophagia (consumption of feces), urophilia (deriving sexual pleasure from urine), masochism, cannibalism, infibulation (genital mutilation), piquerism (literally to "prick," sexual interest in penetrating the skin), exhibitionism, voyeurism, and, of course, pedophilia. Although his claims about the number of his victims were unsubstantiated, he was a suspect in five murders. Ultimately, he confessed to three murders and several stabbings. At trial he pled insanity, saying that he heard voices from God instructing him to kill children. Although his preferred victims were young boys (under age 6), he was convicted of the murder of a 10-year-old girl (Grace Budd), found sane by the jury, and executed by electric chair at Sing Sing in 1936.

The Cleveland Torso Murderer, also referred to as the Mad Butcher of Kingsbury Run, killed and dismembered at least 12 victims in the Cleveland, Ohio area during the mid- to late-1930s, mostly between 1935 and 1938. Although the official number of the killer's victims is 12, the actual number is uncertain. Of the 12 victims, 10 could not be identified and are referred to as John or Jane Doe. Seven of the victims were male and five female. All were adults. All of the victims were decapitated (hence, the "torso" murderer). Although there were two primary suspects, the killer was never apprehended.

Albert "Eddie the Sailor" Dyer lured three young girls into the woods near Inglewood, California, and sexually assaulted and strangled them. These crimes were in late June 1937. He was convicted and hanged at San Quentin Prison.

Jake Bird, the so-called Tacoma Axe-Killer, was a serial killer of women, reportedly murdering as many as 46 women throughout the 1940s. He was ultimately tried and executed for the axe murder of Bertha Kludt (age 53). Although he also murdered Bertha's daughter (Beverly June Kludt, age 17), he was not charged with her murder. He was executed by hanging at Washington State Penitentiary in 1948. Bird reportedly murdered women in Florida, Illinois, Iowa, Kansas, Kentucky, Michigan, Wisconsin, Nebraska, Ohio, Oklahoma, and South Dakota, in addition to Washington.

The Phantom Killer of Texarkana, or Moonlight Murderer, or Phantom Slayer, roamed isolated lover's lanes killing after dark, by moonlight. The killer attacked at least eight and is known to have murdered five in 1946. The victims were all young couples. The women were sexually assaulted. These murders inspired a movie and a play. The Texas Rangers made a valiant attempt to find the killer. Although Youell Swinney was suspected, there was insufficient evidence, and the crimes remained unsolved.

William Heirens, called the "Lipstick Killer," terrorized Chicago in the mid-1940s. Heirens' criminal career began at 13. He was known to police primarily as a serial burglar. After his arrest for one of his burglaries, he was sentenced to three years at the St. Bede Academy, operated by the Benedictine Monks. His test scores were so high that he was encouraged to bypass high school and apply directly to the University of Chicago's special learning program. He was accepted to the program and was to begin classes in fall 1945. He committed his first murder in June 1945, and his "lipstick" murder in December 1945. After he killed Frances Brown, on December 20, 1945, he left a message in lipstick on the wall of Brown's apartment: *For heaven's sake catch me before I kill more. I cannot control myself.* On January 7, 1946, 18 days later, he killed Suzanne Degnan, age 6. He was 16 years old. At the time he confessed to three murders, he was 17 years old. He confessed to the murders in 1946 and spent his life in prison, dying in custody on March 5, 2012 at the age of 83. Two of his victims were adult women.

The most famous single murder of the 1940s was that of Elizabeth Short, a 22-year-old aspiring actress whose body was found cut in half and mutilated near a park in Los Angeles on January 15, 1947. Short became known as the Black Dahlia. Her killer was never found, and her case remains one of the oldest cold cases in Los Angeles. As recently as 2013, the Black Dahlia was back in the news. An article in the *San*

Bernardino Sun (Girardot, 2013) reported an investigation that uncovered further incriminating evidence against Dr. George Hill Hodel. Hodel's son Steve, a former LAPD detective, apparently always believed that his father killed Short.

James Buchanan, age 27, raped and murdered Ilda Koogle, age 60, on April 28, 1948 in East Cleveland. He was arrested on June 30, 1948. Buchanan told the police that during the previous six months he had brutally attacked 16 women. The "Walk of Death" murders occurred on September 6, 1949 in Camden, New Jersey. The killer, Howard Barton Unruh, 28 years old, killed 13 people (including 3 children) during a 12-minute walk through his neighborhood. Unruh was diagnosed with paranoid schizophrenia, found to be "insane," and committed to Trenton Psychiatric Hospital. He died in 2009 at the age of 88.

What has been referred to as "Horror Week" occurred in November 1949. Three children, aged 6, 7, and 17 months, were sexually assaulted and murdered, all in less than one week. Glenda Joyce Brisbois, 7 years old, was kidnapped, raped, and murdered on November 18, 1949 in Burley, Idaho. Her body was left in an irrigation canal. Josephine Yanez, 17 months old, was kidnapped from her parents' car, sexually assaulted, and suffocated in the mud on November 19, 1949 in Fresno, California. Her body was covered with teeth marks. Paul Gutierrez, 25 years of age, was convicted and sentenced to death. Linda Joyce Glucoft, 6 years old, was raped, strangled, slashed, and stabbed to death on November 14, 1949 by Fred Stroble in a neighborhood near Los Angeles. A blood-stained axe, hammer, ice pick, and butcher's knife were recovered near her body. Stroble, a 68-year-old grandfather of the victim's playmate, was convicted of first-degree murder, sentenced to death, and executed on July 25, 1952 at San Quentin Prison. For the news media, Stroble in particular became a symbol of pure evil, and was referred to as a "Sex Fiend" and a "Weeping Werewolf."

It is easy to see how a string of extremely violent crimes could produce widespread fear, if not panic. With reference to Stanley Cohen's book *Folk Devils and Moral Panics*, Feeley and Simon (2008) observed:

> The social world of the USA and other societies at the beginning of the twenty-first century is one of pervasive insecurity that has been described in terms such as "culture of control," "culture of fear," and "governing through crime." In this social world, moral panics are part of the infrastructure of contemporary society.
>
> (p. 46)

Moral Panic

The notion of moral panic was first described by Stanley Cohen in 1972:

> A condition, episode, person or group of persons emerges to become defined as a threat to societal values and interests; its nature is presented in a stylized and stereotypical fashion by the mass media; the moral barricades are manned by editors, bishops, politicians and other right thinking people; socially accredited experts pronounce their diagnoses and solutions; and ways of coping are evolved or resorted to.
>
> (p. 9)

That we panic in response to perceived threats, exaggerate their importance, and express moral panic or outrage toward these "folk devils" (Cohen's term) is well understood and well researched (e.g., Ben-Yehuda, 2009; Cohen, 1972, 1980; Critcher, 2003; Downes, Rock, Chinkin, & Gearty, 2008; Feeley & Simon, 2008; Ferguson, 2010, 2013; Gauntlett, 1995; Goode & Ben-Yehuda, 1994; Jenkin, 1992, 1998; Salerno & Peter-Hagene, 2013; Selvog, 2001; Thompson, 1998; Welch, 2000). Simply stated, moral panic is exaggerated fear of a "folk devil" against which there is moral repugnance (Ben-Yehuda, 2009). Whether the "folk devil" (perceived threat) is Satan, the Black Man, the Jew, the Communist, or the marauding sexual predator, if the threat is seen as pervasive and dire, the consequence may be moral panic. Fear of imminent threat underlies moral panic.

The combination of fear and *anger* appears to underlie moral outrage. Salerno and Peter-Hagene (2013) demonstrated in two studies that the two emotions are interactive (i.e., interaction of anger and fear (or "disgust") predicted moral outrage). The element of anger—when panic turns to outrage—appears to be "associated with an implied culpability" (Szmukler & Rose, 2013, p. 125). That is, "moral outrage derives from what is seen as the cause of the hazard. Such causes include malice (as in terrorist attacks), recklessness, or negligence (as in failures to maintain a railway track)—someone is deemed culpable" (Szmukler & Rose, 2013, p. 126). Szmukler and Rose (2013) provided a clear example—a deer running across the road leads to a car crashing through a barrier onto a railroad track resulting in a derailment and the death of 15 passengers. In the second scenario, the train is derailed because of a faulty track, leading to 15 deaths. The latter scenario will lead to outrage, because it will be assumed that had the track been properly maintained there would have been no accident and hence no deaths. In the former scenario, the accident was strictly fortuitous, a tragic random act. If the tragedy could have been avoided but for the recklessness, negligence, or maliciousness of one or more individuals, the visceral response is anger. In the case of sexual crimes, there are multiple potential targets for alleged negligence—those who freed the offender (the parole board, the court, the experts who pronounced the individual "low risk"), the probation officer, the police.

Moral panic ultimately degrades our principle of human fairness and our capacity for rational judgment. Moral panic can easily override our instinct for equity and justice and cloud our "pre-panic" knowledge that challenges the panic-driven beliefs. Society, as Ferguson (2013) remarked, "spins the moral panic wheel, with preexisting moral beliefs setting the stage for the rest of the process" (p. 67).

Lancaster (2011) captured cogently the "worst case" outcome of this process:

> When fear becomes the normative condition, it inaugurates a broken social order based on mistrust, resentment, and ill will. The pervasive assumption that anonymous, lurking others cannot be trusted undermines goodwill and feeds a sort of poisoned solidarity: we shall all be diligent in monitoring each other for signs of transgression. This rage to surveil and punish reverberates, internalized, in the psyche. It preaches an authoritarian, fear-based ethics that Vygotsky once described as the "policeman of the soul". . . . Fear induces a dread of the other, a tear in the social fabric, and a propensity toward violence . . . . The emergent republic of fear thus constructs an essentially negative sense of community, nation, and social good. . . . Citizenship becomes tantamount to vigilant surveillance, a conception Americans once ridiculed as a defining feature of totalitarian societies. . . . Procedures once deemed anathema to democratic governance become first thinkable, then necessary, and at last unavoidable.
>
> (p. 163)

Moral panic, as we will discuss, is a bad omen when it comes to legislating law. Any significant perturbation in our current *reality*, no matter how seemingly benign, can produce enough of Sophocles' "rustle" to ignite panic. Most panic is short-lived. We look back with the benefit of 20/20 hindsight and laugh at how silly we were. It is highly unlikely, for example, that there would a consensus of opinion today supporting legislation to try individuals accused of being witches. As Feeley and Simon (2008) put it, "Something triggers a threat and if conditions are right, a moral panic can suddenly appear, only to evaporate as suddenly as it arrived" (p. 42). In such a context, laws that emerge from moral panic are not deliberative but fear-driven and can reach a point of obsolescence quickly.

Perhaps a more plausible example than witchcraft was the widespread rustling of our moral feathers during the 1950s around fluoridation of water to reduce dental caries among children (cf. Mausner & Mausner, 1955).

Despite controlled studies over nine years in three communities revealing that fluoridation was safe and highly effective, and despite support from the American Dental Association, the American Medical Association, the National Research Council, and the United States Public Health Service, the widespread fear was that fluoridation held "unknown dangers," was poisonous, and that if everyone was required to drink treated water it was a step toward socialized medicine (Mausner & Mausner, 1955). J. Edgar Hoover, then head of the FBI, went so far as to warn the public to be on guard against the poisoning of public water supplies (AP Dispatch, February 27, 1951, cited in Mausner & Mausner, 1955). Mazur (2004) provides a comprehensive overview of this period.

If we fast-forward a half-century we see a similar modern-day rustling of our feathers around the use of genetic engineering to modify crops (genetically modified food, GMO). Advocates claim that it is our greatest hope to feed an ever-increasing, hungry world. Critics claim that it is a dangerous interference with nature; the foods have not been adequately tested to establish their safety, and there may be unknown deleterious side effects. Despite all of the controversy, GMO foods have now been in supermarkets for 15 years, and many of our most common purchases are foods subject to genetic engineering (e.g., tomatoes, rice, potatoes, corn, soy, and milk). The principal critical claim remains that food derived in part from GMO crops has been insufficiently tested over the long term for its safety. Entirely apart from the science of GMO and whatever hazards might legitimately be claimed, the "risk" has been "socially amplified" (cf. Frewer, Miles, & Marsh, 2002).

It is easy to see the many sources of moral panic seizing center-stage today—climate change (or the denial of the existence of climate change), the Tea Party's "panic" about Big Government (a bloated federal government that taxes and spends voraciously), and, of course, the Big Gorilla, terrorism (and with it, the infringement of individual rights). As always, some of these sources of moral panic have ideological underpinnings (climate change and Big Government). Others, notably bioterrorism and nuclear terrorism, cut across ideological divides, because they pose more obvious existential threats for everyone.

The most recent transpicuous manipulation of fear is intended to affect the outcome of the 2014 midterm elections. The current sources of fear weave together the Ebola (Ebola hemorrhagic fever) epidemic in West Africa deemed a homeland crisis after three cases in the United States *and* the march of ISIS (Islamic State in Iraq and Syria) through Iraq and Syria, also deemed a homeland crisis. Peters (October 9, 2014) reported in *The New York Times*,

> With four weeks to go before the midterm elections, Republicans have made questions of how safe we are—from disease, terrorism or something unspoken and perhaps more ominous—central

> in their attacks against Democrats. . . . Hear it on cable television and talk radio, where pundits and politicians play scientists speculating on whether Ebola will mutate into an airborne virus that kills millions. See it in the black-hooded, machine-gun-brandishing Islamic extremists appearing in campaign ads. . . . Republicans believe they have found the sentiment that will tie congressional races together with a single national theme. The National Republican Congressional Committee is running ads warning that terrorists are streaming across the Mexican border. Republicans . . . have accused Mr. Obama of leaving Americans vulnerable to the Ebola epidemic. Conservative media like . . . *The Daily Caller* has christened him President Ebola.

These fear-based claims are cloaked with a gossamer veil of legitimacy. Legitimate or not, fear is a profoundly potent driving force in motivating behavior, in this case to vote for Republican candidates.

For the present discussion, however, it is also easy to see how a relatively large number of horrific sexual crimes, many committed by "serial" offenders, set the stage for the first wave of Sexually Dangerous Person laws, beginning in the late 1930s. By no means did these sources of "sexual panic" vanish, or even diminish, in later years. As Lancaster (2011) recounted in his Introduction, aptly titled "Fear Eats the Soul,"

> First came the teen male prostitution scares of the 1970s, followed by the AIDS terrors and the satanic ritual abuse and day-care panics of the 1980s. Beginning in the 1990s we have suffered a veritable avalanche. Reportage on violent pedophile predators, the perils of the Internet, the priest abuse scandals, the Michael Jackson trial, and so on made sex crime stories part of the furniture on twenty-four-hour news services, local television news stations, and even newspapers of record.
>
> (p. 3)

Direct application of moral panic to sex offenders was made by McAlinden (2006) in her article "Managing Risk: From Regulation to the Reintegration of Sexual Offenders." Under the heading "The media, 'moral panic' and 'populist punitiveness'," McAlinden remarked that

> Newspaper reporting of sexual offences has given the impression that there has been an unprecedented explosion in sexual crime and that women and children are increasingly at risk of attack by sexual monsters. . . . The sexual offender is demonized as a monster or fiend and is singled out above other dangerous offenders in society.
> (p. 199)

Bribiesca (2007) noted, "Author McAlinden first offers an examination of the socio-political context in which the 'law and order debate' occurs. Chief among the most influential factors is the media's creation of a 'moral panic' that clouds effective strategies amid fear-driven rhetoric" (p. 7).

What is crystal clear is that we have a perverse love–hate relationship with sexual crimes. When we do not feel personally threatened—when the crimes are far away or target a victim group that we are not a part of—sexual offenders and their offenses hold some peculiar fascination, and the weirder or more morbid the offenses (e.g., highly atypical paraphilias), the more fascinated we are by them. We are drawn to read about them, which is precisely why the news media treats them as highly "newsworthy." The "lite side" of child molestation even has entertainment value, most notably in the Dateline NBC reality TV series *To Catch a Predator*. In the dozen episodes between 2004 and 2007, we were treated to sting operations in which decoys pretending to be underage adolescents (generally in the age range of 12–15) lured unsuspecting adult males to their homes under the pretense of sex.

By contrast, when we feel personally endangered or feel that our children are endangered, the threat can grow into panic. And from panic, or the equivalently strong emotion of rage, the demand for corrective action leads inexorably to rapid political responses, often in the form of new or amended laws.

Social Amplification of Risk

The Social Amplification of Risk Framework (SARF), first reported in 1988, was a joint project of Roger and Jeanne Kasperson, Paul Slovic, Nick Pidgeon, Ortwin Renn and their many colleagues (e.g., Kasperson, Kasperson, Pidgeon, & Slovic, 2003; Kasperson et al., 1988; Pidgeon, Kasperson, & Slovic, 2003; Renn, Burns, Kasperson, Kasperson, & Slovic, 1992). Initially, the framework sought to integrate the disparate threads of research on risk perception and risk communication. Hazardous (or risky) events are largely without widespread impact unless *communicated* broadly. Moreover, since some hazardous events have much higher signal value than others (Slovic, 1987, 1992), precisely what is communicated (how the nature of the "risk" is defined in all of its dimensions) influences how it is *perceived*. In the ensuing 15 years, the literature on social amplification of risk has mushroomed (for a poor choice of metaphors). The research literature has generally focused on global diffuse hazards (e.g., extreme meteorologic or geologic events), rare catastrophes (e.g., the explosion of the Challenger Space Shuttle in 1986, the Three Mile Island Nuclear Power Plant accident in 1979, the

Chernobyl Nuclear Power Plant disaster in 1986, and the 2011 earthquake, tsunami and nuclear power plant disaster in Fukushima, Japan), and biocidal hazards associated with the use of herbicides, pesticides, toxic solvents, preservatives and disinfectants.

The heart of SARF is communication. Kasperson et al. (2000) described the structure of SARF thusly: "Social amplification of risk denotes the phenomenon by which information processes, institutional structures, social-group behavior and individual responses shape the social experience of risk, thereby contributing to risk consequences" (p. 237). In this framework, "signal amplification in communications" is critical. Kasperson et al. (2000) stated that "information systems" can "amplify risk events" by "intensifying or weakening signals that are part of the information that individuals and social groups receive about risk; or filtering the magnitude of signals with respect to the attributes of the risk and their importance" (p. 237). As Kasperson et al. (2000) make clear, risk *cannot* be quantified in any "true" or absolute sense; by the same token, the socially amplified "distortion" of risk *cannot* be quantified in any absolute sense.

In the interest of full disclosure, SARF is not without its critics (e.g., Rayner, 1988; Rip, 1988). Rayner (1988), for instance, has criticized the use of amplification as a metaphor, suggesting that it implies the existence of a "true" baseline risk which is then "amplified" (distorted by magnification). Rip (1988) has expressed concern that a focus on "amplification" may have a secondary effect of exaggerating risk.

The impossibility of auguring "true" risk is most clearly evident in the case of criminal violence, wherein the assessment of the probability and magnitude of the behavior are subject to numerous factors that cannot be predicted with any precision (e.g., situational events and victim response). Similarly, distortion of risk is subject to two factors that render it unquantifiable in any meaningful sense: the nature of the distortion is highly variable across information systems, and the filtering of the same risk information by each individual will impact differently (by virtue of personal life experience and by virtue of social and group effects).

Application of SARF, or some variant of SARF, to criminal events is much more infrequent, though clearly as applicable. The overwhelming focus of the literature, criminology as well as psychology, has been on fear of victimization, typically gathering survey data from individuals. Most past analysis, then, has been on what might loosely be called *intra-psychic* amplification (i.e., individual fear of crime), rather than on *social* amplification. The distinction is real. Indeed, Warr (2000) questioned whether fear should—or could—be regulated or controlled (a societal intervention, not a therapeutic one). For Mark Warr, altering fear means altering perceived risk of crime. The goal, at least in theory, is making perceived risk more congruent with objective risk (Warr, 2000). There are innumerable ways, some intentional, others presumably inadvertent, that fear is inflamed, and Warr (2000) discusses many of them:

> The mass media are thus a powerful amplifying mechanism when it comes to crime; information known only to a few can within hours or days become known to thousands or millions. What is the image of crime presented in the mass media? A number of forms of distortion in news coverage of crime have been identified and documented, distortions that tend to exaggerate the frequency and the seriousness of crime. In the real world, for example, crimes occur in inverse proportion to their seriousness; the more serious the crime, the more rarely it occurs. Thus, in the United States, burglaries occur by the millions, robberies by the hundreds of thousands, and homicides by the thousands. In news coverage of crime, however, the emphasis is on "newsworthiness," and a key element of newsworthiness is seriousness; the more serious a crime, the more likely it is to be reported. By using seriousness as a criterion, however, the media are most likely to report precisely those crimes that are least likely to occur.
>
> (p. 467)

> There are entire industries in the United States that rely on fear of crime to sell products and services, from home security systems, anti-auto theft devices, and travelers checks to personal security devices (sprays, alarms, and other weapons), property insurance, and cellular phones. Some firms are responsible and circumspect in the claims they make for their products. Others deliberately exaggerate or dramatize the risks of criminal victimization in an effort to frighten potential purchasers into buying products, some of which are of questionable utility.
>
> (p. 478)

> There is no law, of course, against using fear of crime as a sales tool, and the rule of *caveat emptor* applies to crime prevention as much as any other realm of commerce.
>
> But there is something deeply cynical about exploiting people's concern for their safety (and their loved ones) for monetary reasons. If only as a research question, it would be intriguing to know whether certain segments of the population—the aged, those who live alone (widows and widowers), students, young women—are targeted by such industries for special attention and the degree to which fraudulent claims are used to sell products and services. To be sure, one of the strange ironies of life is that, even if they *are*

> fraudulent and unnecessary, such products may actually function to reduce fear among those who decide to invest in them.
>
> If fear is useful as a sales device, it also has value to politicians, who are sometimes quick to exploit it as a political tool. By some accounts, the 1968 election campaign of Richard Nixon, with its emphasis on law and order, was the first to capitalize on crime and fear of crime for political advantage. In the Bush/Dukakis presidential contest, the infamous Willie Horton commercials appeared to play a pivotal role. Today crime continues to figure heavily in local and national political campaigns, and there appears to be little prospect for change. In a just world, the cynical exploitation of fear for political purposes would be appreciated for what it is. Yet, if nothing else, the eagerness of political figures to capitalize on public fear of crime is testimony to its central place in modern life.
>
> (p. 480)

With reference to Warr's (2000) admonition about exploiting fear of crime by marketing so-called crime prevention devices or products to a naïve public, there are many "anti-rape devices" that have been developed and marketed as well (Murano, 2013).[1] Most of these devices were created in India or South Africa, countries with exceptionally high rates of rape. Two of these devices come from Sweden (#2 and #4), and one comes from China (#3). Needless to say, it is highly unlikely that these devices have been "product tested." What is most remarkable is that *all* of these devices, except for #7, *require* intimate physical contact with the victim. In other words, the sexual assault has already begun. It is inexplicable why a victim would choose a device for protection that would require the assault to go that far (i.e., most of these devices require some degree of vaginal penetration for the device to work), when she could carry mace or a stun gun. Moreover, many of these devices are highly invasive and could cause physical injury to the victim (as well as to the rapist). Given the close physical "proximity" of the offender to the victim, the pain from these devices might well instigate a violent physical attack on the victim that results in further serious injuries.

As highlighted above, prevailing wisdom is that *experience* is a vital determinant of perceived risk (Slovic, Fischhoff, & Lichtenstein, 1982). Biased experiences often lead to inaccurate perception of risk. As Slovic et al. (1982) noted, "Unfortunately, much of the information to which people are exposed provides a distorted picture of the world of hazards" (p. 467). News media coverage of sexual crimes often falls squarely in the camp of biased experience. Warr's (2000) comments above point to the "bottom line" bias of the news media in covering horrific crimes—what draws readership enhances the bottom line, i.e., sales/revenue. When our perceptions of risk of sexual assault are shaped by biased information, our judgment of the magnitude of the risk is likely to be "amplified." Indeed, the availability heuristic would suggest that the very discussion of sexual assault can have the effect of increasing its "imaginability," and thus its perceived risk. Does that mean we adopt the Ostrich strategy? No, of course not. Indifference is avoidance. *Informed* probabilistic judgment is required. In the area of sexual crime, however, informed judgment is more difficult than with most other areas where assessment of risk may be required (e.g., medical side effects of a drug, food contaminants, toxic chemicals in well or ground water, radiation hazards from X-rays, CT scans, or airport body scanners). There are no warning labels or package inserts when it comes to sexual assault, and few, if any, empirically informed, routinely updated, objective sources of information on sexual assault that are readily available. To make matters worse, what fills the vacuum of informed, unbiased information are chilling accounts of isolated crimes.

Sutherland Cycle: Crafting Law in Response to Panic

In his classic article on the diffusion of sex offender laws, Edwin Sutherland (1950a) described the pattern of events that lead to the enactment of these laws. The first event that Sutherland described is a "state of fear" that has "been aroused in a community by a few serious sex crimes committed in quick succession" (p. 144). More often than not, this "state of fear" or panic follows a particularly heinous sex crime, often the sexual murder of a child. The attention given to the crimes by the media exacerbates the fear, which then "readily bursts into hysteria" (p. 145). Sutherland argued that hysteria alone was insufficient to explain the enactment of these laws. Citizens driven by fear and outrage appeal to their legislators directly, or write letters to the news media, or complain vociferously to law enforcement, or band together in committees, or form community crime watches or crime patrols.

Politicians, reacting to public fear and outrage, set up ad hoc committees to "study the problem." These ad hoc committees (Sutherland's 3rd factor) consist of "experts," such as lawyers and mental health professionals. The committees' mission of gathering "facts" (Sutherland's quotation marks) conveys, in his opinion, an appearance of scientific credibility for the recommendations issued by the committee. The committee's recommendations are incorporated into statutes that are intended to address the problem. The role of the public as a catalyst for these laws was clearly evident in the 1940s and 1950s. Apfelberg, Sugar, and Pfeffer (1944) remarked that "the community demands swift, severe punishment for all sex offenders, even when there is little or no injury to society" and

Deutsch (1950) noted that "action against sex crimes usually evolves in an atmosphere of hysteria; such action is often useless and frequently harmful" (cited in Karpman, 1951). A 1948 Massachusetts Report stated that "after a particularly revolting sex crime, the public clamors for harsher penalties" (cited in Sadoff, 1964, p. 249). The cycle that Sutherland described, beginning with fear and outrage from one or more particularly horrendous sex crimes, leading to public outcry, resulting in ad hoc committees that make recommendations, and ultimately producing new laws, has one final stage. Once enacted, the laws are on the books for some lengthy time until the crimes that gave rise to the laws have long since faded in memory, and for a variety of reasons the laws are repealed—until the next horrendous sex crime when the cycle begins anew.

Cass Sunstein (2005) provided a somewhat more simplified version of Sutherland's cycle. Sunstein posed the following question: "Some statistically large risks do not cause a great deal of fear. In many communities, the risks associated with tobacco smoking (a killer of hundreds of thousands of Americans annually) are not salient at all. Why is this?" (p. 92). Sunstein's (2005) answer:

> The question suggests the need to attend to the social and cultural dimensions of fear and risk perception. In many cases of high-visibility, low-probability dangers, such as sniper attacks, shark attacks, and the kidnapping of young girls, the sources of availability are not obscure. The mass media focus on those risks; people communicate their fear and concern to one another; the widespread fact of fear and concern increases media attention; and the spiral continues until people move on.
>
> (pp. 92–93)

Sunstein characterized this in *Laws of Fear* (2005) as "Fear as Wildfire." The governing principle is the availability heuristic (discussed in Chapter 5), the ease with which we can conjure up thoughts or imagine possibilities about some event. The more readily such thoughts come to mind, the more important they must be. Although Galliher and Tyree (1985) were dismissive of Sutherland's explanation for the diffusion of sex offender legislation, there seems to be considerable evidence, experiential if not empirical, to support it. We acknowledge Galliher and Tyree's (1985) observation about the great diversity in media coverage of sex crimes; such diversity would be expected. The basic "elements" of the cycle, however, seem indisputable.

Indeed, the pivotal role of the media in promoting widespread public reaction to crime—often fear—and the connection between public response and legislation were noted in the Report by the President's

Commission on Law Enforcement and Administration of Justice (1967). The Report, commissioned by President Lyndon Johnson, remarked that "the mass media and overly zealous or opportunistic crime fighters may play a role in raising fears of crime by associating the idea of 'crime' with a few sensational and terrifying criminals acts" (p. 52). The Report further observed "the close relationship between worry about crime and the taking of strong precautionary measures" (p. 51).

A striking example is the Beltway Sniper. When John Allen Muhammad and his young companion Lee Boyd Malvo starting shooting motorists in October 2002, terrorizing the Beltway around Washington, DC, Maryland, and Virginia, it took very little to imagine yourself stopping for gas and being shot. Here is one example of a news report on MSNBC dramatizing the shootings:

> Ever since a sniper began picking off people one-by-one, daily tasks like shopping, pumping gas, and mowing lawns have become potentially deadly. Desperate to stay out of the cross-hairs, Washington, D.C. area residents are adjusting where they buy groceries, when they fill their cars, how they exercise. Some even wear bullet-proof vests. . . . It's hard for residents to know what to do to protect themselves.
>
> (http://www.jondube.com/resume/msnbc/snipersshadow.htm)

The probability of being shot was extraordinarily low. Sunstein (2005) reported, "If the snipers were going to kill one person every three days, the daily statistical risk was less than one in one million" (p. 90). The salience, however, was extraordinarily high.

Similarly, there is no icon of danger in the ocean more salient than the Great White Shark. There have over 20 movies capitalizing on our fear and fascination with this savage killer of the deep. Although 14 movies about sharks have appeared since 2000, the "reference point" for all such movies is the classic 1975 movie *Jaws*. Anyone who has seen just one of these movies and then spends a lazy summer vacation basking on the beach is hard-pressed not to think of scenes from the movie. Once again, the probability of being attacked by a shark is very low, but the salience is extraordinarily high.

Sunstein's example of the high risk of mortality associated with tobacco smoking, pairing *high* probability with *low* salience, is a more complex amalgam of base rate neglect and "group think"/social-peer reinforcement (i.e., if many of your family/friends/associates/colleagues smoke and appear to be in good health, the "risk" is far less salient then being shot by the Beltway Sniper or gobbled up by Jaws). The power of clear, easily imaginable, dire threats—a lone sniper with a high-powered rifle and scope killing people, Jaws silently grabbing you and pulling you down below the surface to your hideous death, Al Qaeda terrorists taking down the plane you are on, the ubiquitous Communist lurking in the shadows, programming your brain with diabolical ideas (e.g., the 1956 movie *Invasion of the Body Snatchers*), or Satan taking possession of you—is very hard to overcome.

The political capital accrued by enacting sex offender legislation is undeniable. The New Jersey Supreme Court clearly recognized it in relation to the murder of Megan Kanka: "Clearly, both the Legislature's and the public's increasing awareness of the dangers posed by sex offenders triggered laws here, and elsewhere, as the understanding of the problem was accelerated by the occurrence of highly publicized and horrific offenses" (Doe v. Poritz, 1995). Clearly, it is the responsibility of politicians to enact laws that address problems affecting the safety and security of the public. It is the "acceleration" of the understanding of problems due to "horrific offenses" that frequently undermines the efficacy of the solutions to those problems. Rapid responses may befog rational, deliberative answers. As LaFond (2005) expressed it,

> Terrible crimes often generate instant and widespread law reform in the United States . . . the fierce public anger and virtually unanimous political consensus that these new public policy initiatives were essential for community protection left little opportunity for reasoned reflection on whether they are based on sound empirical knowledge and whether they actually work.
>
> (pp. 9–10)

It appears, at times, that the quick solution may be far more important politically than a deliberative response. In fact, the political response may be calculated and outweigh in importance the effectiveness of the response. In England and Wales,

> the "dangerous offender" risk management agenda of the Criminal Justice Act 2003 also increased the tariff periods of life sentences and introduced imprisonment for public protection (IPP) . . . The year 2003 also saw passage of the Sexual Offences Act. . . . The then Home Secretary described the Act as perfectly illustrating his political strategy: "The whole revision of the sex offense laws [was possible] precisely because I was willing to take on the business of securing confidence. I was on the side of the people, and I knew what I was doing, that I was putting to rest some of the greater fears that people have, and I do believe that that will be the legacy of the time I was here."
>
> (Rutherford, 2008, pp. 68–69)

The chemistry of the media, frightened citizens, and politicians as a driving force behind sex offender legislation is, of course, complex and manifests itself differently from case to case. The "paradigm case" (LaFond, 2005), however, was that of Earl Shriner, precipitating the enactment of the first Sexually Violent Predator legislation in the United States (Washington Community Protection Act of 1990). While in Washington State Prison, Shriner had drawn pictures of torture chambers and revealed to other inmates what horrific crimes against children he would commit after his release. Shriner "had only recently been released from prison 'despite warnings from psychiatrists that he had sadistic, homicidal fantasies about children and was a danger to society'" (Cipolla, 2011, p. 103). An attempt by the State to civilly commit Shriner to a state hospital at the expiration of his criminal sentence was unsuccessful, because he was not considered *mentally ill* (LaFond, 2005). On May 22, 1989, the police arrested Shriner and charged him with abduction, rape, and attempted murder of 7-year-old Ryan Hade. Shriner had cut off the boy's penis, raped him, and left him to die. As LaFond (2005) recounted:

> The public outrage over these horrendous sex crimes—some of which had been predicted and were, in the eyes of many, preventable—proved beyond a reasonable doubt that society needed to do much more to keep convicted sex offenders from committing more sex crimes. To many people, these cautionary tales were simply the tip of the iceberg. They believed there was a national epidemic of sex offenses being committed by dangerous sex offenders released too soon from prison without any control by the police or warning to the public. . . . Politicians were compelled to take action. In June, 1989, Booth Gardner, then Governor of Washington, convened a special task force to study how Washington's law should be changed, under intense political pressure both from victims' rights groups and the media. The case of Earl Shriner became the paradigm case: Dangerous sex offenders must not be allowed to commit another sex crime. One nonnegotiable demand made by law reform advocates was that very dangerous sex offenders would, one way or another, not be released from prison to commit another horrendous sex crime. Another demand was that people had a right to know when a dangerous sex offender was released from prison and living in the community.
>
> (pp. 6–7)

Whether the "cycle" is as Sunstein (2005) described it ("The mass media focus on those risks; people communicate their fear and concern to one another; the widespread fact of fear and concern increases media attention; and the spiral continues until people move on" (pp. 92–93)), or a bit more elaborated as Sutherland (1950a) described it (a "state of fear" is "aroused in a community by a few serious sex crimes committed in quick succession," following a particularly heinous sex crime; the media exacerbates the fear, which "readily bursts into hysteria"; politicians, reacting to public fear and outrage, enact laws that are intended to address the problem), the cycle appears to have the quality of perpetuity, a seemingly ineluctable facet of the human condition.

To illustrate this cycle with a current, ongoing case we will describe in some detail from current news reports a child sexual homicide in Jacksonville, Florida. The elements of the cycle are common. What is remarkable about this case is the accelerated pace of the unfolding of these elements.

Donald Smith, 56 years old, was arrested, and shortly thereafter indicted, on charges of first-degree murder and capital sexual battery in the killing of 8-year-old Cherish Perrywinkle. He was alleged to have committed the crime on June 21, 2013. Smith had been registered as a sex offender in Duval County (Florida) since his 1993 conviction for attempted kidnapping and selling obscene material (Action News Jax, 2013). Smith had subsequent arrests, most recently in 2009, on a charge of child abuse after making obscene phone calls to a 10-year-old girl (Action News Jax, 2013).

On June 23, 2013, two days after Smith allegedly abducted the victim from McDonalds at Wal-Mart, the following column appeared on FamilyFieldGuide.com:

> Rayne Periwinkle, the Jacksonville, Fla., mother whose eight-year-old daughter was murdered after being abducted from a Wal-Mart McDonalds by a pedophile on Friday, is receiving a royal reaming on CafeMom, a popular women's social networking website.
>
> Replies to a rancorous post on the case range from mild disparagement to outright vitriol. Nearly all point a finger at the mother. "Who needs enemies with a mother like that?" one reply said. "Fry her ass and sterilize her so she can't have any more kids to endanger," said another response. The venom goes on.
>
> It's mob mentality. Anonymous accusations. A chance to feel superior. The sad truth is, such hateful comments represent only a small slice of America's current empathy-void. A void that starts when parents lack the skills to nurture their children. It's a cycle. And the cycle repeats itself, unless we are smart enough, and lucky enough, to stop it.

Three days later, Brown (June 26, 2013) posted a column entitled "State Rep calls for change in sex offender checks":

> Pull the delegation together so that we can begin to understand the policy issues, build consensus on solutions that would

> improve safety of our community," says Fernandina Beach State Representative Janet Adkins. . . . While she doesn't have specific plans at this time for what "solutions" lawmakers may be able to craft, she wants to start now speaking with people who work with the system every day to start getting a better understanding of procedures in place.
>
> Particularly disturbing to Adkins is the fact that police performed a routine check on the suspect, Donald Smith, the morning of the abduction.
>
> "Are we really trying to understand what's going on in that individual's head, or are we just putting our eyes on them and saying 'Ok, well, you look ok today'—how in depth is that interview?" she says.
>
> Adkins intends to spend the coming weeks gathering more information, so they can begin drafting legislation in committee meetings in Tallahassee in September.

The Sexually Violent Predator Program (SVPP) in Florida is in the Mental Health Program Office of the Florida Department of Children and Families (DCF). DCF requested a comprehensive review of SVPP by a review panel consisting of three psychologists (Chris Carr, Anita Schlank, and Karen Parker). The review panel submitted its report on September 23, 2013 (cf. http://media.cmgdigital.com/shared/news/documents/2013/09/23/09.23_ SVPP_ Report.pdf).

The following excerpts are from the "Conclusions and Recommendations" of the review panel's report (pp. 39–43):

> As reflected in the statistics, the salient issue is the "false alarm" rate. This is error related to failing to identify offenders who do *not* fall into the highly dangerous and predatory group. These are the 96.4% (135 out of 140) of offenders observed in the OPPAGA study who were deemed to be dangerous but did not reoffend and the 90% (639 out of 710) of offenders in the SVPP study that were deemed to be dangerous but did not reoffend. For those deemed to be so dangerous that they may be committed indefinitely—and cared for at great expense to the state—this false positive rate appears high.
>
> Perhaps the most important question is "Is the SVP Program successful at identifying sexual predators?" Based on the actual numbers (statistics) the Review Team finds the program to be successful in identifying high risk sexual offenders. Out of the 30,000 offenders not recommended for commitment by the SVPP 95.6% did not reoffend, but 4.4% did (as indicated by charge or conviction). This rate of 4.4% is lower than or consistent with the rates of re-offense of routine sex offenders released from prisons

> in Florida and other states. The Adam Walsh Study is a multi-state recidivism study that included 500 offenders from Florida (250 released in 1999–2000 and 250 released in 2004–2005. The 5 year recidivism rate based on charges or convictions for sexually motivated offenses was 5.2%. The 10 year rate was 13.7%.
>
> It is apparent from the above numbers that the type of error that leaves the public at risk (failing to identify offenders who are sexual predators) is far lower than the other type of error (failing to identify offenders who are not sexual predators).
>
> As mentioned earlier in this report, the *Sun Sentinel* neglected to mention that 95.6% of sexual offenders not referred for civil commitment were not charged or convicted of another offense; suggesting that, overall, the commitment process appears to be working extremely well.

The Report went on to recommend that:

> It would be useful if an option was available for there to be a less restrictive alternative to civil commitment, as is available in several other states. In this option the offender is placed directly out in the community on conditional release monitored by probation officers. He has strict guidelines to follow, and any deviation from those guidelines could lead to quick revocation of his conditional release, and placement in the SVP facility. In addition, having a "step-down" transition back to the community for those offenders who have earned release from FCCC is also highly recommended.

One day before the release of the Panel's Report, Kestin and Williams (2013) reported in the *Sun Sentinel*:

> The new findings are part of a broad review of Florida's Sexually Violent Predator Program. The review is due to be released Monday, but the *Sun Sentinel* obtained a draft copy and the state's response. As a result of the review, Esther Jacobo, interim secretary of the Florida Department of Children and Families, ordered immediate changes that include:
>
> - Requiring department screeners to forward to courts cases where there is doubt or ambiguity about whether a sex offender should remain confined.
> - Expanding the offenses that trigger an automatic psychological evaluation—murder and kidnapping—to include attempted kidnapping and attempted murder.
> - Shortening contracts with outside psychologists hired to evaluate offenders from three years to one, and providing more feedback on their work.

> Jacobo went beyond the report's recommendations and put the program under the direction of a non-mental health professional, department attorney Greg Venz. The previous director, psychologist Dan Montaldi, resigned last week after the *Sun Sentinel* questioned the drop in offenders considered for confinement under his leadership, and Montaldi's public comments defending the rights of sex offenders and arguing for a narrow definition of a predator.

By September, politicians began deliberations over further changes in Florida's existing SVP law:

> While what exactly needs to change about the current laws dealing with sex offenders and predators is still up for debate, there is a consensus forming that change needs to happen.
>
> State lawmakers joined with an extensive panel of experts representing law enforcement, the State Attorney's Office, victim's advocates, DCF, mental health and more to tackle the problems in Florida law. This was the first of several meetings State Representative Janet Adkins plans to call on her road to drafting new legislation for the upcoming session.
>
> State Senator Audrey Gibson says the more she's learned about the Perrywinkle case, the more she's convinced something was missed in the suspect's follow-up. She's questioning why the suspect, Donald Smith, was considered a sex offender and not a predator.
>
> "Some things that we need to look at to make sure that we have the categories right," she says.
>
> "We're always scared to just pass new laws when existing laws aren't being followed, but it seems like there are things we can do to make our community safer," he says.
>
> Classification is just one of the ideas Adkins tells me she is taking out of this hearing. Another area she's concerned about is community supervision once an offender is released.
>
> "The concept that community supervision really just mean address verification, let's call it what it is," she says.
>
> She also mirrors the call of many of the experts to possibly have risk assessment done on every offender and predator before they're released in order to best tailor the treatment and supervision warranted when they are out.
>
> "We will continue on this mission," she says.
>
> Adkins is planning on filing legislation in the upcoming session. She couldn't say at this time which of these ideas mentioned might evolve to be the central focus, but tells me she is looking forward to

> having more of these hearings and continuing to learn about new concerns you have.
>
> (S. Brown, September 4, 2013)

According to Dr. Karen Franklin's blog, what reportedly led to the resignation of Dan Montaldi, former director of SVPP, was leaked remarks that he made in an email regarding the difficulty of identifying every truly dangerous sex offender ("He observed that, as a group, sex offenders were 'statistically unlikely to reoffend'."). According to Dr. Franklin, "He went on to say that in a free society, the civil rights of even 'society's most feared and despised members' are an important moral concern" (Franklin, 2013). Kestin and Williams (September 19, 2013) reported in the *Sun Sentinel*, "In writings obtained by the newspaper, Montaldi advocated a narrow definition of a predator and defended the rights of sex offenders—a philosophy that one lawmaker said made his 'skin crawl'."

There are several takeaway messages from this case. In the moment of moral outrage, any defense of the vilified object *will not be tolerated.* Moreover, any suggestion that we cannot act decisively to mitigate "the problem," that we are helpless victims of black swans, that whatever we do will never be enough, *will not be tolerated.* The mere suggestion that sex offenders are "statistically unlikely to reoffend" and that there will always be "black swans" (Franklin, 2013) is experienced as a noxious irritant that inflames. However true the message, the messenger will have his or her head delivered on a platter. The visceral response is outrage, and the equally visceral need is to feel safe—protected from harm. Since "protected" means entrusting our safety to law enforcement, we have only a few (law-abiding) options—recommendations for yet more statutes or revised enforcement/surveillance procedures or stricter/harsher sentencing and management strategies. The quasi-legal or extra-legal option is taking "enforcement" out of the context of law through vigilantism.

The need to comprehend and explain tragedy in a way that makes us *feel safe* (e.g., *it would not happen to me, because I know better*) is also visceral. Only two days after Cherish was abducted from McDonalds, FamilyFieldGuide.com (June 23, 2013) reported that the child's mother was "royally reamed" on CafeMom. "The vitriol included posts such as, 'Who needs enemies with a mother like that?' one reply said. 'Fry her ass and sterilize her so she can't have any more kids to endanger,' said another response. The venom goes on." Presumably, all of this anger stemmed from the fact that the mother allowed Smith, a stranger, to take her daughter to McDonalds. Were it not for the mother's alleged irresponsible behavior, so the argument goes, the child would never have been murdered. Although perhaps true in this case, it does *not* begin to solve the problem of dangerous black swans. This problem was explicitly addressed by Griffin and Stitt (2010), who observed that:

> American crime control policy is powerfully driven by popular outrage over lurid, highly publicized crimes—especially crimes against innocent children. In the wake of the brutal murder of a compelling victim, "memorial crime control" legislation is often passed to satisfy popular demands to address some perceived shortcoming in the justice system's ability to protect the public. The result has been "three strikes" laws, stiff mandatory terms for select offenders, extremely rigorous supervision for sex offenders, and so forth. While gratifying public pressure to "do something," such legislation often creates more problems than it solves, destructively burdening public safety officials and at times even backfiring.
>
> (p. 57)

In advocating a shift away from "memorial crime control" and adoption of "Random Activities Theory" as a model for policy, Griffin and Stitt (2010) noted that,

> Proper understanding of such crimes and their intense impact on public policy is thus an adaptation of Nassim Nicholas Taleb's "Black Swan logic." In *The Black Swan: The Impact of the Highly Improbable*, Taleb argues that the most important historic events are unanticipated flukes ("Black Swans") that seem unthinkable when they occur, have an "extreme impact," and are, owing to the human tendency to impose interpretive order on even chaotic events, perceived to be explicable in retrospect (Taleb, 2007). Under "Black Swan Logic," the most important information is unknown, which is the very reason the "Black Swan" event occurs.
>
> (p. 62)

As far as Donald Smith's alleged murder of Cherish Perrywinkle is concerned, we have two seemingly irreconcilable facts: (1) the expert review panel concluded that Florida's SVPP "appears to be working extremely well," and (2) a repeat offender abducted and murdered a child. For the family of Cherish Perrywinkle, her friends, and the community at large, the task is healing—coming to terms with a wanton act of violence, expressing anger, and restoring a sense of control over fear. The interweaving of fear, feeling helpless, and anger are a well-understood interlocking tapestry of emotions. The incomprehensible grief from loss through violence expresses itself repeatedly in all quarters of society. We are all too familiar with it. It is *not*, however, the foundation upon which law should be crafted. If law is to be an effective vehicle for mitigating violence, it must be astutely informed by the best scholarship, thoughtfully drafted, and uniformly implemented. Reconciliation between the two aforementioned "facts" can always be improved, but not through anger and grief-driven legislation.

> The suspense: the fearful, acute suspense: of standing idly by while the life of one we dearly love, is trembling in the balance; the racking thoughts that crowd upon the mind, and make the heart beat violently, and the breath come thick, by the force of the images they conjure up before it; the desperate anxiety *to be doing something* to relieve the pain, or lessen the danger, which we have no power to alleviate; the sinking of soul and spirit, which the sad remembrance of our helplessness produces; what tortures can equal these; what reflections of endeavours can, in the full tide and fever of the time, allay them!
>
> (Charles Dickens' *Oliver Twist*)

Notes

1 (1a) Anti-rape underwear, which when activated by pressure sensors sends out 82 electric shocks; the underwear comes with its own GPS as well, (1b) anti-rape bra, also with its own sensors that emit electric shocks in response to "pinching and squeezing," (2) "FemDefence tampon," which has a sharp pin that penetrates the perpetrator's penis, (3) hairy leg tights, which make the woman's legs appear to be covered with coarse black hair, (4) anti-rape buckle, described as being like a reverse chastity belt, (5) "Rape-Axe Condom," with jagged teeth that penetrate the perpetrator's penis, (6) "The Injector," has two pneumatic syringes that inject tattoo dye and sedatives into the perpetrator, (7) "Angel Wing Buzzing Anti-Rape Device," an alarm that emits a 90dB tone, (8) "Anti-Molestation Jacket," has a button which, when pressed, discharges 110 volts of electricity, making it similar to a stun gun, (9) "The Snare," a belt-like device with two sharp prongs that severely injures the perpetrator's penis, and (10) "Killer Tampon," has a guillotine blade attached to a hollow cylinder that decapitates the head of the penis.

2

DANGEROUSNESS, RISK, AND THE LAW

This chapter traces the development of the use of "risk" and "dangerousness" as human attributes in American law with a special focus on modern sexually violent predator (SVP) laws. Dangerous or risky *behavior* has always been the straightforward and unproblematic object of the law. But risk or danger, understood not as behavior but as an attribute of a person, has had a much more troubled relationship with the law, and its role in the law has developed along a more circuitous route. Modern SVP laws put risk, understood in this way, front and center.

Much of the law is straightforwardly intended to regulate risky or dangerous behavior. The criminal law is invoked to punish past dangerous behavior, while much health and safety regulation seeks to control how and where risky human activity can take place. But the law has also sought over the years to regulate dangerous *persons*, and this effort has been more problematic. The attractiveness of such regulation of *persons* is clear: it seems better to recognize the human beings with a potential for dangerous behavior and intervene before the potential is manifested, than to wait until after the harm is done to punish the actor. Early and classic examples of this sort of preventive intervention include vagrancy laws (Papachristou v. Jacksonville, 1972). Less obviously, eugenic laws mandating sterilization fall into the same category (Buck v. Bell, 1927), as did the Japanese internment laws (Korematsu v. U.S., 1944) and, indeed, racially based Jim Crow laws in general. Over the past decades, however, most of these laws have been struck down or abandoned. Of central importance, the Supreme Court has established the principle that the law may not criminalize a status; thus, a person may not be punished for being an addict, poor, homeless, a vagrant—or, more generally, for being "dangerous."

But the impulse to identify and control dangerous persons has survived these constitutional constraints in two forms. First, dangerousness continues to be a permissible factor in criminal sentencing. Though dangerousness cannot be a constitutionally adequate predicate for conviction, it may be a factor in determining the nature and duration of punishment.

Dangerousness may be a factor in determining whether a convicted person is sentenced to death, the length of sentence imposed, and the end point of an indeterminate sentence (Cole, 2014; Netter, 2007).

Second, there remains in American law the notion that the deprivation of liberty can be accomplished outside of the "charge and conviction" system of the criminal law. While physical incarceration of individuals within the criminal law is highly constrained by hard-fought constitutional guarantees, such control outside of the criminal law remains an attractive possibility, precisely because it is not subject to the heavy constraints of the criminal justice system. In particular, there remain areas of the law, outside of the criminal justice system, where "risk" as an attribute of the person is a permissible predicate for state deprivation of liberty. The nature of this non-criminal, risk-based intervention is the main subject of this chapter.

We can trace the history of the law's approach to "dangerous people" along several threads. The law long focused on individuals who lacked the usual indicia of reliability and civic personhood: no regular employment or fixed address. Over time, various interventions were permitted, including deportation or removal from a locality and imprisonment. Eventually, the law grew wary of these approaches. In Robinson v. California (1962), the Supreme Court articulated clearly the notion that an individual could not be punished for a status. Around the same time, in Papachristou v. City of Jacksonville (1972), the Court ruled a typical vagrancy statute unconstitutional on the grounds of vagueness. The Court's concern was that the law allowed far too much unguided discretion in enforcement. Both of these decisions came at a time when the Court had awakened to the dangers of legislation based on "outsider" status, a concern born of and inspired by the civil rights revolution.

Long a feature of liberal democracies, outsider-status laws identify a group of people who are outside of the group constituting the "polity," those who are included in the phrase "we the people," so central to our constitutional democracy, and thus who are not entitled to the full quantum of legal rights. These outsiders are not full "civic persons," a status that was illustrated and manifested in the Dred Scott decision (Dred Scott v. Sanford, 1857), affirming the right of the majority to treat outsiders (persons of African descent) as a degraded group, without individualization. This kind of outsider thinking, and its inevitable group-based logic, was clearly articulated in the Supreme Court's shameful rationalization for the Japanese internment:

> Exclusion of those of Japanese origin was deemed necessary because of the presence of an unascertained number of disloyal members *of the group*, most of whom we have no doubt were loyal to this country. It was because we could not reject the finding of the military authorities that it was impossible to bring about an immediate

> segregation of the disloyal from the loyal that we sustained the validity of the curfew order as applying to the *whole group*.
>
> (Korematsu v. U.S., 1944, pp. 218–219)

The antidote for group-based control is to focus on harmful behavior, rather than harmful propensity. The Japanese internment orders put the distinction in high relief. The war environment, so the Supreme Court stated, made it impossible to make individual judgments about loyalty; group-based judgments based on presumed propensity were allowed for that reason. But, of course, this sort of group-based propensity rationale was the accepted basis for the law's tolerance of segregation and differential treatment in many areas (e.g., the tolerance of housing segregation). Thus, as the nation, and the courts, became more sensitive to the fundamental contradiction between the promise of equal protection on the one hand, and race and ethnicity-based policies on the other, group-propensity legislation fell out of favor.

During the same period, another thread of "prevention" legislation became more clearly defined and legitimized. A basic starting point for this discussion is the 1905 U.S. Supreme Court Case of Jacobson v. Massachusetts (1905).[1] Pursuant to the applicable statute, Jacobson was convicted of failing to be vaccinated, and fined $5. He appealed to the Massachusetts Supreme Judicial Court, which upheld the fine against a challenge that it violated Jacobson's constitutional rights (Mariner et al., 2005). On review, the U.S. Supreme Court rejected Jacobson's challenge. The Court characterized the vaccination requirement as a "restraint" of liberty, but justified because "the rights of the individual in respect of his liberty may at times, under the pressure of great dangers, be subjected to such restraint, to be enforced by reasonable regulations, as the safety of the general public may demand" (Jacobson v. Massachusetts, 1905, p. 29). Unsurprisingly, the Court went on to hold that the prevention of smallpox through vaccination was one such circumstance.

Two decades later, Jacobson was cited as constitutional support for the forced sterilization of allegedly mentally deficient women in the infamous case of Buck v. Bell (1927). Citing Jacobson as its main authority, the U.S. Supreme Court said:

> We have seen more than once that the public welfare may call upon the best citizens for their lives. . . . The principle that sustains compulsory vaccination is broad enough to cover cutting the Fallopian tubes . . . . Three generations of imbeciles are enough.
>
> (Buck v. Bell, 1927, p. 207)

To use Jacobson as precedent for forced sterilization required multiple transformations, not the least of which was a shift from one type of "restraint on liberty" to another. In Jacobson, there was no provision in the statute to actually force vaccination on anyone, a fact that was important to the Massachusetts Supreme Judicial Court's decision:

> If a person should deem it important that vaccination should not be performed in his case, and the authorities should think otherwise, it is not in their power to vaccinate him by force, and the worst that could happen to him under the statute would be the payment of $5.
>
> (Mariner et al., 2005, p. 582)

Buck, in contrast, involved forced surgery—cutting the fallopian tubes. The Massachusetts statute deprived Mr. Jacobson of his liberty in the way that most laws do: they prohibit certain conduct, and establish a penalty for those who are convicted of violating the prohibition. Buck, on the other hand, allowed the legal requirements to be enforced directly on the body of the individual.

All criminal prohibitions deprive people of their liberty because they prohibit certain kinds of conduct. Those liberty-deprivations are based on the notion of deterrence: in the face of a criminal prohibition, most people choose to avoid the prohibited conduct, because they do not want to be punished for violating the law. Contrast this with the deprivation of liberty suffered by Carrie Buck on the operating table: direct enforcement on her body, contrasted with the indirect deterrence of the criminal law. The latter leaves "liberty" somewhat intact, in the sense that the choice to obey or violate the law is preserved. The former truncates liberty by tying the fallopian tubes; all choice, and all liberty, is foreclosed.

Instead of standing merely for the rather uncontroversial proposition that the state could design criminal prohibitions for the good of the public, Jacobson, as applied in Buck, authorized the direct, physical, pre-crime incapacitation of individuals to protect the public from predicted harm.

This expanded meaning of Jacobson was solidified in the 1975 concurrence of Chief Justice Burger in O'Connor v. Donaldson (1975), a mental illness civil commitment case in which he said, citing Jacobson: "There can be little doubt that in the exercise of its police power a State may confine individuals solely to protect society from the dangers of significant antisocial acts or communicable disease" (O'Connor v. Donaldson, 1975, pp. 582–583). The transformation of Jacobson continued and was strengthened in Kansas v. Hendricks (1997), the case in which the Court announced its approval of modern SVP laws. This time, the Court was explicit in transforming Jacobson into a principle upholding "physical restraint" in the "civil context" (Kansas v. Hendricks, 1997, p. 346). "There are," the Court stated, "manifold restraints to which every person is necessarily subject for the common good" (Kansas v. Hendricks, 1997,

p. 357). But, as in Buck and O'Connor, the Court did not in any way explain how Jacobson's holding, approving a prohibition in the criminal law, came to legitimize pre-crime deprivation of liberty in the civil context.[2]

In short, the progression from Jacobson through Hendricks has clearly established that the constitution permits restraints of liberty, outside of the criminal justice paradigm, that operate directly on the body of the individual—rather than indirectly through deterrence. These preventive interventions are of necessity based on a finding of "dangerousness," a status, rather than on a conviction for a crime. But the role of dangerousness is complex. Because pre-crime liberty deprivation, outside of the criminal law paradigm, is so threatening to the entire structure of American liberty jurisprudence, the courts have needed to develop a rather elaborate set of constraints as an assurance that preventive detention does not threaten "we the people," but only individuals in some sort of outsider status.

The articulation of the role of dangerousness begins with O'Connor v. Donaldson, in which the Supreme Court appears to hold that dangerousness is a necessary predicate for the state to exercise its "mental health power" through civil commitment laws. Prior to this time, the conceptualization of civil commitment was less clear, and there was confusion about the relationship of civil commitment and guardianship. Both forms of intervention grew out of the state's *parens patriae* power, the power (and perhaps obligation) of the state to look after people (including adults) who lack the capacity to look after themselves. O'Connor made it clear that civil commitment could not be justified simply because the person was mentally incompetent. There had to be some justification based on harm—dangerousness—to others or to self. The meaning and scope of the constitutionally required dangerousness then became a focus of civil commitment legislation and policy, as policy-makers debated what level of dangerousness ought to be required (Gerhardstein, 2012).

Researchers began to clarify the concept of dangerousness and critically examine its application. Among the earliest commentaries on dangerousness is the seminal article "Psychiatry and the Presumption of Expertise: Flipping Coins in the Courtroom," by Ennis and Litwack (1974). Building on a literature that was, as a general matter, critical of psychiatric expertise, these authors reported on several empirical studies of dangerousness prediction. The article came to stand for the proposition that mental health experts are prone to overprediction, there are no generally accepted tools to yield accurate predictions, and that expert predictions of dangerousness were correct one out of three times.

Perhaps the most high-profile attempt to apply the thesis of the "Flipping Coins" article came in a 1983 Supreme Court case, Barefoot v. Estelle (1983). The Court upheld the imposition of the death penalty in a case where the prediction of future dangerousness played a role in sentencing. Though it recognized some of the shortcomings of prediction testimony, the Court was unwilling to hold that reliance on dangerousness prediction violated the constitution. Instead, the Court said that the adversary system would be able to sort out and take "due account of its shortcomings." The same approach has been adopted by appellate courts in the context of SVP commitments (In re Det. Of Campbell, 1999).

Meanwhile, in the late 1980s and early 1990s, several cases that reached the Supreme Court made clear that the breadth of the role of "dangerousness" in social control legislation was an open question. The debate focused on whether, and to what extent, states could use preventive detention to address predicted future dangerousness, or rather were required to limit the deprivation of liberty to the punishment of past dangerous behavior. Some commentators argued for a broad "jurisprudence of prevention," under which the state's right to use preventive detention would be limited only by a balancing test, assessing whether the harm to be prevented justified the deprivation of liberty. Others saw this as a major threat to the moral legitimacy of the criminal law by expanding the permissible scope of non-criminal, "regulatory" restrictions on liberty (Dershowitz, 1974a; Dershowitz, 1974b).

The debate about the jurisprudence of prevention was fueled by the Supreme Court's 1987 decision in United States v. Salerno (1987), in which the Court's reasoning appeared to give strong support to the broad use of preventive detention.[3] The case involved a constitutional challenge to the provisions of the Bail Reform Act of 1984 that allowed pretrial detention based on predicted dangerousness. The Salerno Court considered two competing ways of framing the question of constitutionality. Opponents of the law argued that preventive confinement should be limited to specific categories, such as mental illness commitments, in which preventive confinement has been traditionally allowed. Those categories, they argued, do not include pretrial detention. The Salerno majority opinion rejected this categorical approach, adopting instead a balancing approach. Punishment may be imposed only after conviction for a crime. But the legitimacy of non-punitive confinement (which the Court called "regulatory") is measured by a balancing test in which the benefit to the government (and the public) is weighed against the harm to the person whose liberty is taken away. If the balance tips in favor of the government, regulatory confinement is proper. Under this approach, preventive confinement is not limited to discrete categories, such as mentally ill persons, but can be expanded broadly to address all forms of predicted dangerous activity.[4]

Five years later, in Foucha v. Louisiana (1992), the Court appeared to put limits on the jurisprudence of prevention, making clear that preventive confinement needs to fit some relatively narrow categories, such as commitment for "mental illness." Foucha has come to stand for the proposition that preventive confinement requires dangerousness plus some other factor, such as mental illness.

The Development of Modern Sexually Violent Predator Statutes

The foregoing sets the stage for the development of the modern SVP laws. These laws, and the controversy that has surrounded them, have cast risk assessment and dangerousness in a central role, under a bright light and on a stage that demands—and permits—more analytical sharpness and attention than ever before.

The history begins in the late 1930s as Minnesota and several other states enacted sexual psychopath laws (Leon, 2011). Over the next several decades about half the states enacted similar laws. The espoused purpose of these laws was to create an alternative to punishment for sex offenders who were deemed "too sick to deserve punishment" (Millard v. Harris, 1968, p. 966).[5] The laws were said to reflect new "scientific" understanding of the links between sexual deviance and mental disorder (Brief for the Minnesota Attorney General, State ex rel. Pearson v. Probate Court of Ramsey County, 1940, p. 22).

Twenty-seven states and the District of Columbia enacted some form of mentally disordered sex offender commitment law (Erickson, 1995, p. 3). Contemporary descriptions of these programs indicated that "most of the cases committed under the legislation are minor varieties of sex deviates: peepers, exhibitionists, homosexuals, and the like. The menacing varieties of sex criminals are rarely touched in the operation of these laws" (Burick, 1968, p. 256).

The U.S. Supreme Court examined the Minnesota sexual psychopath statute in 1940. At a time when the Court showed almost no concern about the constitutionality of limitations on personal liberty, the Court upheld the law, but only with a narrow interpretation: the law would be constitutionally suspect, the Court held, unless it was limited to individuals who were "utterly unable to control" their sexual impulses (State ex rel. Pearson v. Probate Court of Ramsey County, 1940). The Court did not explain why this particular limitation was constitutionally required, why the limitation supported the validity of the law, or even what it meant. Further, there is little evidence that this construct had much of a limiting impact on the operation of the laws. In Minnesota, the language was barely mentioned again in any appellate court decision until the early 1990s.

Over time, the use of these laws declined, and their focus shifted from non-violent to violent offenders (Erickson, undated, pp. 10–12).[6] In 1977, the Group for the Advancement of Psychiatry issued an influential report titled *Psychiatry and Sex Psychopath Legislation: The 30s to the 80s* (hereinafter the "GAP Report"). This report, along with reports from the President's Commission on Mental Health, and the American Bar Association's Committee on Criminal Justice Mental Health Standards, recommended the repeal of the sex offender commitment legislation (Brakel, Parry, & Weiner, 1985). The GAP Report characterized sex offender commitment statutes as an "experiment [that] has failed," providing neither effective treatment nor incarcerating truly dangerous individuals (Group for the Advancement of Psychiatry, 1977, p. 942). By the 1980s, most of the states with sexual psychopath commitment laws had either repealed them or had ceased actively using them (Bodine, 1990, pp. 109–110).

But by the late 1980s, a set of societal influences converged to generate an important shift in public policy around sexual violence.[7] The new direction led to a revival of the sex psychopath laws, generally called sexually violent person (SVP) laws. The modern laws are aimed at the "worst of the worst" rather than offenders who were "too sick to deserve punishment." Twenty states and the federal government have enacted in one form or another these SVP laws (Janus & Prentky, 2008, p. 91). Supplementing these civil commitment laws, states have enacted registration and community notification laws (collectively known as Megan's Laws). Pushed by strong incentives from the federal government, all 50 states have enacted some form of registration and notification requirements (Logan, 2003). Many states and local jurisdictions have enacted, or considered, a mélange of other preventive measures, including residential restrictions (Landers, 2008; Laney, 2008), and other temporal and spatial restrictions such as prohibitions on sex offenders using storm shelters (Associated Press, 2005) or going outside on Halloween (Grinberg, 2009; Chaffin, Levenson, Letourneau, & Stern, 2009), and disqualifications from various government benefits (Associated Press, 2009). These laws all share a central feature: to evade the strict constitutional guarantees constraining criminal punishments, they all claim a regulatory label and a non-punitive purpose.

The new laws arose from a complex set of forces in the late 1980s and early 1990s.[8] A key point was the feminist agenda to change societal attitudes and behavior about sexual violence against women (D'Emilio & Freedman, 1997, p. 314). By the late 1980s, feminist-inspired views of sexual violence had transformed social judgments about punishing sex offenders. Existing sentencing guidelines were seen as "inadequate punishment," "too short to permit meaningful treatment of sex offenders in prison" (Office of the Attorney General, State of Minnesota, 1989, p. 10), and providing insufficient "supervised release after the prison doors are opened" (Office of the Attorney General, State of Minnesota, 1989, p. 19).

But while criminal sentences could (and would) be lengthened prospectively, constitutional guarantees such as the protection against double jeopardy prevented states from simply lengthening the sentences that had been previously imposed on offenders. The new sex offender laws aimed to fill the "incapacitation gap" created by this change of viewpoint.

Though the statutory language differs from law to law, the structure of all is similar. [9] SVP laws typically contain four substantive elements and two procedural characteristics. Substantively, the laws aim at individuals who (1) have a history of sexually violent or dangerous conduct; (2) have a mental or personality disorder or "abnormality" which (3) "causes" or "predisposes" the person to (4) a likelihood of future dangerous sexual conduct. The statutes provide little guidance on either the type of mental disorder that qualifies, or the risk threshold for dangerousness, though, as will be discussed in more detail below, some courts have held that a high probability of future harm is constitutionally required. The laws specify procedural protections that are typically higher than standard civil litigation standards, but fall short of the protections required in a criminal prosecution. The laws generally allow the state to force the respondent to testify, and abrogate the rules of privilege and confidentiality to allow the admission of relevant treatment records without the consent of the individual. Some, but not all, states require proof beyond a reasonable doubt and allow for a jury trial. Although details vary, committed individuals can expect to remain committed until the conditions giving rise to the commitment—either the presence of a mental disorder or the prediction of future dangerousness—are ameliorated. Commitment statutes generally require the provision of treatment.[10]

By 1994, a handful of states had adopted SVP laws. Litigation challenging the constitutionality of the laws quickly followed. By the mid-1990s, the laws had been constitutionally vetted and approved by the U.S. Supreme Court. The approval cleared the way for additional adoptions; by 2007, 20 jurisdictions (including the federal government) had adopted SVP laws (Gookin, 2007).

In 1997, the U.S. Supreme Court upheld the constitutionality of the Kansas SVP law in Kansas v. Hendricks (1997).[11] The Court disposed of constitutional challenges on two main fronts. The "substantive due process" challenge argued that the laws extend civil commitment beyond its proper scope. The "punishment" argument asserted that the laws had a punitive purpose, and therefore violated the double jeopardy and *ex post facto* prohibitions of the Constitution.

Substantive due process is a constitutional doctrine that limits the circumstances in which states are permitted to restrict the liberty of individuals. Challengers argued that the Kansas SVP law exceeded the state's constitutional powers because it failed to require a "mental illness" as a basis for commitment. The Court rejected this argument.

While acknowledging that commitment requires some "mental disorder" predicate, the Court held there was no particular constitutional significance to the term "mental illness." The Court stated that the mental disorder predicate for civil commitment is a legal, as opposed to a medical, term. States are given substantial leeway in defining the statutorily sufficient mental abnormality. The "mental disorder" element must "adequately distinguish [persons subject to civil commitment] from other dangerous persons who are perhaps more properly dealt with exclusively through criminal proceedings" (Kansas v. Hendricks, 1997, p. 360).

Several state supreme courts have interpreted this language as imposing a constitutional "volitional dysfunction" test for sex offender commitments. But many commentators argue that "volitional dysfunction" is essentially meaningless. They argue that the courts' use of volitional dysfunction simply serves to limit commitments to repeat offenders—those whose past course of criminal conduct indicates a failure (rather than an inability) to control sexually violent behavior.

Double jeopardy and *ex post facto*: The double jeopardy clause prevents the state from "punishing twice, or attempting a second time to punish criminally, for the same offense" (Kansas v. Hendricks, 1997, p. 368). The *ex post facto* clause "forbids the application of any new punitive measure to a crime already consummated" (Kansas v. Hendricks, 1997, p. 370). Challengers claimed that sex offender commitment laws are really punishment masquerading as civil commitment. Citing statements of commitment proponents (e.g., "these 'animals' should be kept in prison beyond their scheduled sentences and never allowed out"), they argued that the true purpose of commitment laws is to extend the confinement of sex offenders who have served their prison terms. The Supreme Court rejected this argument on the ground that incapacitation of dangerous individuals is a well-accepted purpose of civil commitment.

Challengers also argued that the failure to provide effective treatment to committed individuals is evidence of a punitive intent. Hendricks stated that the availability of effective treatment is not a constitutional prerequisite for civil commitment, explaining that a contrary holding "would obligate a State to release certain confined individuals who were both mentally ill and dangerous simply because they could not be successfully treated for their afflictions" (Kansas v. Hendricks, 1997, p. 366).[12]

Though the constitutional underpinnings of SVP laws appear to put the "mental disorder" and "dangerousness" prongs on equal footing, in reality it is fair to say that most of the focus in the implementation of these laws falls on dangerousness. The mental disorder prong has little or no role in determining who is committed and who is not.

Minnesota's application of the disorder prong of its SVP laws is typical. The Minnesota courts have set few, if any, limitations on the mental disorder predicate for commitment. The laws do not require proof of severe psychiatric illness, criminal insanity, or legal incompetence.

> It is not necessary that the person lack adequate control at all times, if at some times he lacks such control. And the fact that there was a 10-year gap in the person's sex offenses does not show that he had adequate control over his sexual behavior.
>
> (Kirwin, 2005, p. 20)

The Minnesota Court of Appeals held that commitment is not limited "to those individuals who suffer conditions such as psychosis, sleep walking, or brain seizures" (In re Kunshier, 1995, p. 3) or "to those very extreme examples of persons who had cognitive deficits arising from conditions such as severe mental retardation, dementia, or organic brain damage" (In Matter of Patterson, 1995, p. 2). Minnesota law does not require that a person be "mentally ill" or "mentally incompetent" to be committed as a sex offender (Kirwin, 2005, p. 17).

Dangerousness in SVP Laws: Public Policy

Having traced the history and development of "dangerousness" in legal doctrine, we turn to two related topics. First, we explore the public policy implications of the use of risk in SVP laws. Then, we examine how the law receives and processes risk information at an individual or case level. In the final chapters of this book, we ask how those two approaches can best fit together, to produce the fairest procedures, and best public policy, supporting the prevention of sexual violence.

At a policy level, the notion of risk or dangerousness underlying the SVP laws has grown out of society's worry about recidivist sexual violence. This concern has, in turn, led to the conceptualization of the "sexual predator" as the target of legal intervention. These developments have led sexual violence prevention policies to focus on identifying and isolating the "worst of the worst," rather than on policies that are designed systematically to reduce sexual violence.

SVP laws have most often arisen in the context of public outrage over recidivist sexual violence: heinous crimes committed by sex offenders released from prison on parole.[13] Recidivist sex crimes seem to be the most outrageous. We can focus our outrage on the offender—who, after all, should have learned from his punishment—and on the government, which should have known better than to release this (in hindsight, obvious) killer, who was safely imprisoned. Following the template of the path-breaking Washington legislation, much of the recent legislation cites the "high" recidivism rates of sex offenders.

Recidivism is not an irrational matter to consider in designing sex offender policy. Any convicted sex offender is certainly at higher risk for sexual violence than a typical person who has not been so convicted. But the recidivism frame has come to predominate the development of sexual violence policy. It creates a focus on identifying and isolating the "most dangerous," directing our attention away from the societal circumstances that foster sexual violence.

Inherent in the recidivism frame is the widely accepted notion that the recidivism rate for sex offenders is extraordinarily high. In reality, sex offender recidivism is lower than the rate for many other types of criminals. The vast majority of sex offenders, over a three-year period, are not caught in a new sex crime (Langhan, Schmidt, & Durose, 2003, p. 8). But the issue with the recidivism frame goes much deeper. The key problem of our almost exclusive focus on recidivism is that it forces the bulk of sexual violence into the shadows. The fact is that most—the vast majority—of sexual abuse is not sexual recidivism. Of all sexual crimes committed by released prisoners, only 13% are committed by those previously confined for sex offenses. The rest—87%—are committed by prisoners convicted on non-sex offenses (Langhan, Schmidt, & Durose, 2003, p. 7). Further, 86% of sex offenders in prison have no prior history of a sexual offense (Langhan, Schmidt, & Durose, 2003, p. 17). In short, the vast majority of sex offenses are not committed by sex offender recidivists. Thus, we see that the focus on recidivist violence necessarily limits public policy to a small portion of the problem of sexual violence and undercuts any attempt to understand the root causes of sexual violence, and thus the bulk of the problem of sexual violence.

The focus of public policy is further defined by the creation of the category of the "sexual predator." Because preventive detention is an exception to the general rules governing governmental power, the targets of SVP laws need to be understood as "different in kind" from the general population. In part, this difference is demonstrated by their "mental abnormality." Their dangerousness also contributes to the view that sexual predators are "the other." Predator laws reify risk, make it concrete, and ascribe it to the individual. Risk assessment "seeks to bring the future into the present" (Rose, 2002, p. 214), distilling the future into a present "condition" or "propensity." This is necessary because otherwise the law couldn't lock somebody up *now* because of what they might do in the future. While the "causal factors" for violence may be a combination of internal (psychological) and external (environmental) factors (Arboleda-Florez et al., 1998), the resultant "risk" is ascribed solely to the individual. He "is" dangerous, he "has" risk, and it is his "possession" of these characteristics that justifies his incarceration. Pursuant to the SVP laws, we lock people up who "pose a threat to others, not because of what they had done but because of who they are, because their very makeup as a human being made them a threat to 'the community'" (Rose, 2002, p. 209).

As constructed by the predator laws, risk tells us something essential—rather than accidental—about the person. This characteristic—sometimes called "dangerousness"—is portrayed as a stable ingredient of the person, a part of him even if it is not now visible (Harris & Rice, 2003, p. 989). It is this internal characteristic, treated as having long-term stability, that justifies both the prediction of future behavior and the creation of outsider status. The predator is not simply a person who commits a crime, but rather a person whose nature is criminal, "a 'criminal man', a person who by his very nature is driven to commit the most violent of crimes against the most vulnerable of victims" (Petrunik, 1994, p. 19).[14]

In sum, modern sex offender policy zeroes in on individual risk. Our public policy pays inordinate attention to figuring out who are the most dangerous and how we can protect ourselves from them, and very little to determining what are the patterns of sexual violence, and how our social structures allow them to flourish.

The Adjudication of Risk in SVP Cases

We turn our attention now away from the public policy implications of the risk-law interface to a discussion of the adjudication of risk, asking how the law receives and vets risk information in the context of individual cases. We seek to address and understand the tools available to courts for making the judgment assigned to them by the law: separating those for whom SVP commitment is legally appropriate from those for whom it is not. This involves several questions: Does the law articulate an operational legal threshold for risk? Are there adequate legal tools for ensuring that the evidence underlying risk decisions reflects the best available evidence, and that the integrity or quality of the evidence is sufficient? And finally, how effective is the enforcement of these legal standards in actual practice?

We begin with some basic distinctions and definitions that should help us in this examination. To begin, we note that the SVP laws mark a shift from a focus on "dangerousness" to "risk" as the predominant descriptor in the legal context. As two of the authors have discussed previously, we think this change is for the positive.[15] Risk has greater utility and more flexibility than dangerousness for several reasons. First, risk addresses not only the presence of a potential hazard, but also the probability of its occurrence (Prentky & Burgess, 2000, p. 100). It is thus dimensional and continuous, whereas dangerousness is too often thought of in dichotomous terms (i.e., either the offender is dangerous or is not dangerous) (Prentky & Burgess, 2000, p. 100). The increased focus on "risk" also helps clarify that dangerousness is a multi-factor concept. In his 1974 book, Professor Brooks enumerated four components of dangerousness: "(1) the magnitude of harm, (2) the probability that the harm will occur, (3) the frequency with which the harm will occur, and (4) the imminence of the harm" (Bochnewich, 1992, p. 298).

Over 30 years ago, Professors John Monahan and David Wexler sought to clarify the probability standards used in civil commitments[16] (Monahan & Wexler, 1978, p. 37). Monahan and Wexler proposed to subdivide the probability standard into two strands: a substantive aspect, referred to as the standard of commitment, and a procedural aspect, referred to as the standard of proof.

The standard of commitment sets the substantive risk threshold for civil commitment, usually described in terms of the likelihood of dangerous behavior. We can think of the standard of commitment as referring to a "fact" in the real world. It is typically associated with such terms as "likely" and "highly likely." For example, the Massachusetts Supreme Court stated "[a]s used in the statute, however, the term 'likely' is not intended as a standard or burden of proof. Rather, it is descriptive of one characteristic ('likely to engage in sexual offenses') of a sexually dangerous person" (Com. v. Boucher, 2002, p. 50).

The standard of proof, in contrast, is epistemological, and measures the degree of certainty that the trier of fact must have to find that a particular fact is true. The New Jersey Superior Court, Appellate Division stated "[t]he burden of proof, which denotes a degree of certainty of conviction, is a consideration separate and apart from the likelihood of re-offense, which denotes a factual probability" (In re Commitment of W.Z., 2001, p. 114). The standard of proof is operationalized in the courtroom with such phrases as "clear and convincing evidence" and "beyond a reasonable doubt" (Monahan & Wexler, 1978, p. 41; Com. v. Boucher, 2002, p. 50).

As Monahan and Wexler submitted, and as Janus and Meehl discussed, the relationship between these two standards is "intricate and complex." Each standard invokes a notion of probability, but there is often no clear distinction between the two probabilities invoked. For example, when a mental health expert opines that the defendant is "likely" to commit a crime, is she talking about a "fact" in the real world (i.e., a fact about the defendant), or about the level of certainty of her knowledge of the real world (e.g., that she has moderate confidence that the defendant will commit a crime)?

The wide adoption of actuarial risk-assessment instruments helps make this distinction, because they produce numerical scores that explicitly address the real world, and may report, quite separately, information about the level of confidence one should attach to the results (Vars, 2013). But as we point out elsewhere, human judgment and interpretation will inevitably be involved in reporting and interpreting even precise numerical evidence, so the careful distinction that Monahan and Wexler proposed remains an aspiration rather than an accomplished reality.

This discussion of the standards of commitment and proof leads logically to a discussion of the concepts used in the law to evaluate risk-assessment testimony. In other words, how does the law determine whether testimony about risk is of sufficient quality to be considered in an SVP case, and how does the adjudication process determine whether the testimony satisfies the standard of commitment and the standard of proof? These matters are evaluated at three distinct stages of the litigation process, roughly corresponding to the three judgments that must be made.

First, judges make a threshold decision whether to admit or receive particular evidence. This determination provides the clearest opportunity for courts to assess the quality and integrity of the risk-assessment testimony. Key considerations are relevance or "fit," prejudice, and integrity. Courts and legal scholars use various terms when referring to the "integrity" of testimony. Terms such as reliability, validity, dependability, and trustworthiness are frequently used, and some courts simply substitute "general acceptance" of the methods in place of an examination of their integrity (Faigman, 2000). As we discuss in a little more detail below, all SVP jurisdictions have ruled that risk-assessment testimony as a general category—whether wholly clinical or based on actuarial instruments—is sufficiently trustworthy to be admissible.

The second stage corresponds roughly to the "standard of proof," and requires the "trier of fact" (the jury, if there is one; otherwise, the judge) to assess the weight of the evidence. The questions here concern whether, and to what extent, the witness' testimony is credible, and how much influence this testimony ought to have in deciding the ultimate question (here, the legally defined risk posed by the respondent). The finder of fact uses this "weight" assessment to determine whether the evidence is substantial enough to satisfy the "standard of proof."

The third stage is often referred to as the assessment of "legal sufficiency." This requires the application of the standard of commitment to the evidence that has been weighed and sorted out by the trier of fact. In other words, once the trier of fact has determined how much credibility or weight to give to various pieces of evidence, the process determines whether the evidence demonstrates that the risk surpasses the legal threshold set in the standard of commitment.

While these three arenas for the assessment of evidence seem arcane and technical, their deployment has profound consequences on the nature of the legal proceedings, and in particular for the uniformity and transparency of these highly fateful decisions about safety and liberty.

Despite giving lip service to the importance and difficulty of risk assessment, courts have deployed the available tools in a way that minimizes their supervision of this judgment. Courts have imposed few restraints on the admission of risk-assessment testimony and have been reluctant to articulate and enforce legal risk thresholds. As a result, there is little guarantee that risk decisions are based on legal standards that are consistently applied, or are based on the soundest information that science can bring to bear. Let us unpack each of these issues.

To begin, courts are exercising little or no control on risk-assessment testimony at the threshold of admissibility. Despite the relative novelty of actuarial risk-assessment tools, and their evolution over time, courts have erected no serious impediment to their admission (Janus & Prentky, 2003). A typical, and rather recent, example is the decision of the Kansas Supreme Court in In re Girard and Mallard. Applying the "Frye" test—under which scientific evidence is admissible if "the basis of that opinion [is] shown to be generally accepted as reliable within the expert's particular scientific field" (In re Girard, 2013, p. 272)—the Court held, without any significant analysis, that actuarial evidence is scientific. And, citing evidence that actuarial instruments are "widely used," and that courts and academic writing widely support the admissibility of actuarial evidence, the Kansas Court easily concluded that the evidence was admissible.

To our knowledge, only one court has declined to admit any sort of risk-assessment testimony. An Illinois intermediate appellate court refused to admit actuarial scores, but that decision was reversed just a year later by the Illinois Supreme Court with the observation that "there is no question that [actuarial assessment] is generally accepted by professionals who assess sexually violent offenders and therefore is perfectly admissible in a court of law" (In re Commitment of Simons, 2004, p. 1192). Researchers report that "actuarial data are admissible in court over 90% of the time" (Mills, Kroner, & Morgan, 2011, p. 9).

The admissibility of actuarial results should not come as a surprise. The courts have long freely admitted clinical testimony about dangerousness, and one might surmise courts are guided in these decisions not so much by the quality of risk-assessment testimony, but by the clear command of legislatures to base decisions on assessments of risk. As one California appellate court put it: "Where the trier of fact is required by statute to determine whether a person is dangerous or likely to be dangerous, expert prediction may be the only evidence available" (People v. Ward, 83 Cal. Rptr.2d 828, 831 (Cal. Dist. Ct. App. 1999)). It would be remarkable if such legislative commands could be frustrated by evidentiary rulings by courts. Of course, the legislative commands must pass constitutional muster, but as we have pointed out, the Supreme Court has long held that the use of dangerousness testimony does not offend the constitution.

Once risk-assessment testimony has been admitted, the key tool available to courts to supervise risk judgments is the articulation and application of the legal standard for risk, in what we have identified above as the judgment of "legal sufficiency." But here, too, we see courts failing to provide the transparent guidance that would support accountability and uniformity in risk decisions.

Despite the centrality of dangerousness in SVP laws, courts and legislatures have avoided any precise prescriptions for determining how the "most dangerous" will be identified.[17] Several courts have articulated at a rather abstract level some constraints on the likelihood of future violence that is necessary to justify commitment (e.g., "highly likely"), and several courts have designated the kind of violence (e.g., "predatory") necessary (Janus & Prentky, 2003). At least one court has specified the conditions under which danger is to be assessed (i.e., with treatment and under supervision), and a few courts have begun to set some standards for the "validity" of the assessments of risk (Janus & Prentky, 2003). The risk-assessment aspect of SVP cases, however, remains highly discretionary. Real decision-making is situated with juries or trial courts, and few appellate courts intervene to set standards that might lead to some accountability or uniformity in risk thresholds.

Knighton, Murrie, Boccaccini, and Turner (2014) surveyed the 20 states with SVP laws and classified the laws with respect to risk thresholds. They report that states fall into four categories. In the category they call the clearest definition, the state is required to prove that the likelihood of re-offense is "more likely than not." The authors sensibly conclude that this standard requires a probability of re-offense greater than 50%. The authors identify Iowa and Florida as falling into this category.

The second category does not quantify the probability, but clarifies that the legal standard requires proof that re-offense is "highly likely" or some synonymous term. For example, Minnesota, by case law, sets its risk threshold at "highly likely." In a similar vein, California's Supreme Court says that the statutory standard is met if the person presents a "substantial danger," but clarifies that this does not mean a "better than even" chance. Because the courts do not quantify the meaning of "highly likely," it is unclear how decision-makers operationalize this legal standard.

Third, the authors identify a group of states that have explicitly refused to quantify or clarify the statutory standards for risk, leaving that task to the decision-maker at trial. For example, the Illinois Supreme Court emphasized that the standard "cannot be reduced to a mere mathematical formula or statistical analysis." Similarly, the North Dakota Supreme Court explained that "likely to engage" means that the individual's "propensity towards sexual violence is of such a degree as to pose a threat to others" (Grosinger v. MBK, 2002, p. 477). This definition, the Court assures us, "prevents a contest over percentage points" and "allows experts to use the fullness of their education, experience and resources available to them in order to determine if an individual poses a threat to society" (Grosinger v. MBK, 2002, p. 477).

The Massachusetts Supreme Judicial Court explained its reluctance to quantify the risk standard or otherwise explain it, by embracing a "case-by-case" analysis, based on a "number of factors, including the seriousness of the threatened harm, the relative certainty of the anticipated harm, and the possibility of successful intervention to prevent that harm" (Com. v. Boucher, 2002, p. 277). The Court explained that

> while "likely" indicates more than a mere propensity or possibility, it is not bound to the statistical probability inherent in a definition such as "more likely than not," and the terms are not interchangeable. To conclude that "likely" amounts to a quantifiable probability, absent a more specific statutory expression of such a quantity, is to require mathematical precision from a term that, by its plain meaning, demands contextual, not statistical, analysis.
>
> (Com. v. Boucher, 2002, p. 277)

The Minnesota Supreme Court similarly rejected a pointed plea from several judges of the state's Court of Appeals to set out more explicitly some standards for the risk threshold for commitment. In re Ince (2014) presented an ideal case for judicial clarification of the risk threshold standard. The facts in the case were by any measure borderline. Thus, a reasoned judgment from an appellate court, explaining why the case fell on one side or the other of the threshold, would have begun to create a "jurisprudence of dangerousness." The Minnesota Supreme Court declined this clear invitation.

The trial court was presented with facts that at best seemed to be in a gray area for a commitment scheme aimed at the "worst of the worst." The respondent's offenses occurred when he was 17 and 18 years old. He had served a relatively brief prison sentence (which was a "downward" departure from the sentencing guidelines) and was petitioned for commitment at the very last minute prior to the end of this sentence. Apparently for this reason, he was placed on supervised release in the community pending his commitment hearing, for a period of eight months, during which he lived in the community, maintained a job, attended treatment, and refrained from re-offending. On its face, this violence-free period is hardly strong evidence of a distinctive mental abnormality that made it "difficult if not impossible" for him to control his behavior.

Three experts testified about Ince's re-offense risk. Though their testimony varied substantially in the methods and results of their assessments, the Court of Appeals reported that all three agreed that Ince's risk of re-offense satisfied the "highly likely" legal threshold for commitment (In re Ince, 2013, p. 6). Not surprisingly, the appellate court did not explain what the "highly likely" criterion meant, or how the Court ascertained that the experts were using the proper meaning of the term in reaching their conclusions. Rather, it fell back on the standard explanation that

> where the findings of fact rest almost entirely on expert testimony, the [district] court's evaluation of credibility is of particular significance. . . . But whether the evidence is sufficient to meet the statutory requirements for commitment is a question of law, which this court reviews de novo."
>
> (In re Ince, 2013, p. 8)

Here, the Court noted that the district court had based its conclusion largely on a finding that one of the three experts' testimony was "particularly persuasive and convincing," and had "accepted" that testimony while rejecting the testimony of the other experts "only to the extent they did not agree with that of Dr. Marston" (In re Ince, 2013, p. 5). Neither the district court nor the Court of Appeals explained in any detail the basis for crediting one of the three experts and not the other two.

The Court of Appeals then reviewed each of the six "factors" previous case law had established for determining whether the legal standard of "highly likely" had been satisfied, and stated, for each, that the "record . . . supports the district court's analysis of this factor" (In re Ince, 2013, p. 6). Then, the Court stated: "Because the six . . . factors support a conclusion that Ince is highly likely to re-offend, the state has met its burden of proving the statutory factor by clear and convincing evidence" (In re Ince, 2013, p. 7). The Court of Appeals never articulated how the factors were to be analyzed, how they fit together, or how they satisfied the "highly likely" threshold, explaining: "This court defers to the district court's credibility determinations and its opportunity to weigh the evidence" (In re Ince, 2013, p. 14).

By repeating this mantra, the appellate court makes it seem that the real dispute in the trial court was about how to weigh various "factors," and which witness was more "credible." While there may have been some of both kinds of analysis, the key dispute should have focused on an articulation of what the legal standard "highly likely" meant. How else, after all, could the courts determine whether the evidence "supports" the standard? These were not abstract and only potential questions, but questions of legal meaning posed directly by the evidence itself. For example, the experts reported their findings about risk in terms of absolute percent likelihood of re-offending over a specified period of time, and in terms of relative likelihood in comparison to a "typical" sex offender. Yet the Court of Appeals did not set out what the relevance of these quantified measures was to the legal standard. Is "highly likely" an absolute, or a relative, measure? If an absolute, over what period of time is it to be measured? If over a "lifetime," does a 62.4% likelihood meet legal muster? Why or why not? If not on its own, how do the other factors that the Court "weighed" affect the decision? Is "highly likely" translatable into a number? If so, what number? If not, why not? On what basis, or on what methodology, are the factors combined? Do they overlap, or are they orthogonal? How many of them are already taken into account in the actuarial scores? And if they are not taken into account, what is the evidence that they are relevant to risk?

Many of these issues were raised in the concurrence and dissent in the Court of Appeals. Then-Chief Judge Matt Johnson of the Court of Appeals took the unusual step of writing a special concurrence, a well-researched and well-reasoned plea for clearer standards, for the development of a "jurisprudence of dangerousness." He argued that the Minnesota Supreme Court's six-factor test for "highly likely," adopted in the early 1990s, "relegate[s] . . . actuarial tools to the margins of the legal analysis" (In re Ince, 2013, p. 10) and does not address the potential overlap and resultant "double counting" if actuarial tools and the six factors are combined:

> Actuarial risk-assessment tools surely are an imperfect means of predicting a particular person's future behavior, but they appear to provide access to the best prediction presently available. Given the difficulty of the fact-finding task, the case law should allow parties as well as the district courts and this court to take advantage of the best available means of prediction. But the legal analysis prescribed by [the Minnesota court precedent] does not do so and, thus, appears to be inconsistent with the present-day views and practices of professionals in this particular field of work and study.
>
> (In re Ince, 2013, p. 9)

He called out the "confusion that may arise from the lack of guidance concerning the type of risk that is relevant" (In re Ince, 2013, p. 9) citing, in particular, the use of both "relative risk" and "absolute risk" in the expert testimony. His opinion understands and describes the fact that "a person's absolute risk of recidivism, when determined by actuarial tools, depends in part on the base rate of recidivism of a group of comparable sex offenders" (In re Ince, 2013, p. 12).

He points out that the district court's findings "recited only relative-risk statements," which are "incapable of answering the key question in this case: whether Ince is 'highly likely' to reoffend" (In re Ince, 2013, p. 12). He points out that the case "raises an issue concerning the selection of the most appropriate actuarial risk-assessment tool and the most appropriate group of comparable sex offenders from which to obtain a general base rate of recidivism" (In re Ince, 2013, p. 12). He points out, for example, the MnSOST-3.1 yielded a risk of reconviction of 7.12% over a four-year period, but the trial court did not mention this evidence, "let alone attempt to reconcile that evidence with other evidence in the record" (In re Ince, 2013, p. 13).

Finally, Chief Judge Johnson highlighted the "lack of clarity" in the legal term "highly likely":

> For example, in one of this court's recent unpublished cases, two expert witnesses had different understandings of the "highly likely" standard. One expert witness testified at trial that the law requires "[b]asically a better than even chance," while the other expert witness testified at trial that "it's higher than more likely than not but there's no specific number attached to it."
>
> (In re Civil Commitment of Ince, 2013, p. 14)

He concluded:

> The lack of a clear and definite legal standard is in tension with fundamental notions of the rule of law. A statute that may deprive a person of his or her liberty should have "an understandable meaning with legal standards that courts must enforce."[citation omitted] A law should not be so vague and standardless that it leaves . . . judges . . . free to decide, without any legally fixed standards, what is prohibited and what is not in each particular case.
>
> (In re Ince, 2013, p. 14)

Pointing out that "clarifying the meaning of 'highly likely' is unavoidably a matter of line-drawing," the chief judge noted that often such lines are simply recognized "after numerous case-by-case determinations." But, he lamented, "Seventeen years after [the Minnesota Supreme Court articulated the "highly likely" standard], however, the precedential case-by-case determinations on this issue are too few in number and too general in their discussion" (In re Ince, 2013, p. 15).

Judge Johnson's misgivings were bolstered by Judge Stauber's dissent pointing out that the trial court findings are couched within "credibility assessments insulated from appellate review. Given this standard of review, it will continue to be almost impossible to overturn even borderline cases" (In re Ince, 2013, p. 24). Indeed, our review of dozens of cases from 10 SVP states suggests that the weighing, at least as reported in appellate cases, seems to go only one way—granting credibility to the scores when they support commitment, and undermining them when they do not.

Unfortunately, the Minnesota Supreme Court did not accept this clear opportunity to improve accountability and consistency in risk-assessment determinations. The Court's opinion seemed a bit confused about the relationship between the burden of proof and the standard of proof. Similarly, it blurred the conceptual distinction between the risk/dangerousness element and the mental disorder element, suggesting that the highly likely standard was honed even further by the "difficulty controlling" gloss on the mental disorder element. The Court rejected, but without any coherent explanation, the notion that "highly likely" could be related to some quantitative benchmark. Nor did it clarify whether the standard related to relative or absolute risk, or whether or how experts and lower courts should deal with the time horizon for risk assessments.

The Court, to be sure, reversed and remanded Ince's commitment, directing the trial court to explain more clearly its decision. But the Court made no effort to explain why remand was appropriate, other than this was a "difficult task . . . in this unique case." Perhaps the Court thought that the evidence was borderline, in a gray area. Yet even a simple statement of that sort would help, beginning to put some reasoning around the risk-assessment judgment, laying down some points from which all of the stakeholders could begin to ascertain some standard. In the words of Chief Judge Johnson, the Supreme Court could have fostered the beginning of a jurisprudence of dangerousness.

The pattern is similar around the country. Appellate review has not provided meaningful accountability in the judicial risk-assessment process. In our review of 200 appellate cases on risk assessment from 10 states, we found only two successful appeals on risk-assessment issues. In Minnesota, with over 450 appellate cases, there are only 7 cases reversing commitments, and 5 of the 7 occurred in the first years of the SVP program, two decades ago. In re Ince, the 2014 case discussed above, is the only appellate case reversing a commitment because of fault in the risk-assessment methodology.

Some empirical studies help dimension the need for clearer standards for risk assessment.

There is evidence that the selection processes, by which state officials determine which offenders to refer for commitment, are guided to some extent by risk-assessment scores (Boccaccini et al., Do Scores from Risk Measures Matter to Jurors?, p. 260). Boccaccini et al. summarize studies from several states showing that offenders who are referred for full SVP evaluations, those whom mental health evaluators conclude meet statutory criteria for commitment, and those whose cases are chosen for trial by prosecutors have, on average, higher risk scores than offenders who are not selected. Thus, they conclude that risk-measure scores "play a role" in the cases that are brought to trial.

An important study of the Minnesota SVP program conducted by the Minnesota Office of Legislative Auditor reached conclusions that suggest that screeners and prosecutors have highly variable conceptions of the risk threshold for commitment. The report found that per capita petition and commitment rates varied considerably based on geography (judicial districts), and that the variation could not be accounted for by differences in the incidence of sex offenders district by district. Interestingly, the rate of commitments as a proportion of petitions was almost uniform across the state at about 80%, despite the highly variable per capita rate of petition by region. One might have expected a higher rate of petition denials in districts with higher per capital petition rates, as courts sought to impose strict risk-assessment standards to correct lax petitioning standards.

A study in Texas observed that juries committed 100% of the 26 petitions brought during the study period (though one of the commitments came only after a re-trial following a hung jury) (Boccaccini & Turner, 2013). The authors report that this rate of commitment is consistent with Texas SVP results over the life of that state's law: only one jury has ever concluded that an individual subject to a petition did not meet the statutory standards. (Reports indicate that in the Florida SVP scheme, 95% of petitions are granted after trial. In Minnesota, the figure is about 80% (Kestin & Williams, 2013; Office of the State Auditor, 2011).) The same study sought to determine whether the jurors in those cases were influenced by risk-assessment scores (as opposed to clinical judgments) in determining whether respondents met the "likely" standard of Texas. The authors concluded that the scores did not make a difference to the jurors in the study. They hypothesize that since all of the respondents had scores that placed them in the moderate to high range of risk, all of the scores fell above the jurors' perceived threshold for "likely." Alternatively, they suggested that jurors simply do not care about risk in SVP cases. They report that this hypothesis is consistent with prior research showing that mock jurors view the commitment decision in a retributive context, and make a "punishment" decision based on the severity of the individual's past crimes, rather than an assessment of his risk of future crime (Boccaccini & Turner, 2013, p. 266).

A study by Wilson et al. comparing the short-term recidivism rates of offenders released from the Florida SVP program with the rates of offenders released from a Canadian correctional program found that the Florida releasees had a slightly lower rate of recidivism, despite the fact that the two groups had very similar profiles (Wilson, Looman, Abracen, & Pake, 2013).

A study by Knighton et al. sought to determine how actual SVP jurors understand or operationalize the legal standard used in Texas, "likely" to re-offend. The study surveyed 168 jurors who served on 14 SVP civil commitment hearings in Texas between 2009 and 2010, and asked what chance of recidivism they felt meant a sex offender was "likely" to re-offend. The findings showed that all of the jurors felt a 50% chance that the offender might commit another sex crime meant re-offense was "likely." Of the jurors, 53.6% reported a probability of re-offense of just 1% was sufficient to find that an offender was likely to re-offend; 81.7% found that a 15% chance meant re-offending satisfied the "likely" standard; and 97% felt a 25% chance was sufficient.

A recently published study by Minnesota Department of Corrections researcher Grant Duwe endeavored to determine the profile of individuals who have been chosen for civil commitment in Minnesota (Duwe, 2013). The study found that the four-year recidivism rate for the 105 individuals civilly committed between 2004 and 2006 would have been somewhere between 5.2% and 15.6% within four years had they not been civilly committed (Duwe, 2013, p. 6). While this number was slightly higher than the likely recidivism rate for offenders who were not civilly committed, the study concluded that civilly committing those 105 offenders resulted in a reduction of the state's overall four-year sexual recidivism rate of less than half of 1% (reduction from 3.2% to 2.8%) (Duwe, 2013, p. 6).

Moreover, the Duwe study found that the lifetime recidivism rate for the 105 individuals was at most 36%. Conversely, "nearly two-thirds of these offenders would be unlikely to be rearrested for another sex offense in their lifetime if they were released to the community. In other words, for every true positive, there are likely two false positives" (Duwe, 2013, p. 8). Applying this "false positive" rate to the 700-plus people who have been committed, we can conclude that in its 20-year history the Minnesota courts have likely committed over 462 human beings who, had they been released, would not have been arrested for a new sex crime. In exchange, the program has likely reduced the overall rate of recidivism in Minnesota by 0.4%.

Several studies of the Florida SVP program were collected in a special report commissioned by The Florida Department of Children and Families, Substance Abuse and Mental Health (SAMH) Program Office (Carr, Schlank, & Parker, 2013). In one of the studies, researchers followed 140 men who had been screened, referred for commitment, and petitioned in Florida. Before trial, prosecutors had agreed to a "stipulated" conditional release into the community. Followed for periods ranging from one to 10 years, the released offenders had a sexual felony reconviction rate of 3.8% (The Florida Department of Children and Families, 2013). The report observed: "When released into the community, these offenders who were considered to be extremely dangerous predators with disorders that undermined their capacity to control themselves rarely re-offended" (The Florida Department of Children and Families, 2013, p. 23).

A separate study followed 710 offenders who were recommended for commitment in the SVP program and were later released. The study reported that the offender recidivism rate for this group (counting all charges of a sexually motivated crime involving a victim) was 10%. No information on the follow-up period was provided.

The study also compared recidivism rates for offenders who were initially recommended for commitment, but were released after a face-to-face evaluation, with those who were actually petitioned for commitment but later released. It found only a small difference in recidivism rates for these two groups, concluding:

> Such a minor difference is surprising and indicates that the traditional approach to determining SVP status needs to be improved. There are too many false positives (someone determined to fit the SVP definition when he does not, or someone determined to be likely to re-offend but he is not). The re-offense rates of those who were recommended for commitment were hardly different from those who were not recommended.
>
> (The Florida Department of Children and Families, 2013, p. 19)

The report concluded: "These results suggest that individuals are being over-selected for commitment" (The Florida Department of Children and Families, 2013, p. 24).

Conclusion

In this chapter, we have traced the evolution of the law's interaction with dangerousness. Though dangerousness has long played a role in law, modern SVP laws have provided a context in which human risk assessment is explicitly a driving force of public policy. The emergence of these laws has coincided with the development of a robust science of risk assessment. No doubt the SVP laws have provided a ready market for the science, and in that sense we can say that the law has prompted the science. But it is arguable that the science has created some of the conditions that have allowed SVP laws to flourish as well.

The entire SVP enterprise remains highly problematic. Its very foundation—pre-crime, prevention-based confinement—is a huge challenge to the fundamental bargain that American constitutional democracy embraces: strict limits on the power of the state to deprive citizens of their liberty. SVP laws escape this bargain by claiming to target only a small, distinct "outsider" group—sexual predators. But this "outsider jurisprudence" is, in itself, a dangerous throwback to the shameful past of Jim Crow laws, involuntary eugenic sterilization, and internment of Japanese citizens.

The task of this book, however, is not to question the risk-assessment enterprise, but rather, accepting that it exists, to seek to improve it as a tool of the law. In this chapter, we have sought to clarify the structure of the interface between law and science in SVP cases. We have shown that courts and legislatures have several tools available to harness the growing knowledge of risk assessment, but that the legal system has shied away from exercising robust control. As a result, SVP programs are not as carefully focused as they could be on the "most dangerous." There is little accountability and uniformity in the use of this science. Societal efforts aimed at the prevention of sexual violence suffer a dual impairment. Their efficacy is impaired, because the most expensive and highly visible resource for prevention—SVP programs—are not deployed as intentionally and carefully as they should be. And the fairness and justice of the effort is undercut because the "worst of the worst" rationale is shown clearly to be an unattained ideal.

We return, in Chapter 9, to this subject and to our recommendations for courts and policy-makers who seek to more fully attain the benefits of science in this important area of law and public policy.

Notes

1 This section is based on materials published in Janus (2010).
2 Id.
3 Id.
4 End of entry based on Janus (1996).
5 This paragraph is based closely on material from Janus (1996).
6 Janus (2011).
7 Id.
8 Id.
9 Based on Janus (2000).
10 Id.
11 Id.
12 Id.
13 Id.
14 Based on Janus (2007).
15 Based on Janus (2006).
16 Janus and Prentky (2003).
17 This material is based on Prentky, Janus, Barbaree, Schwartz, & Kafka (2006).

3

THE INTERFACE BETWEEN THE LAW AND SCIENCE

Harmonizing the Rule of Law With Good Science

In the sexually violent predator (SVP) context, the relationship between the law and science is particularly fraught. As we have shown in Chapter 2, science is key in furnishing the legitimacy that SVP laws need. Preventive detention is a threat to our normal order, but science seems to provide the categorical classifications that safely confine preventive detention to a small and distinctively different group of mentally disordered dangerous offenders. Of course, we emphasize that science "seems to provide" these classifications, because to a great extent as the law has used them, some of these "scientific" classifications are vague and illusory, lacking scientific substance. Thus, the promise of science in the SVP context is frustrated and unfulfilled. There is no reason to think that the population of SVP detainees is characterized by "mental disorders" that distinguish them from other recidivist sex offenders (or recidivist criminals in general). And while the evidence shows that SVP detainees skew as a population toward the higher end of risk (at least as measured by certain actuarial risk assessment (ARA) instruments), we have suggested that there is good evidence that the law is not in the driver's seat when it comes to risk assessment.

In this chapter, we set out a series of suggestions and recommendations to improve the interface of law and science in SVP matters. Our touchstones are twofold: first, the law must be in charge. The decision to take away someone's liberty is quintessentially a function of the law. This means that science must be kept in its proper place; science is descriptive, not normative. Second, though kept in its proper place, science must have central roles both in setting our public policy regarding sexual violence and in the adjudication of individual cases pursuant to the policy. We must use the best science, and we must use it properly.

Science has key roles in law. The roles fall into two distinct but related arenas. First, science has a role in the legislative, or policy-making, function of law. Public policy ought to be based on science—on an empirically based understanding of the causes and "cures" of sexual violence. The necessarily limited public dollars devoted to the prevention of sexual violence ought to be allocated systematically, guided by science: we ought to be allocating our prevention dollars in a way that, based on empirical evidence, has the best likelihood of preventing the most sexual violence. If we do not design our public policy in this way, we will, by definition, be implementing a policy that permits sexual violence unnecessarily.

Science should not dictate public policy. Science is not normative; it cannot tell us what ought to be. But once we, as a society, decide on what our public goals are, we should be turning to science to help us determine how best to accomplish those ends. In various other writings, we and others have advocated an evidence-based, public health approach to sexual violence prevention policy. At the heart of such an approach is systematic and comprehensive design, rather than the knee-jerk, reactive process that has characterized the development and spread of SVP laws. The public health approach also prescribes careful evaluation of the efficacy of programs, and the dissemination of information on best practices so that effective approaches spread, and ineffective approaches are abandoned.

Unfortunately, current policy-making is often explicitly hostile to science. Consider this example of an extremely hostile reaction to scientific research that did not conform to the politically correct narrative of the day. In 1998, three academic researchers published an article in *Psychological Bulletin*, a peer-reviewed academic journal of the American Psychological Association. The article examined the widely held belief that "child sexual abuse [CSA] causes intense harm, regardless of gender" (Rind et al., 1998, p. 22). Examining 59 studies of CSA, the authors concluded that "[b]asic beliefs about CSA in the general population were not supported" (Rind et al., 1998, p. 22). They concluded that the "negative effects were neither pervasive nor typically intense" (Rind et al., p. 22). The study did not conclude that CSA was *never* harmful, nor did it dispute the fact that many children exposed to CSA do, in fact, suffer harm. Rather, the authors argued for a more careful and scientific definition of CSA, one that would help sort out the true nature of the harm arising from sex between adults and children or adolescents. Finally, the authors emphasized that their study concerned psychology, not morality or legality. "Moral codes of a society with respect to sexual behavior need not be, and often have not been, based on considerations of psychological harmfulness or health" (Rind et al., p. 47). Their findings, therefore, did not imply any change in current legal or moral approaches to CSA.

The article provoked an intensely negative firestorm of criticism. The matter reached as far as the United States House of Representatives, which voted unanimously (355–0) to "denounce" the study. Republican

Rep. Matt Salmon, R-Ariz. sponsor of the resolution, called the article the "emancipation proclamation of pedophiles" (Associated Press, 1999). Referring to the authors of the article, he observed, "Those who excuse this evil conduct, particularly those in positions of influence, are also pretty low on the food chain and deserve the harshest possible condemnation" (Associated Press, 1999).

Though the American Psychological Association, the publisher of the article, initially defended the article as valid science, the organization eventually bowed to the intense pressure and vowed to adopt new procedures for reviewing articles to be published:

> We acknowledge our social responsibility as a scientific organization to take into account not only the scientific merit of articles but also their implication for public policy. Some of the language in the article, when examined from a public policy perspective, is inflammatory.
>
> (American Psychological Association, 1999)

The conservative Family Research Council asked for more: "APA needs to root out the pro-pedophilic academicians who are trying to normalize child abuse" (Family Research Council, 1999).

Many researchers might have taken issue with this article's conclusions. A later review article in the *Journal of Psychiatry and Law* reflected the more prevalent view that "psychological damage associated with childhood sexual abuse is substantial and quite well documented" (Rodriguez-Srednicki & Twaite, p. 336). But this just serves to underline the point that the nature of the harm caused by child sexual abuse is an empirical question. If we want to develop effective programs and policies to assist the victims of sexual abuse, we ought to invite full scientific knowledge of its nature and consequences. The political response to the earlier article placed the moral condemnation of child sexual abuse in direct conflict with increasing empirical knowledge of it. This hostility to empirical knowledge was aptly captured by Republican Rep. Matt Salmon, R-Ariz.: "I don't want to understand pedophiles, I want to put them in prison" (O'Meara, 2009).

A similar disregard of science characterizes the wide adoption of residential restrictions on sex offenders. Authoritative reports from Minnesota, Iowa, Kansas, Colorado, and Florida have shown that there is no empirical reason to think that such geographical restrictions will be effective—and lots of reasons to think that such poorly thought-out broad-brush restrictions may be counter-productive (Colorado Department of Public Safety, 2004; Iowa Department of Human Rights, 2000; Kansas Sex Offender Policy Board, 2007; Levenson & Cotter, 2005; Minnesota Department of Corrections, 2003).

Yet despite these clear warnings, states and localities continue to adopt such residence restrictions. The most striking example is the adoption in California, despite strong media and expert opposition, of Prop. 83 "Jessica's Law" (Jessica's Law, 2006)—imposing, among other things, exactly such broad residency restrictions (California Attorneys for Criminal Justice, 2007; Editorial, 2006; Iowa County Attorney's Association, 2007).

But the relationship between science and public policy is complex. Even good science can mislead the law, causing our policy-makers to adopt unfortunate and maladaptive frames for understanding sexual violence.

At the risk of oversimplification, we can identify two distinct and influential approaches to sexual violence that have emerged in the past several decades. One approach examines sexual violence at a societal level, asking which aspects of our society facilitate or inhibit the sexual victimization of women and children. The second approach looks at the individual sex offender and asks what biological or psychological factors are associated with sexual violence. The first approach will help us understand what societal changes we might take to prevent sexual violence. The second will prompt us to examine interventions at an individual level.

Prominent in the first approach have been feminist theorists and reformers. This approach understands sexual violence as a widespread feature of our society, thriving in intimate relationships and families, socially sanctioned by a "hierarchy of gender." It follows that efforts at prevention must understand the breadth of sexual violence, and must seek to dismantle the gender hierarchy.

These feminist ideas have had a powerful—but limited—influence in reshaping our approaches to sexual violence over the past several decades. The insight that sexual aggression is relatively widespread has received broad acceptance. But the underlying implication—that sexual violence flourishes because of a sexist society—remains the subject of intense controversy.

The second approach to sexual violence is exemplified by the rapid development of ARA tools. As we detail in this book, these scientific approaches prompt us to seek our understanding of sexual violence by looking at—and within—the individual.

There is nothing inherently incompatible between broader societal and narrower individual approaches to explaining and understanding sexual violence. They could easily co-exist. Occupying parallel conceptual worlds, they provide different lenses for understanding and trying to prevent the same social evil. We ought to embrace the truths of both if we want an effective program for addressing sexual abuse.

But if we are not careful, we can allow one approach or the other to occupy our field of vision, obscuring the truths of other frameworks. The actuarial approach allows us—with reasonable accuracy and at reasonable expense—to classify people according to their "risk." But there is a likelihood that with these tools available, our attention will be drawn disproportionately to identifying and neutralizing the "most dangerous," distracting our attention from the societal patterns and root causes of sexual violence.

With these cautions in mind, we can turn our attention to adjudication, the second arena in which law and science interact in the effort to prevent sexual violence. In this aspect of the discussion, we take as our context the existence of SVP laws, and address the processes they use to determine risk, and based on those determinations lock some people up, but not others.

We make two central points. First, the law must be in charge of the adjudication process. Second, the adjudication process must use the best science on risk assessment.

Law must be in charge. The rule of law is a good in and of itself, and it is also a necessary condition for the optimal deployment of prevention resources. SVP laws involve major deprivations of liberty. The constitutional legitimacy of these programs depends on their adherence to the rule of law. In addition, public policy should infuse law with science-based resource allocation policies. The optimal allocation of prevention resources requires adherence to these policies. The rule of law, in other words, is a necessary predicate both for justice and for the optimization of the allocation of prevention resources.

The law has two tasks, and these must be kept conceptually distinct. It must provide a process for determining what risk the respondent poses. This is a complex fact-finding process. It involves the application of the standard of proof to determine the risk the state has proved. This involves assessing the quality, integrity, validity, and credibility of the expert scientific testimony. Second, it must provide a means of determining whether the risk so determined satisfies the legal standard for commitment.

The most important step in ensuring the rule of law is to strictly adhere to the distinction between fact and law, and to understand how that distinction governs the process of adjudicating risk. Many statements characterizing risk are framed in language that could be either factual or legal, such as statements that an individual has "high" risk, or "moderate" risk, or is "highly likely" to offend. These are terms that bridge the vocabulary of psychological expertise and the terms of legal standards. To the extent the words reflect psychological expertise and knowledge, they are properly evaluated under the legal standards for factual assessment in which fact-finders assess the weight and credibility of testimony. On the other hand, to the extent that these terms purport to reflect and apply a legal standard, credibility and weight are the wrong category for evaluation. Mental health experts have no standing to explicate the content of the legal standard, thus their statements about legal standards are not credible, and carry no weight.

For courts to take control of the risk-assessment process, then, requires two conceptually separate inquiries. First, courts must assess the integrity and credibility of the scientific (expert) testimony. Second, courts must determine whether the risk, so determined, meets the legal threshold. The validity, consistency, and internal integrity of the testimony is relevant to the former, but not to the latter. If 100 PhD psychologists testify, with no contradiction and with high credibility, that the respondent is "highly likely" to re-offend, the court still must determine whether the psychologists' understanding of "highly likely" corresponds to the law's prescription.

Court must sort out the factual from the legal. Judging legal assertions to be "credible" is a category mistake. Judging factual statements to be credible is not a category mistake, but, in the SVP risk-assessment context, judging the credibility and weight of an expert's risk-assessment testimony is different from judging the credibility or weight of an event witness' testimony. The latter judgment might be based on intangible nuances of demeanor. The former, on the other hand, ought to turn much more centrally on the integrity and soundness of the science employed by the witness. Expert witnesses are not event witnesses. The "facts" they testify about are largely psychological constructs. The credibility of these "psychological facts" ought to turn on their coherence and clarity, and on their foundation in sound science. Expert testimony must be transparent, not hiding behind opaque conclusory judgments. Experts should demonstrate an awareness of the limitation of their expertise about the meaning of legal standards. They should consciously limit their testimony to facts that have a bearing on the legal standards. They should explicitly distinguish between psychological and legal statements. Courts should discount the credibility of experts who fail these standards.

The key to ensuring that law is in charge of the risk-adjudication process, and that the process is based on the best possible law, is robust appellate review. If it works correctly, appellate review can ensure uniformity in adjudication standards, and the development of a usable "jurisprudence of risk" through the common-law process of rule articulation. But the process of appellate review, and thus the rule of law, can be neutered by the conflation of law and fact decisions, and the overuse of credibility and weight determinations to obscure the assessment of science and insulate the key determinations from meaningful appellate review.

A recent decision by the Minnesota Court of Appeals has clearly adopted the "meaningful appellate review" standard for judging the adequacy of lower court decisions (In re Civil Commitment of Spicer, 2014). This standard provides the beginning of a roadmap for the reform of the risk-adjudication process. The court rejected as insufficient conclusory determinations of credibility and weight. It insisted that trial courts identify and explain the significance of the facts they relied on, and tie those facts specifically to the conclusions of law. Appellate courts should insist that trial courts strictly separate the application of law from the determination of facts. Factual determinations must be explained in terms of the science, and not simply through the unexplained application of opaque terms such as credibility and weight. Trial courts should judge experts on these standards, and appellate courts should judge trial court decisions similarly. Courts should explain their judgments about credibility. Judgments about the weight of testimony should be tied to the legal standard for risk. Testimony that is credible, and that is centrally relevant to the legal standard, should have high weight. Low credibility or peripheral relevance yields low weight.

Above all, experts and trial courts must explain the connection between their factual findings and the legal standards. This requires both an explication of the legal standard and a meaningful analysis of the facts and their relationship to the law.

Trial courts need not deconstruct and re-make the conclusions of experts. What we are suggesting is subtly different. Courts should critically examine expert opinions, assessing them on the standards of science. Courts need not do science; they must be critical consumers of science. This will require testimony about the science being offered—about why it is sound; why other approaches are not sound. And courts must apply the standards of critical thinking such as coherence, clarity, and transparency.

Of course, this prescription becomes more complicated when the fact-finder is a jury rather than a judge. Trial judges as fact-finders are expected to explain their findings. Juries often are not. Still, trial and appellate courts are not without tools to promote the rule of law even in jury trial states. For example, courts could make use of special verdict forms that require juries to answer specific questions. Courts can, in this way, ensure that juries are deciding factual questions, not legal rules. In framing the questions for the jury, judges can pinpoint the key areas of contention; they can set out explicitly the expectation that sound science be used, and should insist that the testimony address the soundness of the science. Courts should be prepared to direct verdicts where the evidence does not clearly show scientific soundness, as well as where the risk testimony, under any interpretation, does not meet legal thresholds. Juries should not be left to determine the meaning of legal terms such as "highly likely."

We acknowledge there will be limits to how well the normal process of trial and appellate decision-making can do in ensuring the best possible science. So we propose the following additional steps, all of which are intended to increase the chances that the best science will be available in SVP risk adjudication.

First, we recognize that a part of the problem of getting good science arises from the adversarial nature of the adjudication process. Research has shown that party identification can introduce bias into expert testimony (Murrie, Boccaccini, Guarnera, & Rufino, 2013). On the other hand, even court-appointed, "neutral" experts bring biases, as well as other potential shortcomings, such as sub-optimal grounding in science. After all, courts might not always choose the best or most competent experts. Adversarial expert testimony provides a safeguard against bias and bad science. Party-hired experts can also facilitate the important function of providing "voice" to respondents, helping to shape the narrative in a way that is most beneficial to a party subject to commitment (Slobogin, 2010). This is not necessarily "bias," but rather part of how our adversarial system deals with the ambiguity and uncertainties of a messy world.

We therefore suggest a hybrid system, in which some of the experts in the risk-assessment process are neutral and some are party-identified. For example, the state of New York has established an independent office retaining neutral experts charged with making referrals for commitment. It operates under a mandate to use the best science (N. Y. Mental Hyg. Law, 2007). Later in the process, if a petition is brought, the respondent can retain his own expert.

Following New York's lead, states should articulate a normative policy requiring the use of the best science. States should foster the development of best-practice standards, which can then serve as guides to courts and experts. States should retain independent experts of unquestioned integrity to audit their risk-assessment systems to determine whether, in fact, they are using sound science. The audits should extend to the adjudication process. A selection of adjudicated cases should be reviewed periodically to determine the quality of the risk-assessment results in the courts.

SVP states should establish specialized courts and lawyers to handle SVP cases. We recognize that there is a danger in centralizing and specializing the adjudication of these cases, because of the isolation and "repeat-player" phenomena that might develop (Galanter, 1974). But the need to incorporate the best science, as well as to develop an adjudicatory system that produces a coherent set of risk-assessment rules, should overweigh this concern.

As a further safeguard, states should evaluate the risk-assessment adjudication process as part of a systematic public policy to address sexual violence. In addition to auditing whether the system uses good science, states should determine whether the process is properly deploying the state's scarce prevention resources appropriately. This would examine whether the "right people" are being selected for the most intensive, most expensive intervention, viewed as part of a more comprehensive systematic approach to sexual violence.

Even with the best science ensured, the rule of law aspiration will be illusory unless the legal threshold for risk, the "standard for commitment," can be articulated in a coherent way that leads to accountability and uniformity of application. For the law to be in charge of risk adjudication, it must articulate a standard that both reflects public policy and provides actionable guidance to judges and the other decision-makers in the SVP selection process. This step has proved elusive. As we have described, legislatures and appellate courts have articulated the legal risk threshold only in the most general terms, and have erected procedural impediments to the development of a jurisprudence of risk through the normal common-law process of case-by-case rule development.

One clear way to set the legal threshold would be to establish a numerical standard, for example 75% likelihood. When the only risk testimony was clinical judgment, assigning a numerical value to the legal standard would have added no benefit: clinical judgments are qualitative, not quantitative, so casting the legal standard in a numerical format adds false precision. The translation between professional judgment and legal standard would have been as unaccountable as it is when the legal standard is a phrase rather than a number.

But with the advent of ARA tools, assigning a numerical dimension to the legal standard becomes much more sensible. The legal standard and the ARA results are both numerical, and thus the translation from legal to professional is less problematic. Of course, even with a numerical legal standard, judgments would not become mechanical or automatic. One would still need to determine whether the ARA number and the legal number were referring to the same thing, whether the ARA number is accurate, how much potential error it contains, etc. But at least the translation between legal and professional would have been accomplished.

Courts and legislatures have refused to quantify the standards. We suspect there are two potential reasons for this refusal, one of which is legitimate and the other not. For example, courts and policy-makers may be worried that the "most dangerous," as identified in the ARA instruments, would not have ARA scores that meet the commonly understood quantitative meaning of "highly probable." Put another way, decision-makers may be afraid that if they set the numerical standard at a level that seems to reflect, in common sense, "highly likely," no one would meet the standard, and that if they set the standard at a level where some people would qualify, the level would seem embarrassingly low. Similarly, the absence of a numerical standard allows courts to delegate these hard decisions—what does "highly likely" mean?—to experts, and in that way to hide the decisions behind judgments of credibility and weight. In short, ambiguity and opacity help the SVP system avoid answering the tough questions.

Ambiguity and opacity are, of course, enemies of the rule of law. But there is a legitimate problem with quantifying the risk standard. It is possible that the legal standard for risk might comprise several orthogonal factors. Clearly, "likelihood" is one of the factors. But it is not unreasonable to suggest, as have some courts, that the severity of potential harm is a second factor. It could also be argued that the imminence of potential harm ought to be a third factor. If the risk threshold is to be understood in this way, then the legal threshold for one of the factors—likelihood—might well vary, depending on the severity and imminence of the predicted harm. The law might tolerate a lower likelihood threshold where the potential harm is murder, but demand a higher threshold where the potential crime is fondling.

If the multifactor nature of risk underlies the reluctance of courts to adopt a numerical standard, the first step is for courts to acknowledge that they are adopting such a definition of risk. But that will require courts to acknowledge that some sexual violence is more severe than others. Acknowledging this may not be as easy as it sounds. There are important voices that assert that all sexual abuse leads to severe harm. The reaction of the U.S. House to the Rind et al. study, referenced above, is an example of this sort of approach. There is authority to the contrary. The recent Minnesota Court of Appeals case, Lingl (In re Civil Commitment of Lingl, 2012), as well as an older Minnesota Supreme Court case, Rodriguez (In re Rodriguez, 1993), ventured to make comparisons and distinctions about severity among criminal sexual conduct.

Courts must simply decide which of these contrasting positions they will adopt. If the former—all sexual abuse is equal—then this impediment to adopting and articulating a clear numerical standard for risk is removed. If the latter, courts then must undertake to construct a set of rules and guidelines for distinguishing among types of sexual violence, and using those distinctions to modulate the likelihood threshold for SVP cases.

This acknowledgement opens the door for courts to begin to establish benchmarks in the classic manner of common-law adjudication. As each case is adjudicated, courts can assess and explain the similarities and differences in likelihood and severity to prior cases. What is it about the present case, for example, that makes the predicted harm more severe than in the prior precedent, and therefore the likelihood threshold lower than in the prior case?

When risk assessment was nothing more than the *ipse dixit* of psychiatrists, the law could, with only slight embarrassment, abdicate its responsibility for assessing risk to the opaque expertise of the mental health expert. But as risk assessment has developed into a science, this abdication becomes more of a choice than a necessity. Science opens a window into the iffy process of locking people up for crimes they might commit in the future. No longer can judges hide behind the sage but mysterious psychiatric assessment of the human mind. In the old days, all of the vagueness and uncertainty and potential error were hidden in the expert's inscrutable exercise of professional judgment. Now, law has the tools to understand and assess that process.

Further, the empirical approach that has grown with the development of risk-assessment research can be applied equally to assessing how well the law is functioning *as a system*. Are the SVP laws contributing to the reduction of sexual violence? Are they contributing on a scale commensurate with their cost?

Courts have reflected their discomfort with the science by using the tools of procedure and evidence to blunt its impact. These tools—characterizing disputes about risk as weighing evidence and judging credibility, failing to insist on the best science, refusing to articulate, even in incremental ways, what the standards for risk are—all of these serve to hide the uncomfortable truths from systemic and public view.

If we hope to introduce legitimacy and accountability to the SVP system, and if we aspire to a system for sexual violence prevention that is designed to be smart and optimally effective, then we must cease to avert our gaze, and embrace both the rule of law and the proper role of good science.

4

AN INTRODUCTION TO VIOLENCE RISK ASSESSMENT WITH SEX OFFENDERS

Introduction

The next four chapters of our book will examine the use of actuarial risk assessment instruments (ARAIs) in the assessment of recidivism risk in sex offenders. This section of the book takes an admiring but critical look at the ARAIs. The development of these risk assessment instruments (e.g., Hanson & Thornton, 1999; Quinsey, Harris, Rice, & Cormier, 1998) has coincided (approximately over the decade of the 90s) with the enactment and promulgation of legislative measures in the US to manage sex offenders. Sexually violent predator (SVP) laws are now in place in many of the American states. Courts operating under the jurisdiction of these laws require that forensic evaluators conduct evaluations of SVP candidates as to their risk for sexual recidivism and to present opinion evidence at trial concerning the risk posed by the individual. Among forensic psychologists and psychiatrists, it is now well accepted that ARAIs are an improvement over expert but subjective clinical judgment alone in estimating risk. Currently, virtually all SVP evaluations and trial testimony involve the use of ARAIs in one form or another. In turn, SVP courts have come to admit ARAI evidence, despite legal challenges to their admissibility (Janus & Prentky, 2003).

These two historical developments (ARAIs and SVP courts) have been mutually facilitative. Use of the ARAIs, being empirically supported and generally accepted in the forensic mental health community, has reinforced the constitutionality and apparent fairness of the SVP laws. In turn, the demand for the ARAIs by the courts has encouraged the widespread use and popularity of the ARAIs among forensic psychologists and psychiatrists, leading to their further scientific development and improvement. Some authors have referred to the "cottage industry" surrounding the use of ARAIs by forensic evaluators in the SVP courtroom (Grisso, 1987, p. 831).

In the first of these chapters, we distinguish between what we mean by "risk" and what the public would understand as risk. We describe the history of the development of actuarial risk prediction in forensic mental health, we review studies of sex offender recidivism, and we describe the various approaches used by forensic experts to make clinical risk predictions. In the second of these chapters, we illustrate the empirical development and evaluation of a brief ARAI, and illustrate the evaluation of predictive accuracy using receiver operating characteristic (ROC) analysis. We review the most popular and most often used ARAIs and we examine the empirical data supporting their use, particularly independent cross-validation studies. We discuss the effects of aging on sex offender recidivism risk and the recent development of the ARAIs which have incorporated a revised age item. Finally, we summarize the state of the art of sex offender risk prediction as of the end of the year 2012.

In the third of these chapters, we highlight the importance of recognizing that actuarial assessment occurs in two distinct stages. In the first stage, referred to by Meehl (1954) as "classification," the clinician uses an actuarial instrument to assign an offender to one of several ranked categories. This stage of actuarial assessment provides a measure of "relative risk" in which we can say that offenders in higher-ranked categories are higher risk relative to offenders in lower-ranked categories. The second stage of actuarial assessment attempts to assign a level of "absolute risk," usually presented as percent recidivism, to each of the ranked categories assigned in Stage 1. We discuss the problems that have arisen in attempts to establish an absolute level of risk. We describe various approaches to solving this issue, including a "frequentist" approach, a "Bayesian" approach, and a "logistic regression" approach. We discuss the strengths and weaknesses of each approach and conclude that, at present, we can estimate levels of absolute risk, but errors of measurement are high.

In the fourth chapter, we discuss the importance of theory in the future development of actuarial risk assessment. We begin by recognizing the fact that the ARAIs were developed in the absence of any theory of recidivism risk, and we describe what we see as the problems resulting from the absence of theory. We describe the role of aging as a risk factor and its confound with the other risk factors, sexual deviance and antisocial orientation. We describe the results of the disentangling of aging from the other risk factors and the impact on our theoretical understanding of recidivism risk in sex offenders. We make suggestions as to where the field can progress from here, and how the SVP courts should use ARAIs now and in the future.

In the present chapter, we begin with a definition of "risk," we describe a historical account of actuarial assessment, and we demonstrate how an actuarial instrument is developed and validated through a process known as "incremental predictive validity." Throughout this chapter, we develop our definition of "risk." First, we consider how the general public might define risk, and we refer to this as colloquial (non-expert) risk. Then we define risk in scientific terms, as a statistical expectation expressed as a probability (0.00 to 1.00) or as a percentage.

Colloquial Risk

The notion of risk is at once both deceptively simple and complicated. Webster's Unabridged Dictionary first defines risk simply as "The chance of injury, damage, or loss. A dangerous chance; a hazard." The notion of risk permeates virtually every domain of human behavior and experience.

Although we may not consciously define our decisions in terms of risk, we make risk-based decisions all the time. We risk getting a speeding ticket when we drive 20 mph over the limit; we risk serious injury, even death, when we tail-gate at high speed; we may not wear our seat-belt when we know we are only driving a half-mile down the street to the "7/11" for a quart of milk; we answer our mobile device or we return a call while driving; we decide to drive after having two beers; we decide not to replace that left rear tire that the mechanic said was worn. We make decisions about how much automobile or homeowner's insurance to carry, or whether to carry professional liability, or life, or disability, or long-term care insurance. We decide whether to pay for natural disaster insurance (e.g., earthquakes or hurricanes). Standing at the cash desk while purchasing a new electronic device, we make a decision about whether to purchase an extended warranty.

We make multiple critically important health-related decisions every day. Should we have unprotected sex? Should we smoke cigarettes or drink alcohol? Should we eat that delicious triple hamburger and/or king-size basket of French fries, each with a gram of sodium, when we have hypertension? Should we enjoy that egg yolk or the foie gras soufflé when we have atherosclerosis? Many of our recreational decisions involve an element of risk (e.g., backcountry skiing under chancy conditions, cliff jumping, whitewater racing, base jumping, BMX, ice/rock climbing, etc.). In all of these examples, and many more, there is a possibility of a "worst case" outcome. People do fall off cliffs, homes do burn down, and fatal auto accidents do happen. But in most of these daily multiple risk-related decisions, we are blissfully unaware of the actual probability of a bad outcome. We do not calculate, or we cannot calculate, the likelihood of the potential ill effects of our behavior. These everyday risks may cause us fleeting worry or anxiety, but we make decisions that determine our exposure to possible bad outcomes every day without a great deal of thought or consideration.

The vast majority of the time, we glide through life making adequate risk-related decisions without any serious consequences. We don't generally "think" about risk in terms of the probability of a bad outcome. We buy automobile insurance because the law requires it, not because we imagine ourselves in a catastrophic accident. We buy homeowner's insurance because our mortgage company demands it, not because we imagine the possibility of our house burning down.

The risks that we *are* consciously aware of and the risks that cause us the greatest worry and anxiety are those considered *dire* and over which we have no control. For example, we might worry about groundwater contamination from a toxic waste disposal site in the next county or a radiation leak from a nuclear reactor in the next town. We might be anxious in the short term about an impending hurricane or tornado or in the long term about food shortages due to global warming.

Slovic (1987) described three basic constructs that are related to our perception of risk: (1) *dread*—characterized by a "perceived lack of control" over some catastrophic event with potentially fatal consequences and the perceived "inequitable distribution of risks and benefits" (p. 283), (2) *unknown risks*—risks "judged to be unobservable, unknown, new, and delayed in their manifestation of harm," such as a contamination from a chemical spill, and (3) *number of people potentially exposed to the risk or in harm's way*. Although there are many other factors that undoubtedly determine perception of risk, these three are fundamental.

Ironically, the more sophisticated our society becomes technologically and scientifically, the more potential risks seem to be revealed and the more we worry about them. Wildavsky remarked, some 35 years ago, "How extraordinary! The richest, longest lived, best protected, most resourceful civilization, with the highest degree of insight into its own technology, is on its way to becoming the most frightened" (1979, p. 32). Thirty-five years later, we are, if anything, even more vigilant, if not fearful, of myriad risks, from credit card fraud and identity theft to climate change and terrorism. Indeed, we can add to the list a modern-age "problem"—we are outliving our retirement savings, resulting in *longevity risk*. The retirement services industry now provides a vast array of products, plans, and investment tools such as deferred income annuities as a hedge against our living longer (is this the opposite of life insurance?).

Given this array of different potential sources of risk, one thing we may be reasonably confident about is that the construct of risk itself is subjective, value-laden, and multidimensional (Slovic, 2000). Simply stated, we do not all *experience* risk the same way; the *experience* of risk is inherently subjective. As Slovic (2000) pointed out, humans invented the notion of risk to cope with the real and imminent dangers they faced. Although the dangers were "real," the risk associated with those dangers was variable, not immutable, and not "objective." The same remains true today.

The fear we experience in relation to the release of a potentially "dangerous" sex offender into our community is a fear of such dire risk. The public's broadly conceived notion of risk posed by sex offenders includes such factors as uncertainty, "dread" (fear), the perceived potential for catastrophe, one's sense of control (or lack of it), and the number of people potentially impacted by the adverse outcome (Slovic, 2000). We cannot control the event, and we are unable to calculate the actual risk to our children or other family members.

The Science of Risk

"Risk" does not necessarily mean the same thing to experts as it does to the public. In contrast to the public, an expert's perceptions of risk are not determined by these dimensions or the characteristics that underlie them. Instead, experts see risk as synonymous with expected mortality (Slovic, 2000, p. 394). Webster's Unabridged Dictionary expands its definition of risk, and its second definition is more detailed: "In insurance, (a) the chance of loss; (b) the degree of probability of loss; (c) the amount of possible loss to the insuring company: in full, amount of risk." So in common usage, risk reflects the possibility of some unwanted, typically adverse outcome. But its more specialized definition includes an implied determination of the probability of the adverse outcome. In the present context, "expected mortality" is the equivalent of "expected re-offense." Insurance companies employ actuaries to calculate the likelihood of loss to determine the premiums required to cover the expected loss, and hopefully provide for a tidy profit. In the present context of criminal behavior, courts ask forensic experts to estimate the likelihood or probability that an offender will re-offend to support its mandate to protect the public from sexual crime.

Assessing risk involves making a prediction. As we have seen, risk involves the possibility of a future adverse event. If the adverse event has already happened, it is no longer a risk, but is now a certainty. Life insurance companies make predictions as to how long an insured person will live to determine the required premium to be charged. When a forensic expert assesses the risk that a released sex offender poses to the safety of a community, the expert is making a prediction as to how the released offender will behave in the future.

Clinical Versus Actuarial Prediction

In his seminal work published 60 years ago, Paul Meehl (1954) initiated the modern scientific investigation of risk prediction by making the historic distinction between clinical and actuarial prediction. Approaches to predicting human behavior have been broadly categorized as either clinical or mechanical (Dawes, Faust, & Meehl, 1989; Grove & Meehl, 1996). The fundamental difference between these two approaches is the method by which risk factors are identified, scored, and combined in making the final prediction (Grove & Meehl, 1996; Marchese, 1992). Clinical prediction is difficult to define. Clinical judgment refers to the ways in which clinicians make predictions where information is available in an informal format and decisions are made in a subjective way. Different clinicians make decisions according to different methodologies, and individual clinicians may use different methods at different times. In this approach, the clinician selects the variables relevant to the criterion of interest (e.g., violent re-offending) for a given population (e.g., adult male offenders) and determines the decision-making process by which these variables are scored and combined to make a prediction (e.g., likelihood of violent re-offending). Given the evaluator's discretion in this prediction approach, this approach to assessment has been described as informal, subjective, and impressionistic (Grove & Meehl, 1996), and clinical judgment is not subject to precise specification (Grove, Zald, Lebow, Snitz, & Nelson, 2000, p. 19).

In contrast, actuarial prediction can be described in detail. In defining actuarial prediction Meehl (1954) stated,

> We may order the individual to a class or set of classes on the basis of objective facts concerning his life history, his scores on psychometric tests, behavior ratings or check lists, or subjective judgments gained from interviews. The combination of all these data enables us to classify the subject; and once having made such a classification, we enter a statistical or actuarial table which gives the statistical frequencies of behaviors of various sorts for persons belonging to the class. The mechanical combining of information for classification purposes, and the resultant probability figure which is an empirically determined relative frequency, are the characteristics that define the actuarial or statistical type of prediction.
>
> (p. 3)

In the actuarial approach, the individual evaluator will follow a set formula in selecting and scoring risk factors that have been empirically validated. Grove and Meehl (1996) refer to

> mechanical or statistical methods that have been developed using optimized prediction formulas derived from multiple regression or discriminative analysis or simple unit weighted sums of predictors and other mechanical schemes that yield precisely reproducible predictions.
>
> (p. 296)

Actuarial science became a formal mathematical discipline in the late 17th century in response to increased demand in the insurance industry for long-term predictions of mortality by age, and is now used in a wide variety of financial and business disciplines (Cunningham, Herzog, & London, 2011). Meehl's paper sparked a debate on the relative value of clinical versus actuarial prediction that continues in various forms today. The obvious question arising from the distinction between clinical and mechanical methods of prediction is which of the two general approaches has led to greater predictive validity. This is a question that has been posed and answered numerous times, and the consistent finding has been that mechanical prediction is generally equal or superior to clinical prediction (Borum, Otto, & Golding, 1993; Dawes et al., 1989; Marchese, 1992; Sawyer, 1966). Direct comparisons of clinical and actuarial predictions in forensic settings have generally demonstrated the superior accuracy of the latter (Gardner, Lidz, Mulvey, & Shaw, 1996; Menzies, Webster, McMain, Staley, & Scaglione, 1994; Mossman, 1994). From their meta-analysis of 136 studies within the fields of psychology and medicine, Grove et al. (2000) reported that, depending on the specific analysis, mechanical prediction substantially outperformed clinical prediction in 33–47% of studies examined. Although clinical predictions were sometimes found to be as accurate as mechanical predictions, clinical predictions were found to be superior to mechanical prediction in only a few studies (6–16%; p. 19). Grove et al. (2000) could discern no common characteristics across the small number of studies in which clinical predictions outperformed mechanical ones. Accordingly, they concluded:

> The general superiority (or at least material equivalence) of mechanical prediction . . . holds in general medicine, in mental health, in personality, and in education and training settings. It holds for medically trained judges and for psychologists. It holds for inexperienced and seasoned judges.
>
> (p. 25)

This issue has been addressed recently in the area of risk prediction with sex offenders by Hanson and Morton-Bourgon (2009) who conducted a meta-analysis of the sex offender recidivism literature examining the accuracy of various approaches to sex offender risk assessment. They found that actuarial approaches are superior in accuracy to all other approaches. We think it is now generally accepted that actuarial methods make more accurate predictions than clinical methods, and this general acceptance has extended to the SVP courts with which we are familiar.

The Prediction of Sexual Violence

Monahan and Steadman (1994a) formalized the notion of statistical prediction of future violence by defining three closely related components: *risk factors*, the variables that predict violence; *harm*, the outcome being predicted, including the nature and seriousness of the sexual violence to be predicted; and *risk level*, the probability that the individual will go on to engage in criminal sexual behavior.

Risk factors are those characteristics of the offender that increase the likelihood of future violence. According to Monahan and Appelbaum (2000), risk factors have two necessary characteristics. First, the risk factor must be identified and present before the criterion outcome occurs, as in prior to the offender's release to the community. And second, there must be a statistical correlation between the risk factor and the criterion outcome. In the context of the present discussion, risk factors are quantifiable features of sex offenders that are identified and quantified prior to their release from custody and which correlate with future sexual offenses. Of course, these correlations have been obtained by empirical research with offenders who were released some time ago and have had opportunities to re-offend during a period of living in the community. It is these empirically determined correlations that allow the forensic examiner to make predictions concerning similar offenders being released today.

Harm is the second component identified by Monahan and Steadman (1994a), and this component concerns the sexual violence that can be predicted by risk factors. The literature refers to this harm as recidivism (from the Latin *recidivus* meaning "recurring"). Recidivism occurs when a person repeats an undesirable behavior after they have been punished for that behavior, or after they have received treatment or some other rehabilitation designed to prevent or eliminate that behavior. In the research literature on sex offender recidivism, it is common to make a distinction among three kinds of recidivism: *Any recidivism* refers to any kind of criminal re-offense, including property crime as well as a violent crime; *Sexual recidivism* refers to the re-commission of a nominal sexual crime such as sexual assault or rape; and *Serious or violent recidivism* refers to any crime involving physical contact with the victim, including both sexual and nonsexual violent crimes (Hanson & Bussiere, 1998; Hanson & Morton-Bourgon, 2005).

For the third component, risk level, Monahan and Steadman (1994b) described a probability statement, usually quantified as a continuous percentage or a proportion. Borum (1996) defined the *base rate* as the percentage or proportion of offenders within a given population released to the community who recommit an offense of a specific type over a given period of time (p. 946). Base rates for a given kind of re-offense will vary from sex offender subgroup to subgroup according to

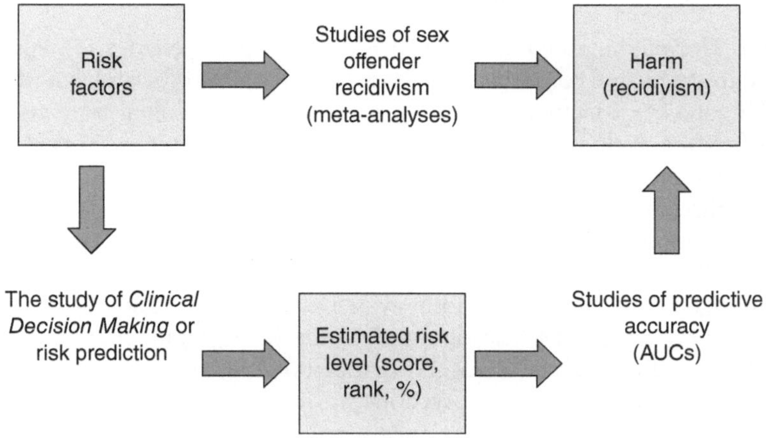

Figure 4.1 Monahan and Steadman's model of risk prediction.

the specific characteristics of the group. In the absence of any additional risk-relevant information, risk level can be construed as the base rate of a particular kind of recidivism (e.g., sexual recidivism) for a group of offenders (e.g., male child molesters) having specific characteristics in common (i.e., risk factors). And risk level is dependent on the amount of time the offender has to re-offend. It should be obvious that a sexual re-offense is more likely if the offender is given a longer opportunity to act, and base rates of recidivism are therefore higher when the follow-up period is longer (Borum, 1996). Therefore, risk represents a probability estimate for the occurrence of a specific act of recidivism (any, sexual, violent), in a group of offenders sharing a similar pattern of risk factors (e.g., male child molesters) over a specified period of time (e.g., five years; Hanson et al., 2003; Monahan, 1996; Monahan & Steadman, 1994a; Quinsey et al., 1998).

Monahan and Steadman (1994a) go on to distinguish three kinds of studies pertinent to risk assessment, based on the relationships among the three entities identified above. Figure 4.1 presents our adaptation of the original figure presented by Monahan and Steadman (1994b, p. 3). These studies include: (1) studies of the relationship between risk factors and recidivism, exemplified by the meta-analyses of sex offender recidivism (Hanson & Bussiere, 1998; Hanson & Morton-Bourgon, 2005), (2) studies of the relationship between risk factors and risk prediction, exemplified by the studies of clinical decision-making (Mulvey & Lidz, 1984, 1985), and (3) studies of the relationship between risk prediction and recidivism, exemplified by the studies of prediction accuracy (e.g., Barbaree, Seto, Langton, & Peacock, 2001; Hanson & Morton-Bourgon, 2009). We will discuss these three kinds of studies in turn.

Studies of Sex Offender Recidivism

What information about an offender is relevant and necessary to make an accurate prediction concerning his recidivism? Empirical research has identified a core set of factors that are valid predictors of criminal recidivism in all offenders, including: history of antisocial behavior, antisocial personality pattern including antisocial cognitions, antisocial associates, family/marital conflict, dysfunctional behavior at school or work, low levels of leisure and recreation, substance abuse and offender age (Andrews & Bonta, 2010, p. 500; Bonta, Law, & Hanson, 1998; Gendreau, Little, & Goggin, 1996; Hanson, Scott, & Steffy, 1995; Lipsey & Derzon, 1998). These risk factors have been referred to as "the big eight" (Andrews & Bonta, 2010).

There is also evidence to suggest that certain types of violence have distinct predictors. For example, psychopathy, prior sexual offenses, and phallometrically assessed sexual deviance have been shown to be particularly associated with sexual recidivism (Rice, Harris, & Quinsey, 1990; Rice, Quinsey, & Harris, 1991), as has a diagnosis of paraphilia and degree of sexual preoccupation with children (Prentky, Knight, & Lee, 1997).

Karl Hanson and his colleagues (Hanson & Bussiere, 1998; Hanson & Morton-Bourgon, 2005) have conducted a number of meta-analytic reviews of the large sex offender recidivism literature and these provide a comprehensive summary of the research on predictors of various types of recidivism among sexual offenders. In their 1998 meta-analysis, based on 61 studies and 23,393 offenders, they reported that the strongest predictors of sexual recidivism were measures of sexual deviancy, and the strongest predictors of nonsexual violent recidivism and general (any) recidivism were juvenile delinquency and a history of prior violent offenses.

Later, Hanson and Morton-Bourgon (2005) reported the results of a subsequent meta-analysis of 82 recidivism studies involving 1,620 findings from 29,450 sexual offenders. These authors sought to evaluate a broad array of potential risk factors to see what kinds of variables were predictive of recidivism. To that end, both authors coded variables identified as potential risk factors from each study in the meta-analysis using a standard list of variables and explicit coding rules. Risk factors were first coded into specific individual variables (e.g., sexual interest in boys), and these narrowly defined factors were then combined into more general (superordinate) categories (e.g., antisocial orientation, sexual deviancy). The general categories were as follows (from Hanson and Morton-Bourgon, 2005):

1 *Sexual deviancy*: deviant sexual interests, such as children, rape, and other paraphilias, as well as sexual preoccupations and gender dysphoria;
2 *Antisocial orientation*: antisocial personality (e.g., antisocial personality disorder), psychopathy, Minnesota Multiphasic Personality Inventory Scale 4, antisocial traits (e.g., lifestyle instability, substance

abuse, hostility), and a history of rule violation (e.g., childhood criminality, history of nonsexual crime, violation of conditional release);

3 *Sexual attitudes*: tolerance of sexual crime, support for adult–child sex, and low sex knowledge;
4 *Intimacy deficits*: poor social skills, negative social influences, conflicts in intimate relationships, emotional identification with children, and loneliness;
5 *Adverse childhood environment*: conflicts with and separation from parents, neglect, and physical and sexual abuse;
6 *General psychological problems*: internalization of psychological problems (e.g., anxiety and low self-esteem, as well as major mental illness); and
7 *Clinical presentation*: denial, minimization, lack of victim empathy, low motivation for treatment, and poor progress.

Table 4.1 presents a summary of the results of the meta-analysis. The measure of the extent to which the risk factor predicted recidivism was calculated as *d*, the standardized difference between the mean of the recidivists and mean of the non-recidivists divided by the pooled standard

Table 4.1 Factors associated with recidivism among sexual offenders

	Type of recidivism			
Category of risk factor	*Sexual*	*Violent nonsexual*	*Violent*	*Any*
Sexual deviancy	.30+/–.08 (5,053;32)	–.05+/–.17 (1,385;10)	.19+/–.08] (3,155;17)	.04+/–.08 (6,555;19)
Antisocial orientation	.23+/–.04 (23,012;65)	.51+/–.07 (8,283;24)	.54+/–.05 (13,065;28)	.52+/–.04 (15,988;43)
Sexual attitudes	.16+/–.12 (2,370;14)	.17+/–.22 (732;6)	.14+/–.11 (1,598;9)	.24+/–.10 (1,053;9)
Intimacy deficits	.15+/–.11 (2,852;22)	.12+/–.21 (2,852;6)	.12+/–.21 (822;6)	.10+/–.10 (1,715;15)
Adverse childhood environment	.09+/–.08 (7,259;27)	–.02+/–.17 (2,256;7)	.14+/–.08 (5,041;14)	.11+/–.07 (5,044;15)
General psychological problems	.02+/–.10 (3,208;19)	.21+/–.14 (2,089;8)	.00+/–.10 (1,974;10)	–.04+/–.11 (1,658;11)
Clinical presentation	–.02+/–.09 (5,094;24)	.16+/–.20 (2,090;5)	.09+/–.09 (3,849;12)	.12+/–.08 (4,714;18)

Note
Values are averaged *d* values, followed by their 95% confidence interval and (in parentheses) the total sample size and number of studies (*k*). Reproduced from Hanson and Morton-Bourgon, 2005 with permission.

deviation of the two groups; *d*s ranged from near zero (not predictive) to just over 0.50 (significantly predictive). As can be seen from the table, different risk factors predict different recidivism outcomes in sex offenders, and some presumptive risk factors do not predict recidivism at all. In predicting a sexual re-offense, offender characteristics of sexual deviance and antisocial orientation were the strongest predictors, sexual attitudes and intimacy deficits were moderate predictors, and, somewhat unexpectedly, adverse childhood environment, general psychological problems, and clinical presentation were not predictive of recidivism. For violent nonsexual re-offense, the strongest predictor was antisocial orientation, with general psychological problems as a more moderate predictor.

Static Versus Dynamic Risk Factors

Hanson (1998) identified two general types of risk factor: static predictors and dynamic predictors. Static predictors are variables statistically related to recidivism that are either historical in nature (and thus cannot themselves be changed with interventions) or are features of the offender that are very unlikely to change over time. Examples of static predictors for violent re-offense would include a history of criminal convictions and a history of juvenile delinquency and antisocial behavior (Quinsey et al., 1998). Dynamic predictors are also variables that are statistically related to recidivism but the value of these variables can change over time. More specifically, changes in the value of these dynamic variables are statistically related to changes in the likelihood of violence. Examples of dynamic predictors for sex offenders include attitudes supportive of sex with children, association with criminal peers, and substance use (Hanson & Harris, 2000). A further distinction can be drawn between stable and acute dynamic predictors. According to Hanson (1998), stable dynamic factors have the potential to change but the changes are slow and the particular values of these variables can endure for long periods (e.g., deviant sexual preferences or alcoholism). In contrast, acute dynamic factors are rapidly changing states (e.g., anger, sexual arousal, or intoxication) that immediately precede sexual crimes (Hanson, 1998).

Beech and Ward (2004) have argued quite convincingly that the distinction between static and dynamic risk factors is an artificial one, an argument that seems to have been recently accepted by Hanson and his colleagues (Mann, Hanson, & Thornton, 2010, p. 194), where these authors concede that there is very little empirical support for the distinction between static and dynamic risk factors. According to this argument, an offender engaging in antisocial behavior may create a record that cannot be changed (e.g., criminal convictions, behavior problems in elementary school) resulting in a static risk factor, or they may express antisocial attitudes and beliefs recorded by the probation officer as a dynamic risk factor. However, the underlying antisocial predisposition is common to both factors, and the extent to which the underlying predisposition is subject to change is an empirical question. The distinction between static and dynamic risk factors depends more on the nature of the recording or method of assessment rather than any substantive differences among risk factors. For many static risk factors, the historical record of antisocial behavior cannot change, but that does not mean that the underlying risk predisposition cannot change.

A distinction that is more important to make, relating to the differences between static and dynamic risk factors, is between long-term and short-term prediction. Different research designs have been used to investigate two fundamentally different approaches to risk assessment. Static risk factors have been shown to predict violence in research designs involving long-term (5 to 20 years) follow-up between the clinical assessment and recording of the risk factor and the recidivism outcome being predicted (e.g., Quinsey et al., 1998). Most of the scientific research on risk assessment has focused on the identification of risk factors using research designs involving long-term follow-up, and empirically these investigations have found static factors to be superior to dynamic factors. In contrast, dynamic factors have been shown to predict violence in research designs that involve shorter follow-up times. The values of the risk factors are monitored continuously over several weeks or months and changes in these values are detected prior to a violent incident (Quinsey, Coleman, Jones, & Altrows, 1997; Hanson, Harris, Scott, & Helmus, 2007). A change in an offender's mood, perhaps to one in which hostility is markedly increased or substantial interpersonal distress is noted, may indicate that a violent act is imminent and crisis intervention is warranted.

Mann et al. (2010) conclude the discussion of static and dynamic risk factors by stating:

> We propose that another way to understand risk factors . . . is by adopting the concept of *psychologically meaningful risk factors*. Such risk factors can be conceptualized as individual propensities, which may or may not manifest during any particular time period. Like the traditional concept of trait, propensities are enduring characteristics that lead to predictable expressions of thoughts, feelings, or behaviors. Although propensities are characteristic of individuals, these propensities can also be recognized by individuals' transactions with others and the environments in which they live.

Studies of Risk Prediction

The fortune teller has "knowledge" of—and will predict—the future. However, for most of us, soothsaying and prophesizing, the generally discredited art of fortune telling, is taken with a large grain of salt. Predicting and forecasting are a routine part of everyday life; we make predictions all the time. Generally, these predictions are guesses, informed by past experience rather than tea leaves, runes, tarot cards, a crystal ball, or a Ouija board. Our everyday predictions, to the extent that they rely on a large enough pool of past experiences, are generally reliable, but we are not surprised when our predictions do not pan out. Predictions of criminal behavior may also be based on the predictor's past clinical experience, and these judgments have been referred to as clinical or intuitive, but humans (experts or otherwise) have a limited ability to assess future risk of harmful behavior.

Risk assessment has been aptly referred to as "the mother of all uncertainties" (Bailar & Bailer, 1999, p. 273). Uncertainty in behavioral risk assessment can be traced to two main sources. First, limitations in risk assessments stem from the fact that the future is inherently unknowable. Future circumstances, sentinel events, environmental changes, and unforeseen personal and interpersonal developments may affect risk so that future sexual crimes are to some extent unpredictable. And second, clinical risk assessment is, by definition, an exercise in human judgment. The susceptibility of human judgment to error has been the subject of considerable empirical scrutiny (cf. Garb, 1998), and numerous sources of error in clinical judgments have been described (e.g., Garb, 1998; Grove, Zald, Lebow, Snitz, & Nelson, 2000); many were discussed in Chapter 3. Although the former limitation (the ever-cloudy crystal ball) is inescapable, the fallibility of human judgment is something we can do something about.

There have been numerous descriptions of the various approaches to risk assessment and, except for one, these various approaches depend to varying degrees on clinical judgment. For example, Doren (2002) identified six different approaches to risk assessment of the sex offender, including: (1) at one end of the continuum of subjectivity, *unstructured/unguided clinical judgment*, (2) at the other end of the continuum, a *purely actuarial approach*. This approach does not involve clinical judgment at all. Then, in between these extremes were approaches that combined empirically determined rule-based reasoning with expert or professional clinical judgment. These are (3) *guided clinical judgment*, (4) *anamnestic risk assessment* (based on a study of the individual life history and whether identified risk factors were still present), (5) *research-guided clinical judgment*, and (6) *the clinically adjusted actuarial approach*.

In contrast to clinical or intuitive judgment, empirically based prediction relies on statistical inference, using one or more statistical prediction rules. As we indicated earlier, judgments based on statistical prediction rules tend to be far more reliable than clinical judgment (Hanson & Morton-Bourgon, 2009). Nevertheless, we take the position that forensic evaluations in the real world involve a complex interplay between statistical prediction and informed expert judgment. There are various models describing how empirical prediction is integrated into the forensic expert's judgment. Here, we describe five different models.

Hanson, Morton, and Harris (2003) identified *empirically guided clinical assessment* as one frequently used approach to risk assessment for sex offenders. In conducting these assessments, the evaluator uses risk factors that have been shown empirically to have a significant statistical relationship with the outcome to be predicted (as, for example, in Table 4.1). After rating the offender on the relevant risk factors, the evaluator makes a subjective judgment to derive the final risk level. In this approach, a clinician would use the factors identified in Table 4.1 (specific risk factors contained within the superordinate risk factors, sexual deviance and antisocial orientation) together with their own knowledge of the offender to make predictions of future recidivism. If the offender had little evidence of the risk factors, she would perhaps assess the risk as low. If on the other hand the offender had prominent features of these risk factors, her evaluation would be of higher risk. While empirically guided clinical assessment represented an historic advance over previous approaches (unguided and unstructured clinical judgment), the outcome studies have shown that this approach is not optimal (Barbaree et al., 2001; Hanson & Morton-Bourgon, 2009).

During the past 25 years, numerous ARAIs have been developed that have been empirically validated in predicting recidivism in sex offenders. When used by professionals with appropriate training, these instruments represent the current state of the art in sex offender risk assessment. These instruments have been developed using different approaches, and the instruments are currently used in different ways by different evaluators.

Hanson and Morton-Bourgon (2007) identified four different approaches to the use of formal risk assessment instruments. These different approaches vary in the way items are selected for inclusion in the instrument and the way item scores are combined to determine the final estimate of risk. In the *structured professional judgment* (SPJ) approach, the items are rationally selected on the basis of a theory of risk and are based on risk factors that have been shown empirically to predict recidivism, but the final estimate is a subjective judgment made by the expert assessor (Hanson & Morton-Bourgon, 2007, 2009). In the *mechanical or conceptual actuarial* approach, similar to the SPJ approach, the items are rationally selected based on the empirical evidence and a theoretical understanding of sex offender recidivism, but here explicit rules are provided for combining the item scores into an overall evaluation of risk. In the *empirical actuarial* approach, the items are selected based on their empirical relationships with recidivism outcome and explicit rules are provided for combining the item scores into an overall evaluation of risk. In the empirical actuarial approach, the items have no necessary face validity and no necessary connection with any theory of recidivism. They are selected and weighted based on their empirical relationship with recidivism outcome. And finally, in the *adjusted actuarial* approach, the actuarial method is used to determine a probability of recidivism and then this probability is adjusted up or down based on consideration of risk factors that are external to (not included in) the actuarial instrument used (Hanson et al., 2003). These approaches to risk assessment can be better understood as we consider the process an evaluator goes through in conducting a risk assessment.

The process of risk assessment can be thought of as occurring in seven steps (Barbaree, Langton, Gopnik-Lewinski, & Beach, 2013). These steps are presented for each of the approaches to risk assessment described above and contained in Table 4.2. Not all evaluators use all steps, and different evaluators use each step differently. That being said, all evaluators using any of the different approaches emphasize the importance of reviewing complete, up-to-date information on the individual being assessed.

We begin with Step 1 (Information Gathering and Review). All of the information available on the individual being assessed is gathered and reviewed. A primary source of information available to the evaluator is that which is acquired directly from the person being evaluated in interview. However, evaluators are encouraged not to depend solely or even primarily on information provided by the person being evaluated, since they often have motivation to present information in a self-serving light. The evaluator must seek and review additional information including police reports, crown briefs, transcripts from court proceedings, clinical reports, hospital reports and records, correctional facility reports and records, etc. The risk evaluator is expected to have a detailed familiarity with all of the information available on the individual being evaluated. Whatever approach is taken to the risk assessment itself, it is accepted by evaluators using all of the various approaches to risk assessment that risk evaluations should be based on all the available risk-relevant information. When information is missing or felt to be unreliable, information must be sought from collateral sources. The evaluation report should detail the missing information and an appropriate caveat concerning the potential effect of the missing information should be included in the report. An excellent description of the information-gathering and organization process is described in Quinsey et al. (1998, 2006).

In Step 2 (Identifying Risk Factors/Items), the information is organized into risk-relevant categories around known risk factors or risk items specified in risk assessment instruments. For example, if the evaluator is basing her evaluation of risk at least in part on the individual's history of antisocial behavior, then information concerning previous criminal history, juvenile delinquency, institutional infractions, history of violence, etc. will have to be gathered together and reviewed to make an appropriate evaluation. For those evaluators using a structured approach to risk assessment, the evaluator will have chosen a risk assessment instrument that specifies the risk factors/items and what information is required to assess

Table 4.2 The steps in the process of risk assessment of the sex offender, for each of five different approaches to risk assessment (adapted from Barbaree et al., 2013)

	Steps						
	1	2	3	4	5	6	7
Approaches to risk assessment	*Info*	*Identifying risk factors*	*Factor/item scoring*	*Assigning a composite score*	*Determining relative risk*	*Determining absolute risk*	*Adjustment/ override*
Empirically guided clinical	√	Empirically determined	Clinical	Clinical	No	No	No
Structured professional judgment	√	Risk factors determined rationally	Mechanical	Clinical	No	No	No
Conceptual actuarial	√	Risk factors determined rationally	Mechanical	Statistical	Possible	Possible	No
Empirical actuarial	√	Risk factors determined empirically	Mechanical	Statistical	Yes	Yes	No
Clinically adjusted empirical actuarial	√	Risk factors determined empirically	Mechanical	Statistical then clinical	No	No	Yes

the individual on that factor or item. For the most often used ARAIs, instrument developers have provided manuals describing risk factors and related items contained in the instrument.

In Step 3 (Scoring Risk Factors/Items), the information available on each of the risk factors is analyzed and the evaluator assigns a score for each risk factor or item. For many structured risk instruments, the process whereby the score is derived is a *mechanical* process in which the strict rules for scoring are laid out in the scoring manuals provided by the instrument developer(s). While the scoring is mechanical, it is not necessarily straightforward. Risk assessment instruments are provided with scoring manuals, and extensive training on scoring items is available for some instruments. For example, on some risk instruments, an item might call for the evaluator to indicate whether the individual had ever been married. The risk assessment instrument may provide a manual for evaluators in which all terms are defined in detail (i.e., what is marriage). The evaluator would then determine a response for this item from the available information.

In Step 4 (Assigning a Composite Risk Score), the scores from the various factors or items are combined into a final risk score. In a *clinical* approach to the derivation of a composite score, the evaluator reviews the item and factor scoring and then assigns a final composite score, usually in some categorical system (low, moderate, high), based on their expert opinion. However, if the scores are combined through a process of mathematical calculation, this is referred to as a *statistical* combination. The item or factor scores may be combined in a straightforward way such as the addition of item or factor scores (a linear combination with all factors and items having the same weight). On the other hand, the risk assessment instrument may call for a combination of item or factor scores in which each factor or item is weighted differently in accordance with weightings that have been derived previously using a statistical method relating item and factor scores to recidivism outcome (e.g., VRAG, Quinsey et al., 1998, 2006).

In Step 5 (Determining Relative Risk), the individual's score derived from the above process of evaluation is compared with the distribution of scores made available by the developers of the risk assessment instrument, resulting in the individual being assigned a measure of relative risk, including a *percentile ranking* (Hanson, Lloyd, Helmus, & Thornton, 2012) or a *risk ratio* (Hanson, Babchishin, Helmus, & Thornton, 2012). Most readers will be familiar with the concept of percentile ranking. Percentile ranks are usually calculated as the percent of the sample whose risk score is the same as or below that obtained by the individual being evaluated. Recently, Hanson and his colleagues have suggested that risk ratios are a superior measure of relative risk and we will review this suggestion later in Chapter 5.

In Step 6 (Determining the Absolute Risk), the risk for recidivism is provided in percentage terms or in a statement of probability. The percentages have been empirically derived by the test developers and these percentages represent the percentage of their samples who have obtained the same score of the individual being evaluated who have recidivated over specified periods of time (e.g., 5, 10, and 15 years). These risk levels are expressed as a percentage (i.e., 45%) or a probability (i.e., 0.45) and are often provided by the instrument developers in tabular format similar to actuarial life tables.

For those evaluators who adhere to the adjusted actuarial approach, adjustments to the actuarial result are done in the final step, Step 7 (Adjusting the Actuarially Estimated Probability of Recidivism). In this step, the probability of recidivism specified in Step 6 is adjusted, if required, either up or down, based on consideration of risk (or protective) factors that are external to (not included in) the actuarial instrument used (Hanson et al., 2003). For example, the evaluator might have used the Static-99 to determine a level of risk, but on interview finds that the offender has particularly strong attitudes in support of sexual interactions between adults and adolescents. Since sexual attitudes supportive of sexual abuse are not included in the Static-99 (they are external to the instrument), she might increase her estimate accordingly. In most of these situations, the size of the adjustment is not empirically based or determined but is estimated by the evaluator using their own clinical judgment.

Recently, Hanson and Morton-Bourgon (2007) conducted a meta-analysis of the accuracy of recidivism risk assessments for sexual offenders based on 577 findings from 79 distinct samples. Calculating the size of effects over these diverse studies, these authors concluded that empirical actuarial instruments were superior in their ability to predict recidivism in sex offenders compared with all other methods, including conceptual actuarial measures and structured professional judgment.

Summary and Conclusions

In this chapter, we have provided the reader with an introduction to the assessment of violence risk in sex offenders. We began by defining risk, comparing risk as the public would define it with a scientific understanding of risk, as a statement of the probability of an adverse outcome over a specified period of time. We adopted actuarial risk prediction as conceived of originally by Meehl (1954) and later by Monahan and Steadman (1994) in which empirically determined risk factors provide for the statistical prediction of adverse outcomes. We defined recidivism as the reoccurrence of both sexual and nonsexual offenses by offenders released from custody over a defined period of follow-up. We described a number of recognized approaches to risk assessment that occurs in seven distinct steps, and we described how each approach uses either a clinical judgment or a mechanical/statistical methodology at each step. We emphasized Meehl's description of actuarial assessment as occurring in two stages, namely a first stage in which known risk factors are used to classify offenders into ranked categories of relative risk and a second stage in which empirically derived levels of absolute risk are determined for each risk category. The next three chapters examine this model of risk prediction to see how well it applies to the real world of sex offender risk assessment.

5

THE DEVELOPMENT AND EVALUATION OF ACTUARIAL RISK ASSESSMENT INSTRUMENTS

Introduction

In the second of these four chapters on risk assessment, we discuss the empirical development and evaluation of actuarial risk assessment instruments (ARAIs). First, we describe the empirical development and evaluation of a brief actuarial scale (BAS). Second, we discuss how evaluation of predictive accuracy of ARAIs is accomplished using receiver operating characteristic (ROC) analysis. Third, we review the most popular and most often used ARAIs, and examine the empirical data supporting their use, particularly independent cross-validation studies. Fourth, we discuss the effects of aging on sex offender recidivism risk and the recent development of the static instruments which have incorporated a revised age item. Finally, we summarize the state of the art of sex offender risk prediction as of the end of the year 2012.

Illustrative Data Set

In this book, we are going to provide a number of illustrative demonstrations to elucidate the points we are making. These demonstrations will be done using a specific data set. A number of years ago, one of us (HB) was contracted to establish and run a treatment program for sex offenders in a Canadian medium-security penitentiary, and this led to access to pertinent clinical, psychometric, legal, and demographic information concerning the treatment participants. The eventual sample of participants in the data set comprised adult male sex offenders who were offered assessment and treatment at the Warkworth Sexual Behavior Clinic (WSBC) during its first eight years of operation (1989–1996). The clinic was located in Warkworth Penitentiary, a medium-security federal penitentiary in Ontario, Canada. Of the 806 offenders offered assessment and treatment, 571 participated in either assessment or treatment. All sexual offenders incarcerated at Warkworth Penitentiary were eligible for treatment at the WSBC and were encouraged to participate by their case managers. Offenders who did not consent to participation ($n = 235$) were not admitted to the program and are not included in this data set. All 571 sexual offenders agreed to the use of their file information for research as part of their written consent to assessment and treatment at the WSBC. The sample included all sexual offenders seen at the WSBC for whom relatively complete file information was available. Ninety-five sexual offenders were excluded for various reasons (death, deportation, major inconsistencies in file information, offender not released by end of follow-up period). Data on recidivism outcomes were obtained for 476 sexual offenders who had been released to the community and therefore who were at risk of reoffending during the follow-up period.

The group of 476 sexual offenders was composed of 175 rapists (offenders who had sexually assaulted females aged 16 years or older, exclusively), 155 extra-familial child molesters (offenders who had sexually assaulted extra-familial children, aged 15 years or younger), 93 familial offenders (offenders who had sexually assaulted biologically related and/or step-children aged 15 years or younger, exclusively), 45 mixed offenders (offenders who had sexually assaulted females aged 18 years or older and children aged 13 years or younger, while being five or more years older than the child victim at the time of the abuse), five sexual offenders with adult male victims (offenders who had sexually assaulted a male aged 18 years and older), and three offenders with non-contact sexual offenses (e.g., a conviction for indecent exposure). Due to the lack of empirical evidence demonstrating the validity of the risk assessment instruments with non-contact sexual offenders or sexual offenders with adult male victims, these last two subsets (offenders with male victims aged 18 years or older and non-contact sexual offenders) were removed, leaving a final sample of 468 sexual offenders. This sample has been used in numerous studies in the published literature. (See asterisks in the References for this book.)

The Development of a Brief Actuarial Scale: A Demonstration

Previous authors have published descriptions of brief actuarial scales. The Rapid Risk Assessment of Sex Offender Recidivism (RRASOR; Hanson, 1997) is an actuarial instrument that includes four items: male victim, unrelated victim, previous sexual offense, and offender age. The Screening Scale for Pedophilic Interests (SSPI; Seto & Lalumiere, 2001; Seto, Harris,

Rice, & Barbaree, 2004) also includes four items: any male child victim, more than one child victim, any prepubescent victim (under 12 years of age), and any extra-familial victim.

We are going to take the reader through the exercise of constructing a brief actuarial instrument. For demonstration purposes, we will be using only a subset of data contained in the sample described above. Specifically, we will be using the participants in the sample who had only victimized children (we are excluding here any offender who victimized an adult). Beginning with an *n* of 248, and excluding three offenders with missing data, the resulting *n* for this subgroup of child molesters is 245.

Single bits of information can be, by themselves, predictive of sexual recidivism. Our illustrative actuarial scale will contain three bits of information (i.e., three items). In the Hanson and Bussiere (1998) meta-analysis involving 61 follow-up studies, a number of factors predictive of recidivism among sexual offenders were identified. Sexual offense recidivism was best predicted by measures of sexual deviancy and general criminological factors. Table 4.1 in Chapter 4 listed numerous predictive factors. For example, we have known for a long time that sex offenders who have only ever offended against family members (incest offenders) are at very low risk for future recidivism. (See Hanson & Bussiere, 1998, p. 352, studies = 21, *n* = 6,889.) Put another way, if an offender has ever offended against an unrelated victim, their risk for recidivism is higher. This risk factor is represented by items in many of the ARAIs, and specifically exemplified by Static-99R item #8. In our sample of child molesters, using Static-99R item #8 as the grouping factor, offenders with unrelated victims had a higher recidivism rate (14.6%) than offenders who did not have an unrelated victim (2.3%). Therefore, this item is significantly related to sexual recidivism, $\textit{chi square}_{(df=1)} = 9.201$, $p<.01$.

Similarly, we have known for a long time that sex offenders who have ever offended against a male victim are at higher risk for recidivism than offenders who have never offended against a male victim. (See Hanson & Bussiere, 1998, p. 352, studies = 19, *n* = 10,294.) This risk factor is represented by items in many of the ARAIs, and specifically exemplified by Static-99R item #10. In our sample, using Static-99R item #10 as a grouping factor, offenders with at least one male victim had a higher recidivism rate (19.1%) compared with offenders with no male victims (5.1%). Therefore, this item is significantly related to sexual recidivism, $\textit{chi square}_{(df=1)} = 12.075$, $p<.001$.

Finally, we have known for a long time that offenders with previous charges or convictions for sexual offenses are at higher risk for recidivism than offenders who are serving time for a first known sexual offense. (See Hanson & Bussiere, 1998, p. 352, studies = 29, *n* = 11,294.) This risk factor is represented by items in many of the ARAIs, and specifically exemplified by Static-99R item #5. In the scoring instructions for this item, the response is graded from 0–3 depending on the number of previous charges or convictions for sexual offenses. For the purposes of this demonstration, we have recoded the item as a "0" or a "1," distinguishing between offenders who have no previous charges or convictions for sexual offenses (coded as 0) and offenders who have previously been charged or convicted of a sexual offense (coded as 1). In our illustrative data set, using the revised Static-99R item as a grouping factor, offenders with previous charges or convictions for at least one sexual offense had a higher rate of recidivism (23%) compared with first-time sexual offenders (1.4%). Therefore, this recoded Static-99R item #5 was significantly related to sexual recidivism, *chi square* $_{(df=1)} = 30.414$, $p<.001$.

Now that we have demonstrated that each individual item is significantly related to recidivism, we will address the issue of whether the combination of these items is related to recidivism. Adding these three items (each score as a "0" or a "1") to construct our scale, the scale score varies from 0–3. To follow the example of the developers of actuarial instruments, we will go on to demonstrate that different scale scores are associated with different levels of recidivism. Figure 5.1 presents the five-year sexual recidivism rates for offenders assigned to each of the four BAS score groups. As you will see, recidivism rates increase with increases in the BAS scores, and this increase is statistically significant, *chi square* $_{(df=3)} = 39.083$, $p<.001$.

Studies of Predictive Accuracy

How well do we predict the future behavior of sex offenders? This question raises a prior question: how do we assess our ability to predict the future behavior of sex offenders? We quantify our ability to

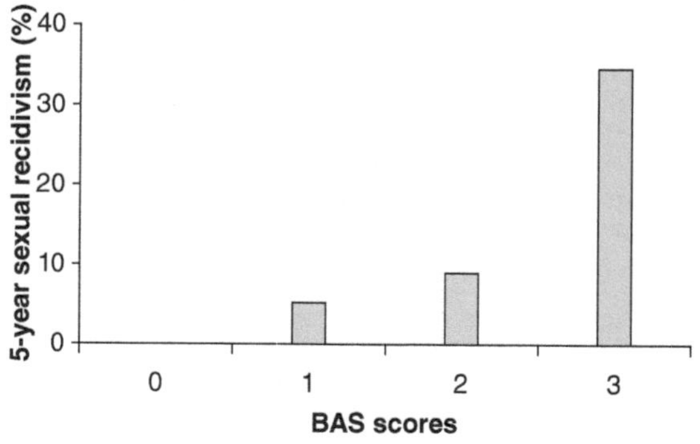

Figure 5.1 Five-year recidivism rates for groups assigned to each BAS score value.

Note
For offenders with a BAS score of zero, there were no recidivists.

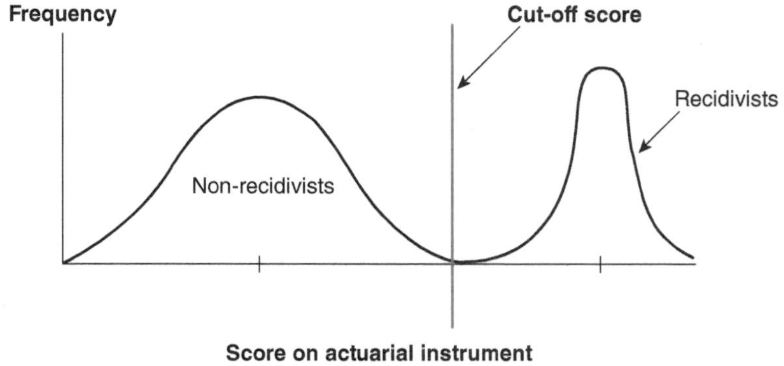

Figure 5.2 An idealized view of optimal group discrimination in scores on the hypothetical actuarial instrument.

predict recidivism in sex offenders using a statistical calculation known as receiver operator characteristic (ROC) analysis (Hanley & McNeil, 1982; Mossman, 1994; Rice & Harris, 1997). The ROC curve plots the trade-off between true positives and false positives across a test's measurement range. The resulting statistic is referred to as the "area under the curve" or AUC. Let's work our way through a ROC analysis of an illustrative attempt to predict sexual recidivism.

What would test score distributions look like in the case of perfect prediction by the test? Figure 5.2 represents an idealized frequency distribution of scores. In the case of perfect prediction, the distribution is bimodal, with a complete separation of test scores resulting from the recidivists and non-recidivists. An arbitrary cut-off score (sometimes referred to as a cut score) is chosen as a score that is above the highest score for the non-recidivists, and below the lowest score for the recidivists, representing a boundary that separates one distribution from the other. It would be wonderful if we could devise a test that produced this bimodal non-overlapping distribution of test scores, but unfortunately perfect prediction never happens, at least not in the real world of sex offender risk assessment.

Figure 5.3 represents the two distributions of scores as they more often occur in the real world. In this figure, the distribution of scores overlap, so many of the recidivists have scores that are lower than many of the non-recidivists, and many non-recidivists have scores higher than recidivists. Here, it is not clear where the cut score should be placed as there is no score that divides the two distributions cleanly. However, a cut score can be placed in the figure as a vertical line. Different values of cut scores can then be contemplated so that the cut score is represented as a vertical line that can be moved up and down the test scale, depending on the choice of the examiner making the prediction.

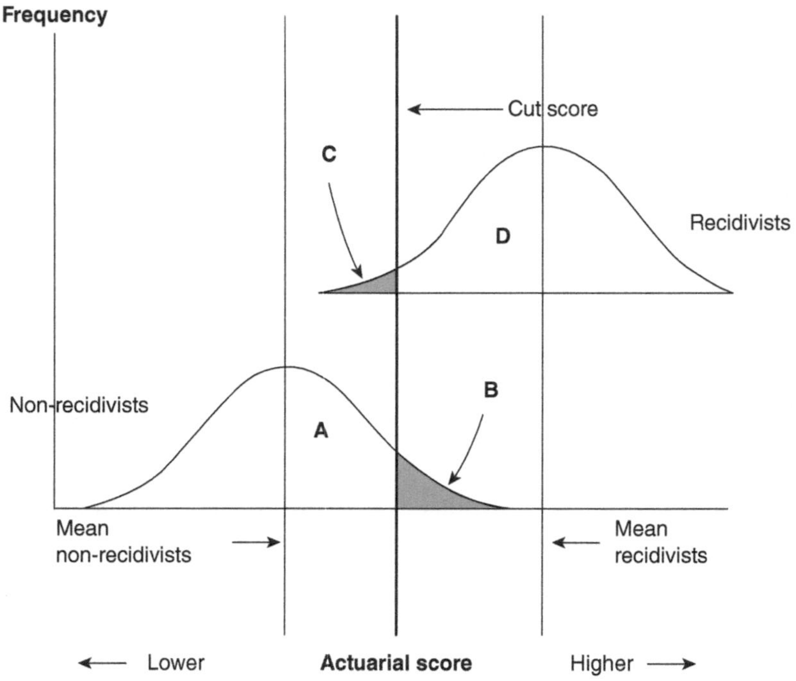

Figure 5.3 An idealized view of sub-optimal group discrimination in scores on a hypothetical actuarial instrument.

The cut score divides each sample (recidivists and non-recidivists) into two groups, one group that is predicted by the test to recidivate (scores above the cut score), and the other group that is predicted by the test to not recidivate (scores below the cut score). This produces a four-group division of the sample that is represented in the figure by the letters A, B, C, and D. This grouping of the whole sample of sex offenders is often represented in a 2 × 2 Classification Table, as in Table 5.1. On the vertical dimension, actual group membership is represented (recidivists, non-recidivists) and on the horizontal dimension the prediction made by the test (recidivist, non-recidivist) is represented. The same four groups are represented in the quadrants of the table, namely: Group A are non-recidivists who were predicted by the test to not recidivate; Group B are non-recidivists who were predicted by the test to recidivate; Group C are recidivists who were predicted by the test to not recidivate; and Group D are recidivists who were predicted by the test to recidivate.

A number of important statistics can be calculated from this table. These statistics tell us a great deal about the test's ability to predict

Table 5.1 Classification Table

	Group assignment by actuarial assessment		
	No recid	*Recid*	*Total*
Actual group membership			
Non-recidivists	A	B	A+B
Recidivists	C	D	C+D
Total	A+C	B+D	A+B+C+D
Specificity = A/(A+B)*100			
Sensitivity (TPR) = D/(C+D)*100			
FPR = B/(A+B)*100			

recidivism. The test's *sensitivity* is the percentage of recidivists who were predicted by the test to recidivate (D/ (C+D)*100). Some people refer to the test's sensitivity as the "true positive rate" or TPR. The test's *specificity* is the percentage of non-recidivists predicted by the test to not recidivate (A/ (A+B)*100). The quality of a test measurement used for prediction can be summarized by its sensitivity and specificity, and the higher each percentage is, the better.

A complementary term to specificity is the "false positive rate," or FPR, which is the percentage of non-recidivists predicted by the test to recidivate (B/ (A+B)*100). These terms are complementary because the specificity of a test plus its FPR should equal 100%. Again, the quality of a predictive test can be thought of in terms of its TPR and FPR; a high-quality test maximizes its true positive rate and minimizes its FPR.

Figure 5.4 presents frequency distributions for the BAS in our illustrative sample separately for the non-recidivists (upper panel) and recidivists (lower panel). As can be seen, the two distributions overlap considerably. However, the modal score among the recidivists (3) is higher than the bimodal scores for the non-recidivists (0 and 2). The mean BAS score for the recidivists is 2.52 and for the non-recidivists is 1.28, a difference that is statistically significant ($F_{(1, 239)} = 33.93$, $p<.001$). So the scale is promising, because the scores are significantly higher for the recidivists compared with the non-recidivists. Let's see how it does as a predictor of recidivism.

Let's imagine that a forensic researcher wanted to see how good this scale is as a predictor of sexual recidivism. She might choose a cut score of 0.5. By doing so, she is saying that she predicts that all offenders with scores of 0 will not recidivate, and offenders with scores above 0 will recidivate. Using data from our illustrative sample of sex offenders, Table 5.2 (upper panel) presents the resulting Classification Table. Calculating cell percentages across the rows, you will see that with the cut score of 0.5, the test's specificity is

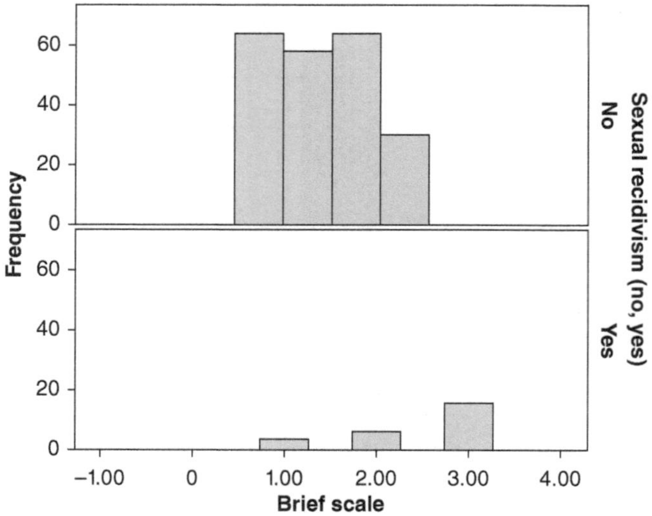

Figure 5.4 Frequency distributions for BAS scores for non-recidivists (top panel) and recidivists (bottom panel).

29.62%, its sensitivity (TPR) is 100%, and its FPR is 70.37%. Now let's imagine that she chose a cut score of 1.5. The resulting Classification Table is presented in the middle panel in Table 5.2. Here the test's specificity is 56.48%, its sensitivity (TPR) is 88%, and its FPR is 43.51%. Finally, let's imagine that she chose a cut score of 2.5. The resulting Classification Table is presented in the bottom panel in Table 5.2. Here the test's specificity is 86.11%, its sensitivity (TPR) is 64%, and its FPR is 13.89%.

A ROC curve is plotted in Figure 5.5. The figure is a two-dimensional space with the TPR as a proportion represented on the ordinate (vertical dimension) and the FPR as a proportion represented on the abscissa (horizontal dimension) and with the 0.00 for both scales anchored at the origin (lower left). Then, the TPRs and FPRs are calculated and plotted for every possible cut score. In our sample, the range of BAS scores ranged from 0 to 3. Since cut scores are designed to divide the sample into two groups cleanly, and since the scores are all integers, the three cut scores are .5, 1.5, and 2.5. Then, the paired proportions (TPR, FPR) are plotted in the two-dimensional space. Two additional points are plotted, for a cut score below the lowest score in the sample (–1.00) and a cut score above the highest score (4) in the sample. The TPR and FPR for the first of these will both be 1.00, because with a cut score below the lowest score, all individuals in the sample are predicted to be recidivists, and the TPR and FPR for the second of these will

Table 5.2 Classification Tables for the BAS with three cut scores

	Using BAS scores to predict cut score = 0.5		
Actual group membership	*No recid*	*Recid*	*Total*
Non-recidivists	64	152	216
	29.63%	70.37%	100%
	0	25	25
Recidivists	0.00%	100.00%	100%
	64	177	241
Total	26.56%	73.44%	100%

Specificity = 29.62%
Sensitivity = 100% (true positive rate)
False positive rate = 70.37%

	Using BAS scores to predict cut score = 1.5		
Actual group membership	*No recid*	*Recid*	*Total*
Non-recidivists	122	94	216
	56.48%	43.52%	100%
	3	22	25
Recidivists	12.00%	88.00%	100%
	125	116	241
Total	51.87%	48.13%	100%

Specificity = 56.48%
Sensitivity = 88% (true positive rate)
False positive rate = 43.51%

	Using BAS scores to predict cut score = 2.5		
Actual group membership	*No recid*	*Recid*	*Total*
Non-recidivists	186	30	216
	86.11%	13.89%	100%
	9	16	25
Recidivists	36.00%	64.00%	100%
	195	46	241
Total	80.91%	19.09%	100%

Specificity = 86.11%
Sensitivity = 64% (true positive rate)
False positive rate = 13.89%

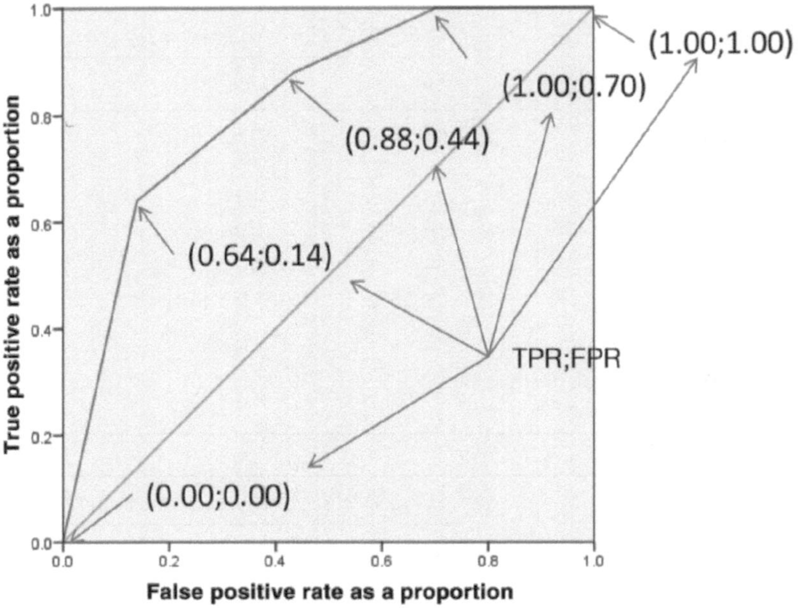

Figure 5.5 ROC curve for three-item actuarial scale with child molesters. TPR and FPR values are plotted as proportions.

both be 0.00, because with a cut score above the highest score, all individuals in the sample will be predicted to be non-recidivists.

Again, this curve plots the trade-off between true positives and false positives across a test's measurement range. An AUC value of .50 (represented by the diagonal line) indicates a "chance" relationship between predictor and outcome. An AUC value of 1.00 would indicate "perfect" prediction. Reasonably good AUC values lie between .70 and .80. The further the curve extends up into the upper-left corner, the higher the TPR and the lower the FPR, and the better the predictive relationship is found to be. One way to think about the AUC value is that it represents the probability that a recidivist selected randomly from the sample will have a higher score on the test than a randomly selected non-recidivist. In this particular case, predicting sexual recidivism in our sample using the BAS scores, the AUC is .82, $p<.001$.

To provide another example of a ROC curve for ARAIs, we will present the ROC curve for the Static-99R (the most popular and often used ARAI at present, to be described in more detail in this chapter), using the sample of child molesters we used for the development and evaluation of the BAS. The plot of the true positive and false positive rates calculated in this table is presented in Figure 5.6.

Table 5.3 Classification Table for the Static-99R

	Actual					
	Non-recidivists		*Recidivists*			
Predicted	*Non-recidivists*	*Recidivists*	*Non-recidivists*	*Recidivists*	*FPR*	*TPR*
Cut score						
–3.5					1.00	1.00
–2.5	2	203	0	24	0.99	1.00
–1.5	6	199	0	24	0.97	1.00
–0.5	29	176	0	24	0.86	1.00
0.5	57	148	0	24	0.72	1.00
1.5	94	111	1	23	0.54	0.96
2.5	120	85	5	19	0.41	0.79
3.5	147	58	7	17	0.28	0.71
4.5	173	32	15	9	0.16	0.38
5.5	189	16	17	7	0.08	0.29
6.5	199	6	19	5	0.03	0.21
7.5	201	4	21	3	0.02	0.13
8.5	205	0	21	3	0.00	0.13
9.5	205	0	23	1	0.00	0.04
10.5					0.00	0.00

Note
FPR and TPR values are entered as proportions.

Incremental Predictive Validity

An important concept inherent in the empirical development of an actuarial scale is incremental validity. It is defined as follows: A measure has incremental validity to the degree to which it increases the ability to predict an important phenomenon (Haynes & Lench, 2003, p. 457). These authors further define incremental predictive validity as the degree to which a measure can account for a higher proportion of variance in a variable measured later. The empirical development of risk prediction scales is a good example of incremental predictive validity.

To illustrate the concept of incremental predictive ability, we return to our BAS. Following the scoring instructions for the Static-99R, each of the items 8 and 10 are scored as a "0" or a "1," and as we indicated above, we recoded item #5 so that it is scored as a "0" or a "1." For illustrative purposes, using our child molester data set, we have calculated three two-item combinations or scales (items 8 and 10, 8 and recoded 5, and 10 and recoded 5), each with scale scores varying from 0 to 2. Finally, we

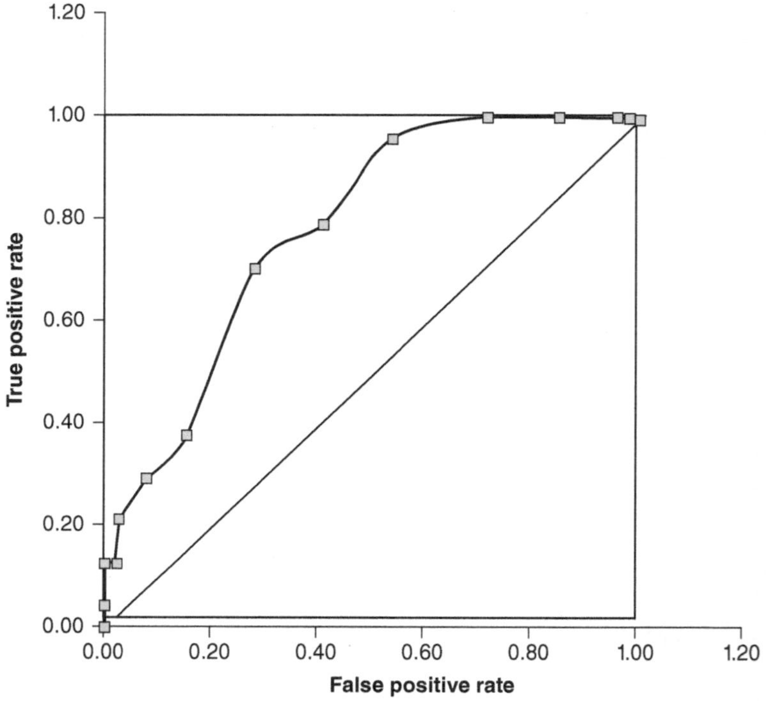

Figure 5.6 ROC curve plotted for the Static-99R used with a sample of child molesters (*n*=241; AUC=0.78).

calculated a three-item scale score (adding items 8, 10, and recoded 5). Examination of Table 5.4 reveals what we mean about incremental validity. Two of the three two-item combinations have AUCs in the mid-.60s, while their combination AUC is in the low .70s. Combining all three items yields a scale with an AUC in the low .80s. The AUC for the three-item scale is significantly higher than the AUCs for two of the three individual items, and significantly (p<.05) higher than the combination of the items 8 and 10 on its own.

Table 5.5 presents additional results of our analysis. All figures in the table in "bold" represent the percent recidivism found for different specific identifiable groups. In the first entry, we present the base rate of recidivism for this group of 245 child molesters (10.2%), over an average of approximately five years. If we know nothing at all about the individuals in this sample, our best guess concerning their likelihood of recidivism would be approximately one in 10.

Table 5.4 AUCs for one, two, and three-item actuarial scales

	Static-99 item#	*AUC*	*Standard error*	*Significance level*	*95%CI*	
					Lower	*Upper*
Single item predictors						
Any unrelated victim	8	0.66	0.05	0.013	0.56	0.75
Any male victim	10	0.67	0.06	0.006	0.56	0.79
Any previous conviction/ charge	recoded 5	0.79	0.04	0.000	0.71	0.87
Combining 2 items						
	8 + 10	0.73	0.05	0.000	0.64	0.83
	8 + recoded 5	0.80	0.04	0.000	0.72	0.88
	10 + recoded 5	0.81	0.04	0.000	0.73	0.89
Combining 3 items						
	8 + 10 + recoded 5	0.82	0.04	0.000	0.74	0.90

Immediately below, we present the subgroups of offenders formed by the application of the first actuarial item, "Any unrelated victim." For offenders with only related victims, the recidivism rate is 2.0%, while for offenders with any unrelated victim, the recidivism rate is 14.6%. Now, our ability to make predictive statements is improved. If we know that the offender has only offended against a member of his own family, his recidivism rate will be expected to be extremely low (about 1 in 50). However, in comparison, if we know that the offender has offended against a child outside his own family, his recidivism risk increases to about 1 in 7. Adding information about offenders that has predictive validity increases our ability to estimate the likelihood of recidivism.

The more information we add, the better we are able to estimate that likelihood. For the two-item scale that includes information concerning the gender of the victim, our estimates of recidivism vary from 1 in 70, to 1 in 12, to 1 in 4.5. Finally, our ability to discriminate between subgroups of offenders with considerably different recidivism rates increases again with the addition of information concerning their previous sex offense history. For the subgroup of offenders with unrelated victims, male victims, and a previous history of sexual offenses, our estimate of the likelihood of recidivism goes up to approximately 1 in 3.

Table 5.5 Recidivism rates for score value groups on a three-item actuarial scale

	Score = 0		*Score = 1*		*Score = 2*		*Score = 3*	
	N	%	N	%	N	%	N	%
Base rate	25	**10.2**						
	N = 245							
Add relationship to victim	2	**2.3**	23	**14.6**				
	N = 87		158					
Add gender of victim	1	**1.4**	8	**8.1**	16	**22.2**		
	N = 71		99		72			
Add previous convictions/charges	0	0	3	**4.9**	6	**8.6**	16	**34.8**
	N = 64		61		70		46	

Empirical Development of ARAIs for Sex Offenders

There have been two major research groups who have been working steadfastly and diligently on the programmatic development of sex offender ARAIs over the past 20 to 25 years: (1) the Research Department at the Mental Health Centre Penetanguishene (now Waypoint Centre for Mental Health Care), and (2) the Static-99 research group headquartered at Public Safety Canada (formerly the Department of the Solicitor General for Canada).

The Research Department at Penetanguishene was established in 1975 by Vern Quinsey. Marnie Rice and Grant Harris followed in the role of Director of the Research Department. Between 1975 and 1990, Vern and his colleagues published numerous studies of recidivism by patients released from the maximum-security facility at Penetanguishene. The first recidivism studies specifically focusing on sex offenders appeared in the early 1990s (Rice, Harris, & Quinsey, 1990; Rice, Quinsey, & Harris, 1991), and the first publication describing the Violence Risk Appraisal Guide (VRAG) was published in 1993 (Harris, Rice, & Quinsey, 1993). This group has been actively conducting and publishing research on the recidivism of sex offenders ever since. The most comprehensive account of their critically important work is described in their book on the appraisal of violence risk published by the American Psychological Association (Quinsey, Harris, Rice, & Cormier, 1998, 2006), and the third edition of this book is currently in production. This group has been responsible for the development of the VRAG and the companion Sex Offender Risk Appraisal Guide (SORAG), and they have recently developed an improved revised actuarial scale for sex offenders, the VRAG-R.

The Static-99 group has been led by Karl Hanson and includes his colleagues David Thornton, Leslie Helmus, and Andrew Harris, among others. Karl began this work with the development of the Rapid Risk Assessment of Sex Offender Recidivism (RRASOR), the four-item actuarial instrument previously mentioned. David Thornton joined Karl in the development of the Static-99, which involved the combination of the four items from the RRASOR with items contained in an instrument (Structured Anchored Clinical Judgment) that Thornton had been using in the UK (Hanson & Thornton, 2000). This group has gathered together very large data sets from around the world from investigators who have conducted independent cross-validations of the Static-99. The group has worked conscientiously to provide detailed scoring instructions and standardized life tables for the Static-99 in a comprehensive scoring manual that has evolved over the years. This group has also been diligent about providing advice and assistance to users of the Static-99. The development of the Static-99 has been supported by a number of very influential meta-analyses of the sex offender recidivism literature (Hanson & Bussiere, 1998; Hanson & Morton-Bourgon, 2004, 2005, 2009). The Static-99 was revised in 2011 (Static-99R; Helmus, Thornton, Hanson, & Babchishin, 2012) to account for the influence of aging on recidivism risk, and this group has also developed a second-generation instrument, the Static-2002 and Static-2002R.

We all owe a debt of gratitude to these two research groups for infusing risk assessment with empiricism and in so doing moving the field a quantum step past the days of pure clinical judgment. Sex offender risk assessment today is, in varying degrees, a mechanically assisted task, attributable in large measure to the contributions of Quinsey, Hanson, and their respective colleagues.

Actuarial Scales Circa 2010

In a meta-analysis of sex offender recidivism studies, Hanson and Morton-Bourgon (2004) identified the five most commonly used actuarial instruments as the VRAG, the SORAG (Quinsey et al., 1998), the RRASOR (Hanson, 1997), the Static-99 (Hanson & Thornton, 1999), and the Minnesota Sex Offender Screening Tool-Revised (MnSOST-R: Epperson, Kaul, Huot, Hesselton, Alexander, & Goldman, 1998).

The VRAG and SORAG were the first of these to be developed. The VRAG (Harris, Rice, & Quinsey, 1993) was developed to assess risk for violent recidivism (including sexual offenses involving physical contact with the victim) among mentally disordered offenders. The SORAG (Quinsey et al., 1998) is a modification of the VRAG and was developed using a similar method to assess risk for violent recidivism among adult sexual offenders. On the basis of the VRAG and SORAG total scores, individual offenders are assigned to one of nine ascending risk categories (bins) ranging from 1 (lowest risk) to 9 (highest risk). The actuarial development of the VRAG and SORAG has been described in detail in Quinsey et al. (1998).

The SORAG is a modification of the VRAG, with 10 common items, and was developed using a similar method. The SORAG has 14 items: living with both biological parents until age 16, elementary school maladjustment, history of alcohol problems, marital status, nonviolent offense history, violent offense history, sexual offense history, sex and age of index victim, failure on prior conditional release, age at index offense, meeting DSM-III criteria for any personality disorder, meeting DSM-III criteria for schizophrenia, phallometrically measured deviant sexual interests, and PCL-R score (Quinsey et al., 1998). Total SORAG scores can range from –27 to +51. Individuals are assigned to one of nine risk categories based on their scores; ranging from 1 (lowest) to 9 (highest).

The RRASOR has four items: number of prior charges or convictions for sexual offenses; age upon release from prison or anticipated opportunity to re-offend in the community; any male victims, coded as yes or no; and any unrelated victims, coded as yes or no (Hanson, 1997). Total scores can range from 0 to 6; the item weights reflect the magnitude of the item's independent relationship with sexual recidivism. The instrument was developed using samples of adult males who had been convicted of at least one sexual offense.

The Static-99 has 10 items, including the four RRASOR items (Hanson & Thornton, 1999). The additional items are prior sentencing dates, any convictions for non-contact sexual offenses, index offense of non-sexually violent nature, prior non-sexually violent offense, any stranger victims, and cohabitation status. The Static-99 was developed for adult males who were known to have committed at least one sexual offense. Total scores can range from 0 to 12; individuals are assigned to one of seven risk categories based on their score (individuals with scores of 6 or more are combined). Ordinal position among these risk categories ranging from 0 (lowest) to 6+ (highest) was submitted to the ROC analyses. (The Static-99 has recently been revised to accommodate new empirical evidence regarding the effects of aging on sex offender recidivism risk. We will discuss the Static-99R after our review of the effects of aging.)

The MnSOST-R has 16 items, 12 scored from historical information and four scored from institutional information (Epperson et al., 1998). Unlike the other instruments described here, the MnSOST-R is not scored for offenders with only related victims (i.e., incest offenders). The historical items are number of sex/sex-related convictions, length of sexual offending history, offender under supervision at time of any sexual offense, any sexual offense committed in a public place, force or threat of force used in any sexual offense, any sexual offense within a single incident that involved multiple acts perpetrated on a single victim, number of different age groups victimized across all sexual offenses, victim aged 13 to 15 years and offender five or more years older, victim was a stranger in any sexual offense, adolescent antisocial behavior, substantial drug or alcohol abuse in year prior to arrest, and employment history. The institutional items are discipline history while incarcerated, involvement in substance use treatment, involvement in sex offender treatment, and age at time of release. Like the VRAG and SORAG, item weights for the MnSOST-R are based on the empirical relationship between each item and the outcome of sexual re-offense in the development sample, using a method adapted from Nuffield (1982). Each point represents an increment or decrement of 5% from the base rate of sexual recidivism in that sample (artificially set at 35%, after a minimum follow-up time of six years, by oversampling recidivists). The selection of the items and derivation of their weights is described in detail by Epperson et al. (1998). Total MnSOST-R scores can range from –14 to +30. In the latest update of this instrument, individuals can be assigned to one of six risk categories based on their total score; the ordinal position among these risk categories, ranging from 1 (lowest) to 6 (highest), was submitted to ROC analyses.

The Static-2002 (Hanson & Thornton, 2003) was conceived as an improvement to the Static-99 (Hanson & Thornton, 2000), an ARAI that is used across jurisdictions and research contexts in North America as well as Europe and Asia (R. K. Hanson, personal communication, June 11, 2003). Hanson and Thornton (2003) identified four reasons for the revision. First, they wanted to increase the coherence and introduce conceptual clarity to the measure. This should, in part, assist evaluators in determining whether variables external to the measure but present as features in a given case require consideration in a comprehensive risk assessment. The second reason was to improve the consistency of the scoring criteria. As Hanson and Thornton (2003) noted, the Static-99 was the product of combining two earlier risk assessment scales, each with its own scoring rules, complicating training and potentially affecting rater reliability in applied contexts. A third reason for a revision was the possibility of rare cases that had to be scored counter-intuitively; Hanson and Thornton (2003) provided the example of an offender whose score must be lowered when he commits a new sexual offense following an index offense involving nonsexual violence. The fourth reason given for undertaking a revision was an interest in improving upon the predictive accuracy of the Static-99. Development of the Static-2002 followed a similar procedure to that used in the development and validation of the RRASOR (Hanson, 1997) and the Static-99. Multiple data sets were used (10 with a total size of 4,596) in the scale construction. With the emphasis on ease of data collection and the simplest empirically based coding methods, Hanson and Thornton (2003) again identified variables from meta-analytic work as well as other ARAIs according to their univariate relation with recidivism, which were then combined into content area subscales. Among these, the subscales shown using multivariate analyses to add incrementally to the others were then weighted equally. The resulting scale consisted of 13 items across five content areas. (The Static-2002 has recently been revised to accommodate new empirical evidence regarding the effects of aging on sex offender recidivism risk. We will discuss the Static-2002R after our review of the effects of aging.)

Independent Cross-Validation of Sex Offender ARAIs

Tables 5.6 and 5.7 present AUCs reported for the six sex offender ARAIs by cross-validation studies published in the peer-reviewed literature. Cross-validation studies use samples of sex offenders that were not involved in the development of the instrument in question. Table 5.6 presents AUCs for predictions of sexual recidivism. Table 5.7 presents AUCs for predictions of violent recidivism. As can be seen from these tables, most AUCs indicate moderate but statistically significant prediction with significant AUCs ranging from the mid-.60s to the mid-.70s. Very few studies reported non-significant AUCs. The Static-99 has received the most attention but the instruments receiving the least attention (Static-2002 and MnSOST-R) have at least four studies published evaluating their predictive ability.

Hanson and Morton-Bourgon (2009) conducted a meta-analysis of the sex offender recidivism literature, examining the accuracy of sex offender risk assessment. This review compared the accuracy of various approaches with the prediction of recidivism among sexual offenders. On the basis of a meta-analysis of 536 findings drawn from 118 distinct samples (45,398 sexual offenders, 16 countries), empirically derived actuarial measures were more accurate than unstructured professional judgment for all outcomes (sexual, violent, or any recidivism). The accuracy of structured professional judgment was intermediate between the accuracy found for the actuarial measures and for unstructured professional judgment. The effect sizes for the actuarial measures were moderate to large by conventional standards (average *d* values of 0.67–0.97).

The Effects of Aging on Sex Offender Recidivism Risk

Very recently, interest has been focused on the age of offenders at the time of their release from custody. Hanson (2002) has examined the effects of age at release on rates of sexual recidivism in a large sample of sex offenders. Dividing his sample into nine age cohorts (18–24, 25–29, 30–34, 35–39, 40–44, 45–49, 50–59, 60–69, and 70+), Hanson plotted the rate of recidivism over age cohorts. The results indicated that sex offenders'

Table 5.6 AUCs reported in cross-validation studies published in the peer-reviewed literature for six risk assessment instruments predicting sexual recidivism

Actuarial risk assessment instrument			*VRAG*	*SORAG*	*RRASOR*	*STATIC-99*	*MnSOST-R*	*STATIC-2002*
Published article	N	*Country*						
Allan et al. (2006)	538	Australia			.71*	.78*		
Allan et al. (2007)	495	New Zealand				.72*		
Barbaree et al. (2001)	215	Canada	.61*	.70*	.77*	.70*	.65	
Bartosh et al. (2003)	186	US		.58	.63*	.64*	.59	
Beech et al. (2002)	140	UK				.77*		
Bengtson & Långstöm	121	Denmark				.62*		.67*
Craig et al. (2006)	85	UK			.50	.59		
De Vogel et al. (2004)	122	Netherlands				.71*		
Ducro & Pham (2006)	147	Belgium		.64*		.66*		
Eher et al. (2011)	263	Austria		.72*		.75*		
Endrass et al. (2009)	89	Switzerland				.76*		
Friendship et al. (2003)	2557	UK				.70*		
Hanson et al. (2014)	475	US				.82*		
Harris et al. (2003)	289	Canada	.65*	.66*	.59*	.62*		
Helmus & Hanson (2007)	706	Canada				.76*		.76*
Långström (2004)	1303	Sweden			.73*	.72*		
Langton et al. (2007)	468	Canada	.61*	.66*	.68*	.64*	.70*	.71*
Looman (2006)	258	Canada		.69		.63		

(continued)

Table 5.6 (continued)

Actuarial risk assessment instrument			*VRAG*	*SORAG*	*RRASOR*	*STATIC-99*	*MnSOST-R*	*STATIC-7007*
Published article	N	*Country*						
Nunes et al. (2002)	258	Canada		.70*		.65*		
Parent et al. (2011)	590	US	.66*	.69*	.70*	.71*	.68*	.69*
Rettenberger & Eher (2006)	202	Austria			.68*	.74*		
Rettenberger & Eher (2007)	254	Austria		.73*				
Rettenberger & Eher (2010)	394	Austria		.69*	.74*	.74*		
Rice & Harris (1997)	159	Canada	.62*					
Sjostedt & Langstrom	1400	Sweden				.76*		
Sjostedt & Langstrom (2002; only rapists)	51	Sweden	.58		.73*			
Skelton et al. (2006; Static- 99 Lite)	1133	New Zealand				.78*		
Stadtland et al. (2005)	134	Germany				.66*		

Note
*indicates a statistically significant AUC

Table 5.7 AUCs reported in cross-validation studies published in the peer-reviewed literature for six risk assessment instruments predicting violent recidivism

Actuarial risk assessment instrument			*VRAG*	*SORAG*	*RRASOR*	*STATIC-99*	*MnSOST-R*	*STATIC-2002*
Published article	N	*Country*						
Allan et al.	495	New Zealand				.62*		
Barbaree et al. (2001)	215	Canada	.65*	.73*	.65*	.70*	.58	
Bartosh et al.(2003)	186	US		.64*	.74*	.73*	.54	
Bengtson & Långström (2007)	121	Denmark				.71*		.70*
Craig et al. (2006)	85	UK			.58	.62		
De Vogel et al. (2004)	122	Netherlands				.54		
Ducro & Pham (2006)	147	Belgium		.72*		.68*		
Eher et al. (2011)	263	Austria		.75*		.73*		
Friendship et al. (2003)	2557	UK				.70*		
Harris et al. (2003)	289	Canada	.73*	.73*	.56*	.63*		
Helmus & Hanson (2007)	706	Canada				.73*		.76*
Langton et al. (2007)	468	Canada	.70*	.71*	.59*	.64*	.64*	.70*
Looman (2006)	258	Canada		.69*		.56		
Nunes et al. (2002)	258	Canada		.69*		.69*		
Parent et al. (2011)	590	US	.70*	.68*	.50	.61*	.68*	.59*
Rettenberger & Eher (2006)	202	Austria			.67*	.76*		

(continued)

Table 5.7 (continued)

Actuarial risk assessment instrument			*VRAG*	*SORAG*	*RRASOR*	*STATIC-99*	*MnSOST-R*	*STATIC-2002*
Published article	N	*Country*						
Rettenberger & Eher(2007)	254	Austria		.76				
Rettenberger & Eher (2010)	394	Austria		.72*	.66*	.71*		
Rice & Harris (1997)	159	Canada	.77*					
Rossegger et al. (2013)	137	Switzerland		.69*				
Sjostedt & Langstrom (2001)	1400	Sweden			.63*	.74*		
Sjostedt & Langstrom (2002; only rapists)	51	Sweden	.69*		.62			
Smid et al. (2014)	397	Netherlands		.63*	.68*	.72*		.76*
Stadtland et al. (2005)	134	Germany				.71*		
Urbaniok et al. (2006)	79	Switzerland	.73*					

Note
*indicates a statistically significant AUC

risk for recidivism decreases with age at release. Barbaree, Blanchard, and Langton (2003) examined sexual recidivism in a sample of sex offenders (*n* = 477) released from a Canadian federal penitentiary and followed for an average of almost five years. They divided their sample into age cohorts (21–30, 31–40, 41–50, and 51+) and found that recidivism decreased as a linear function of age at release.

Fazel, Sjöstedt, Långström, and Grann (2006) followed all adult male sex offenders released from prison in Sweden from 1993 to 1997 (*n* = 1,303) and recorded criminal convictions for an average of 8.9 years. They divided their sample into age cohorts (<25, 25–39, 40–54, 55+). The rates of violent recidivism decreased significantly in older-aged cohorts. Thornton (2006) followed a large nationally representative sample (*n* = 752) of sex offenders for a period of 10 years after their release from prison in the UK. Dividing his sample by age cohort (<18, 18–24, 25–39, 40–59, 60+), he found that the rate of sexual recidivism declined with age.

Hanson (2006) followed a very large sample (*n* = 3,425, compiled over eight separate samples) of sex offenders released from prison in North America and the UK. Hanson calculated five-year recidivism rates for different age cohorts (18–24, 25–39, 40–49, 50–59, 60+) and found significant reductions in recidivism with age.

Prentky and Lee (2007) followed a group of rapists and child molesters who had been civilly committed in a specialized treatment facility in Massachusetts, dividing their sample into five age cohorts (18–30, 30–40, 40–50, 50–60, and 60+). Both groups showed significant decreases in recidivism rates with age. Rapists showed reductions in rates of recidivism throughout the span of ages from the 20s to 60+, whereas child molesters showed an increase is recidivism rates from the 20s to the 40s, followed by a decrease from the 40s to 60+. Based on these studies, it would be reasonable to conclude that when sex offenders are released from custody at different ages, they show age-related decreases in recidivism.

Skelton and Vess (2008) followed all sexual offenders (*n* = 5,880) released from New Zealand prisons between January 1, 1990 and December 31, 2004. The average length of time these offenders were followed was 10.4 years. These authors divided their sample into six age bands, under 20, 20–30, 31–40, 41–50, 51–60, and 60 and older. Sexual recidivism rates decreased over age.

Lussier and Healey (2009) followed 553 adult males convicted of a sexual offense released from custody at the Regional Reception Centre in the Province of Quebec, a maximum-security federal Canadian institution. These authors divided their sample into five age cohorts, 20–29, 30–39, 40–49, 50–59, and 60 and older, according to their age at release. After following this sample from their release into the community for an average of 55 months, sexual recidivism was found to decrease over age.

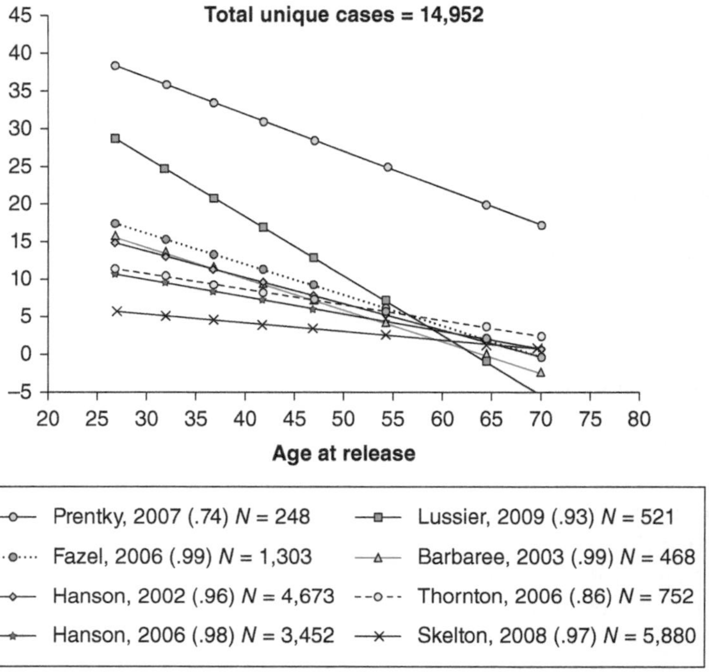

Figure 5.7 Eight studies on age and recidivism.

Comparing the results of these studies is difficult because each used a different set of age class intervals, and a different follow-up period. We conducted the following set of calculations to present these findings in a common format. Figure 5.7 presents the results of these eight studies. We used data from each published article to calculate a regression equation for each set of data. Using the regression coefficients for each study, we calculated eight regression lines using the age class intervals used by Hanson (2002), the first of these studies. Most of these studies had follow-up periods approximating five years, and for those with longer follow-up periods, we adjusted the recidivism rates proportionally.

These reductions in recidivism among sex offenders are consistent across studies (Barbaree & Blanchard, 2008) and are very similar to reductions in recidivism (both violent and nonviolent) in the aging non-sexual criminal population (Hirschi & Gottfredson, 1983; Moffitt, 1993; Sampson & Laub, 2003). According to Wollert (2006), the aging effect has been recognized as one of the most robust findings in the field of criminology. In a seminal and influential article, Hirschi and Gottfredson (1983) pointed to the "invariance" of this relationship in that crime rates decreased with age for offender groups who (a) lived in different centuries, (b) came from different countries, (c) differed with respect to age and gender, (d) were at large in the community or incarcerated, and (e) committed different types of crimes (Wollert, 2006). Age-related reductions in the rate of recidivism in sex offenders are also consistent with a large body of literature examining human sexuality, indicating that sexual behavior decreases in the aging male (e.g., Rowland, Greenleaf, Dorfman, & Davidson, 1993). Barbaree and Blanchard (2008) linked age-related reductions in blood levels of bio-available testosterone to decreases in sexual behaviors as a possible explanation for the effects of aging on sex offender recidivism and proposed the addition of "maturation" as a risk factor distinct from previously specified static and dynamic risk factors (Hanson, Morton, & Harris, 2003).

The Development of the Static-99R and Static-2002R

By 2010, the then current ARAIs treated the age of the offender in different ways. The VRAG/SORAG coded age at index offense. The MnSOST-R coded age as being a dichotomous variable, under or over 30 years of age-at-release. The RRASOR and the Static-99 coded age as being a dichotomous variable, under or over 25 years of age. Therefore, if the ARAIs considered aging as a risk factor, they did not include any information concerning any changes in recidivism risk beyond the age of 25–30.

In response to the growing evidence for the effects of aging on sex offender recidivism risk, Helmus, Thornton, Hanson, and Babchishin (2012) sought to develop a revised scoring system for two risk assessment tools (Static-99 and Static-2001) that would more accurately describe older offenders' risk of recidivism. Using data from 8,390 sex offenders derived from 24 separate samples, age was found to add incremental predictive validity to both Static-99 and Static-2002. After creating new age weights, the resulting instruments (Static-99R and Static-2001R) had only slightly higher relative predictive accuracy. The absolute recidivism estimates, however, provided a substantially better fit for older offenders than the recidivism estimates from the original scales.

Some authorities (Doren, 2002; Harris & Rice, 2007a) have argued strongly against considering aging as a mitigating factor in forensic risk assessment. Analyzing data from their samples of violent offenders used in the development of the VRAG (Quinsey, Harris, Rice, & Cormier, 1998), Harris and Rice (2007a) reported that age at release did not add to the predictive equation after actuarial scores and age at first offense were entered into the equation. Accordingly, these authors concluded that (a) there is no meaningful effect of aging on recidivism in sex offenders, (b) age at release provides no useful additional information concerning recidivism risk, and (c) evaluators using actuarial assessment in the conduct of their forensic evaluations should not make adjustments in their estimates of risk for the older offender. Instead, Harris and Rice (2007a) attribute recidivism risk entirely to stable enduring traits, consistent with their earlier statement that

> the preponderance of scientific evidence supports the idea that the majority of variance in violent criminal conduct (including sexual aggression) can be attributed to genetically and physiologically based enduring traits that, once initiated, exhibit life-long persistence under conditions so far observed.
>
> (Harris & Rice, 2003, p. 208)

Nevertheless, the general acceptance of the Static-99R and Static-2002R in practice in the sexually violent predator courtroom indicates that the field as a whole has accepted that aging has a mitigating effect on recidivism risk in sex offenders.

Summary and Conclusions

Earlier, in Chapter 4, we described Meehl's (1954) seminal work distinguishing between clinical and actuarial prediction and his description of actuarial assessment. In the quote that we referred to, Meehl suggested that actuarial assessment consists of two stages. In the first stage, a stage he referred to as "classification," an individual is scored using some actuarial instrument, and classified according to their score on the instrument. Most of our discussion to this point in our chapter pertains to Meehl's first stage of actuarial assessment. So far, we have focused on the development of the actuarial items, the scoring of the instrument, and the resulting accuracy of these instruments in identifying eventual recidivists. This stage allows evaluators to classify offenders and to make distinctions between and among offenders in terms of their level of "relative" risk.

Two ways of quantifying relative risk have been proposed. Hanson, Lloyd, Helmus, and Thornton (2012) proposed percentile ranks as a non-arbitrary metric for quantifying risk. These authors computed percentile ranks for Canadian sexual offenders based on their scores on the most popular sexual offender risk assessment tools (Static-99, Static-99R, Static-2002 and Static-2002R). They found that the distribution of Static-99 scores was highly stable in international comparisons of sexual offenders from Canada (1990 to 2005; $n = 2{,}011$), Sweden (1993 to 1997; $n = 1{,}278$), and California (2008 to 2010; $n = 37{,}600$). These authors recommended that evaluators presenting percentile ranks should consistently provide recidivism base rate information so that decision-makers do not confuse the rarity of a score with estimates of absolute recidivism risk.

Second, Hanson, Babchishin, Helmus, and Thornton (2012) found strong evidence for a relative risk interpretation of Static-99R scores using eight samples from Canada, the UK, and Western Europe (n = 4,037 sex offenders). Each increase in Static-99R score was associated with a stable and consistent increase in relative risk (as measured by an odds ratio or hazard ratio of approximately 1.4). Hazard ratios from Cox regression were used to calculate risk ratios that can be reported for the Static-99R. Hanson et al. (2012) recommended that evaluators consider risk ratios as a useful, non-arbitrary metric for quantifying and communicating risk information. As with percentile ranks, to avoid misinterpretation they recommended that risk ratios be presented with recidivism base rates.

Once we have assigned the offender to a level of relative risk (Joe is higher risk than Sam but lower risk than Peter), we turn our attention to Meehl's second stage of actuarial assessment, a stage he alluded to but did not describe in detail. He referred to looking up the absolute level of risk (a numerical probability of recidivism, sometimes expressed as a percentage) in a life table, the equivalent of mortality tables as used by insurance companies. Meehl gave short shrift to Stage 2 of the actuarial assessment, we presume because he assumed the construction of the life tables would simply be a matter of empirical determination. Find a large sample of offenders with the characteristics of the classification in question and follow them in the community over a period of time and calculate their recidivism rate. Do that for each classification category, and the result is a life table. Likewise, Monahan and Steadman (1996), in their landmark paper, refer to "risk level" as being the desired outcome of the statistical prediction equation and their discussion implies a straightforward calculation of absolute risk.

In Chapter 6, we address the issues involved in establishing the level of "absolute risk" (probability of percentage recidivism) for each actuarial score value. As we will show, the determination of absolute risk is not straightforward and remains a question to this day.

6

USING ACTUARIAL RISK ASSESSMENT INSTRUMENTS TO ESTIMATE ABSOLUTE RISK

Introduction

Earlier, in Chapter 4, we described Meehl's (1954) seminal work distinguishing between clinical and actuarial prediction and his description of actuarial assessment. As we indicated at the end of Chapter 5, Meehl conceived of actuarial assessment as consisting of two stages. In the first stage, which he referred to as classification, individuals are scored using some actuarial instrument, and classified according to their score on the instrument. Virtually all of our discussion in Chapters 4 and 5 pertained to Meehl's first stage of actuarial assessment. The only allusion we made to Meehl's Stage 2 was in our Figure 5.1 wherein we plotted absolute recidivism rates for each score value group resulting from our brief actuarial scale (BAS). In discussing Meehl's Stage 1, we have focused on the development of the actuarial items, the scoring of the instruments, and the resulting accuracy of the actuarial risk assessment instruments (ARAIs) in identifying eventual recidivists. This stage allows evaluators to classify offenders as to their level of relative risk. Now that we have assigned the offender to a level of relative risk (Joe is higher risk than Sam but lower risk than Peter), we turn our attention to establishing the absolute level of risk by determining a numerical probability of recidivism, often expressed as a percentage. In other words, if we release 100 sex offenders into the community for a period of five years, how many will be charged or convicted of a sexual re-offense? The reader will remember that this last step in actuarial prediction was called for in Monahan and Steadman's (1994a) model of statistical prediction.

Recently, Karl Hanson and his colleagues (e.g., Hanson, Babchishin, Helmus, & Thornton, 2012; Helmus, Hanson, Thornton, Babchishin, & Harris, 2012) have distinguished between the two stages of actuarial assessment in some detail, in terms of the information that each stage provides, the scales of measures obtained from each, the statistical analyses used to evaluate each, and the implications of the distinction on reporting outcomes. Borrowing from terms coined in actuarial biomedical research (Gail & Pfeiffer, 2005), Helmus et al. have referred to Stage 1 of actuarial assessment as "discrimination" (Meehl's "classification") and to Stage 2 of as "calibration." As Helmus et al. (2012, p. 1149) state, virtually all (actuarial assessment of sex offender risk) research to date has focused on discrimination, which considers the extent to which recidivists can be differentiated from non-recidivists and the extent to which offenders can be categorized into subgroups ranked according to relative risk. They go on to say,

> There is surprisingly little research examining calibration, which is the ability of risk scales to estimate absolute recidivism rates associated with the Stage 1 categories (i.e., What is the likelihood of recidivism associated with each risk score?) This is concerning given the importance of absolute recidivism estimates for certain contexts, such as civil commitment in the United States.

Following Hanson and Helmus et al.'s direction, we will refer hereafter to this second stage as "calibration."

This chapter is highly statistical in nature and may not be for every reader of this book. For some readers who are very familiar with the ARAIs and their use in the sexually violent predator (SVP) courtroom, this chapter may not present anything they did not already know. For some readers, those of you with less interest in numbers, statistics, or mathematics, this chapter may be a hard slog. We recognize that some of you will not take the time to digest the material herein. If you want a summary of the point we are trying to make here, it is this: Estimating absolute recidivism rates for groups of offenders with different scores on ARAIs is an activity fraught with complex difficulties, and in the end, our estimates have a degree of error associated that some will say is unacceptably high. Some approaches to calibration are better than others and our knowledge continues to develop. This chapter attempts to present these complex difficulties in a user-friendly fashion, so that a motivated reader with a modicum of mathematical or statistical reasoning ability will come away with a good appreciation of the difficulties scientists have had in making these critically important estimates.

The Frequentist Position

Meehl (1954), initially, and Monahan and Steadman (1994a) 40 years later, described a model of actuarial assessment in which the actuarial score values obtained in Stage 1 led, through the collection of data, to an empirically derived probability of recidivism. These probabilities were based on recidivism outcomes observed by the instrument developers in their developmental samples. Specifically, instrument developers would follow their sample of offenders in the community over various periods of time (5, 7, 10, 15 years) and record the percentage of each type of recidivism. For users of the actuarial instruments, these probability (or percentage) figures were presented as entries in the actuarial or life tables for each actuarial score value group and for the various follow-up periods. These life tables were typically provided in the ARAI's manual containing instructions for scoring and assigning probabilities of recidivism.

Recognizing that the probabilities derived from the instrument development work required independent replication, Dennis Doren (2004a) investigated the degree to which the risk percentages for each instrument score replicated across different samples and different underlying sexual recidivism base rates. Doren sought data from numerous investigators who had conducted independent cross-validation studies of the Rapid Risk Assessment of Sex Offender Recidivism (RRASOR) and the Static-99 and who had followed offenders post release and recorded sexual recidivism. Independent cross-validations are studies designed to evaluate the actuarial instrument in question (1) conducted by investigators who are independent of the instrument developer(s), and (2) which involved samples of offenders that were not used in the development of the instrument. Doren calculated recidivism rates for each score value for each sample and noted the base rates for each sample. His findings indicated that the recidivism rates associated with actuarial scores from the independent samples yielded percentage recidivism rates similar to the entries in the available life tables. Moreover, the score-wise recidivism rates (rates of recidivism recorded for each actuarial score value) seemed to be stable across varying base rates. On this basis, Doren's conclusions were consistent with the assumptions made by Meehl, Monahan, and Steadman and others. The assumption that recidivism rates associated with actuarial score values are more or less consistent and can be estimated by repeated sampling of the population of interest is referred to here as the "frequentist" position (Harris & Rice, 2013), a position that is often contrasted to the Bayesian Position (Held & Bové, 2014, p. 51).

Bayesian Inference and Bayes' Theorem

Thomas Bayes' *An Essay Toward Solving a Problem in the Doctrine of Chances* was published posthumously by the Royal Society in 1763. As a minister, Bayes did not believe that the world was inherently uncertain. Bayes believed firmly in a rational world, and that the more information (data) we acquired, the closer we could come to understanding the world. In essence, he believed, our degree of understanding "the truth" was probabilistic, the divinity of nature was rational, and our comprehension was imperfect. The degree to which we could predict accurately that the sun would rise the next morning was a function of the data that we had. The more and the better the data, the greater the probability that our prediction would be accurate.

Bayes revised classic probability theory to include *prior* information along with present sample (or case) information to improve probabilistic estimates. We present Bayes' Theorem here couched in terms that would apply to sex offender risk assessment so that its relevance can be immediately apprehended. The Theorem states that the probability of a specified condition (e.g., high risk) given the presence or absence of certain signs (e.g., risk factors) can be determined as:

$$P(C|S) = \frac{P(S|C) \times P(C)}{P(S|C) \times P(C) + P(S|noC) \times P(noC)}$$

where:

$P(C|S)$ = probability that O has condition C (high risk), given that O has S (the risk factors)

$P(S|C)$ = probability that S (risk factors) is present when the condition C (high risk) is present

$P(C)$ = *prior* probability of having C (high risk)

$P(S|noC)$ = probability that S (risk factors) is present without condition C (high risk) being present

$P(noC)$ = *prior* probability of not having condition C (high risk)

This remarkably simple algebraic formula, composed of only three known variables and one unknown, is a means of calculating conditional probabilities. Given the simplicity of this theorem, it is remarkable how much impact Bayes' Theorem has had, forming the basis of an influential epistemology with a sizable following that has come to be known as "Bayesian inference." A recent feature article on the front page of the *New York Times* (The Odds, Continually Updated, September 29, 2014) described the vast array of problems to which Bayesian inference has been applied. The simple logic underlying Bayesian inference is that the likelihood of an event is a function of (a) the likelihood of the occurrence and nonoccurrence of certain conditional events (risk factors), and (b) the likelihood of occurrence and nonoccurrence of the event itself (i.e., a re-offense).

The Bayesian approach to a problem starts with the formulation of a statistical model that is proposed as the best description of the natural phenomenon of interest. Bayesian inference is an approach to statistics in which all forms of uncertainty are expressed in terms of probability. The proposed model may depend heavily on prior determined empirical "facts" expressed as probabilities, it may depend entirely on the Bayesian's subjective beliefs concerning the likely probability, or the model may be made up of some combination of facts and beliefs. The model at this stage is described as based on "priors," or knowledge that is available prior to the collection or examination of the data. Bayesian reasoning can be contrasted with frequentist reasoning which relies solely on the evidence as it is collected with no reference to prior facts or beliefs. Bayesian reasoning continues by examining the data observed relating to the probabilities of interest. Application of Bayes' Theorem results in conditional probabilities for specific events. These conditional probabilities are known as "posterior" probabilities. From this distribution of posterior probabilities, Bayesians can compute predictive distributions for future observations. Bayes' Theorem is often applied iteratively. After applying the Theorem, the resulting posterior probability can then be treated as a prior probability, and a new posterior probability computed from new evidence, a procedure termed "Bayesian updating." The critical point about Bayesian inference, then, is that it provides a structured way of combining new evidence with prior beliefs, through the application of Bayes' Theorem.

One way to apply Bayes' Theorem to risk assessment of sex offenders is to consider the base rate of recidivism to be the prior knowledge, and the Bayesian model of risk assessment sets out to calculate the conditional probability of recidivism for each actuarial score value. It has been said that, in the absence of any additional information, the best estimate of recidivism for an individual is the base rate of the group from which the individual has been selected (Quinsey et al., 1998). With the application of Bayes' Theorem, a conditional probability of recidivism is calculated for each ARAI score value, or the probability of recidivism "given" a particular actuarial score value. The conditional probabilities are the "posteriors" in the Bayesian analysis of actuarial assessment.

It is important here to distinguish between Bayesian inference and Bayes' Theorem. Bayesian inference is more than Bayes' Theorem. As described above, Bayesian inference quantifies uncertainty by reporting probabilities for things we are uncertain of, given specified premises. Later in the book we will discuss Bayesian inference as it might apply to sex offender risk assessment in the SVP courtroom. However, in the remainder of this chapter, we restrict our consideration to Bayes' Theorem. In this section of the chapter, we hope to raise awareness and understanding of Bayes' Theorem and its application to actuarial assessment of sex offenders. Understanding the calculations and principles enunciated here will increase understanding of the realities of actuarial assessment. The importance of Bayes' Theorem to actuarial assessment has been articulated much more elegantly and presented in a more sophisticated way by earlier authors (Mossman, 2006; Donaldson & Wollert, 2008). This section of our chapter is based on their work. Importantly, we recognize Rich Wollert's role as an advocate for the importance of Bayes' Theorem/Bayesian reasoning in actuarial assessment in the SVP courtroom. Despite this advocacy, the importance of Bayes' Theorem is largely unknown or ignored.

Two years after Doren's (2004a) article argued that score-wise recidivism rates were independent of the base rate, Doug Mossman (2006) published a rejoinder based on Bayes' Theorem. Later, Donaldson and Wollert (2008) made the same points as Mossman using a slightly different methodology. These two articles make an important argument that should be understood by users of actuarial instruments. We will refer to Mossman's, Donaldson's, and Wollert's position as the "Bayesian" position.

We are going to try to increase appreciation for the significance of Bayes' Theorem using an illustration. Table 6.1 presents a "Bayes Calculator" (our Excel spreadsheet is available upon request from any of the authors) based on the calculations presented in Mossman's article. Here, we will use the BAS we developed as an illustration in Chapter 5 (pp. 90–98) as a representative actuarial instrument with four score values. The cells in the first four columns contain data we obtained from the BAS (the data presented in Chapter 5, Figure 5.1, p. 92), using the sample of child molesters we described in Chapter 5, pp. 89–90.

The table makes certain calculations based on Mossman's (2006) article. We will take the reader through each step in turn. The first column (Column A) contains the score values from the BAS, ranging from 0 to 3. In the next column (Column B), labeled R+, we entered the number of individuals in each score group who recidivated. In the next column (Column C), labeled R–, we entered the number of individuals in each score group who did not recidivate. By adding across these two columns for each score value, we obtained the total number of individuals within each score group and these totals are presented in Column D. We also calculated the total recidivists and non-recidivists and total *n*, and these totals are entered at the bottom of the relevant column.

The 5th column (Column E) contains the probability of recidivism for each score group which we calculated by dividing the entry in the R+ column (Column B) by the number of individuals in the particular score group (Column D). As can be seen, and as expected, the probability of recidivism increases with higher scores. The next two columns calculate "conditional probabilities," in the first column using only data from the recidivists, and in the second column using only data from the non-recidivists. Considering only those individuals who recidivated, we calculated the probability of an individual obtaining a particular score value, given that they recidivated. In Mossman's notation, we calculated $P(G_i \mid R+)$, or the probability of score "i" (0, 1, 2, 3) given R+. For example, for

Table 6.1 Our Bayes Calculator for sex offender actuarial assessment

	Recidivism (yes/no)		*Total* N	*Empirical P(R+)*	*P(G_i|R+)*	*P(G_i|R–)*	*LR_i*	*Posterior odds*	*Probability*
	R+	*R–*							
Actuarial score									
0	0	64	64	0.0000	0.0000	0.2963	0.0000	0.0000	0.0000
1	3	58	61	0.0492	0.1200	0.2685	0.4469	0.0517	0.0492
2	6	64	70	0.0857	0.2400	0.2963	0.8100	0.0938	0.0857
3	16	30	46	0.3478	0.6400	0.1389	4.6080	0.5333	0.3478
Total	25	216	241						

Calculation of base rate (prior) odds
P(R+) = 0.1037
1–P(R+) = 0.8963

O_{br} (R+) = P(R+)/(1–P(R+)
= 0.1157

Posterior odds = $LR_i \times O_{br}$ (R+)

the score group "0," we divided the number of recidivists with that score (0) by the total number of recidivists (25). And so on, for all score groups. The results are contained in Column F.

Now, considering only those individuals who did not recidivate, we made the same calculations. For each score group, we calculated the probability of score "i" (0, 1, 2, 3) given R–. For example, for the score group "0," we divided the number of non-recidivists in that score group (64) by the total number of non-recidivists (216). And so on, for all of the remaining score groups. The results of these calculations are contained in Column G.

Before going on to our next set of calculations, we need to introduce the concept of "odds." The relationship between the probability that an event will occur and the odds of an event occurring is as follows: the odds of an event occurring is the probability of the event occurring divided by the probability of the event not occurring. (The probability of an event occurring is notated as p; the probability of an event not occurring is notated as $1-p$; the two probabilities have to add to 1.) Therefore, converting a probability to an odds is given as $p/(1-p)$. A probability of zero is the same as the odds of zero. Probabilities between 0 and 0.5 equal odds less than 1.0. A probability of 0.5 is the same as odds of 1.0. As the probability goes up from 0.5 to 1.0, the odds increase from 1.0 to infinity. If the probability is 0.75 then the odds are $0.75/(1-0.75) = 3$. To convert odds (O) back to probability, divide the odds by $1+O$; or $P = O/(1+O)$.

Getting back to our Bayes Calculator, we calculated the odds of recidivism for each score group. In Column H, for the score value of "0," we entered the product of the division of Column F (the probability of scoring "i" given recidivism of 0.000) divided by the entry in Column I (the probability of scoring "i" given non-recidivism of 0.2963). These calculations were then made for all score groups and entered in Column H. The values in Column H are known as likelihood ratios (LRs) and as pointed out by Mossman and reiterated by Donaldson and Wollert (2008, p. 213),

> These likelihood ratios are the slope coefficients for a risk instrument's receiver operating characteristic curve, which may be derived by plotting the value of the true and false positive rates for each cutting score on the y and x axes respectively, of a two-dimensional graph where the vectors range from 0% to 100%.

These LRs across the score groups represent the discriminative ability of the actuarial instrument (Mossman, 2006). If all LRs were equal, if all of the slopes were the same, then there would be no discriminatory power to the test at all. Put another way, if all of the slopes were equal, the receiver operator characteristic (ROC) curve would be equivalent to the straight line along the diagonal and the area under the curve (AUC)

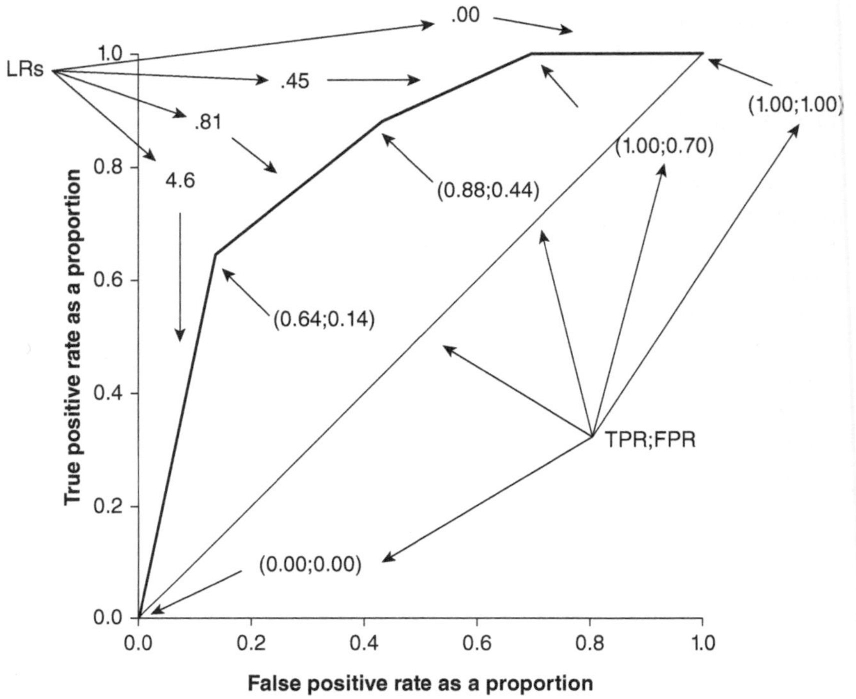

Figure 6.1 ROC curve for three-item actuarial scale with child molesters.

would be 0.50, indicating a chance prediction. The larger the difference between the lowest LR and the highest LR, the greater the discrimination. In respect of the ROC curve, a low value for the lowest LR (the flat slope at the upper-right corner of the curve) and a high value for the highest LR (the steep slope at the lower left aspect of the curve) would occur when the ROC curve goes substantially into the upper-left corner of the two-dimensional space, as happens with higher AUCs. Remember, the gold standard for actuarial assessment is where the instrument achieves a high true positive rate (approaching 1.00) and a low false positive rate (approaching 0). In the ROC curve, the gold standard is located in the upper-left corner of the two-dimensional space. The more the ROC curve extends into that upper-left corner, the better.

Here, in Figure 6.1, we re-present our ROC curve for our BAS with some additional pertinent information. Figure 6.1 presents the ROC curve derived from the data we generated in the development of the BAS in Chapter 5 (pp. 90–98). Using the methodology for plotting ROC curves described in Chapter 5 (pp. 92–100), we calculated the sensitivity and specificity of the instrument for each possible cut score value (0.0, 0.5,

1.5, 2.5, 3.5) and these points are added to the figure originally presented in Chapter 5 (p. 98). This figure also presents the LRs (0.0, .45, .81, and 4.6) and it can be seen that the LRs represent the slopes of the ROC curves in the relevant segments of the curve.

Now, what does all this have to do with recidivism rates in each score group? The answer is that recidivism (expressed as an odds ratio) is the product of the LR for that score group multiplied by the base rate (expressed as an odds ratio). To calculate the base rate odds ratio, we used the usual formula for converting a probability to an odds, namely $p/(1-p)$. As in the example in Table 6.1, the base rate of recidivism expressed as a probability or P(R+) is 25/241 or 0.1037. So, to convert it to an odds ratio: O_{br} = 0.1037/(1–0.037)= .1157.

To calculate the posterior odds for each score group (Column J), we multiplied the LR for that group (LR_i) times the 0_{br}. For the group with a score of "1," we multiplied .4469 times .1157 equals .0517. The same calculation was made for each of the score groups and entered into Column J. The entries in Column J represent posterior odds, and to convert them back into probabilities we divided each O_i by $1+O_i$ or $P(R_i) = O_i/(1 + O_i)$. So, for the "1" score group, O_0 =0.0517/(1+0.0517) = .0492. These entries were made for each score group in Column K. All forms of Bayes' Theorem result in the following general formula: The posterior odds are equal to the prior odds (base rate) multiplied by the LRs for the specific conditions (score values).

You will notice that the entries in Column K, the posterior probabilities for each score group, are the same as the entries in Column E, the empirical recidivism rates we calculated for each score group prior to the implementation of Bayes' Theorem. This demonstrates (proves?) that the recidivism rates for each score group (expressed as an odds ratio) are a joint product of the LR (odds ratio) for that score group times the sample base rate (expressed as an odds ratio). On this basis, the Bayesians would argue with those (e.g., Doren, 2004a) who claim that absolute score-wise recidivism rates are independent of the base rate. As the base rate increases, so will the recidivism rates associated with each actuarial score. This is not a hypothesis or theory; it is a mathematical reality based on Bayes' Theorem (Donaldson & Wollert, 2008; Mossman, 2006).

Estimating Absolute Recidivism Rates: Bayes Correction

So the lesson from this illustrative set of calculations is that the absolute recidivism rates attached to each actuarial score value are the product of the base rate odds multiplied by the LR for the relevant score value. Therefore, for score-wise absolute recidivism rates to be stable across samples, either the Bayesian coordinates (LRs and base rates; Donaldson & Wollert, 2008) have to be stable from sample to sample, or the Bayesian coordinates have to change in complementary ways from sample to sample to produce stable recidivism rates. Although this latter circumstance seems unlikely, both of these possibilities are subject to empirical evaluation.

With respect to base rates, the likelihood of them being stable across diverse samples is low. Many factors influence base rates. For example, longer follow-up times would lead to higher base rates and samples vary considerably in their follow-up times. Jurisdictions vary in the rigor with which they investigate and prosecute sexual crimes. This issue has been put to the empirical test. Helmus, Hanson, Thornton, Babchishin, and Harris (2012) conducted a meta-analysis evaluating absolute recidivism rates across 23 samples with a total of 8,106 sex offenders. Their study examined absolute and relative risk estimates for Static-99R and 2002R. Logistic regression coefficients for Static-99R and 2002R were combined through meta-analysis (8,106 sex offenders; 23 samples). While Static-99R and 2002R both demonstrated remarkably consistent relative predictive accuracy across studies (consistent with the AUCs we report in Chapter 5, Tables 5.5 and 5.6), both scales demonstrated large and significant variability in absolute recidivism rates across studies, both in terms of base rates and in terms of rates attached to each actuarial score value (score-wise recidivism rates). Over the 23 samples, five-year follow-up base rates varied from a minimum of 0% to almost 30%, with a mean base rate of 11.5% (*SD*=7.8). Figure 6.2 depicts these 23 base rates in rank order from lowest to highest to illustrate the nature of the distribution of base rates. The black line depicts the statistical mean (average)

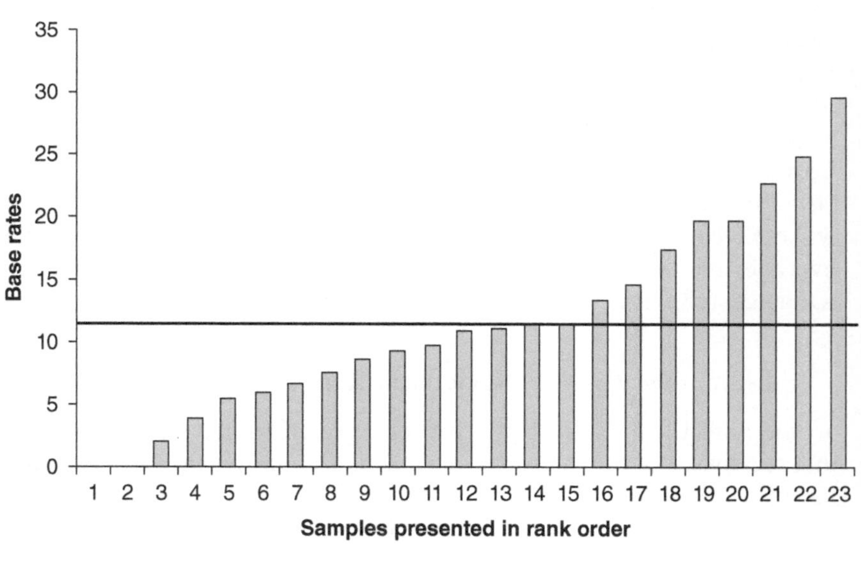

Figure 6.2 Base rates for 23 samples.

of the distribution. Examination of the distribution tells us that the mean does not represent very many of the base rate values. In other words, the base rates are not clustered around the mean with a small number of outliers. Instead, the density of the base rates is roughly equal across the range of values.

Besides the five-year rates, Helmus et al. (2012) also provided ten-year base rates for 15 samples, and these base rates varied widely as well. Our new understanding of Bayes' Theorem and its relevance to actuarial assessment helps us understand that, with varying base rates across samples, the absolute rates attached to each score value must vary as well.

If base rates vary widely, it is important to consider if LRs are stable across samples for specific actuarial instruments. Mossman (2006) described LRs as an integral part of the AUC, as described above, and he described the distribution of LRs over the actuarial score values as representing the ability of the actuarial instrument to discriminate among score value groups in recidivism risk. Since AUCs are reasonably consistent across samples (see Tables 5.6 and 5.7 in Chapter 5, pp. 107–108), it is reasonable to suggest that the LRs generated by an actuarial instrument might be stable across samples. If the base rates vary but the LRs for a particular actuarial instrument are consistent across samples, then absolute score-wise recidivism rates could be estimated using Bayes' Theorem to adjust absolute rates attached to each score value. Harris and Rice (2013) investigated whether a "Bayesian correction" could estimate absolute recidivism rates attached to actuarial scores for samples with different base rates. They followed Mossman's article (and calculations) by multiplying the base rate odds for the particular sample by each of the score value LRs from different samples. Harris and Rice reported the results of numerous attempts at using Bayes correction and concluded that such estimates are reasonably good in some circumstances but that the estimates do not approximate the empirical findings in many circumstances.

In fact, the Bayesian correction does not work because neither of the Bayesian coordinates (base rate or LRs) is stable across diverse samples (Mossman, personal communication). LRs can only be consistent across samples when there is consistency in the distribution of recidivists and non-recidivists across score groups as well as consistency in the score-wise recidivism rate (Helmus & Babchishin, submitted for publication; Helmus & Thornton, 2014). LRs would be expected to change depending on the distribution of cases across score groups in different samples, even if the probability of recidivism per risk score remains identical. This is obvious from the Bayes rule. If base rates change but score-wise recidivism rates remain the same, then LRs must change. Helmus and Thornton (2014) provide a convincing illustration of this point.

We present our own illustration of this point in Table 6.2, using data from our BAS example. In Panel 1 in Table 6.2 the first column presents the percent recidivism for each BAS score group. The second column presents the total *n* in the groups categorized in each score group of the BAS. By multiplying the percentage by the *n* for each group, we calculate the R+ (the number of recidivists) for that bin, and by subtracting the number of recidivists from *n* for the group, we calculate the number of non-recidivists for that group. In Panels 2 and 3, we hold the percent recidivism constant (Column 1) and vary the distribution of offenders across the BAS score groups. In Panel 2, we add 20 *n* to each of the two higher-score bins, and we subtract 20 *n* from each of the lower-score bins. Notice that the total *n* adding across score bins remains constant.

In Panel 3, we subtract 20 *n* from each of the two higher bins and we add 20 *n* to each of the two lower bins. In summary, Panel 2 presents a distribution of scores across the bins that represents higher risk overall compared with Panel 1, the original distribution. Panel 3 presents a distribution of scores across the bins that represents lower risk overall compared with the original. Now, we calculate a set of LRs for Panels 2 and 3 and compare them with the original. These LRs are presented for comparison in the bottom panel of Table 6.2. Bayesian coordinates (base rates and LRs) are measures that are specific to particular samples and do not generalize from one sample to the next. Importantly, this means that the Bayesian coordinates do not generalize from a standardized sample to other independent samples. Therefore, Bayesian coordinates (LRs and base rates) are not helpful for us to use to estimate score-wise absolute recidivism rates.

Estimating Absolute Recidivism Rates: Logistic Regression

When Monahan and Steadman (1994a) suggested statistical prediction as the proper basis for making statements of the potential for violence in forensic patients, they likely had simple linear regression or multiple linear regression in mind. These statistical methods were widely taught in graduate programs in Psychology and other disciplines in the mid to latter half of the 20th century. These regression techniques calculate predicted values of a dependent variable (predicted outcome) as a straight-line function of the value of the independent variable (predictor variable(s)), minimizing the summed squared deviations (least squares) between actual and predicted values of the dependent variable. These regression techniques are used when both the predictor variable(s) and the outcome or predicted variable are continuous variables with at least an interval level of measurement.

In the case where we are trying to estimate the probability of recidivism, the outcome variable is not continuous but dichotomous. When sex

Table 6.2 Changes in likelihood ratios with changes in the distribution of cases across brief actuarial scale scores

Panel 1: Calculation of LRs based on current distribution of BAS scores

Current Recid%	N	*R+*	*R–*
0.00%	64	0	64
4.92%	61	3	58
8.57%	70	6	64
34.78%	46	16	30
	241		

Panel 2: Calculation of LRs after adding 20 n *to each of the 2 higher bins and subtracting 20* n *from each of the 2 lower bins*

Recid%	N	*R+*	*R–*
0.00%	44	0	44
4.92%	41	2	39
8.57%	90	8	82
34.78%	66	23	43
	241		

Panel 3: Calculation of LRs after subtracting 20 n *from each of the 2 higher bins and adding 20* n *to each of the 2 lower bins*

Recid%	N	*R+*	*R–*
0.00%	84	0	84
4.92%	81	4	77
8.57%	50	4	46
34.78%	26	9	17
	241		

Panel 4: Resulting LRs

BAS score	*Risk level*		
	Original panel 1	*Higher panel 2*	*Lower panel 3*
0	0.000	0.000	0.000
1	0.447	0.323	0.684
2	0.810	0.615	1.146
3	4.608	3.371	6.976

offenders are released into the community, they either recidivate (Score=1) or they do not (Score=0). There are two statistical techniques that have become more widely known and used in recent years that have been designed to make accurate predictions when the predictor variables are continuous (as is the case of actuarial scores and scales representing other potential risk factors) but when the predicted variable or outcome is binary (as in the case of recidivism). Logistic regression is used for predicting binary outcomes of the dependent variable based on one or more predictor variables that may be either continuous or categorical. The second statistical technique is Cox regression, used in situations with multiple continuous predictor variables and a dichotomous outcome variable and where the time to outcome (recidivism) is known. We will focus here on logistic regression.

Logistic regression treats the dependent variable as if it were the outcome of a Bernoulli trial, such as flipping a fair coin repeatedly. Logistic regression is a form of regression analysis in which the binary dependent variable is converted into a logit (Hosmer & Lemeshow, 2000). Logistic regression calculates the natural logarithm of the odds of the dependent variable being a case (i.e., a "head," or in the case of ARAIs, a recidivist). This odds ratio, referred to as the logit or log-odds, is a continuous outcome variable that can be thought of as a transformed version of the binary dependent or outcome variable. The transformed and now continuous variable is fitted to the predictors using linear regression analysis. Then, the predicted value of the logit is converted back into the predicted odds via the inverse of the natural logarithm. Therefore, although the observed dependent variable in logistic regression is a zero-or-one variable, the logistic regression estimate is the odds that the dependent variable is a case (recidivist).

Logistic regression has some parallels to the Bayes' Theorem example we were working with above. Logistic regression is a way of calculating the conditional probability of recidivism "given" a certain value of the predictor variable, or in our case, the actuarial score. Logistic regression analysis provides two log-odds ratios. B_0 is the equivalent in linear regression to the "Y intercept." In the case of logistic regression with recidivism data, B_0 is the log-odds of recidivism when the ARAI score is equal to zero. B_1 is the equivalent in linear regression to the "slope." B_1 estimates the average increase in recidivism (expressed as a log-odds) associated with each one-unit increase in the ARAI score. B_1 is an estimate of predictive accuracy, and has been suggested as a replacement for the AUC statistic we described in Chapter 5 (Helmus et al., 2012).

For the purpose of illustration, we will present the results of a logistic regression analysis of our sample of child molesters to estimate absolute score-wise recidivism rates for the Static-99R. Since we are interested in estimating recidivism rates for a particular period of follow-up, we have to observe one restriction on the use of logistic regression. The sample must include offenders who have all been in the community at risk for a certain period of time. In our previous analyses of recidivism data, we have been working with a file in which the offenders had been in the community at risk for recidivism for an average of five years, but the follow-up periods ranged above and below that average. In the present analysis, we will be working with a file of offenders who have all been in the community at risk for three years. Therefore, we are using logistic regression to estimate three-year recidivism rates.

Table 6.3 presents the results of our logistic regression of three-year recidivism rates for our sample of child molesters. The upper panel presents the Statistical Package for the Social Sciences (SPSS) output for the analysis in which we entered the Static-99R scores (truncated at –1 and 6 due to small *n*) as the predictor variable. The critical entries in this table are presented in the third column labeled "B," containing the B_0 (–4.313) and the B_1 (0.468). Remember that the first of these *B*s is sometimes referred to as the intercept and represents the recidivism rate (as a log-odds) for offenders with Static-99R scores of zero. The second of these *B*s is sometimes referred to as the slope and represents the average increase in recidivism rate (as a log-odds) with each unit increase in Static-99R score. The Wald statistics are tests of the significance of Static-99R as a predictor of recidivism.

The lower panel presents the transformation of the dependent variable as required in logistic regression. We present these data to illustrate how logistic regression calculates the estimates we are interested in. Column 1 presents the Static-99R score values, and Columns 2 and 3 present the recidivists and non-recidivists in each score group. Column 4 presents the percentage recidivism in each group. The transformation of the dependent variable proceeds as follows. Column 5 converts the percentage recidivism into a probability. Column 6 converts the probabilities into odds (we described the difference between probability and odds earlier in this chapter). In Column 7, the odds are converted to log-odds (the natural logarithm of the odds).

Then, logistic regression performs the usual linear regression calculation. For each Static-99R score, a predicted value of the log-odds is calculated, as Y (predicted log-odds) = intercept + (slope × Static-99R score). These predicted values are presented in Column 8. If you plot these predicted logits over the Static-99 scores, you will see that they form a straight line.

Then, in Columns 8 to 11, logistic regression reverses the logarithmic transformation back from log-odds to percentage recidivism. Column 9 contains the transformed values from the natural logarithm contained

Table 6.3 Logistic regression estimating child molesters' three-year score-wise absolute recidivism rates for the Static-99R

Panel 1: SPSS output: Variables in the equation

		B	S.E	Wald	df	Sig.	Exp(B)	95% C.I. for EXP(B)	
								Lower	Upper
Step 1[a]	Static-99R	0.468	0.159	8.693	1	0.000	1.597	1.17	2.18
	Constant	−4.313	0.705	37.439	1	0.000	0.013		

[a]Variable(s) entered on step 1: Static-99R.

Panel 2: Linear regression performed on tranformed dependent variable (logit)

	Sexual recidivism		Actual				Predicted			
Static-99 R score	N of no	N of yes	Percent recidivism	Probability of recidivism	Odds of recidivism	Logit or log-odds	Logit or log-odds	Odds	Probability	Percent
	To calculate:		%	%/100	p/(1−p)	*ln* p/(1−p)	$y = B_0 + x(B_1)$	EXP_{Logit}	Odds/(1+Odds)	p*100
−1	29	0	0.00%	0.0000	0.0065	−5.0360	−4.7810	0.0084	0.0083	0.83%
0	28	0	0.00%	0.0000	0.0110	−4.5099	−4.3130	0.0134	0.0132	1.32%
1	37	1	2.63%	0.0263	0.0270	−3.6109	−3.8450	0.0214	0.0209	2.09%
2	28	2	6.67%	0.0667	0.0714	−2.6391	−3.3770	0.0341	0.0330	3.30%
3	28	1	3.45%	0.0345	0.0357	−3.3322	−2.9090	0.0545	0.0517	5.17%
4	31	3	8.82%	0.0882	0.0968	−2.3354	−2.4410	0.0871	0.0801	8.01%
5	16	2	11.11%	0.1111	0.1250	−2.0794	−1.9730	0.1390	0.1221	12.21%
6	19	4	17.39%	0.1739	0.2105	−1.5581	−1.5050	0.2220	0.1817	18.81%

B_0 (Intercept) = −4.313
B_1 (Slope) = 0.468

in Column 8 to the odds in Column 9, which are in turn transformed back to probability in Column 10, and percent recidivism in Column 11. These transformations are opaque in the SPSS output, but the contents of Column 11 can be saved using SPSS. When you are in the point and click menu for binary logistic regression, there is a "save" option where you can save the predicted probabilities (Helmus, personal communication).

Figure 6.3 plots the results of the logistic regression used to estimate three-year score-wise recidivism rates. The dark trace plots the actual recidivism rates for each score value. The lightest trace plots the estimated recidivism rates as calculated by logistic regression. For a comparison, we conducted a linear regression on the percentage recidivism rates and the resulting plot is presented in the figure as the straight line trace.

As you can see, the observed recidivism rates show a generally increasing level of recidivism from the lowest score (–1) to the highest score (6+). However, the increase is variable. For example, the group with a score of 3 has a lower rate of recidivism than adjacent score groups. This irregularity is expected in small samples. Our sample, with an *n* of 229, is a small sample, so a smooth increasing curve would not necessarily be expected. Regression analyses serve to estimate the shape of the curve given much higher *n*. Our linear regression line provided estimated recidivism rates for each score value, and the estimates are, by design, located on a straight line.

Our logistic regression line is an increasing positively accelerating curve (not a straight line). Both the linear and logistic regression lines are estimates of the absolute recidivism rates for the range of Static-99R scores.

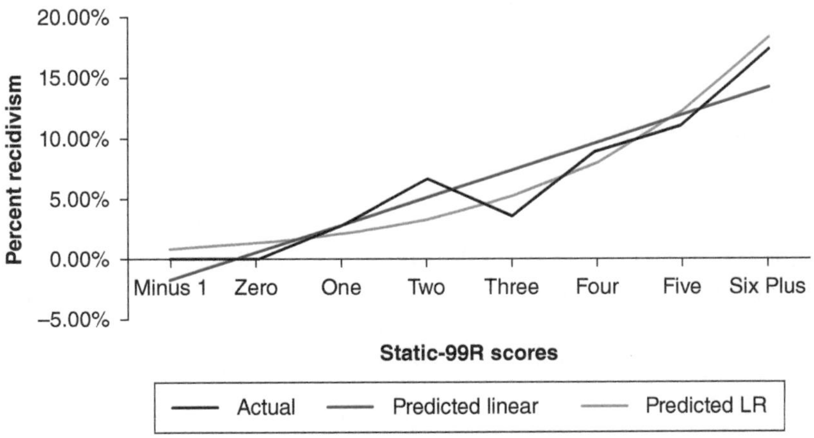

Figure 6.3 Estimating three-year absolute recidivism rates using the Static-99R, linear regression, and logistic regression.

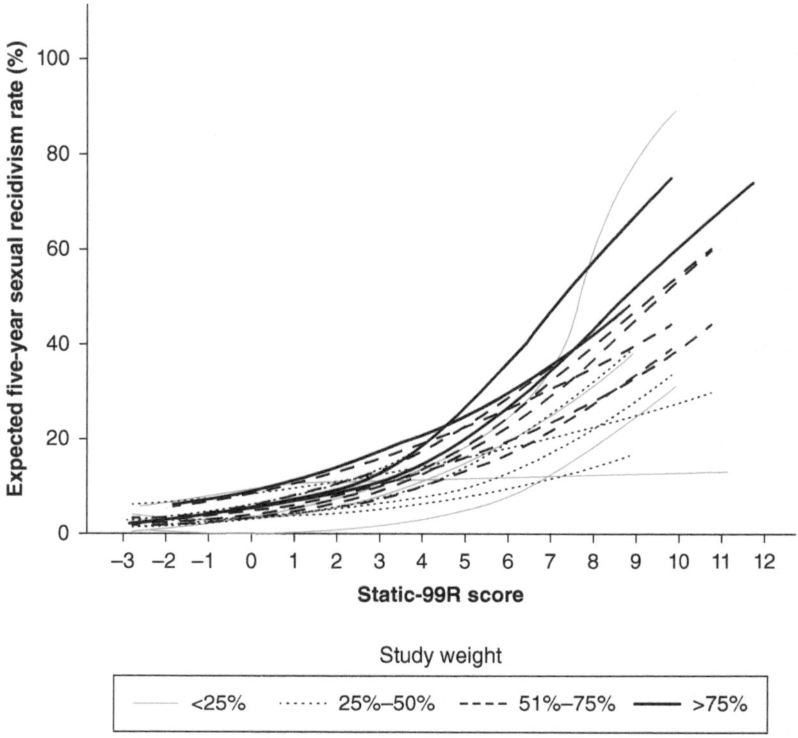

Figure 6.4 Logistic regression results from each sample. Taken from Helmus et al. (2012), reprinted by permission of Sage Publications (Copyright © by International Association for Correctional and Forensic Psychology).

Helmus et al. (2012) have conducted logistic regression on 23 samples (n = 8,106). They calculated the results of B_0 and B_1 by plotting five-year recidivism rates over Static-99R scores. We present their findings (their Figure 3) in our Figure 6.4. As can be seen, the shapes of their plots of these 23 logistic regressions are similar in shape, and similar to the plot of our analysis presented in Figure 6.3. However, the curves do not reflect similar levels of recidivism across samples and this is especially true for higher Static-99R scores. As an example, for the Static-99R score of 5, estimated rates of recidivism range from less than 5% to more than 25%. Helmus et al. (2012) concluded that predicted recidivism rates within each risk score demonstrated large and significant variability across studies (samples).

Confidence Intervals

One of the advantages of logistic regression is that it provides the opportunity to calculate confidence intervals (CIs) around each estimate. When we calculate CIs, we make the assumption that our estimate of the rate of recidivism is exactly that, an estimate. Our estimate is a statistical approximation to the "true" recidivism rate for that ARAI score value. CIs provide us with boundaries around our estimate within which the true value (population parameter) is expected to lie. We can specify statistically how precise our estimate is. To put this another way, CIs provide us with a way to communicate our confidence that the true recidivism rate is within our stated boundary. For example, the 95% CI around an estimate indicates that the true rate (population parameter) will be contained within the lower and upper CI boundaries 19 times out of 20.

Helmus and Hanson (2007) have provided a detailed description of how to conduct and interpret the results of logistic regression. They provided the formula for the calculation of CIs taken from an authoritative text on logistic regression (Hosmer & Lameshow, 2000). To calculate CIs for each Static-99R score group, we have to add (for the upper limit) and subtract (for the lower limit) the value 1.96 times the standard error of the logit, as follows:

$$95\%\ \text{Cl} = \text{logit} \pm (1.96\ (SE_{logit}))$$

You may remember from introductory statistics that in the normal distribution (distribution of Z), 95% of the sample is contained between plus and minus 1.96 standard deviations. The same is true for the distribution of the standard error. What we are looking for then is 1.96 standard deviations of the standard error of the logit on either side of our estimate (the logit) for each Static-99R score value.

To calculate the standard error of the logit, use the formula:

$$SE_{logit} = \sqrt{(SE_{B0})^2 + 2 \cdot x \cdot r \cdot SE_{B0} \cdot SE_{B1} + x^2 (SE_{B1})^2}$$

To make this calculation, you will need the standard error of both Bs and the correlation of the estimates (r; an estimate of the relationship between B_0 and B_1), which can be derived from the logistic regression analysis. X refers to the Static-99R score. Standard errors of the logit are therefore calculated separately for each risk score.

From our logistic regression estimating three-year absolute recidivism rates for child molesters, we made the calculations of the CIs described above. Figure 6.5 presents the estimates and the upper and lower limits of the 95% CIs for the eight Static-99R scores (–1 to 6+). The middle line represents the recidivism estimates for each score group. The lower line represents the lower limit and the upper line represents the upper limit to the 95% CI. For example, for the score of 4, the estimate is about 8%, the lower limit is about 5%, and the upper limit is about 14%. Therefore we could conclude that, on the basis of the logistic regression

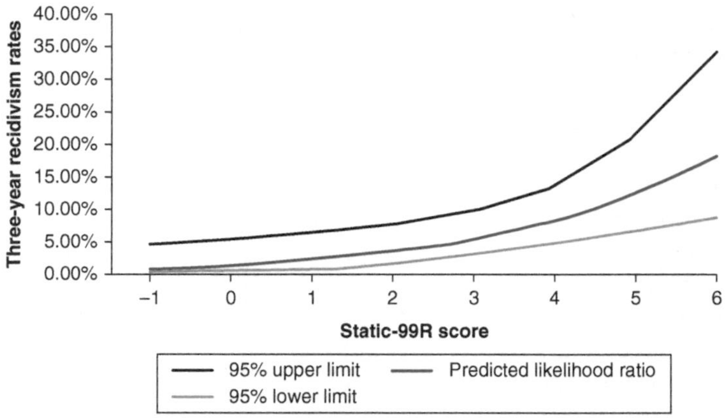

Figure 6.5 Estimating the three-year rate of recidivism (and 95% CI) using logistic regression.

analysis of our sample, the best estimate of the three-year rate of recidivism for a child molester with a score of 4 is 8% and the "true" three-year rate of recidivism for individuals with a score of 4 will be somewhere between 5 and 14% nineteen times out of twenty.

Summary and Conclusions

This chapter has dealt with Meehl's Stage 2 of actuarial assessment, a stage that has come to be known as calibration. When we calibrate an ARAI, we are making estimates of score-wise recidivism rates. The frequentist position holds that repeated sampling of recidivism rates in various samples will eventually provide a precise estimate of score-wise recidivism rates. Empirical research reviewed in this chapter has revealed that score-wise recidivism rates, as well as sample base rates, vary widely from sample to sample. Application of Bayes' Theorem has taught us about the axiomatic relationships between score-wise rates and base rates that exist within specific samples. Some authors had expressed the hope that LRs might be stable from sample to sample and that score-wise recidivism rates might be calculated across samples of varying base rates using a Bayesian correction. However, research and logic have shown us that these Bayesian coordinates, both base rates and LRs, can vary widely among samples, and calibration cannot be helped by the Bayesian correction.

This chapter described how logistic regression can be used to calibrate ARAIs, with the added feature of providing CIs. Therefore, even though base rates and score-wise recidivism rates vary widely across samples, at least we are in a position to estimate the error rate. Being able to estimate error has been seen as a crucial feature of scientific evidence introduced at trial by experts (Daubert v. Merrel Dow Pharmaceuticals).

One of the prominent features of the development of the ARAIs is the fact that they have been developed through an entirely empirical process without the guidance of any theory of recidivism risk. This empirical development is both a strength (ARAIs work and their use is not complicated by theoretical controversies) and a weakness (current ARAIs are not optimal in the sense that there are no obvious theories to guide improvement and further development of the ARAIs). In the next chapter, Chapter 7, we will focus our critical examination of the ARAIs on the problems that result from the absence of theory from the scientific process.

7

THE IMPORTANCE OF THEORY IN ASSESSING RISK

Introduction

In the previous three chapters, we have presented a brief history of actuarial assessment of risk for recidivism in sex offenders. We described how actuarial risk assessment instruments (ARAIs) were developed and illustrated our description with the development of our own brief (three-item) actuarial scale for child molesters. We described how ARAIs are evaluated for accuracy and we surveyed the literature focusing on independent cross-validations of several ARAIs. We examined the problems experienced in calibrating ARAIs, specifically the fact that estimates of score-wise recidivism rates are characterized by large error rates. In this chapter, we examine some other problems with ARAIs, and make the claim that many of these problems arise because these instruments were developed in the absence of any theory of recidivism risk. We underscore the importance of theory in science, and we speculate on what solutions to problems might be found with the guidance of a theory of risk.

Problems with Actuarial Assessment

The development of actuarial risk assessment tools is perhaps the most significant scientific development in Forensic Psychology. Beginning with Paul Meehl's landmark monograph in 1954, the transparent inadequacy of pure clinical judgment was recognized and scholars responded with concerted efforts to infuse decision-making with empiricism. If there ever was an "inflection point" in the assessment of dangerousness, this was it. We fully recognize the enormous progress that has been made since. It appears, however, that the scientists have bumped up against the proverbial glass ceiling over the past decade, while the forensic practitioners are quite content to rest on the laurels of past success. The evolutionary nature of science is, by definition, not static, and neither is the science of risk assessment. It is our strong conviction that more is required to bring about the next "quantum" improvement. In this chapter we examine what we regard as multiple, significant problems with actuarial assessment of sex offenders.

First, as we documented in the previous chapter, the score-wise estimates of recidivism vary widely. Second, while the reliability and validity of these instruments are an improvement over clinical judgment, the improvement is small. These instruments result in only moderate predictive accuracy. Moreover, as we noted above, we seem to have hit a ceiling in the value of area under the curve (AUC) values reported for ARAIs (AUC values in the mid-.70s, with some studies finding AUC values in the mid to high .60s). Recent innovations in ARAIs (e.g., Static-2002, VRAG-R) have not significantly improved our predictive ability. Third, because the items on these instruments are static in nature, the instruments may be appropriate for assessing long-term risk, but are not helpful in assessing change resulting from acute events that rely on dynamic factors, systemic change brought about by a treatment, or change brought about by external controls or interventions.

Fourth, a related problem, the scores resulting from actuarial assessment do not provide meaningful information concerning the nature of the risk factors that give rise to the risk. The completed assessment, as we have seen, ranks the individual in their level of risk, and provides estimates of the likelihood of recidivism within boundaries set by confidence intervals. However, no information is provided that conveys an explanation of the individual's risk. The field aspires to more; Mann et al. (2010) make reference to "psychologically meaningful" risk factors, and Barbaree et al. (2009) describe "conceptually meaningful" risk factors.

Fifth, different scales rank offenders differently. Barbaree et al. (2006a) examined the consistency of ranking of a sex offender's risk for recidivism by the various actuarial instruments. Percentile ranks were computed for $n = 262$ sex offenders using five actuarial risk instruments commonly used with adult sex offenders (RRASOR, Static-99, VRAG, SORAG, and MnSOST-R). Proponents of a purely actuarial approach to evaluation would expect relatively consistent ranking by instruments, especially among instruments that have been developed using the same recidivism outcome (violent recidivism versus sexual recidivism). However, Barbaree et al. reported that the average range of ipsative percentile ranks (comparing across the five percentile ranks within individuals) was almost 50 percentile ranks. In other words, it was not uncommon for one ARAI to rank an offender at the 90th percentile and another ARAI to rank the same offender at the 40th percentile rank. The most problematic consequence of this issue is raised when the use of multiple instruments yields different outcomes in the same evaluation. Which assessment is more valid? Unfortunately, the literature provides little information on how often such discrepant outcomes should be expected to occur and little guidance for the clinician as to how to interpret or resolve such differences when they occur.

Sixth, the actuarial instruments have no relationship to any theory of sex offender risk. As we described in the previous chapters, the process of selecting and weighting actuarial items was completely independent of theory. In fact, at the time of the development of the ARAIs, there was no extant theory of recidivism risk in sex offenders. Developers of ARAIs may have drafted items based on their knowledge of the empirical literature on recidivism, and their informed expectation that items reflecting antisocial orientation and sexual deviance would likely predict recidivism, but their choices were not based on any formal theory of recidivism. As Hanson and Morton-Bourgon (2004a) noted, in the empirical actuarial approach, the items have no face validity. Items were selected and weighted based on their empirical relationship with recidivism outcome. In Chapter 5, we described the empirical development of the actuarial instruments as an example of *Incremental Predictive Validity*. We demonstrated how bits of information about a sex offender chosen entirely from our knowledge about the information's relevance to recidivism can allow for a prediction to be made about the offender's likelihood of recidivism. We showed how combining bits of information can increase our ability to predict recidivism.

If all we want ARAIs to do is predict recidivism, this situation may not be seen to be too serious. However, if, as scientists, we wish to develop assessment tools that allow for hypothesis testing and theory building, actuarial tools as presently available do not help very much. This lack of connection to theory is the most serious problem because it leads back to or is the cause of the other problems. From a scientific perspective, a connection to risk theory would allow for hypothesis testing and theory building and might lead in turn to the improvement of predictive validity, consistency in assessment across instruments, and the development of risk scales that are sensitive to change. Additionally, from a clinical perspective, a connection to risk theory would allow clinicians to evaluate the individual's risk factors as potential targets in treatment and would allow evaluators to communicate a case formulation (Hart & Logan, 2011) along with their risk assessment. It is interesting to us that while the development of ARAIs has been devoid of theory, the development of dynamic risk instruments has been guided by theory (e.g., Hanson & Harris, 2000, 2001) and the literature on dynamic risk factors has contributed to theory (Hanson & Morton-Bourgon, 2005; Mann et al., 2010).

Science and the Importance of Theory

Science is a formal approach to the development and accumulation of knowledge through the scientific method. The *Oxford English Dictionary* defines the scientific method as "a method or procedure that has characterized natural science since the 17th century, consisting [of] systematic observation, measurement, and experiment, and the formulation, testing, and modification of hypotheses." The defining characteristic of science that distinguishes it from other methods of "knowing" is the use of empirical data to test hypotheses derived from theory. A scientific theory is a formal statement of "current knowledge" about some aspect of the natural world. A theory is articulated in such a way that it can generate falsifiable hypotheses. From their chosen theoretical framework, scientists propose hypotheses as explanations of natural phenomena. Hypotheses are stated in a form that makes explicit predictions concerning the outcome of an experiment or study. Then, hypotheses are tested by the gathering and analysis of data. A theory is supported when its predictions are confirmed and challenged when its predictions prove false. As additional scientific evidence accumulates, a theory may be rejected or modified if it does not fit the new empirical findings. A good theory can explain a wide range of empirical phenomena while at the same time being elegantly simple (Occam's Razor).

The scientific development of an assessment instrument can and should involve the critical influence and guidance of theory. A good example of the scientific development of a forensic assessment instrument that will be familiar to most of our readers is the work leading to the development of the Psychopathy Checklist Revised (PCL-R; Hare, 2003). (See a detailed account of the development of the PCL-R in Skeem, Polaschek, Patrick, & Lilienfeld, 2011.) Canadian psychologist Robert Hare began with the description of psychopathy provided by Herve Cleckley (1976). Cleckley had based his conception of psychopathy on his extensive clinical experience with psychiatric patients and he proposed 16 diagnostic criteria (see a categorized list of diagnostic criteria in Patrick, 2006, p. 612). Hare's original PCL contained 22 items. Based on an analysis of data collected with this item set including standard psychometric analyses (item-total correlations; Hare & Neumann, 2008), and based on his own clinical experience with offenders in a correctional setting, Hare revised the item set as the 20-item PCL-R (Hare, 1991, 2003) and demonstrated that it was possible to score personality characteristics reliably. The development and promulgation of the PCL-R as a reliable and valid measure of psychopathy has allowed for an explosion of scientific studies on psychopathy, examining its essential nature including its component parts, etiology, biological underpinnings, and possible genetic sources of variance. This literature is a model of good science, with theory generating hypotheses and empirical studies testing hypotheses, and our understanding of psychopathy has blossomed. In Chapter 5 we referred to the development of ARAIs as an example of incremental predictive validity. In contrast, the psychopathy literature has been described as a good example of "construct validation"

(Skeem et al., 2011, p. 143). To see the depth and quality of this literature, refer to the volume edited by Patrick (2006).

Theories of Sex Offender Risk

The pure actuarial approach fosters a uni-dimensional conception of risk; recidivism risk is the only relevant dimension. On the other hand, theoretical accounts of actuarial risk (Doren, 2004a; Beech & Ward, 2004; Mann, Hanson, & Thornton, 2010) propose a multidimensional conceptual framework for factors underlying recidivism risk. After an extensive review of the literature, Doren (2004a) concluded that there appeared to be at least two superordinate dimensions which he identified as sexual deviance and psychopathy/general criminality. In fact, antisocial behavior and sexual deviance have been used for decades as explanatory concepts for sexually abusive behavior (i.e., Marshall & Barbaree, 1984, 1990), and for rationalizing classification systems for sex offenders (Knight & Prentky, 1990). Rice and Harris (1997; replicated in Harris et al., 2003) have pointed to the potent combination of psychopathy (a correlate of antisocial behavior) and sexual deviance in predicting recidivism in sex offenders. Both of the large meta-analytic studies of the sex offender recidivism literature (Hanson & Bussiere, 1998; Hanson & Morton-Bourgon, 2005) identify deviant sexual interests and antisocial orientation as important predictors of sexual recidivism. It is likely, therefore, that actuarial items empirically selected for ARAIs reflect these two risk dimensions.

After a similarly extensive review of the literature in which they paid particular attention to theoretical accounts of sexual assault, Beech and Ward (2004) presented an integrated model of risk in sex offenders, a model that included developmental factors, vulnerability factors they refer to as traits, dynamic state factors, and contextual risk factors or triggering events. These authors used their model to categorize items from commonly used actuarial instruments into the following categories: psychosocial adjustment, sexual self-regulation, level of interpersonal functioning, self-management/impulsivity/hostility, and a contextual factor that included items relating to alcohol or substance abuse. These categories reflect numerous aspects of sexual deviance and antisocial behavior. These multidimensional accounts of risk are in keeping with modern theories of sexual assault (e.g., Knight & Sims-Knight, 2003; Malamuth, 2003).

The Relationship Between Putative Risk Factors and Actuarial Items

Theories of recidivism risk encourage us to think of the relationship between the individual actuarial items and the theoretical constructs

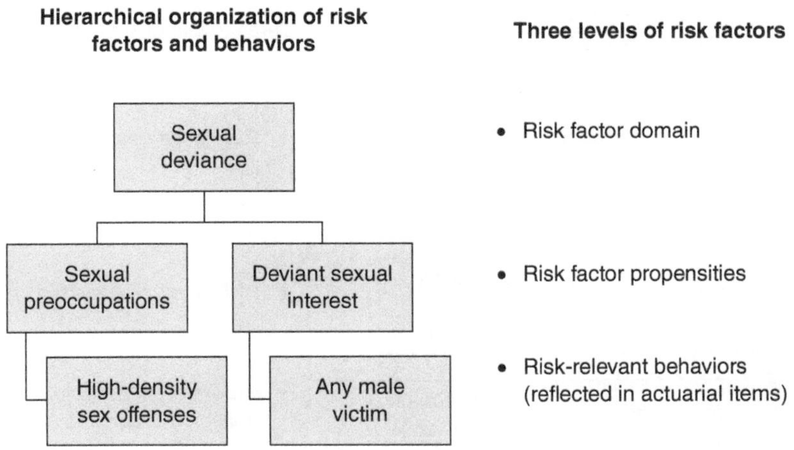

Figure 7.1 The relationship of risk factors to actuarial items.

proposed by theory. In the usual (non-actuarial) approach to developing assessment instruments, items would be developed on the basis of theories of recidivism, and would reflect behaviors that were under the influence of the underlying theoretical risk factors.

Figure 7.1 presents a pictorial account of what the relationship of theory to an item might look like. Sexual deviance is seen here as a superordinate risk factor, referred to here as a risk factor domain. This figure represents a hierarchical arrangement in which the larger risk domain is composed of numerous more narrowly defined risk factors, described as risk propensities (after Mann, Hanson, & Thornton 2010).

Mann et al. propose numerous propensities that might be thought of as comprising the sexual deviance risk domain, including sexual preoccupations, sexual preferences for prepubescent or pubescent children, sexualized violence, multiple paraphilias, offense supportive attitudes, and emotional congruence with children (Mann et al., 2010, pp. 199–200). The figure depicts two propensities, sexual preoccupations and deviant sexual interest. These propensities, according to theory, lead on to risk-related behaviors, which in turn affect the scoring of actuarial items. In the figure, sexual preoccupations lead on to high-density sex offenses (SVR-20 item #12), and deviant sexual interests lead on to the choice of a male victim (Static-99, item #10).

Figure 7.2 depicts a similar organization for the risk domain antisocial orientation. Mann et al. propose a number of risk propensities that might fall into the antisocial domain, including: lack of emotional intimate relationships with adults, lifestyle impulsiveness, poor problem-solving,

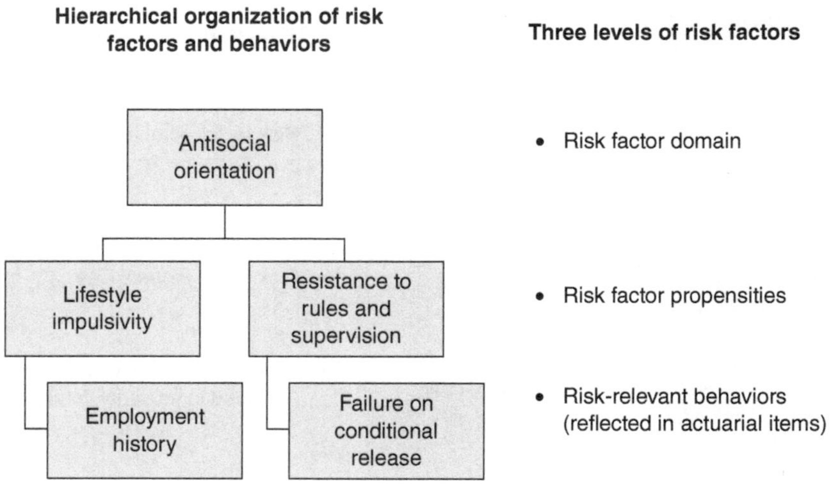

Figure 7.2 The relationship of antisocial orientation risk factors to actuarial items.

resistance to rules and supervision, grievance/hostility, and negative social influences. These propensities lead on to risk-related behaviors, which in turn affect the scoring of actuarial items. In the figure, lifestyle impulsivity leads on to employment problems (MnSOST-R item #12), and resistance to rules and supervision leads on to failure on conditional release (SORAG, item #9).

When actuarial items are developed without regard to theory and with no planned or postulated relation to underlying theoretical constructs, the only basis for their inclusion in the actuarial instrument is their relationship to recidivism outcome. Relations with underlying risk factors are left to chance and are largely unexplored. Examination of these relations reveals an important problem with the empirical (non-theoretical) development of actuarial tools.

The problem that arises from the empirical selection of actuarial items is that two or more risk factors can be confounded in the item's prediction of recidivism. Table 7.1 examines some statistical details regarding our sample's score on a specific actuarial item, item #2 on the Static-99. The item divides the sample into those individuals who have ever lived with a lover for at least two years and those who have not. In our sample, this item divides our large sample into two groups with significantly different rates of sexual recidivism, 8.9% versus 18.6%. This difference in the Static-99 developmental samples is what led this item to be included in the Static-99. You can imagine why this actuarial item might predict recidivism. Mann et al. have identified "Lack of emotional intimate

Table 7.1 Comparing married and unmarried sex offenders

	Static-99 item #2				
	Ever lived with partner/ lover for at least 2 years?				
	Yes	*No*	*Significance*		
% Recidivism (sexual)	8.9%	18.6%	AUC = .589, $p < .05$		
% Recidivism (serious)	23.3%	31.9%	AUC = .542, ns.		
				r *with sexual recidivism*	r *with serious recidivism*
Socioeconomic status (Blishen)	34.1 (8.9)	30.6 (8.8)	$F(1,448) = 12.85, p < .001$	–.06	–.13 **
Employment status (% employed)	70.4%	57.2%	$X2(1) = 6.4, p < .025$	–.02	–.08
Prior psychiatric history	48.7%	56.7%	$X2(1) = 2.4$, n.s	.09 *	.05
Length of current sentence (months)	57.3 (38.7)	58.7 (28.4)	$F(1,452) < 1$, n.s.	–.07	–.09
# Prior non-violent non-sex offenses	5.9 (8.3)	6.1 (7.5)	$F(1,460) < 1$, n.s.	.00	.16 **
# Prior violent non-sex offenses	1.05 (2.43)	.83 (1.36)	$F(1,459) < 1$, n.s.	.00	.14 **
# Prior sex offenses	.76 (1.6)	.97 (2.0)	$F(1,460) = 1.36$, n.s	.15 **	.09
Total # of victims	3.2 (4.2)	4.0 (9.6)	$F(1,460) = 1.48$, n.s.	.01	–.07
Age (years) at assessment	40.1(10.3)	30.4 (7.7)	$F(1,459) = 86.32, p < .001$	–.12 *	–.26 **
Age (years) at first criminal conviction	26.6 (12.1)	21.6 (6.2)	$F(1,459) = 18.27, p < .001$	–.14 **	–.26 **
Age (years) at release from custody	42.1 (10.7)	32.9 (8.4)	$F(1,460) = 78.9, p < .001$	–.13 **	–.27 **

Note
*$p<.05$
**$p<.01$

relationships with adults" as a risk propensity which we have classified above in the risk domain of antisocial orientation.

Table 7.1 explores some additional statistical comparisons between the two groups. It is important to recognize that *any* statistically significant difference between these two groups on any dimension potentially reflects a risk factor that might contribute to the differences in recidivism risk. As can be seen, the group composed of individuals identified as "never having lived with a partner/lover for more than two years" was also composed of individuals identified as being of lower socioeconomic status and as having less stable employment. These two differences between groups are not related directly to the inability to form intimate relations. Instead, these two differences would seem to be related to other risk factor propensities in the antisocial domain, such as lifestyle impulsivity which might lead to a higher recidivism rate. Now we have two theoretical risk factor propensities identified as potentially responsible for the difference in recidivism risk. When these two risk factor propensities are contained within the same risk factor domain, this might not seem to be too great a problem. When two risk factor propensities come from two different risk factor domains, the confound between the propensities potentially detracts from our ability to extract meaning from the assessment.

Many of the comparisons in Table 7.1 do not show a statistically significant difference between groups. For example, the groups do not differ in past psychiatric history and several aspects of their criminal histories are not different. However, the final three comparisons (age at assessment, age at first criminal conviction, and age at release) show highly significant differences between groups: the group with the higher rate of recidivism is younger at assessment, younger at their first criminal conviction, and younger when they were released from custody. One of these age variables is theoretically related to the risk factor domain antisocial orientation. It is well known that individuals with the more serious criminal histories begin their criminal careers at a younger age (e.g., Quinsey et al., 1998, 2006). So, this age variable might be seen to be part of the antisocial orientation risk domain. The other age variables, especially the age-at-release variable, seem not to be related to either of the risk factors, antisocial orientation or sexual deviance, but rather to suggest another risk factor altogether, namely maturation (Barbaree & Blanchard, 2008).

Barbaree and his colleagues (Barbaree, Langton, & Blanchard, 2007; Barbaree, Langton, Blanchard, & Boer, 2008; Barbaree, Langton, Blanchard, & Cantor, 2009) examined the confound between actuarial risk and aging. They describe a confound between risk factors as the situation that arises when a risk item or risk scale can be interpreted as being predictive of recidivism due to the influence of two or more risk factors. Barbaree et al. (2007, 2008, 2009) pointed to the correlations between

Table 7.2 Some actuarial items with negative correlations with age at release

Actuarial	*Item#*	*Item*	N	r
MnSOST-R	10	Adolescent antisocial behavior	407	–0.364**
MnSOST–R	12	Employment history	414	–0.358**
Static-99	7	Any stranger victims	462	–0.341**
VRAG/SORAG	6/9	Failure on conditional release	460	–0.294**
VRAG/SORAG	3/3	History of alcohol problem	468	–0.214**
Static-99/RRASOR	6	Any unrelated victims	465	–0.212**
VRAG/SORAG	12/14	PCL-R score	448	–0.206**
VRAG/SORAG	2/2	Elementary school maladjustment	447	–0.200**
MnSOST-R	3	Under supervision when they commit	407	–0.197**

Note
$^{**}p < .001$

actuarial item scores and age at release as revealing an important potential confound between commonly accepted putative risk factors (antisocial orientation and sexual deviance) and aging. They reported that of the 36 unique non-age items contained in the VRAG, SORAG, RRASOR, Static-99, and MnSOST-R, 31 (88%) have significant correlations with age at release.

Table 7.2 lists a number of ARAI items that have negative correlations with age at release. For these items, offenders who had been scored as positive on these items were younger than offenders who had not been scored positive. These ARAI items are recognizable as reflecting risk factor propensities within the antisocial orientation risk domain. These correlations point to a confound between risk factor propensities contained in two different risk factor domains, namely antisocial orientation and maturation (aging). Table 7.3 lists a number of ARAI items that have positive correlations with age at release. For these items, offenders who had been scored as positive on these items were older at release than offenders who had not been scored as positive. These ARAI items are recognizable as reflecting risk factor propensities within the sexual deviation risk domain. These correlations point to a confound between risk factor propensities contained in two different risk factor domains, namely sexual deviance and maturation (aging).

Why would actuarial items reflecting antisocial orientation and sexual deviation have significant but opposite correlations with age at release? Barbaree et al. (2007, 2008, 2009) described a number of important relationships between aging and actuarial risk that might assist us in answering this question. These relationships include: (1) risk for recidivism decreases with age in sex offenders, (2) rapists are younger than

Table 7.3 Some actuarial items with positive correlations with age at release

Actuarial	*Item#*	*Item*	N	r
MnSOST-R	7	# of different age groups victimized	404	0.376**
MnSOST-R	1	# of sex-related convictions	414	0.334**
MnSOST-R	6	Multiple acts on single victim	405	0.254**
Static-99	8	Any male victims	465	0.217**
MnSOST-R	8	Offended against a 13 to 15-year-old	403	0.211**
Static-99	1	Prior sex offenses	466	0.158*
MnSOST-R	2	Length of sex-offending history	409	0.144*
SORAG	7	# of convicts for sexual offenses prior	463	0.143*
SORAG	13	Deviant sexual preferences	393	0.118*

Notes
**$p<.001$
*$p<.05$

child molesters in the sex offender samples we have examined, (3) risk factor propensities within the antisocial orientation risk domain are more prevalent in rapists than child molesters, and (4) risk factor propensities within the sexual deviance risk domain are more prevalent in child molesters than rapists. These facts lead to the result that antisocial risk factors are more prevalent in younger offenders and sexual deviance risk factors are more prevalent in older offenders. Hence the correlations we see in Tables 7.2 and 7.3. We will now review each of these findings.

Risk for Recidivism Decreases With Age

As we indicated in some detail in Chapter 5, a large body of evidence has recently accumulated indicating that recidivism in sex offenders decreases with the age of the offender at the time of their release from custody (Barbaree, Blanchard, & Langton, 2003; Fazel, Sjöstedt, Långström, & Grann, 2006; Hanson, 2002, 2006; Prentky & Lee, 2007; Thornton, 2006). These reductions in recidivism among sex offenders are consistent across studies (Barbaree & Blanchard, 2008). Age-related reductions in the rate of recidivism in sex offenders are also consistent with a large body of literature examining human sexuality indicating that sexual behavior decreases in the aging male (e.g., Rowland, Greenleaf, Dorfman, & Davidson, 1993). In a recent publication, we (Barbaree & Blanchard, 2008) linked age-related reductions in blood levels of bio-available testosterone to decreases in sexual behaviors as a possible explanation for the effects of aging on sex offender recidivism, and proposed the addition of "maturation" as a risk factor distinct from previously specified static and dynamic risk factors (Hanson, Morton, & Harris, 2003).

Figure 7.3 The rates (arrests per 100,000 population) of arrest for forcible rape plotted over the age of the male person arrested. In age class intervals containing more than one year, the rate is calculated as an average yearly rate. (Reprinted with permission from Barbaree & O'Shaughnessy, 2013, p. 958.)

Rapists are Younger Than Child Molesters

In the US, persons under the age of 18 accounted for 15% of all those arrested for the crime of *forcible rape* in 2008 (FBI Uniform Crime Report, 2009). Figure 7.3 plots the rate of arrest for forcible rape per a 100,000 population over the age of the male arrested. As can be seen, the rate of arrest increases from a very low rate for 10 to 12-year-olds to a peak of about 3.5 arrests per a 100,000 population for 18 and 19-year-olds. The rate then decreases with the age of the person arrested. For men aged 25 and older, the annual rate of arrest remains steady at the low rate of one per 100,000.

In contrast to youthful rapists, empirical studies of child molesters appear to show that the average child molester studied is older than 40 years of age. As an illustration of this point, we conducted an informal survey of recent studies of child molesters published in the journal *Sexual Abuse: A Journal of Research and Treatment* and found that the mean age of all but one of the samples of child molesters was over 40, and the exception was near 40 (Elliot, Beech, & Mandeville-Norden, 2013; Long, Alison, & McManus, 2012; McKillop, Smallbone, Wortley, & Andjic, 2012; Schmidt, Gykiere, Vanhoeck, Mann, & Banse, 2014). Mokros, Dombert, Osterheider, Zappalà, and Santtila (2010) compared mean ages of sex offender (child molesters) and non-sex offender volunteers sampled from among patients in a forensic psychiatric hospital at the time of their participation in the research study. Child molesters were older (*Mn* = 42.9 years) compared with the non-sex offenders (*Mn* = 32.3 years).

When direct statistical comparisons have been made comparing the ages of rapists and child molesters, rapists have been found to be younger. For example, Hanson (2002) reported ages at release from custody and compared rapists, extra-familial child molesters, and incest offenders. Rapists (*Mn* = 32.1, *SD* = 8.9) were younger than the extra-familial child molesters (*Mn* = 37.1, *SD* = 11.5) and incest offenders (*Mn* = 38.9, *SD* = 9.9). Due to the large sample sizes, differences between all the groups were statistically significant at $p<.001$ even though the average age difference between the two child molesters groups was only 1.8 years. Feelgood, Cortoni, and Thompson (2005) compared age at assessment among different offender groups and found that child molesters (*Mn* = 43.5 years) were older than rapists (*Mn* = 36.0 years) and non-sexually violent offenders (*Mn* = 31.8 years).

Table 7.4 presents an analysis of age data from our sample, comparing rapists and child molesters. Various measures of age are presented here, including age at index offense, age at assessment, age at first criminal conviction, and age at release from custody. In the table, the sample of 468 sex offenders are divided into four different sex offender subgroups, namely: rapists, extra-familial child molesters, incest offenders, and mixed-age offenders (*rapists* had sexually assaulted adult women, *extra-familial child molesters* had sexually assaulted children outside their own family relationships, *familial child molesters* had sexually assaulted their own biological or step children, and *mixed offenders* had sexually assaulted both female adults and children of either sex). Means and standard deviations for each age variables are given for each sex offender subgroup in our data set. The table also presents the results of t-tests comparing the rapists with the extra-familial child molesters and incest offenders combined. As can be seen, all of these comparisons were statistically significant, and the rapists were found to be younger than the child molesters in every respect.

Another way of looking at this phenomenon is to examine the relative proportion of offenders in subgroups in different-aged cohorts. We divided our illustrative sample into age-at-release cohorts (21–30, 31–40, 41–50, and 51+ years of age at release from custody), as reported in Barbaree, Blanchard, and Langton (2003). Figure 7.4 presents the numbers and percentages of offenders in each sex offender subgroup in each of the four age-at-release cohorts. As can be seen, for offenders released from custody during their 20s, the vast majority (almost 70%) were rapists and mixed offenders, whereas the minority were child molesters (<25%). For offenders released from custody when they were older than 50, the vast majority were child molesters (over 80%), and rapists comprise a small minority of these older offenders (<12%). This finding replicates a previously published report by Dickey, Nussbaum, Chevolleau, and Davidson (2002). They found that the number of rapists among offenders over 40 years of age in their sample was smaller, proportionally, compared with pedophiles and sadists.

Table 7.4 Rapists are younger than child molesters

		Age at:							
		Index offense		*Assessment*		*First criminal conviction*		*Release*	
Sex offender subtypes	N	Mn	SD	Mn	SD	Mn	SD	Mn	SD
Rapists	175	28.9	7.5	32.2	8.1	20.9	6.6	34.8	8.8
Extra-familial child molesters	155	33.0	9.6	40.6	10.7	27.5	11.9	43.1	11.3
Familial child molesters (incest)	93	32.5	7.8	43.7	9.8	31.7	13.9	45.7	9.6
Mixed age victims	45	30.7	8.7	36.5	9.1	22.2	6.6	40.0	11.1
Total	468	31.2	8.6	37.7	10.5	25.4	11.1	40.2	11.0
Contrasts *(t)*		4.44		10.54		8.34		9.54	
df		460		463		463		464	
Significance		<.001		<.001		<.001		<.001	

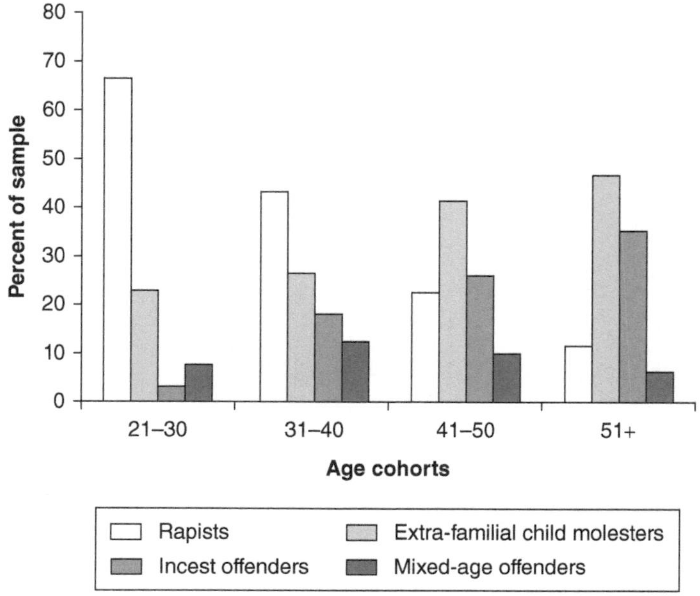

Figure 7.4 The relative proportion of a sex offender sample ($n = 468$) for each offender subtype in each age cohort.

Table 7.5 Sex offender subtypes differ in their Mean Total PCL-R Scores and Factor 2 Scores

		PCL-R		*PCL-R*	
		Total scores		*Factor 2 scores*	
Sex offender subtypes	N	Mn	SD	Mn	SD
Rapists	163	18.85	7.3	8.66	4.1
Extra-familial child molesters	147	15.19	7.2	5.91	4.6
Incest offenders	90	13.34	5.1	4.92	3.5
Mixed offenders	42	18.71	6.1	8.35	3.3
Overall *F* (df)		$F(3,438) = 16.45$ $p<.001$		$F(3,438) = 21.55$ $p<.001$	

Antisocial Orientation is More Prevalent in Rapists and Sexual Deviance is More Prevalent in Child Molesters

Table 7.5 presents a comparison among our sex offender subtypes on their PCL-R scores, both total scores and Factor 2 scores. As can be seen in the

Table, PCL-R total scores and Factor 2 scores differed significantly among the subtypes. Tukey post-hoc comparisons indicated that the rapists (rapists and mixed offenders) had higher total and Factor 2 scores compared with the child molesters (extra-familial and incest offenders). It has been reported previously that rapists are more likely to be diagnosed as antisocial personality disordered than child molesters (Eher, Rettenberger, & Schilling, 2010; Francia et al., 2010).

We then calculated two standardized risk factor scales. Items with positive correlations with age at release ($n = 11$) were combined in the sexual deviance scale, and items with negative correlations with age at release ($n = 20$) were combined in the antisocial behavior scale. For each scale, item scores were standardized then combined to produce a mean standardized score. Table 7.5 presents means and standard deviations for these standardized scale scores comparing four sex offender subgroups. Sex offender subgroups were significantly different in their antisocial behavior and sexual deviance scales, *F*'s (3,464) = 50.75 and 82.68, respectively, both $p<.001$. Post-hoc Tukey tests indicated that rapists and mixed offenders had the highest antisocial behavior scales scores, whereas the familial child molesters had the lowest antisocial behavior scale scores. Extra-familial child molesters and mixed offenders had the highest sexual deviance scale scores, whereas rapists had the lowest sexual deviance scale scores.

Antisocial Orientation is More Prevalent in Younger Offenders and Sexual Deviance is More Prevalent in Older Offenders

Figure 7.5 presents mean scale scores comparing age-at-release cohorts. As reported in Barbaree et al. (2009), age-at-release cohorts differed in

Table 7.6 Sex offender subtypes differ in the risk factor-scale scores: Rapists are higher on antisocial behaviour and lower on sexual deviance

		Risk factor scales			
		Antisocial behavior		*Sexual deviance*	
Sex offender subtypes	N	Mn	SD	Mn	SD
Rapists	175	0.60	0.83	−0.70	0.79
Extra-familial child molesters	155	−0.23	0.93	0.64	0.94
Incest offenders	93	−0.91	0.59	−0.01	0.67
Mixed offenders	45	0.03	0.84	0.54	0.66
Overall *F* (df)		$F_{(3,464)} = 74.82$ $p<.001$		$F_{(3,464)} = 82.68$ $p<.001$	
Planned contrast rapists vs child molesters		$t(464) = -14.15$ $p < .001$		$t(464) = 12.54$ $p < .001$	

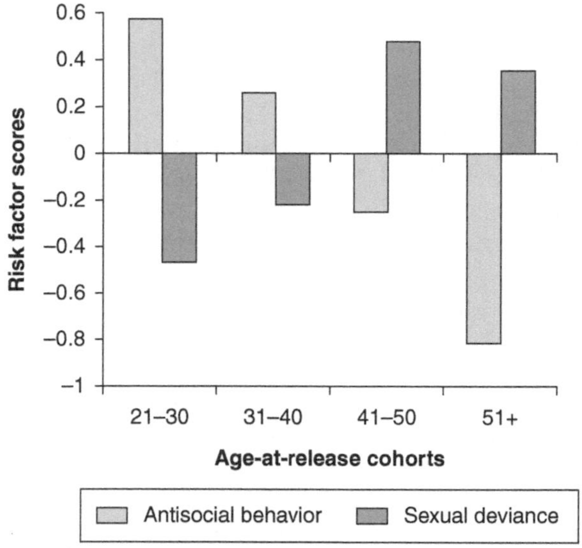

Figure 7.5 The distribution of risk factor scores across-age-at release cohorts.

their antisocial behavior and sexual deviance scale scores, *F*'s (3,464) = 37.40 and 22.71, respectively, both $p<.001$. Partitioning the main effect using trend analysis indicated that, for the antisocial behavior scale, scale scores decreased in a linear fashion from the youngest to the oldest cohort, F_{linear} (1,464) = 144.02, $p<.001$, and deviations from linearity in this relationship were not significant, $F_{non\text{-}linearity}$ (2,464) <1.35, ns. For the sexual deviance scale, scale scores increased from the youngest to oldest cohort. Trend analysis indicated a significant linear trend, F_{linear} (1,464)= 64.00, $p<.001$, but the trend included a significant non-linear component, $F_{non\text{-}linearity}$ (2, 464) = 7.63, $p<.01$. Post-hoc comparisons using the Tukey test indicated that the two older age-at-release cohorts had significantly higher sexual deviance scale scores compared with the two younger age-at-release cohorts.

Figure 7.5 nicely illustrates the significant and opposite correlations between each risk factor domain and age at release. Actuarial items reflecting antisocial orientation are negatively correlated with age at release because these items are more likely to be scored positively when assessing younger offenders. Similarly, actuarial items reflecting sexual deviance are positively correlated with age at release because these items are more likely to be scored positively when assessing older offenders.

The Effects of Aging are Embedded in ARAI Scores

Barbaree and his colleagues (2007, 2008, 2009) went on to argue that, because of the confound, the effect of aging was embedded in actuarial risk item scores. They argued that if aging has the effect of decreasing recidivism risk, then antisocial items were helped by aging and sexual deviance items were hampered by aging in their prediction of recidivism. For antisocial items, there were two risk factors contributing to their predictive ability, antisocial orientation and a young age. For sexual deviance items, higher scores for sexual deviance predict recidivisms while the effects of aging counteracted that effect.

To test this hypothesis, Barbaree et al. used semi-partial correlation as a statistical technique to separate the effects of aging from actuarial risk. They regressed item scores on age at release and saved the residuals as age-corrected actuarial scores. Barbaree et al. reported that for the VRAG/SORAG (Barbaree et al., 2007), the SVR-20 (Barbaree et al., 2008), and the five most often used actuarial instruments for sex offenders (Barbaree et al., 2009), age-corrected actuarial items were modified in their ability to predict recidivism. For antisocial items, age correction had the effect of reducing their predictive ability. This makes sense if the original scores were predictive on the basis of antisocial orientation and aging. With age correction, the remaining scores had only the antisocial orientation factor to lead to their prediction of recidivism. For sexual deviance items, age correction had the effect of improving their predictive ability. This makes sense if the original sexual deviance scores were hampered by aging. Removing the effects of aging made these items more able to predict recidivism (see Barbaree et al., 2007, 2008, 2009).

Factor Analyses of Actuarial Item Scores

If there was a straightforward relationship between actuarial item scores and risk factors, certain statistical analyses would likely reflect those relationships. For example, factor analyses of actuarial item scores would be expected to find clusters of items coalescing around underlying risk factors. Indeed, the empirical literature confirms this expectation. Using a sample of sex offenders from the UK, Roberts, Doren, and Thornton (2002) factor analyzed 10 actuarial items taken from the Static-99 and an actuarial instrument widely used in the UK, the Risk Matrix 2000. This analysis resulted in three clearly identifiable factors: general criminality, sexual deviance, and detachment. These authors used factor scores in a logistic regression analysis to predict sexual recidivism. In this analysis, all three factors were unique significant predictors of sexual recidivism.

Three factor analyses of actuarial items have been reported using sub-samples of the participant sample used in the demonstrations presented here (our illustrative data set). First, Langton, Harkins, Peacock, and Barbaree (2003) conducted a principal component analysis (PCA) of 31 non-redundant actuarial items from four actuarial risk instruments (SORAG, 11 items; RRASOR, two items; Static-99, two items; MnSOST-R, 10 items) and one guided clinical risk assessment instrument (six items, VASOR; McGrath, Hoke, Livingston, & Cumming, 2001). Langton et al. found three clearly identifiable factors: sexual deviance, lifestyle maladjustment/instability, and detached predatory behavior, replicating the results reported by Roberts et al. (2002). In a Cox regression analysis, sexual deviance was a significant predictor of sexual recidivism, while lifestyle maladjustment/instability and detached predatory behavior were significant predictors of serious (violent plus sexual) recidivism. Second, as part of a study attempting to optimize predictive accuracy using combinations of actuarial information, Seto (2005) conducted a PCA on 19 rationally selected actuarial scale items, resulting in three interpretable factors: antisociality, atypical sexual interests, and demographics. Finally, Barbaree, Langton, and Peacock (2006) conducted a PCA using the 38 non-redundant static items contained in the five actuarial instruments that have been shown to have predictive ability (VRAG, SORAG, RRASOR, Static-99, and MnSOST-R). These authors found six interpretable components: antisocial behavior, child sexual abuse, persistence, detached predatory behavior, young and single, and male victim(s). Using receiver operator characteristic (ROC) analysis, they found that antisocial behavior was a significant predictor of violent recidivism, whereas persistence and child sexual abuse were significant predictors of sexual recidivism.

Factor Analysis of Age-Corrected ARAI Items

Barbaree and Langton (unpublished manuscript) reasoned that if the effects of aging are embedded in actuarial item scores, these factor analyses on uncorrected actuarial item scores would likely be somewhat compromised. They reasoned that a factor analysis on age-corrected items scores might be more informative. The following section of the chapter presents a summary of their findings. They conducted a PCA on the age-corrected actuarial items (residuals) from Barbaree et al. (2007, 2008, 2009). The following three tables present the resulting 13 factors, organized according to conceptual meaning. The first table presents factors relating to the risk factor domain "unstable and antisocial lifestyle." The next two tables present factors relating to the risk factor domain "sexual deviance." The factor analysis revealed a sexual deviance factor that would be expected from our earlier discussion, and this factor has to do with the deviance of sexual interests. But the factor analysis also revealed three factors that had to do with the impulsivity of the sexual offenses.

Table 7.7 presents six factors relating to antisocial and unstable behavior. These items in their totality are reminiscent of Factor 2 of the PCL-R, including general criminality and unstable deviant lifestyle. The first of the six factors includes all items relating to non-sexual criminal convictions, and high scores on this factor would indicate a high degree of general criminality. Then, the remaining factors reflect unstable lifestyle,

Table 7.7 Risk factor domain: Antisocial and unstable lifestyle

Factor	*ARAI*	*Item #*	*Item details*	*Factor loading*	*Eigen-value*	*% of variance*
2	Risk Factor Propensity: Non-Sexual Criminal Convictions				3.120	7.270
	SVR-20	9	Past non-sexual violent offenses	0.890		
	Static-99	4	Prior non-sexual violence—Any convict	0.882		
	SORAG	5	Cormier-Lang Score for non-violent offenses	0.544		
	Static-99	6	Prior sentencing dates	0.531		
	SVR-20	10	Past non-violent offenses	0.473		
4	Risk Factor Propensity: Substance Abuse				2.580	6.000
	SVR-20	5	Substance abuse problems	0.810		
	SORAG	3	History of alcohol problems	0.800		
	MnSOST-F	11	Pattern of drug or alcohol abuse	0.705		
5	Risk Factor Propensity: Non-Compliance With Supervision				2.350	5.470
	SVR-20	11	Past supervision failure	0.812		
	SORAG	9	Failure on conditional release	0.756		
	MnSOST-F	3	Under supervision when they committed any sex	0.705		
6	Risk Factor Propensity: Anti-Social Developmental Trajectory				2.070	4.830
	MnSOST-F	10	Adolescent antisocial behavior in the file	0.610		
	SORAG	1	Lived with both biological parents to age 16	0.605		
	SORAG	2	Elementary school maladjustment	0.587		
	SVR-20	6	Suicidal/homicidal ideation	0.568		
	SORAG	14	PCL-R score	0.406		
10	Risk Factor Propensity: Employment Instability				1.770	4.110
	MnSOST-F	12	Employment history	0.846		
	SVR-20	8	Employment problems	0.683		
8	Risk Factor Propensity: Marital Status				1.980	4.600
	Static-99	2	Ever lived with a lover for at least 2 years	0.855		
	SORAG	4	Marital status	0.854		

Table 7.8 Risk factor domain: Deviant sexual behaviour

Factor	*ARAI*	*Item #*	*Item details*	*Factor loading*	*Eigen-value*	*% of variance*
7	Risk Factor Propensity: Male Child Victim				2.050	4.770
	Static-99	10	Any male victim	0.825		
	VRAG	9	Sex of victim	0.819		
	SORAG	8	History of sex offenses against only females	0.516		
13	Risk Factor Propensity: Pedo-Hebephilia				1.480	3.440
	MnSOST-R	8	Offended against a 13–15-year-old victim	0.790		
	MnSOST-R	7	Number of different age groups victimized	0.563		
11	Risk Factor Propensity: Deviant Sexual Preferences					
	SORAG	13	Deviant sexual preferences	0.813	1.670	3.870
	SVR-20	1	Sexual deviation	0.696		
12	Risk Factor Propensity: Violence During Sexual Offenses				1.580	3.660
	SVR-20	15	Use of weapons or threats of death in sex offenses	0.661		
	Static-99	4	Index non-sexual violence	0.609		

including substance abuse, non-compliance with supervision, developmental factors leading to antisocial orientation, and problems with meeting adult responsibilities.

Table 7.8 presents four sexual deviance factors reflecting deviant sexual behavior. These include deviance with respect to male child victims, sexual behavior directed toward children, deviant sexual preferences as reflected in phallometric laboratory assessment, and the use of force or violence in the commission of sexual offenses.

Table 7.9 presents factors that reflect impulsivity or lack of control over sexual impulses. The first factor is titled "high drive-impaired inhibition." The first item is from the SVR-20 and reflects an increasing frequency and severity of sexual offending. The second factor reflects a failure in inhibition by the fact that the individual is offending against strangers in a public place. Finally, the third factor reflects a failure in inhibition in the sense that the individual is offending despite being apprehended, charged, and convicted for a sexual offense in the past.

Conceptually Meaningful Risk Scales Predict Recidivism

Factor analysis of age-corrected actuarial items takes the information contained in actuarial item scores and reorganizes the information into multiple conceptually meaningful scales. The question arises: do these conceptually meaningful scales predict recidivism, and if so, do they do so as well as the original actuarial instruments from which they were derived? Barbaree and Langton (unpublished manuscript) combined factor scores for each of the risk factor propensity scales in the previous three tables to calculate standardized scale scores for each of the risk factor domains contained in Tables 7.7 to 7.9. Table 7.10 presents AUCs for each of the risk factor domain scale scores, a standardized scale representing age at release ($Z_{\text{age risk}} = Z_{\text{age at release}} \times (-1)$), and a scale that represents a combination of the four risk scales.

As can be seen, the familiar risk factor domain of antisocial orientation is a significant predictor of both sexual and violent recidivism, and the sexual impulsivity risk factor domain is predictive of sexual recidivism, as we would expect. Age at release is predictive of both sexual and violent recidivism. Importantly, the combination scale has an AUC of 0.71 for both sexual and violent recidivism, which is equivalent to the AUCs we reviewed in Chapter 5 (Tables 5.5 and 5.6) and the actuarial instruments' ability to predict recidivism in our own sample (Barbaree, Seto, Langton, & Peacock, 2001; Langton et al. 2007). Barbaree and his colleagues have taken the information contained in actuarial item scores and partitioned this into conceptually meaningful risk factors. Partitioning was done by removing the effects of aging from the actuarial item scores and adding the effects of aging back as an independent risk factor.

Table 7.9 Risk factor domain: Sexual impulsivity

Factor	*ARAI*	*Item*	*Item details*	*Factor loading*	*Eigen-value*	*% of variance*
1	Risk Factor Propensity: High Drive-Impaired Inhibition				3.220	7.480
	SVR-20	16	Escalation in frequency and severity of sex offenses	0.789		
	MnSOST-R	1	Number of sex-related convictions incl index	0.732		
	SVR-20	12	High-density sex offenses	0.704		
	MnSOST-R	2	Length of sex-offending history (1–6 years)	0.589		
	MnSOST-R	6	Multiple acts on a single victim	0.531		
	SVR-20	13	Multiple sex offense types	0.516		
3	Risk Factor Propensity: Stranger Assault in a Public Place				2.780	6.460
	MnSOST-R	9	Stranger victim	0.928		
	Static-99	9	Any stranger victim	0.927		
	MnSOST-R	4	Sex offense committed in a public place	0.548		
	Static-99	8	Any unrelated victim	0.433		
9	Risk Factor Propensity: Persistence Despite Punishment				1.860	4.330
	SORAG	7	Number of convictions for sex offenses prior to index	0.721		
	Static-99	5	Prior sex offenses	0.691		

Table 7.10 Conceptually meaningful risk factor domain scales predicting sexual and violent recidivism

Derived scales	*AUCs for sexual recidivism*	*AUCs for violent recidivism*
Antisocial orientation scale	.61*	.66***
Sexual deviance scale	.57	.50
Sexual impulsivity scale	.64**	.57
Age-at-release scale	.61*	.69***
Combination scale	.71***	.71***

Notes
*$p<.05$
**$p<.01$
***$p<.001$

Conceptually Meaningful Risk Factors: Static Versus Dynamic Risk

Over the past 15 years, a great deal of work in the field of risk assessment for sex offenders has attempted to identify dynamic risk factors (e.g., Hanson & Harris, 2000, Hanson, Harris, Scott, & Helmus, 2007). This area of the field has been predicated on the idea that the actuarial risk instruments were based entirely on static risk and that the actuarial instruments did not allow for measuring change due to treatment or intervention. The STABLE-2007 and the ACUTE-2007 were designed to assess and monitor changes in risk status over time by assessing "dynamic" risk factors. These risk factors were divided into two categories depending on how stable the behaviors were. "Stable" dynamic risk factors were described as skill deficits or learned behaviors that correlate with sexual recidivism but that can be changed through treatment or supervision. Examples of stable dynamic risk factors are sexual preoccupations or lack of concern for others. "Acute" dynamic risk factors were thought to be transient states that would only last hours or days. Examples of acute dynamic risk factors are alcohol intoxication or anger. These factors are rapidly changing intrapersonal stresses perhaps triggered by environmental conditions or events that have been shown by empirical research to be related to sexual re-offense (Hanson & Morton-Bourgon, 2005). Hanson, Harris, Scott, and Helmus (2007) describe the development of the STABLE-2007 and ACUTE-2007 instruments for evaluating these dynamic risk factors. Their research indicates that these instruments produce AUC values for sexual re-offense of .76. STABLE-2007 and ACUTE-2007 assessments were found to add predictive power above and beyond that available to assessments of static risk alone (based on the Static-99).

Table 7.11 Items from current risk assessment instruments for sex offenders

Stability of item response	*Static*[1]	*Stable*[2]	*Acute*[3]
Conceptually meaningful risk factor domains			
Antisocial and unstable lifestyle	Non-sexual criminal convictions		Substance abuse
	Substance abuse	Lack of concern for others	Rejection of supervision
	Non-compliance with supervision	Lack of cooperation with supervision	
	Antisocial developmental trajectory		
	Employment instability		
Sexual deviance	Male child victim	Sexual pre-occupations	Sexual pre-occupations
	Pedo-hebephilia		
	Deviant sexual preferences		
	Violence during sexual offenses	Hostility toward women	
Sexual impulsivity	High drive/impaired inhibition	Poor cognitive problem solving Sex as coping	
	Stranger assault in a public place		
	Persistence despite punishment		
Social relations	Marital status	Negative social influences Rejection/loneliness	
Emotional state		Negative emotion/ hostility	Emotional collapse hostility
Environment			Victim access Collapse of social supports

Notes
1From a PCA of static items (Barbaree & Langton, unpublished manuscript) contained in the most commonly used actuarial instrument for sex offenders
2From the STABLE-2007
3From the ACUTE-2007

Our development of conceptually meaningful risk factors based on the factor analysis of age-corrected actuarial items provides us with an opportunity to describe the relationship between static, stable, and acute risk factors. Table 7.10 presents these risk factors in a matrix. Along the horizontal dimension, the stability of the risk factors varies from static to stable to acute. The risk factor domains as presented above are listed in the vertical dimension.

A theory of recidivism risk in sex offenders would assist in the rationalization of assessment items along the item stability dimension within risk factor domains and propensities. Current ARAIs contain items that record historical behaviors that cannot be changed, and these are required to make long-term predictions. Current measures of dynamic risk contain items worded in such a way as to allow recording changes in behavior. A good theory of recidivism risk would guide the development of further items of both a static and dynamic nature.

Summary and Conclusions

In this chapter, we identified a number of serious problems encountered with ARAIs, and suggested that these problems are due, at least in part, to the fact that the ARAIs were developed in the absence of any theory of recidivism risk. One of the critical consequences of this circumstance is that we know little about the relationship between ARAI items and putative risk factors. Much of the current chapter examined the relationship between ARAI items and the risk factors, antisocial orientation and sexual deviation. We referred to these as risk domains. This examination was a review of the logic and findings reported earlier by Barbaree and his colleagues (Barbaree et al., 2007, 2008, 2009).

We described the confound between aging and the risk factors, and described how the effects of aging on recidivism risk are embedded in actuarial scores. We described in some detail how Barbaree and his colleagues demonstrated the statistical separation of the aging effects from the risk factors. We described a PCA (Barbaree & Langton, unpublished manuscript) that showed how the actuarial items coalesced around conceptually meaningful risk factor propensities (Mann et al., 2010), and how the risk factor propensity scores predicted sexual recidivism with AUCs as high as those obtained with the original ARAIs. We showed how the conceptually meaningful risk factors mapped onto the empirically validated dynamic risk factors that have been proposed on the basis of theory.

We have maintained that although the ARAIs were developed without theory, ARAI data can be analyzed in such a way as to uncover the relationship between item scores and theoretical constructs. This leads to the possibility of using ARAI data to test hypotheses derived from theory and to build and validate a theory of recidivism risk.

We have adopted the theoretical position that views recidivism risk as if it were organized in a hierarchy, with the superordinate risk factor domains, aging, antisocial orientation, and sexual deviation, as containing risk factor propensities. The Barbaree and Langton factor analysis sorted ARAI items into conceptually meaningful risk factor propensities that could be easily sorted conceptually into the two risk factor domains, antisocial orientation and sexual deviance.

The reorganization of actuarial "statistical information" into conceptually meaningful scales means that a risk assessment can be much more informative. Imagine an ARAI assessment that not only tells you where the offender is ranked in terms of risk, but also provides his percentile rank on scales derived from the risk factor domains. Evaluators could present a risk profile and integrate the risk factor information into a narrative account of the underlying risk factors leading to his level of risk. Clinicians could use the profile in their case formulation, and treatment providers could use the profile to begin to identify likely criminogenic needs. Additional testing with the dynamic risk instruments could elaborate on the formulation and identification of treatment targets.

As we began the chapter, so will we close it, by saying that the development of the ARAIs has been the single most significant development in Forensic Psychology. However, we believe that further development and improvement of risk assessment demands the use of a good theory of recidivism risk, and the theory must be tied to the instruments that we use.

8

RISK JUDGMENTS UNDER CONDITIONS OF UNCERTAINTY

Heuristics and Biases

Perched on the Rocky Shoals of Risky Decision-Making

There is no better way to introduce this chapter than to frame the often subtle ambiguity of the examiner's forensic role with the sage advice of Murray Cohen and his colleagues over 35 years ago:

> It is a perilous, narrow path between the requirements of social order and the expression of individual freedom. To balance order and liberty properly is a sociopolitical, not a clinical issue, and this must be done by society's courts and legislatures. The clinician should neither be given nor attempt to usurp society's right to determine the risks it is willing to take in resolving the conflict between safety and liberty.
>
> (1978, p. 39)

Risk and risk assessment are terms deeply embedded in the vocabulary of forensic practice. As Cohen, Groth, and Siegel pointed out in 1978, and Monahan (1985) several years later, it falls entirely within the province of lawmakers and adjudicators to affix the bright lines of risk and to judge those defendants who cross the lines. The task of the forensic examiner would be clarified, albeit perhaps not simplified, if assessment of risk was replaced, as Monahan (1985) long ago suggested, with "providing an estimate of the probability of future violent behavior" (p. 10). It would be up to the court to decide if the estimated probability "crossed the line." Although the distinction itself may seem subtle, it would remove, or at least reduce, the examiner's psychological burden of determining whether the defendant is *too risky* to be returned to society. *That decision* would be left to the court.

As it stands, however, forensic examiners routinely provide risk assessments, and it is with the larger problem of how such assessments may be improved that we begin by discussing how such assessments unwittingly fall victim to the common missteps of human judgment. These missteps take the form of biases and heuristics. Deriving from the same Greek word for *eureka*, heuristics, in the vernacular, are simply precepts or maxims with no scientific basis, often called "rules of thumb." Hastie and Dawes (2010) referred to our "*cognitive toolbox* of mental heuristics stored in long-term memory," cognitive tools that "are efficient, but sometimes inaccurate procedures for solving a problem . . . *cognitive tools* [that] are acquired over a lifetime of experience" (p. 88). These "evolved capacities," as Gigerenzer (2008a) referred to them, are "frugal" (based on limited information).

Kahneman and Tversky (1972), who devoted their careers to explicating the nuances of rational decision-making with limited information under conditions of uncertainty, underscored the occasional downside to heuristics, noting that when judgments are made under conditions of uncertainty, we do not "follow the calculus of chance or the statistical theory of prediction. Instead, [we] rely on a limited number of *heuristics* which sometimes yield reasonable judgments and sometimes lead to severe and systematic errors" (p. 237). Heuristics are an integral part of the human condition; most of the time they serve us well, assisting with quick, adequate answers. Under specifiable conditions, such as uncertainty and, in particular, uncertainty compounded by risk, heuristics can lead us astray, and the results, as Kahneman and Tversky noted, can be severe. "Heuristics are very useful things, but they necessarily produce biases and blind spots. For instance, the heuristic 'When you encounter a dangerous animal, run away!' is often a useful guide but not when you meet a grizzly bear" (Silver, 2012, p. 267).

Heuristics reduce complexity in the decision-making process, generally to a constructive end. As Silver (2012) points out, even the grand masters of chess rely on heuristics. For Silver, chess is exemplary of the constraints on the human capacity for processing information. Although chess, as a game, is deterministic, the complexity of the options demands heuristics, even for the grand masters. Forecasting weather, at least in theory, is also deterministic. The problem is not so much the limitations of information processing; the much greater problem is incomplete or imperfect knowledge. In particular, knowledge about "initial conditions" (discussed shortly as the butterfly effect) is lacking. In the case of predicting risk of criminal behavior, it is woefully lacking. We argue that this simple principle of Lorenz—that small changes in input can rapidly produce large changes in output—is an Achilles heel of risk prediction.

From a theoretical standpoint, the most influential contribution to understanding accuracy and bias in human judgment is signal detection theory (Green & Swets, 1966; Swets, 1992). A starting assumption of signal detection theory (SDT) is that the preponderance of all human reasoning and decision-making occurs with some degree of uncertainty. For SDT, uncertainty is noise, and the task is to identify the signal against a background of noise. Given the presence of uncertainty or noise, SDT offers a precise methodology for examining the accuracy of decision-making. Noise is defined essentially as anything that complicates detection of the signal by introducing uncertainty as to whether the signal is present.

In SDT, typically the forecast or decision as well as the outcome ("truth") are binary. As with all 2 × 2 contingency tables, the options are limited to four possibilities: (1) the individual detected the signal when it was present (a "hit" or True Positive), (2) the individual failed to detect a signal and the signal was in fact absent (a "correct rejection" or True Negative), (3) the individual reported detecting a signal when in fact there was no signal (Error: "false alarm" or False Positive), and (4) the individual failed to detect a signal when one was present (Error: "miss" or False Negative). In SDT, the two critical values are the "Hit" rate and the "False Alarm" rate, yielding a PPP index or Positive Predictive Power (Hits / (Hits + False Alarms) × 100). PPP = the accuracy of predictions that individuals will detect the signal when present. In the current case, this is the accuracy of predictions that individuals will be violent or will re-offend. In SDT, a receiver operating characteristic (ROC) curve is fitted by plotting the hits against the false alarms for different values of the criterion (e.g. different ROC curves would be plotted for different signal strengths).

In the present context, a "hit" is a correct judgment that the "signal" (violence or high risk) is present, and background noise is everything that undermines the accuracy of those judgments. Noise could be easily (and obviously) understood as misleading evidence introduced at trial or used as a foundation for reaching and supporting a judgment. Noise can also be the myriad biases or heuristics that steer us away from accurate judgments. It is to those sources of noise that this chapter is devoted.

Wray Herbert (2010) recounted a compelling story of three savvy backcountry skiers who ventured out to the virgin slopes of Utah's Wasatch Mountain Range on February 12, 1995. The most experienced of the three was Steve Carruthers. Carruthers had skied these same mountains many times before. A storm had left around two feet of new snow the day before. After about two hours of skiing, the three stopped and talked about the best ways to traverse the mountains. Within one hour of discussing their strategy, the skiers set off an avalanche and Carruthers was dead. The area where the skiers were was well known as avalanche terrain, and the timing was bad—February was known as high risk. Ian

McCammon, a friend of Carruthers, an experienced backcountry skier and a scientist, set out to understand what went wrong. McCammon examined the details of 700 avalanches in which there were fatalities. He coded risk factors associated with the avalanches and as much information as was available on the 1,355 skiers that died. McCammon published his findings in a paper titled "Evidence of heuristic traps in recreational avalanche accidents." He had found six "poor choices" that should not have been made by experienced skiers. These poor choices or shortcuts to quick decision-making are heuristics. Herbert (2010) described a few of them:

> Consider the "familiarity heuristic" . . . if something comes quickly to mind, trust it. It must be available in your memory for a reason, so go with it. The basic rule of thumb is that familiar equals better equals safer. That's a very useful rule for, say, grocery shopping . . . . It's also a useful rule for ER physicians, airline pilots, and soccer players—people who have to make rapid-fire decisions and are trained to quickly identify familiar patterns and react . . . . They [the 3 skiers] were so familiar with the terrain that it seemed safe—simply because it always had been safe before. It was familiar, and thus unthreatening . . . . So, familiarity and comfort can be traps. But the fact is, Carruther's decision-making really started to go wrong long before he even started waxing his skis. It started when . . . he or one of his buddies said, "Hey, let's take a run out to Gobbler's Knob tomorrow." At that point, they triggered another powerful cognitive tool, known as the "default heuristic" or "consistency heuristic" . . . once they made that initial decision, the cold calculation stopped . . . we have a powerful bias for sticking with what we already have, not switching course . . . we rely on stay-the-course impulses all the time, often with good results. Constant switching can be perilous, in everything from financial matters to romantic judgments, so we have become averse to hopping around.
>
> (p. 12)

Overview and Historical Perspective

Scholarship on judgment and decision-making has evolved over the past six decades, with at least four epochs of seminal contributions:

1 Paul Meehl's 1954 classic monograph *Clinical Versus Statistical Prediction: A Theoretical Analysis and a Review of the Evidence*;

Ward Edwards' 1954 Psychological Bulletin article "The Theory of Decision Making" (cf. Weiss & Weiss, 2009); Meehl and Rosen's (1955) *Psychological Bulletin* article on antecedent probability; Herbert Simon's 1955 paper on bounded rationality "which in effect defines the problem that the field has been trying to solve ever since" (Kahneman, 1991, p. 142) (cf. Rancan's (2013) article on the contributions of Franco Modigliani and Simon to the use of decision theory under uncertainty for behavioral economics).

2 The early papers by Daniel Kahneman and Amos Tversky (e.g. Kahneman & Tversky, 1972, 1973; Tversky & Kahneman, 1971, 1972, 1973, 1974), and a remarkably prescient article by Saleem Shah in 1978 citing Kahneman and Tversky's 1973 *Psychological Review* article and Tversky and Kahneman's 1974 article in *Science.*

3 John Monahan's classic 1981 book *Predicting Violent Behavior: An Assessment of Clinical Techniques*, Monahan's 1984 paper in the *American Journal of Psychiatry* and a chapter by Monahan in Charles Patrick Ewing's 1985 book *Psychology, Psychiatry, and the Law: A Clinical and Forensic Handbook.*

4 A veritable explosion of influential, innovative books on risk and decision-making from 2000 to the present, a sampling of which includes: Ariely, 2008; Baumeister & Tierney, 2011; Belsky & Gilovich, 2000; Coates, 2012; Dawes, 2001; Fischhoff, 2012; Fischhoff & Kadvany, 2011; Gigerenzer, 2002, 2007, 2008b; Hastie & Dawes, 2010; Kahneman, 2011; Kasperson & Kasperson, 2005a, 2005b; Lichtenstein & Slovic, 2006; Pidgeon, Kasperson, & Slovic, 2003; Posner, 2010; Reyna & Zayas, 2014; Roeser, 2010; Silver, 2012; Slovic, 2000, 2010; Taleb, 2007; Tetlock, 2005.

There are many more that could be included, and we apologize for inadvertent and unintended omissions.

The message seems clear: the confluence of highly sophisticated, programmatic research over the past six decades has culminated in a rich trove of documented findings on many aspects of risky decision-making, related heuristics and biases, and decisions made under varying conditions of uncertainty. Chapter 8 takes advantage of some of this empirical largess and applies it to a unique problem—*not* Wall Street traders, *not* lay investors, *not* gamblers, *not* meteorologists, *not* geologists, *not* environmental or health hazard scientists, *not* professional athletes, but to those who evaluate risk posed by sex offenders.

Evaluation of *risk* in sex offenders invariably boils down to one key question—what is the likelihood of a future sex offense? The ability of mental health professionals to accomplish this task proficiently and reliably has been the subject of interminable debate and controversy, and yet necessity dictates that the practice must continue. Since this niche of risky decision-making has not, by and large, been the beneficiary of the past half-century of research on decision-making, it is our goal to introduce the reader to some of the pivotal findings that bear on the evaluation of risk of "dangerousness" behavior. As one could readily imagine, covering 50 years of complex research would necessitate vastly more space than we have been allotted by our publisher. As a compromise, we touch only briefly on selected important heuristics and areas of bias, and (hopefully) connect the dots to evaluation of criminal behavior.

Meehl: A Watershed Moment and the Ensuing Great Debate

If there is one single catalyst for the clinical vs. actuarial debate it must be Paul Meehl's 1954 monograph on clinical vs. statistical prediction. The evidence presented by Meehl in 1954 alone would seem sufficient to have characterized the case as "open and closed." In the 1996 preface to the re-printing of Meehl's book, he says:

> This little book made me famous—in some quarters infamous—overnight; but while almost all of the numerous prizes and awards that my profession has seen fit to bestow upon me mention this among my contributions, the practicing profession and a large segment—perhaps the majority—of academic clinicians either ignore it entirely or attempt to ward off its arguments, analyses, or empirical facts. Thus I am in the unusual position of being socially reinforced for writing something that hardly anybody believes!

Two years later, delivering the Cattel Award address before the Association for Psychological Science in Chicago, Meehl (May 23, 1998) once again remarked, "The clinical-statistical problem has also been solved, although most clinicians haven't caught on yet. . . . I do not know of any controversy in the social sciences in which the evidence is so massive, diverse, and consistent" (p. 6). Meehl cited in his talk a major meta-analysis of 136 empirical studies covering a wide predictive domain; in no more than 5% of these 136 studies was the clinician's judgment more accurate than statistical prediction rule-based decisions (Grove, Zald, Lebow, Snitz, & Nelson, 2000). Meehl then queried whether 1,360 studies might be adequate to convince the skeptics. Three years later, Dvoskin and Heilbrun (2001) observed that the "Great Debate" lives on.

That same year, Monahan and his veritable A-Team of colleagues (Monahan et al., 2001) concluded that "the general superiority of statistical over clinical risk assessment in the behavioral sciences has been known for almost half a century" (p. 7). Prentky, Janus, Barbaree, Schwartz, and Kafka (2006) noted similarly that "the predictive efficacy of actuarial methods of risk assessment is superior to clinically derived assessments of risk. In large measure, the superiority of actuarial risk assessment arises from the elimination or reduction of the many sources of error" (p. 372). The sheer number and diversity of papers/books weighing in on this "Great Debate" are truly remarkable (e.g. Dawes, Faust, & Meehl, 1989, 1992; Dershowitz, 1970; Diamond, 1974; Dvoskin & Heilbrun, 2001; Ennis & Litwack, 1974; Falzer, 2013; Grove & Meehl, 1996; Gardner, Lidz, Mulvey, & Shaw, 1996; Grove et al., 2000; Harcourt, 2007; Hastie & Dawes, 2010; Kahneman & Tversky, 1982; Klein, 1976; Kleinmuntz, 1968a; LaFond, 2005; Lidz, Mulvey, & Gardner, 1993; Litwack & Schlesinger, 1999; Meehl, 1954; Monahan, 1976, 1981; Monahan & Steadman, 1994a; Monahan et al., 2001; Plous, 1993; Price, 1997; Quinsey & Maguire, 1986; Sarbin, 1943, 1944; Swets, Dawes, & Monahan, 2000; Wollert, 2001).

In 1976 Klein posed the question: "Given the conclusiveness of the evidence that through either clinical or actuarial techniques we are unable to accurately predict violent behavior, the question of why this is so still remains" (p. 117). By way of answering his own question, Klein quoted from the 1948 publication *Assessment of Men: Selection of Personnel for the Office of Strategic Services*, a document of the problems encountered recruiting (and predicting) the best candidates for the needs of the war effort, particularly selecting ideal candidates for clandestine and covert operations:

> It is easy to predict precisely the outcome of the meeting of one known chemical with another known chemical in an immaculate test tube. But where is the chemist who can predict what will happen to a known chemical if it meets an unknown vessel? And even if all the properties of all the chemicals resident in a given laboratory are exactly defined, is there a chemist who can predict every chemical engagement that will take place if Chance, the blind technician, is in charge of the proceedings?
>
> (p. 8)

Klein (1976) drew from this passage *interactivity* (complex interactions): "When people interact, they do not interact as do two known chemicals in the immaculate test tube" (p. 117). Klein went on to say:

> Until such time as we can predict with accuracy what is now the unpredictable—the social situations which one will meet in the future—it is unlikely that we shall be able to predict violence with the degree of accuracy which is necessary if we are to justify intrusive forms of social control.
>
> (p. 117–118)

Some commentators have been unabashedly sardonic, as in the comment of Kleinmuntz (1968b) that:

> Clinicians tenaciously cling to the opinion that patients communicate with, or signal to, them in numerous nonverbal modes, and they tend to believe that they must see, and sometimes even "smell out," their patients' diseases in order to arrive at an accurate diagnosis.
>
> (p. 149)

The Ennis and Litwack (1974) paper on "flipping coins in the courtroom" has often been cited, as has Monahan's (1976) now antiquated conclusion that dangerousness as a criterion for civil commitment was "doomed." Even Hastie and Dawes (2010) were prompted to remark that: "There are many reasons for the resistance to actuarial, statistical judgment models. First of all, they are an affront to the narcissism (and a threat to the income) of many experts" (p. 62). Others have been more charitable. Kahneman, Slovic, and Tversky (1982c) stated in the Preface to their book, for example, that the "furious controversy" inspired by Meehl's 1954 book

> was probably *not* the demonstration that clinicians performed poorly in tasks that they should not have undertaken. Rather, it was the demonstration of a substantial discrepancy between the objective record of people's success in prediction tasks and the sincere beliefs of these people about the quality of their performance.

Clearly, the broader question, inspiring this Great Debate, has been the question of whether mental health professionals are equipped to be making these judgments at all. Monahan and Cummings concluded in 1975 that "The empirical fact of the invalidity of violence prediction suggests that neither the interests of society nor the interests of the identified individual are being served by social policies based on the prediction of violence" (p. 162). The respective professional organizations (American Psychiatric Association, 1974; American Psychological Association, 1978) registered their concerns. Ned Megargee (1981) quipped, "The identification of the potentially violent individual with sufficient accuracy to warrant preventative detention . . . is an impossible quest" (p. 181), prompting Grisso and Appelbaum (1992) to ponder whether it is in fact unethical to make predictions of future violence. Parenthetically, they concluded that it was *not* unethical. The most damning statements, however, appear in the early papers of Chuck Ewing (1983, 1985), who did find that auguring such predictions was unethical: "The psychiatrist or psychologist who makes a prediction of dangerousness violates his or her ethical obligation to register judgments that rest on a scientific basis" (1983, p. 418). And by 1984 Monahan observed: "Dark clouds began to form in our crystal balls" (p. 10). These same troubling questions were re-visited again 12 years later by Mossman and Hart (1996).

One of the few commentators of the time who was supportive of the special disciplinary expertise of mental health professionals was Tom Litwack (1984), who reminded us that psychiatrists and psychologists possess unique skills such as conducting clinical/forensic interviews and psychological testing that laypersons do not possess. Mulvey and Lidz (1985) described two factions at the time: "abolitionists" who held that *dangerousness* as a criterion was hopelessly mired in methodological and operational quicksand and, as such, should be discarded as a standard for civil commitment; the counterargument came from the "ameliorationists" who held that mental health professionals could not possibly disown the responsibility for evaluating *dangerous* people, and the only reasonable course of action was to improve the efficacy of their decisions. None other than the unlikely ameliorationist Robyn Dawes (1982) agreed, remarking that:

> People are important. The statistical model may integrate the information in an optimal manner, but it is always the individual (judge, clinician, subject) who chooses the variables. Moreover, it is the human judge who knows the directional relationship between the predictor variables and the criterion of interest or who can code the variables in such a way that they have clear directional relationships. The linear model cannot replace the expert in deciding such things as "what to look for," but it is precisely this knowledge of what to look for in reaching the decision that is the special expertise people have.
>
> (p. 394)

Perhaps the most moderating voice was that of Saleem Shah, who, long before it was fashionable to entertain a "middle ground" between clinical and mechanical judgment, argued that "there is no reason why information provided by actuarial tables and similar devices could not be combined with specifically identified and empirically tested clinical information" (1978, p. 230).

Steve Hart (2009) posed the didactic though arguably provocative question:

> If it is impossible, even with the assistance of astounding measurement instruments and supercomputers, to predict with a high degree of precision which teapots will drip, when Microsoft stocks will rise or fall, when it will next rain in Lisboa, or when the toss of a 100-escudos coin will turn up the figure of Pedro Nunes, how can we think it is possible to make precise quantitative predictions regarding whether a person will commit an act of violence? Yet, on my home continent at this time it is fashionable for forensic psychologists, both clinical and academic, to conceptualize the clinical task of risk assessment as the *prediction* of violence.
>
> (p. 62)

We do not adopt a "predictionist" approach. We prefer what we might call a "rationalist" approach, which, in the present context, is "Dawesian," to coin a new term. The ameliorationist stance is that rendering judgments about likelihood of violent behavior is inextricably woven into the fabric of the criminal justice system. At least for now, it is ineluctable and inexorable. Courts will require it, and forensic psychologists (and a smaller cadre of forensic psychiatrists) will be more than willing to provide it. Out of realism, not fatalism, we conclude that if it is to happen, *it can be done better*. If we abandon our efforts to improve the efficacy of our judgments, either the process will stagnate in a suboptimal state or worse, the process will revert back to pure clinical risk assessment based on inklings and hunches. We very much appreciate, however, Hart's (2009) warning, "Some of us who work with adults, in our scientific zeal, have allowed ourselves to be used as a justification for draconian political decisions and social policies" (pp. 66–67). As is hopefully evident in this book, we share that concern.

Monahan's 1981 Book

The import of Monahan's 1981 book is simply that it is, to the best of our knowledge, the first—and remains one of the very few—discussions of sources of bias among those retained to evaluate criminals. Monahan (1981) pointed to five primary factors that contribute to overprediction of violent behavior: (1) political influences, (2) illusory correlations, (3) cultural differences, (4) conceptual and contextual problems, and (5) low base rates. Several of these—illusory correlations and base rates—we address separately in this chapter.

Political Influences we allude to on various occasions. Political Influences refers to the potential consequences for the examiner if the individual re-offends. If the examiner was insightful enough—or lucky enough—to have judged the individual at high risk of re-offending, there will be *no* consequences. Ever. We are not aware of any instance in which an examiner has suffered social, political, or legal (law suit) repercussions from finding that a defendant is high risk. If the examiner found the individual was *not* at high risk and the individual is released and re-offends, the consequences may include negative media coverage, embarrassment, and, in rare instances, even lawsuits. These adverse repercussions seem disproportionately to occur when the individuals are sex offenders, and the "degree of adversity" of the fallout is invariably a function of the severity of the re-offense. For a sex offender to re-offend by taking the life of the victim is all the more intolerable when the professional has judged the offender *not* to be "high" risk. To avoid the possible adverse repercussions of making a mistake, judgments are frequently biased in the "conservative" direction (defined here as a reluctance to find someone *not* dangerous or *low* risk). Saleem Shah (1975, 1978) observed long ago that because of social and political pressure, the recommended decision rule is "better safe than sorry." Erring on the conservative tends to increase the potential false positive error region and decrease the potential false negative error region, or, as Monahan said, lead to overprediction. When nonregressive predictions are made under conditions of uncertainty, the customary response is to predict conservatively. Stated otherwise, by avoiding a possible "bad" outcome, we tip the judgment scale toward a false positive error.

Phillips and Edwards (1966) defined conservatism somewhat differently—a reluctance or "slowness" to revise a prior probability estimate when presented with new data, or as Plous (1993) stated it, "Conservatism is the tendency to change previous probability estimates more slowly than warranted by new data" (p. 138). The matter of conservatism in human information processing is a subject of some controversy. In a spirited debate on the topic, Ward Edwards and his colleagues argued the merits of the phenomenon, with Edwards maintaining the "cause of conservatism is human misaggregation of the data" (Kleinmuntz, 1968, p. 18). Edwards was maintaining that the problem lies in the inability to combine—or aggregate—the meaning of new data with the meaning of existing data when deciding how to weigh the import of the new data. Although the substance of the laboratory research under scrutiny in the 1960s debate operationalized "conservatism" quite differently from how it is used here, Edward's speculation about misaggregation certainly applies in the broadest sense. How to weigh new data—from irrelevant or unimportant to trivial or minor to conclusion altering, to borrow from Malcolm Gladwell—"tipping point" data clearly characterizes what forensic experts routinely face. As much as extant empirical data may shed light on this question, there is, unfortunately, a hefty subjective element. The expert's prior conviction about the risk of the defendant, typically influenced by the "side" that hired the expert, will tend to minimize or exaggerate the importance of new data.

Political Influences has a potentially chilling effect on *all* expert judgments, not just with sex offenders. The *New York Times* reported on October 27, 2012 that a judge in Italy convicted seven scientists of manslaughter and sentenced them to 6 years in prison for failing to give proper warning before an earthquake (April 9) that killed 309 people in the city of L'Aquila (Diacu, 2012). The scientist's "crime," deserving imprisonment, is that in late March, in response to small seismic events, the expert judgment was that a major earthquake was unlikely. Freudenburg (1988) commented, in this regard, that "The empirical world is not always so tidy; scientists are sometimes subjected to distinctly unscientific pressures, and scientific results are not immune to being used by persons who may not fully share a scientific commitment to the fair and balanced reporting of evidence" (p. 46).

Cultural Differences refers to the mistakes in judgment that arise when the examiner and the examinee are of different racial or ethnic backgrounds. The most common instance is when the examiner is a Caucasian male psychologist or psychiatrist from a middle- or upper-middle-class upbringing and the examinee is an African-American or Hispanic from an inner-city, low socioeconomic status family. Resentment around racial or ethnic differences may undermine rapport. Indeed, even the street language used by the examinee may be so alien to the examiner that rapport is undermined. Even when rapport is good, however, the examinee's life experiences may be so foreign to the examiner that the relevance of those life experiences for predicting violence may be very poorly understood and easily misinterpreted by the examiner. From the meta-analysis of Hanson and Bussiere (1998), for instance, the correlations between general recidivism and having a negative relationship with one's mother and father were .14 and .00, respectively, and the correlation with general family problems was .06. Given the pervasiveness of family dysfunction among the poor, one could easily miscalculate the risk-relevance of such dysfunction and give far more weight to it than is warranted. Similarly, Bonta, Law, and Hanson (1998) reported in their meta-analysis that the relationship between any substance abuse and general and violent recidivism was .11 and .08, respectively. Again, given the ubiquity of exposure to—and use of—substances in the inner city, one could easily attribute far more risk significance to a history of substance use than is justified.

Conceptual and Contextual Problems refers to the training and indoctrination of most mental health professionals, principally psychologists and psychiatrists, who render judgments about risk of offense-related behavior. Mental health professionals are all trained to examine and diagnose psychopathology. Consequently, risk of engaging in violence is conceptualized as a trait and described in terms of clinical signs and symptoms. The medical model, strictly adhered to, potentially limits the scope of the examination of risk-relevant factors, thereby excluding social, situational, and interactional variables. In more updated parlance, we may be overlooking dynamic risk factors. Thirty years after Monahan (1981) described *Conceptual and Contextual Problems* as a biasing concern, we have moved to an increasingly complex relationship between risk and diagnosis and civil law that commits those deemed at high risk. As we have discussed in Chapter 1, the statutory role of diagnosis (the 2nd prong) is essential for constitutional authority but in practice by experts is subordinated in importance to the 3rd prong (risk). The full breadth and scope of psychiatric nosology (DSM-V) has been functionally shrunken to the exclusion of all but a handful of diagnoses, principally a few paraphilias. Paradoxically, although medical certification via the DSM-V provides the imprimatur the court seeks, the rigorous application of the DSM-V is nil.

From the vantage of a mathematical sociologist, Freudenburg (1988) argued that scientists were just as subject to human error as the general public when it came to estimating risk. Freudenburg (1988) identified three problem areas, two of which were described by Monahan (1981): (1) "statistical vulnerability of low-probability estimates" and (2) "monetary and political pressures" (p. 46). The third area mentioned by Freudenburg (1988) was "calibration and overconfidence" (p. 41). Each of these areas will be further discussed in this chapter.

Rendering Judgments Under Uncertainty

Butterflies and Chaos Theory

The earliest-known written version of a popular nursery rhyme dates back to around 1390. The oft-repeated version of that rhyme is the one that Benjamin Franklin inscribed in 1758 in his *Poor Richard's Almanack*, preceded by the words, "A little neglect may breed great mischief." At the time, the American colonies were having "problems" with the English Parliament, roughly 17 years before the start of the Revolutionary War.

> For want of a nail, the shoe was lost,
> For want of a shoe, the horse was lost,
> For want of a horse, the rider was lost,
> For want of a rider, the battle was lost,
> For want of a battle, the kingdom was lost,
> And all for the want of a horseshoe nail.

This charming children's nursery rhyme carries a poignant message about the "chaotic" nature of life events as they unfold from beginning to end.

The nursery rhyme is an exceptional introduction to Chaos Theory, as noted by Gleick (1987). A superb real-world example was provided by Williamson (2008):

> There are real-life historical examples of the truth behind this proverb. Consider this: On the bloodiest day in American history—September 17, 1862—the Civil War Battle of Sharpsburg (also known as Antietam) resulted in nearly 23,000 casualties. After crossing the Potomac River into Maryland on September 9, 1862, Confederate General Robert E. Lee divided the 45,000-man Army of Northern Virginia and spelled out the location for each group on written dispatches (Special Order No. 191) for delivery to various commanders. These dispatches were delivered by couriers on horseback to the commanders except for one that was accidentally dropped from the courier's pocket when he stopped along the way to relieve himself. Unfortunately for General Lee, this dispatch was found by a Union soldier just a few days later in an envelope wrapped around three cigars near a fence. This misplaced secret dispatch reached Union Army Commander George B. McClellan, giving him and his 90,000-man army the exact locations of their enemy, leading to a strategic Union victory . . . for the want of a rider . . . , for the want of a message.
>
> It is important to remember that such root-cause thinking is typically seen in hindsight. It is highly unlikely that anyone would have warned that cigars in a message envelope would have led to foiled military plans and to the loss of a Civil War battle.

(The root cause, of course, was not cigars in a message envelope but the carelessness of the courier to allow the dispatch to drop from his pocket and failing to notice that he had lost it.)

In science, as in all of life, a chain of events can reach a crisis point in which very small changes become magnified, producing outcomes far in excess of the original events. In the world of science, this phenomenon is occasionally referred to as *the butterfly effect*, a term originating with Edward Lorenz, a mathematician and meteorologist who developed mathematical models of weather using a set of differential equations. A serendipitous discovery that very small changes in input can rapidly produce enormous changes in output led Lorenz to discover the phenomenon of "sensitive dependence on initial conditions," referred to more colloquially as the butterfly effect. The term itself comes from the title of an academic paper that Professor Lorenz gave in 1972, entitled: "Predictability: Does the Flap of a Butterfly's Wings in Brazil set off a Tornado in Texas?"

Lorenz will long be remembered in the scientific community, however, as the pioneer of Chaos Theory, which describes systems that are both *dynamic* (i.e., the behavior of the system at Time 1 influences the behavior of the system at Time 2) and *nonlinear* (i.e., the systems are exponential rather than simply additive). As James Gleick (1987) expressed more poetically in his marvelous book *Chaos*, "Errors and uncertainties multiply, cascading upward through a chain of turbulent features, from dust devils and squalls up to continent-size eddies that only satellites can see" (p. 20).

The butterfly effect itself has captured the artistic imagination of pop culture, appearing (with varying degrees of correctness) in numerous movies and television shows. One of the most easily recognized and widely seen was the 1993 movie *Jurassic Park*, in which Dr. Malcolm (Jeff Goldblum) attempts to explain Chaos Theory to Dr. Sattler (Laura Dern), using the butterfly effect as an example. The simple message: Jurassic Park is a highly unpredictable nonlinear dynamic system!

Chaos Theory, with its many applications, from predicting weather to predicting the stock market, provides a model for attempting to understand an underlying order of highly complex systems (or patterns) that appear "chaotic" (i.e., without order). Fundamental precepts of Chaos Theory can be successfully applied to the awesome complexity of human behavior, and perhaps provide some insight into the demands and challenges of predicting sequences of events leading to atypical, often low-frequency criminal offenses. Highly imperfect prediction results from a simple A/B pattern: A (prior) to B (index) to C (predicted outcome). In classic Chaos Theory, criminal behavior is often both dynamic and nonlinear.

In a simplistic example that I often use with my (RAP) students, an ex-rapist, now living comfortably in the community with his wife, arises one morning late for work after a late evening "with the boys," is chastised by his wife for staying out late and excessive drinking on a work day, gets into a fight with his wife, leaves the house not only later than he was before but angry, and arrives at work where he is "chewed out" by his supervisor for his periodic tardiness. By the time 5:00pm rolls around he has been stewing for a half-dozen hours. He drops in at a local bar "just to unwind" before going home. By the time he leaves the bar mildly intoxicated, his risk of re-offending is substantially higher than it was at 9:00am when he woke up. All of these events over the course of the day are not in any mathematical sense additive. They are nonlinear. The incidental first event was staying out too late with his buddies and drinking excessively. Although this first event constituted poor judgment, it alone was not "fateful" (pivotal). He could have set the alarm, forced himself to get up in plenty of time to take a cold shower, shaken off the "afterglow" of the night before, had breakfast with his wife and arrived at work on time.

Once he had gotten up late, a cascade of subsequent events followed. In sum, criminal behavior, especially low-frequency criminal offenses, tend to be dynamic and follow nonlinear patterns.

Judgments of Risk Under Uncertainty

We auger judgments of risk against a backdrop of uncertainty. Ironically, *certainty* was part of the majesty of science for Sir William Blackstone. As Boorstin (1958) noted, "The certainty, uniformity, and reasonableness which made law a science, also were guarantees of its regard for the feelings of human nature" (p. 145). With the advent of an increasingly mature science of risk assessment, the certainty of science once prized by Blackstone has evolved into the *science of uncertainty.*

As Hastie and Dawes (2010) commented, "We not only underappreciate uncertainty in the world outside of us, we are also prone to illusions of consistency, reliability, and certainty about the world inside our own heads. There can be little doubt that we think we are more logical, rational, and consistent than we really are" (p. 325). Uncertainty, we should hasten to add, is not a uniformly cruel task master. As Hastie and Dawes (2010) note, life without uncertainty would be dreadful; it would be dull, boring, without surprises, indeed without challenges. In the realm of risk analysis, however, uncertainty *must* be regarded as the ever-present impediment to our reckoning. In this realm, we want *no* surprises; we want life to be routine, if not dull and boring.

As conceptualized by Nate Silver (2012), uncertainty is simply risk that is difficult to measure or assess. Risk refers to some unknown outcome; assessing the likelihood of that outcome is estimated with varying degrees of *certainty.* Certainty (or uncertainty) is simply a dimensional expression of what we believe to be the knowns and unknowns that affect a given outcome, ranging from the house edge (or vig) in casinos to the next wacko who walks into a shopping mall, or movie theater or school, and starts shooting. Uncertainty is an incontrovertible fact for "all forms of life" and "at all levels of biological complexity" (p. 509) (Kahneman & Tversky, 1982). As such, scholarship on predictions or judgments under conditions of uncertainty is voluminous, dating back 30 to 40 years (e.g., Kahneman & Tversky, 1973; Nisbett & Ross, 1980; Ross, 1977). Uncertainty, simply stated, reflects the unavoidable condition of partial information about the likelihood or odds of some risk. When it comes to evaluating criminals, the extant information ("discovery") is not merely partial; it is of unknown quality. Information that you believe may be critical is often unavailable, unobtainable, or inadmissible. Indeed, information that you have relied upon may be inadmissible at trial. Uncertainty, moreover, is equally characterized by law *and* science (Saks & Neufeld, 2011).

The appearance of science in the courtroom is the collision of *two* uncertain worlds.

Joslyn and LeClerc (2013) noted that the general public have a reasonably good understanding of the uncertainty in predicting the weather, commenting that:

> the general public correctly expect more uncertainty for longer lead times and a high false alarm rate for warning forecasts . . . [the] evidence suggests that despite the fact that people receive predominantly deterministic forecasts, they are well aware of the uncertainty involved and have developed strategies for estimating it.
>
> (p. 309)

Not only are the public aware of uncertainty with respect to weather forecasts, meteorologists are as well. Silver (2012) noted that:

> variations on the term *uncertain* or *uncertainty* were used 159 times in just one of the three IPCC [Intergovernmental Panel on Climate Change] 1990 reports. . . . Although climatologists might think carefully about uncertainty, *there is uncertainty about how much uncertainty there is.*
>
> (p. 389–390, author's italics)

There is an important distinction to be made. We, as consumers of weather forecasts, have all *experienced* uncertainty in weather prediction. We have all been subject to meteorologic "miscalculations" that left us without an umbrella when one was sorely needed. Weather forecasters get it right much of the time, and when they don't we take these occasional mistakes for granted. This is not true for crime forecasters. Those who predict criminal behavior invariably have no *experience* with their miscalculations. Feedback that it "rained" on our expert judgment rarely is forthcoming.

In their classic paper on "Violent Storms and Violent People," Monahan and Steadman (1996) pointed out that availability of feedback was identified by the National Research Council's Committee on Risk Perception and Communication as one of the five reasons that weather forecasters excel at what they do. Monahan and Steadman (1996) then suggest that many of these same factors underlying the success of meteorologists are relevant for those who assess risk of violence, including availability of feedback. Their argument is that reduced time in hospitals and increased outpatient commitments and other forms of supervised community-based management have improved documentation of outcomes. Although true, this does not speak to the virtual impossibility of documenting outcomes in the "other" system housing the violent—prisons. Prison stays for violent offenders are anything but short, and indeterminate sentences for sex offenders may extend incarceration for decades. There is no provision for the systematic follow-up of those released, and certainly no systematic provision for reporting back to the expert who cast an opinion many years prior. Moreover, we might note, a bit whimsically, that the scientists that develop, test, and revise risk assessment scales for offenders, unlike their counterparts at the National Center for Atmospheric Research, do not have an IBM Bluefire supercomputer in their lab that generates 77 trillion calculations per second. Yes, the retort is obvious—all of the aggregated data in the world on sex offenders would not warrant such a computer!

Kahneman and Tversky (1982) described four variants of uncertainty. The last two variants concern "external uncertainty," which

> can be assessed in two ways: (i) a distributional mode, where the case in question is seen as an instance of class of similar cases, for which the relative frequencies of outcomes are known or can be estimated; (ii) a singular mode, in which probabilities are assessed by the propensities of the particular case at hand.
>
> (p. 517)

Kahneman and Tversky (1982) noted that, "people generally prefer the singular mode, in which they take an 'inside view' of the causal system that most immediately produces the outcome, over an 'outside view,' which relates the case at hand to a sampling schema" (p. 518).

This distinction is easily transferrable to the sexually violent predator (SVP) arena. We suggest that forensic experts too prefer the singular mode (ii). Indeed, as psychologists or psychiatrists, we are trained to prefer the singular mode (i.e., we evaluate "individuals," not "classes"). Experts assess the risk of the individual, however, in the distributional mode (i) using tables of norms from standard psychological tests or life tables from actuarial risk assessment scales. This works satisfactorily some of the time but misses the mark when the individuals are distributional outliers. Presumptive singular mode cases (ii) are treated as part of a class of all similar cases, resulting in serious base rate violations (i.e., treating as singular, putative outliers). The consequence, of course, is relying on a class of cases with known base rates (or, at least, estimated base rates using extant data on the class) when the case at hand falls outside the class (e.g., much older than the class; much higher than average number of sexual assaults than the class [as with "serial" offenders]; much higher degree of violence than average for the class [as with child killers compared with all other child molesters]). These base rate violations will invariably result in prediction errors.

Coates (2012) pointed out three situations that signal "threat" and trigger "a massive physiological stress response": novelty, uncertainty, and uncontrollability (p. 217). These evolutionary, hard-wired responses were critical for survival. When confronted by novelty, uncertainty, or uncontrollability, there was no time to kick back and contemplate; vigilance, preparedness, and response readiness were required. Freezing was not an adaptive response. Fast forwarding a dozen millennia, we retain similar hard-wired responses, only to different threat signals. Given the vast increase in complexity of modern life, the number of potential threats signaling uncertainty has increased exponentially. Indeed, uncertainty is a defining feature of modern life, from jobs to relationships to retirement portfolios to health concerns to personal security. Just as the volatility of the market signals uncertainty to traders, the volatility of the courtroom signals uncertainty (and uncontrollability) to expert witnesses.

Hastie and Dawes (2010) offered the following advice: "judgments are likely to be more accurate if the judge can step back, take an outside view, and think distributionally and probabilistically, even if the thought process is only qualitative" (p. 160) . . . "Our primary advice about how to make better judgments under uncertainty is focused on creating effective external (diagrammatic and symbolic) representations of the situation being judged" (p. 163). Plous' (1993, p. 228) advice for advancing the accuracy of our risk judgments under uncertainty is, as he put it, "something lightweight, durable, and easy to apply":

Stop to consider reasons why your judgment might be <u>*wrong*</u>

Although all judgments about the likelihood of a criminal to re-offend involve some degree of uncertainty, the most profoundly troubling evaluations involve individuals that we fear may be *black swans* capable of committing a horrific crime but with no clear behavioral track record to justify our concerns.

Base Rate/Probability Neglect

Accounting for Black Swans

In *Fooled by Randomness*, Taleb (2005) introduced the black swan with characteristic flair:

> Reality is far more vicious than Russian roulette. First, it delivers the fatal bullet rather infrequently, like a revolver that would have hundreds, even thousands, of chambers instead of six. After a few dozen tries, one forgets about the existence of a bullet, under a numbing false sense of security. The point is dubbed in this book the *black swan problem.*
>
> (p. 26)

Two years later Taleb (2007) published his *New York Times* bestseller *The Black Swan*. Although Posner (2010) commented in his book, *Stalking the Black Swan*, that black swans have been most frequently associated with the research of Benjamin Graham and David Dodd (e.g., Graham & Dodd, 1940), it has clearly been Taleb who has made the black swan a celebrity.

Although there are real black swans, they are scarce, living primarily in Australia. It is their scarcity, and indeed the conviction of Europeans that all swans were white until a Dutch mariner voyaged to Australia in the early 17th century, that contributed to the black swan becoming a symbol of the rare or improbable event. The black swan represents more than a rare event, however; it represents a rare event that is *highly consequential.* Posner (2010) stated that:

> Turbulent weather is one apt metaphor for the difficulty in forecasting the fundamental world. But there are other kinds of nonlinear forecasting challenges, some of which may resemble avalanches or earthquakes: *tranquility reigns for long periods and is followed abruptly and unpredictably by extreme outcomes.*
>
> (p. 10)

Although the lessons of the black swan have been most often applied to the marketplace, applications to all realms of risk-focused decision-making—e.g., the business world, security and intelligence agencies, corporate and federal regulators, geologists, meteorologists, and behavioral scientists—are obvious. In the physical world, "big data" sets yield algorithms that forecast events such as hurricanes and tornadoes with reasonable accuracy. With the help of supercomputers, scientists are able to identify most relevant factors that predict occurrence, thereby limiting the unknowns. The greater the unknowns (and the unknowables), the greater the potential sources of error.

Seasonal storms are routine events; they become black swan events when the proverbial "perfect storm" chains a rare combination of factors that results in extreme storms. As Joslyn and LeClerc (2013) remarked, "although uncertainty estimates may be helpful for typical seasonal weather, they may not be appropriate for rare, destructive weather" (p. 311). Slovic, Fischhoff, and Lichtenstein (2000) noted that:

> Holmes (1961) found that 50% of the damage from major floods was caused by floods with probabilities of occurrence in any year of less than .01. The city of Skopje, Yugoslavia was leveled by earthquakes in the years AD 518, 1555 and 1963, and the mudflow that took 25,000 lives in Yungay, Peru had swept across the same valley between 1,000 and 10,000 years before.
>
> (p. 41)

The Fukushima Daiichi Nuclear Power Plant disaster is an example of the "perfect storm," wherein the Tohoku earthquake produced a devastating tsunami. The now common reference to "perfect storms" comes, of course, from the 1997 non-fiction book by Junger about the fate of the fishing boat the Andrea Gail caught in the convergence of three powerful storm systems in the early winter of 1991 (October 30). It was this freak occurrence that led to it being dubbed *the perfect storm*. The storm, said to be stronger than any in recorded history in the area (Gloucester, MA), was called the "storm of the century." The tragedy was popularized in the 2000 movie of the same name. The perfect storm was a classic black swan event.

The explosion of the Space Shuttle Challenger on January 28, 1986 is another such *rare but catastrophic* event. Plous (1993) recounted:

> Before the shuttle exploded on its twenty-fifth mission, NASA's official launch risk estimate was 1 catastrophic failure in 100,000 launches (Feynman, February, 1988). This risk estimate is roughly equivalent to launching the shuttle once per day and expecting to see only one accident in three centuries
>
> (p. 217)

Other examples of highly consequential rare "events" include the 1987 worldwide stock market crash, the financial crisis of 2008, the explosion and sinking of the Deepwater Horizon oil rig and consequent spill off the Gulf of Mexico on April 20, 2010, the 1979 Three Mile Island nuclear power plant meltdown, the September 11, 2001 terrorist attack on the United States by Al Qaeda and the 1986 Chernobyl nuclear power plant disaster. Plous (1993) cited Rylsky (1986) as stating that Vitali Skylarov, Minister of Power and Electrification in the Ukraine, remarked "The odds of a meltdown are one in 10,000 years" two months prior to the Chernobyl disaster (p. 217). In most cases, these were "freak" catastrophic events; as such, they may be thought of as one-off. Although it is possible to develop a data set to improve prediction, the data set will inevitably include a highly heterogeneous collection of similar events (e.g., all deep water oil spills, all nuclear power plant accidents). Examining the Chernobyl nuclear power plant disaster and the Three Mile Island nuclear power plant meltdown, for example, would have been of little help in predicting what happened at Fukushima Daiichi.

Black swan events are typically so rare as to be "one-off" from any statistical standpoint. As a statistical outlier, accurate prediction of such rare events is typically unattainable. Nate Silver (2012) contrasted baseball and politics "as data-rich fields that yield satisfying answers" with terrorism, noting that in the latter case, "terrorist groups try to conceal their intentions—Al Qaeda was known to be especially effective at this"

(p. 426). When data vital to prediction are unavailable, incomplete, or distorted (intentionally or otherwise), accuracy is severely undermined. As forensic practitioners, we are almost always contending with incomplete discovery and questionable, distorted, or dubious self-report.

From the standpoint of accurately assessing the likelihood of rare events, Taleb (2005) is of the conviction that "Our brain is not cut out for nonlinearities . . . . Our emotional apparatus is designed for linear causality. . . . Owing to this nonlinearity, people cannot comprehend the nature of the rare event" (p. 179). This does *not* imply for Taleb that all outcomes are random events. There are certainly nonrandom paths leading to positive outcomes, but for Taleb (2005) "very few people have the mental stamina to follow them" (p. 179).

The very catastrophic nature of these events elicits strong emotional responses, often of an accusatory nature, about the "failings" of an individual or individuals who could have (or should have) prevented the tragedy. It seems to be a quirk of human nature to point fingers of blame when wrought by extreme emotions. In truth, however, most of these rare or improbable events could not have been predicted without the benefit of hindsight. Statisticians occasionally refer to these rare extreme events as "fat tails" (i.e., they are "significant" events but they occur in the tail of the Gaussian distribution). Similarly, "quants" refer to these events as "tail risk."

Although our main focus is on the *low* base rate problem (the "rare" or black swan event), the issue of base rate *neglect* (that most people pay little or no attention to base rates when making decisions) has also been the subject of some controversy, with Koehler (1996) arguing that conventional wisdom that most people ignore base rates is a fallacy. Our present concern is less the neglect of base rates than the mis-estimation and misapplication of base rates by forensic examiners. A second (related) concern is the application of Bayesian analysis, which is often used to aggregate base rate data (cf. Fischhoff & Beyth-Maron, 1983; Meehl & Rosen, 1955). As Koehler (1996) stated, "base rate information does not map unambiguously into the Bayesian framework in most real world problems" (p. 1). There is, as Koehler pointed out, a considerable difference between creating normative rules for aggregating probabilistic data, such as prior odds, and *applying* those rules in real cases. We address this problem in Chapter 6 by offering an illustrative model for inputting probabilistic information.

The Distribution of Black Swan Criminal Events

Crime rarely conforms to Gauss' normal distribution. Crime is much more accurately captured by Pareto's power law distribution (e.g., Schroeder, 1991) or the closely related J-curve (e.g., Clarke, 1996), both characterized by a marked positive skew. In both distributions there are a few atypical (or extreme) events on the left side and a very long tail of more common (or much less extreme) events on the right side. In popular terms, this has also been referred to as the "80/20" rule (Kock, 1999), wherein 20% of something is responsible for 80% of some outcome. Although the ratio is rarely 80/20, the principle holds—a small proportion of something accounts for a large proportion of something else. The power law distribution has been applied to everything from earthquakes (a very few earthquakes cause most of the damage) to wealth (a very small proportion of the population holds most of it) to crime (a small number of offenders are responsible for a disproportionate amount of crime) (Eck, Clarke, & Guerette, 2007).

One of the most often cited longitudinal studies of delinquent youth illustrating the J-curve or power law distribution was conducted by Marvin Wolfgang (Wolfgang, Figlio, & Sellin, 1972). This birth-cohort study involved close to 10,000 boys in Philadelphia. About one-third of the boys (n = 3,475) had had at least one documented contact with the police. A very small proportion of the entire cohort (6%) were charged with five or more offenses. When restricted to only those with a prior contact with the police, the proportion was still relatively small (18%). Out of the entire cohort, 627 (6%) were chronic offenders, responsible for 71% of the homicides, 77% of the rapes, 70% of the robberies, and 69% of the aggravated assaults.

The prospective longitudinal Cambridge Study in Delinquent Development (CSDD), conducted by West and subsequently by Farrington, followed 411 boys, most 8–9 years old, from 1961 until 1981 (e.g., Blumstein, Farrington, & Moitra, 1985; Farrington, 1986; Farrington, 1981). Extensive data were gathered on most of the boys (n = 395). The boys were interviewed and tested at ages 8, 10, and 14, and again at 16, 18, 21, and 24. Similar to the Philadelphia Cohort Study, about one-third of the youths in the CSDD sample were convicted at least once. Again similar to the Philadelphia Cohort Study, 7% of the youth accounted for about half of all the offenses in the study and were labeled "chronic offenders."

The Pittsburgh Youth Survey began in 1987 with 1,500 youths in the first, fourth, and seventh grades (Loeber, Farrington, Stouthamer-Loeber, Moffitt, & Caspi, 1998). The study, directed by Loeber, followed about 500 boys from ages 7 to 17 and another 500 boys from ages 13 to 23. Almost the entire sample (87%) reported at least 1 and at most 20 delinquent acts. Although this study relied on self-report, the results were similar to the CSDD: about two-thirds of the youths reported no delinquent acts; of those that did, the range was from 1 to 20. Once again, a power law frequency distribution described both the entire sample and when the two-thirds of youths reporting no delinquency were removed.

Moffitt's (1991) longitudinal study of 1,037 New Zealand children compared the base rates of persistent and temporary antisocial behavior problems. The boys were rated as "very antisocial" by three sources (parents, teachers, youths), and 5% of the boys met these selection criteria. Moffitt found clear evidence that the temporal stability of delinquency was attributable to these 5% of the youths whose behavior was most extreme and most persistent.

In a seven-year retrospective longitudinal study of 667 boys in the child welfare system that had been flagged for sexually inappropriate and coercive behaviors (Prentky, Pimental, & Cavanaugh, 2009; Prentky et al., 2010), we found evidence of the same power law distribution of re-offenses:

Total # of Sexual, Victim-Involved Offenses at Follow-Up (skew = +3.64, se = .472)

0	1	2	3	4	13
96.4%	1.9%	0.7%	0.3%	0.4%	0.1%

Total # of Victims at Follow-Up (skew = +4.04, se = .098)

0	1	2	>2
75.6%	9.0%	4.9%	4.3%

Total # of Separate Incidents at Follow-Up (skew = +3.52, se = .098)

0	1	2	3	4	5	6–25
59.5%	10.5%	5.2%	5.5%	2.4%	4.3%	6.3%

These findings do not, of course, apply only to juveniles. The same distributions are noted with adult offenders. Piquero (2000), for instance, examined data from the Philadelphia Collaborative Perinatal Project Birth Cohort, looking at offense skewness across gender. Piquero (2000) found (1) a small group of offenders was responsible for a large proportion of the offenses, (2) chronic offenders (≥ 5 offenses) evidenced an earlier onset age of offending, and (3) both of these findings were invariant across gender (although male skewness was higher compared with females). The male chronic offenders in Piquero's (2000) study represented 2.5% of the entire cohort and were responsible for 226 of the 443 (51%) contacts with police. The female chronic offenders represented 1.0% of the entire cohort and accounted for 63 of the 144 (44%) police contacts.

The power law distribution even applies to crime locations (Eck & Weisburd, 1995). Hegarty (2010) reported a wide range of these studies, all converging on the same power law distribution: (a) a study of bars in Shawnee, Kansas found that 20% of the bars accounted for 62% of the reported bar-related crime, (b) a study of stores in Danvers, Connecticut found that 20% of the stores accounted for 85% of the reported shoplifting, (c) a Jacksonville, Florida study found that 20% of the 269 apartment complexes with at least one reported crime accounted for 47% of the crime (which would have been much higher had all apartment complexes been included), (d) a Chula Vista, California study of motels in the city found that 19% of the motels accounted for 51% of the police calls, (e) a Seattle, Washington study over a 14-year period found that 4–5% of the city's blocks accounted for 50% of the reported crime, (f) a study of shootings in Boston over a 30-year period found that the 7,359 incidents took place in only 11.5% of the city (i.e., no shootings occurred in the other 88.5% of the city), and (g) a Minneapolis, Minnesota study found that 3% of the addresses in the city accounted for 50% of police calls over a 1-year period.

In attempting to assess the sexual re-offense risk posed by sex offenders, be they juveniles or adults, we are implicitly, as well as explicitly, trying to capture the *most persistent* of the offenders. If the base rate hovers around 15% over 5 years for adult offenders (Hanson & Bussiere, 1998; Hanson & Morton-Bourgon, 2005) and 10% over 5 years for juvenile offenders (e.g., Caldwell, 2007, 2010; Heilbrun et al., 2005; McCann & Lussier, 2008; Reitzel & Carbonell, 2006; Viljoen, Mordell, & Benetau, 2012), *we may reasonably conclude, with a very small true positive target, that a high false positive rate is virtually inevitable.*

Rare Events Under Scrutiny in the Courtroom

The most important threats to public safety from criminals are those with very low probabilities and very high consequences. Mental health professionals tasked with assessing risk of violence (or "dangerousness" or simply "re-offense") are beset by the *black swan problem.* Psychologists and psychiatrists are well aware of the potential for "extreme events," *dread* them, call them by names unmentionable in polite conversation, and assiduously avoid them by erring conservatively. Extreme criminal "events" are statistically negligible, but the perceived consequences of being "wrong" are so profound we override all rational appreciation of the probability of the event. In so doing, predicting statistically rare (but extreme) criminal offenses end up, more often than not, false positives. Parenthetically, our use of the word *dread* was not hyperbole. Slovic (2000) introduced a factor that he referred to as "dread risk." The higher the score of a potential hazard on "dread risk," the higher its perceived risk, and "the more people want to see its current risks reduced, and the more they want to see strict regulation employed to achieve the desired reduction in risk" (p. 226). Camerer and Kunreuther (1989) also noted that events that are perceived as most risky are those that "evoke dread" (p. 578).

The relationship between fear of very violent (but rare) criminal offenses and ignoring or discounting the probability of those offenses was addressed quite clearly in the Report by the President's Commission on Law Enforcement and Administration of Justice (1967)—almost 50 years ago. The Commission noted that

> the public fears most the crimes that occur least often, crimes of violence . . . the annual rate of all index offenses involving either violence or the threat of violence is 1.8 per 1,000 Americans. This is minute relative to the total accidental injuries calling for medical attention. . . . A recent study of emergency medical care found . . . that as many as 20,000 Americans die unnecessarily each year as a result of improper emergency care . . . on a straight statistical basis, the closer the relationship the greater the hazard. In one sense the greatest threat to anyone is himself, since suicides are more than twice as common as homicides.
>
> (pp. 51–52)

The Commission further observed that "the fear of crimes of violence is not a simple fear of injury or death or even of all crimes of violence, but, at bottom, a fear of strangers," and "this fear of strangers has greatly impoverished the lives of many Americans, especially those who live in high-crime neighborhoods in large cities" (p. 52).

Forensic examiners tend to be *most* vulnerable to a false positive mistake when the client has a known extreme prior, even though the likelihood of a repeat offense similar in gravity to the prior is relatively small (with the obvious exception of known "serial" offenders). Simply stated, overcoming the gravity of the prior and placing it in proper probabilistic context can be a daunting challenge. The *opposite* problem is an extreme index offense, and no known history of priors that remotely resemble the index offense. This is often the "golden black swan," exemplified by a child abductor that sexually assaults and murders his victim. These perpetrators often present with little or no known history of extreme violence. Some may even be unknown to the criminal justice system; their past may be shady but not so dark that it brought them to the attention of law enforcement. If they were known to the police, it was not for the extreme offense that they are now being tried for. The violent index crime is something of a black swan in that it arrives without any clear track record; it appears "rare" in the context of the individual's collective life experiences and deeds.

Lancaster (2011) provided comparisons of probabilistic outcomes (based on frequency estimates) for many events resulting in death or serious injury to children. He noted that there are "about one hundred high-risk abductions of children by strangers every year, and about half end in murder" (p. 77). He then went on to compare these 100 abductions, or 50 child abduction/murders with child fatalities, resulting from: (a) disease or congenital illness ($n = 36{,}180$), (b) motor vehicle accidents ($n = 7{,}981$), (c) drowning ($n = 1{,}158$), (d) accidental suffocation or strangulation ($n = 953$), (e) fire ($n = 606$), (f) firearm accidents ($n = 167$), or (g) death at the hands of a family member ($n = 1{,}500$). (National Maternal and Child Health center for Child Death Review, "United States Child Mortality, 2002," n.d., www.childdeathreview.org/Nat<#213>1%data%20Webpage%202002_files/US2002.pdf; U.S. Department of Health and Human Services, Child Maltreatment Annual Reports: www.acf.hhs.gov/programs/cb/stats_research and U.S. Department of Health and Human Services, Child Abuse and Neglect Fatalities: Statistics and Interventions, Child Welfare Information Gateway, April 30, 2010, www.childwelfare.gov/pubs/factsheets/fatality.cfm.)

Lancaster (2011) concluded that, "In real terms, a child's risk of being killed by a sexually predatory stranger is comparable to his or her chance of being struck and killed by lightning (1 in 1,000,000 versus 1 in 1,200,000)" (p. 77). Or, according to these estimates, 30 times as many children are killed by family members as by stranger child predators. (Statistical Assessment Service, "Phony numbers on child abductions," STATS.org, August 1 2002, www.stats.org/stories/2002/phony_augol_02.htm (accessed October 5, 2009); John D. Whittaker (June, 1986), "Evaluation of Acceptable Risk," Journal of the Operational Research Society, 37(6), 542.)

Unlike illness, car accidents, firearm accidents, drowning, and fires, all of which are generally understood to be *accidents* (unless malfeasance is suggested), and naturally grieved by the child's family, the death of a child at the hands of a child predator, no matter how infrequent statistically, is experienced as an imminent, dire threat to the entire community. Willing ourselves to believe that our own children are safe from car accidents, fires, serious illness, firearm accidents, and drowning is far more easily accomplished than believing that our children are safe from the unknown child predator. Although we believe, rightly some of the time, that it is within our control to avoid catastrophic accidents like drowning, firearm accidents, fires, and car accidents, Hastie and Dawes (2010) remarked that the "pervasive tendency to see much more structure than is actually present and to imagine we have much more control over events than we do in hundreds of important naturally occurring situations is still a puzzle" (p. 155).

Clearly, however, a stranger abducting our child is regarded (understandably) as being outside of our control. The community impact of these stranger abductions is so profound that politicians frequently enact laws named after the victim, as if this assuages the pain of the parents and family of the child and reassures the community that action has been taken. Understandably, we *need* to believe that this was not a random act of evil, which would imply an absence of control. One of the three experiences, along with uncertainty and novelty, signaling threat and eliciting a massive physiological stress response is *uncontrollability* (Coates, 2012). "Loss of control in a threatening situation provokes the most terrifying stress response" (Coates, 2012, p. 219). Given the stark reality of uncertainty and loss of control in the face of a dire threat, insensitivity to, or awareness of, a proper base rate for these acts of evil is *only human.*

Forecasting violent human behavior is invariably fraught with unknowns and unknowables; what is unknown (or unknowable) triggers feelings of loss of control and hence vulnerability, which can arouse fear. Camerer and Kunreuther (1989) spoke directly to this point:

> Risks that are uncontrollable or unknowable (ambiguous perhaps) are feared even when they are statistically unlikely. A familiar example is air travel, which is uncontrollable by passengers but is much safer on a per mile basis than driving a car.
>
> (p. 578)

The answer is obvious—no matter how much riskier it is to drive a car, *you are behind the wheel and feel that you are in control*, even if you exercise no control over all of the other cars on the road.

An interesting corollary is firearms—not ownership per se but *reason* for ownership. Gallup (2013) conducted a poll on gun ownership between October 3 and 6, 2013, with 37% of respondents reporting that they owned a gun. The proportion is comparatively low; the only year since 1965 when fewer respondents reported owning a gun was in 1999 (34%–36%). What is remarkable, however, is the *reason* reported for owning a gun: Collecting guns/hobby (1%), work-related, police, military, etc. (only 3%), target shooting (just 8%), hunting (36%), personal safety/protection (60%). Almost two-thirds of the respondents who owned a gun reported personal safety as a reason. We may infer, as Camerer and Kunreuther (1989) did, that perceived risk from harm (presumably due to crime), no matter how statistically unlikely, is feared, and owning a gun is a way to restore some sense of control.

The most robust axiom of predicting human behavior is *past is prologue to the future*, i.e., accuracy relies on past similar behavior, or in the present context, past bad behavior predicts future bad behavior. Thus, the higher the base rate of past criminal behavior, the greater the probability of future criminal behavior. This axiom is the precise antithesis of what we frequently face with the rare crime or black swan problem, wherein there was no known track record of prior violent acts (or a track record sufficiently minimal that it would not have brought the individual to the attention of law enforcement). Quinsey's (1980) suggested solution to the low base rate of violent behavior was to rely on the "intra-offender" factor of multiple releases (i.e., with a given offender, multiple failed releases increase the base rate for that offender). Although clearly true, it does not solve the black swan problem.

Ideally, in predictive terms (not in practical, social, or ethical terms), we would prefer a base rate of 50%. What we often see, however, is a seemingly disturbed, perhaps moody individual, sometimes (not always) with major mental illness, who has been harboring fantasies of violence for a long time unbeknownst to anyone, with a history of eccentric, erratic, dysfunctional behavior, sometimes (but not always) criminal but rarely of the extreme violence manifest in the index offense. As such, the index offense for this individual would be a "rare" or isolated event in their history. Based on this person's history alone, one would be hard pressed to predict an outcome of extreme violence.

> Popular wisdom often warns of the old neighbor who appears to remain courtly and reserved, the model of an excellent citizen, until you see his picture in the national paper as a deranged killer who went on a rampage. Until then, he was not known to have committed any transgression. There was no way to predict that such pathological behavior could emanate from such a nice person.
>
> (Taleb, 2005, p. 109)

In the recent case discussed in Chapter 1 of Donald Smith, accused of killing Cherish Perrywinkle in June 2013 (Florida), Smith is reported by the media to have "a long criminal history." By media report, he does have a lengthy criminal history, dating to 1977, when at age 21 he was arrested for "lewd and lascivious behavior on a child under 16," followed in 1993 by "attempted kidnapping" (trying to lure three young girls into a van filled with pornography), a 2003 arrest for stolen property, and finally in 2009 "impersonation of a public employee (DCF) and attempted child abuse by mental harm" (making obscene phone calls to a young child). If this is an accurate portrayal of his known criminal history, he clearly was known to the criminal justice system as a child molester, with three known sexual offenses prior to the murder. Two of the three offenses (lewd and lascivious, and making obscene phone calls) appear to have been what are generally called "nuisance" sex offenses (hands-off). Only one offense would have set off alarm bells—his 1993 attempted kidnapping. In sum, although he had a track record of child sexual interest and criminal activities dating back to 1977, he had no (known) behavior—reported by the media—that even remotely suggested the possibility of extreme violence/homicide (with the lone exception of the 1993 offense, and we have no idea what his intentions were in that attempted kidnapping).

By marked contrast, we need not lose sleep over the re-offense risk of a man who presents with numerous prior arraignments for criminal conduct. I (RAP) was once asked to evaluate such a young man in his late twenties with 128 arraignments for every crime imaginable, a true "cafeteria-style" criminal with a hefty PCL-R score. It was one of the most enjoyable, relaxing evaluations that I have ever done. No fancy mechanistic scales were needed, though I did walk through a PCL interview. I felt no internal conflict, no stress over *likelihood*. I engaged the young man in a three-hour conversation about his life; he dripped of guile and grandiosity covered with a rich coat of charm. I took copious notes, not to shore up my opinion but to present to my graduate students as a marvelous teaching case. He was certainly not a black swan, just an outlier with a prodigious capacity for violating the law.

Most of the forensic clients that we evaluate present with one, maybe two, known priors, not dozens. One or two known priors, when the priors are sexual offenses, are not viewed statistically as "rare" or isolated events. All risk assessment scales for adult sex offenders give "points" for priors, even one prior. In most realms of *lawful* behavior, doing something two times is not generally an adequate basis for predicting a third time. For instance, let's propose that the "client" is a college student who, on a lark, went to a local community airport on a pleasant Saturday morning and jumped out of an airplane—hopefully with a parachute. Assuming that the student had done this on *one prior* occasion, you are asked to predict whether the student will go sky diving a 3rd time. Clearly, doing anything only twice in your life, even if you are only 20 years old, must be considered "rare," or at least highly infrequent. Your initial take on this assignment might be a high degree of skepticism. There are some behaviors, however, that are considered so anomalous—out of the "norm" in this case for college students—that "only twice" may take on a different meaning. If you were asked to evaluate a 20-year-old college student who had been apprehended twice for "mooning," you might wonder: Once, probably a prank or a dare, but twice? Maybe something else is going on here?

The more extreme the criminal behavior, the more likely we are to conclude that even once "is enough." Homicide is the obvious example. Homicide is a rare event, which is why three murders "qualifies" the offender for the FBI's honorific title of "serial." Does serial move us outside the realm of "rare" when it comes to prediction? One answer is "No." The label is simply conferred upon those who engage in behavior that is so intolerable to civil society that it puts them in a different "class." Another answer is "Yes." One murder might be situationally determined or passion-driven, or self-defense. But three murders? Highly unlikely. Far more likely that three murders are motivated by entrenched psychopathology (e.g., a deep reservoir of poorly managed, extreme anger, psychopathy, sexual sadism, etc.) that, unchanged, places the individual "at risk" of further such crimes.

Even in serial murder, however, the killings are "rare" events relative to all other criminal behaviors in the life of the offender. Predicting "when," "where," and "under what circumstances" the next murder will occur is extremely difficult. Unlike earthquakes and monsoons, *there are no algorithms for murder based on "big" datasets.* If every earthquake and every monsoon was uniquely driven by its own constellation of forces, prediction would be vastly more complicated (and less accurate). Such is the problem with human dangerousness: Accounting, on a case-by-case basis, with the storms of emotions swirling inside, the conditions igniting those emotions, the situational events that mitigate or aggravate management of those emotions, situational events that encourage—or deter—a crime, victim response, etc. contrive to make a crime more, or less, likely to occur. Most of these factors fall into the predictive black hole of unknowns or unknowables. All that we can reasonably infer, in the presence of a minimal prior track record of criminal behavior, is the internalized "will" to engage in the same or similar behaviors evidenced in the past.

As distasteful as it may be, *there will always be black swan crimes that no one could have predicted.* Taleb (2007) admonished us that there are highly improbable events that could not have been anticipated (or extrapolated) from existing (including all past) data. Forensic examiners—psychologists and psychiatrists—are not empowered with an indwelling electrode that informs them of the innermost secret thoughts, fantasies, and yearnings of the defendant. As such, we are haunted by the reality of black swan crimes. It is with Kierkegaardian *fear and trembling* that we contemplate whether the client sitting in front of us is capable of such a crime. As some forensic examiners have experienced, false negative mistakes can subject us to ridicule in the media and possibly even a law suit. Beyond the fear of "fallout," which is predominantly self-serving, there is also a sense of moral obligation to prevent these catastrophic crimes. The net result: an irresistible Siren tugging us toward the rocky shoals of false positive error, a danger zone pointed out repeatedly since the 1970s (e.g., Cocozza & Steadman, 1974, 1976; Fagin, 1976; Monahan, 1975; Shah, 1978).

Base Rate Accuracy

As critical as base rates are in predictive accuracy, it is the *reliability* of those base rate estimates that are determinative. The application of a spurious or misguided base rate is worse than no base rate at all. This is indeed troubling, since there appear to be twin messages of equal prominence—on one hand, including an estimation of the base rate is essential; on the other, "Everyone knows, Doctor, that base rates underestimate the number of actual sexual offenses. Isn't that correct, Doctor?" Defense experts agreeing with the prosecutor that rapes are dramatically under-reported is now a routine part of cross-examination. Curiously, now that the expert has readily agreed, the cross moves on, rarely touching upon the implications of what the defense expert has agreed to. Prosecutors should be mindful that they have merely cracked open the door. As experts, we must more than acknowledge this obvious fact. We must address its relevance for our formulations of risk that rely on science, which in turn relies on a unique subsample of individuals that the defendant/respondent may or may not be similar to. Similarly, when asked about recidivism rates, we must be clear that reported rates are based on these small, unrepresentative samples of offenders who are reported, caught, prosecuted, and incarcerated. To take this argument to the next level, the recidivism studies that follow up these incarcerated individuals are estimating their failure rates on *reported* re-offenses.

It harkens back to the notion of Susan Estrich's (1987) "real rape." The theory of *real rape* is simple—"legitimate" rapes are the ones that are pronounced so by the criminal justice system. These rapes, according to the theory, are a very small and *unrepresentative* minority of all sexual assaults of women. Estrich (1987) argued, undoubtedly correctly, that rapes will be regarded as *real rapes*—by everyone, from victims to police, prosecutors, jurors, and the community at large—when the crime is violent, the offender is a stranger, resistance is overt, and injury is sustained and documented. This composite of "requirements" for *real rape* excludes the preponderance of marital rape, date rape, acquaintance rape, "non-violent" stranger rape in which the victim acquiesces, and "party" rape in which the victim is deprived of consent by intoxication. Despite staircasing legislation, this cultural definition of rape remains, pervading not just society but the criminal justice system too. This small subsample of rapists serve the purpose of crafting social and cultural attitudes and stereotypes about rape (and rapists), as well as providing the empirical gruel for estimating incidence/prevalence, designing and validating risk assessment scales, developing treatment programs, and of course enacting legislation.

We have no massive data field to mine. Our knowledge base is founded upon a micro-sample of the estimated extant population of individuals who engage in unwanted sexual behavior. The majority of offending individuals are unknown and hence unaccounted for in our markedly skewed data field. This reality has obvious implications for the science of risk assessment.

We might note in passing that this "phenomenon" of under-reporting is nothing new. A half-century ago Giulio DiFuria and Hayden Mees (1964) observed in *The American Journal of Psychiatry* that,

> At any given time we can be sure that several thousand men are in custody somewhere in the United States for committing a sexual offense. Multiply that number by several score and we may approach the number of men who are actively practicing

> illegal sexual behavior. No accurate figure can be given for either of these statements, obviously, for several reasons, but primarily because more often than not both the public, in the form of laws and officials, and the victims are too embarrassed to discuss it, let alone make records of it. . . . Victims, wives and neighbors who could make a complaint against sexually deviant men do not do so because of the scandal. The offenders are often too embarrassed and too frightened to seek help for their problems.
>
> (p. 980)

Heuristics

Representative Heuristic

The *representative heuristic*, first described by Kahneman and Tversky in 1972, applies to individuals who

> evaluate the probability of an uncertain event, or a sample, by the degree to which it is: (i) similar in essential properties to its parent population; and (ii) reflects the salient features of the process by which it is generated.
>
> (p. 431)

Kahneman and Tversky hypothesized, in other words, that event A will be judged more probable than event B *if A appears more representative than B*. The *representative heuristic*, in the simplest terms, is "latching onto a single salient variable" while ignoring other important variables (Posner, 2010, p. 69).

Determining what is and what is not *representative* can be highly subjective. These subjective determinations are often reasonably accurate (i.e., some *representative*-based predictions of outcomes are in fact more likely than other outcomes). Kahneman and Tversky (1973) noted, however, that this is *not* always the case,

> because there are factors (e.g., the prior probabilities of outcomes and the reliability of the evidence) which affect the likelihood of outcomes but not their representativeness. Because these factors are ignored, intuitive predictions violate the statistical rules of prediction in systematic and fundamental ways.
>
> (p. 238)

Davis and Follette (2002) noted that

> attorneys invite judges and juries to rely on the representativeness heuristic to decide their verdicts. Attorneys argue, "This person

> has all the characteristics of a murderer/bad parent/thief, therefore (s)he must (will) be one!" It is in this sense that we use the term "intuitive profiling."
>
> (p. 134)

Davis and Follette (2002) further clarified their use of "intuitive profiling":

> The use of intuitive profiling to assess guilt relies on the following logic: "If persons who commit embezzlement are likely to be in debt, then persons who are in debt are likely to be embezzlers," or "If most A's are B's, then most B's are A's." Logically, of course, these conclusions are erroneous.
>
> (p. 134)

One (of many) examples in the evaluation of sex offenders that readily comes to mind is the relation of victim gender to risk among child molesters. Prevailing wisdom tells us, though the empirical evidence is somewhat inconclusive, that child molesters with same-sex (male) victims pose the greatest risk for re-offense while child molesters with opposite-sex (female) victims pose the lowest risk, with child molesters having mixed-gender victims falling somewhere in between. When evaluating a child molester with only boy victims, victim gender becomes *representative* of high risk. As Kahneman and Tversky pointed out, however, ignoring prior probabilities and the reliability of the evidence could seriously affect one's judgment of risk. Although the *representativeness* of victim gender remains, the predicted probability of a high-risk outcome may be erroneous. This should be fairly obvious, given that roughly two-thirds of child molesters with same-sex victims are not identified as re-offenders.

One of the most indisputably high-risk child molesters that I (RAP) ever encountered was a 63-year-old man with a lifelong record of sexually offending against *girls*. He had been arraigned on yet new charges when he eloped. The PA State Police tracked him down to North Carolina. The North Carolina State Police found him living in an abandoned school bus; when they arrived he had already left, leaving behind cartons of child pornography. The NC State Police tracked him to Tennessee. The TN State Police found him living on a farm; when they arrived he again had already left. He was picked up on a random tag check in Miami, and returned to Philadelphia. It was at that point that I was contacted by the Sex Crimes Unit. This man hardly required an evaluation. He exemplified what professionals—as well as lay people—would regard as the *highest risk* of all child molesters. Child molesters with a preference for opposite-sex victims can be as recidivistic and dangerous as child molesters with a preference for same-sex victims.

The above example admittedly reflects tail risk, so "extreme" that no examiner would downplay the offender's risk because of his victim gender preference. We are repeatedly confronted, however, not by extreme cases but by nominal ones falling under the bulbous part of the risk curve (e.g., a child molester with one known prior offense against a boy and an index offense involving a boy). For these cases, the overwhelming majority of the ones we see, the representative heuristic poses a very real challenge. Indeed, its potential influence cannot be underestimated. As Kahneman and Tversky (1972) long ago noted, "The biasing effects of representativeness are not limited to naïve subjects. They are also found (Tversky & Kahneman, 1971) in the intuitive judgments of sophisticated psychologists" (p. 433).

Research on the *representativeness* heuristic reveals a number of ways to improve the efficacy of our judgments (Plous, 1993, p. 119–120): (1) Beware of highly detailed descriptions of crimes—the same details that appear *representative* decrease their likelihood, (2) Base rates, once again, are especially critical when they are low. Parenthetically, base rates also pose a serious problem when very high: "When base rates are extreme, *representativeness* is often a fallible indicator of probability," (3) Be mindful of regression toward the mean; extreme behavior is not the "norm" even for violent offenders. In simple terms: Beware of over-focusing on one single highly salient variable or factor; predictions based on a single salient factor are vulnerable to the *representativeness* heuristic.

Law of Small Numbers

The "law of small numbers" was coined by Tversky and Kahneman (1971) with a tongue-in-cheek reference to the better-known "law of large numbers" (the larger the sample randomly drawn from the population, the closer the sample mean will be to the population mean). The law of small numbers, commonly associated with the representative heuristic, is the belief that the law of large numbers also applies to small numbers. Kahneman and Tversky (1972) stated, "Statistical significance is commonly viewed as the representation of scientific truth. Hence, a real effect (in the population) is expected to be represented by a significant result (in the sample) with insufficient regard for the size of the sample" (p. 433). In sum, samples are assumed to be highly representative of the population from which they were drawn, irrespective of the size of the sample, or even the method by which the sample was drawn. The law of small numbers should come to mind when considering the size of the reference groups used for generating probabilistic estimates in the life tables of actuarial risk scales. Assuming that the reference groups are highly representative (similar to the population in all risk-relevant characteristics) may lead to the inductive fallacy (Taleb, 2005) (overconfidence in our ability to infer characteristics of the population from the observed characteristics of the individual).

Availability Heuristic

In *The Sign of the Four*, a Sir Arthur Conan Doyle Sherlock Holmes mystery, Dr. John Watson meets Miss Mary Morstan for the first time when she knocks on the door at 221B Baker Street. Dr. Watson first observed "a blonde young lady, small, dainty, well gloved, and dressed in the most perfect taste. There was, however, a plainness and simplicity about her costume which bore with it a suggestion of limited means." Konnikova (2013) commented,

> Right away, the image stirs up memories in his head of other young, dainty blondes Watson has known—but not frivolous ones, mind you; ones who are plain and simple and undemanding, who do not throw their beauty in your face but smooth it over with a dress that is somber beige, "untrimmed and unbraided." And so, Mary's expression becomes "sweet and amiable, her large blue eyes were singularly spiritual and sympathetic." Watson concludes his opening paean with the words, "In an experience of women which extended over many nations and three separate continents, I have never looked upon a face which gave a clearer promise of a refined and sensitive nature." Right away, the good doctor has jumped from a color of hair and complexion and a style of dress to a far more reaching character judgment. Mary's appearance suggests simplicity; perhaps so. But sweetness? Amiability? Spirituality? Sympathy? Refinement and sensitivity? Watson has no basis whatsoever for any of these judgments. Mary has yet to say a single word in his presence. All she has done is enter the room. But already a host of biases are at play, vying with one another to create a complete picture of this stranger. . . . This tendency is a common and powerful one, known as the availability heuristic.
>
> (p. 41–42)

The availability heuristic was first described by Tversky and Kahneman (1973, 1974) as a method by which decision-makers "assess the frequency of a class or the probability of an event by the ease with which instances or occurrences can be brought to mind" (1974, p. 1127). The availability heuristic can simply be understood as the tendency to magnify the likelihood of events when they are readily imagined and to underappreciate the likelihood of events that are distantly removed. The more easily thoughts, images, and fantasies come to mind, the more "probable" they are. That is, the more that something is a "headline grabber" (Plous, 1993, p. 122), the more "available" it will be. As such, airplane crashes are far more "available" than car crashes, despite the dramatic difference in frequency.

When we employ the availability heuristic we are effectively assessing the degree of risk according to the possibilities that easily come to mind

(Tversky & Kahneman, 1972, 1973). As Sunstein (2005) and numerous others have pointed out, the availability heuristic can lead to serious risk assessment errors as a result of combined fear and base rate neglect. Indeed, Plous (1993) remarked, "When it comes to probability and frequency estimates, no heuristic is more central than the availability heuristic" (p. 130).

The two principal heuristics for facilitating intuitive judgments of probability, *representativeness* and *availability*, were contrasted by Kahneman and Tversky (1972):

> The major difference between the two heuristics lies in the nature of the judgment which underlies the evaluation of subjective probability. According to the representative heuristic, one evaluates subjective probability by the degree of correspondence between the sample and the population, or between an occurrence and a model. This heuristic, therefore, emphasizes the generic features, or the connotation, of the event. According to the availability heuristic, on the other hand, subjective probability is evaluated by the difficulty of retrieval and construction of instances . . . it focuses.

Although we discuss the concept of *familiarity* in greater depth in relation to the broader consideration of the affect heuristic, it should be noted that the availability heuristic is importantly affected by familiarity as well as salience. That is, how "available" our thoughts are about risk-related possibilities is partly a function of our familiarity with those possibilities as well as the salience of those possibilities. All three constructs were sewn together by Plous (1993):

> (1) The more *available* an event is, the more frequent or probable it will seem; (2) the more *vivid* a piece of information is, the more easily recalled and convincing it will be; and (3) the more *salient* something is, the more likely it will be to appear causal.
>
> (p. 178)

The relation between salience and causal attribution has been firmly established (Taylor & Fiske, 1978) and is potentially very important in forensic contexts.

Vividness

"Vividness" is how "imaginable" something is (e.g., the clarity of the image or the ease with which the image comes to mind). Vividness, "a close cousin of availability" (Plous, 1993), can be a powerful tool in influencing opinion: "The power of vivid information is widely appreciated by advertising executives, politicians, and many other 'professional persuaders.' One area in which vividness can be absolutely pivotal is a court of law" (p. 127). Prentky et al. (2006) also commented that vivid detail, for experts as well as juries, can be misleading and frequently detracts from the objectivity and reliability of an opinion. Vivid detail can have a potent psychologically biasing effect that is explained by the availability heuristic.

In one of the earliest demonstrations of the potential power of vividness in the courtroom, Reyes, Thompson, and Bower (1980) examined the influence of vivid vs. pallid information on mock jury decisions. In a controlled study, Reyes, Thompson, and Bower manipulated evidence in a drunk driving case such that the facts of the case were either vivid or more pallid. The side—either defense or prosecution—that used the vivid evidence prevailed in mock jury verdicts. Moreover, the advantage of vividness was even more pronounced when the verdicts were reported 48 hours *after* the evidence had been presented—when the vivid evidence would remain more clearly in the minds of the jurors than the pallid evidence.

> In one of the most significant jury trials in recent history (*Silkwood v. Kerr-McGee Corp.*, 1984), the famous attorney Gerry Spence told jurors to think about the situation in terms of a zookeeper who carelessly left a cage door unlatched, allowing a ferocious lion to escape and attack a hapless woman who had the bad fortune to be in harm's way. The story about the negligent zookeeper "told" the jurors what to do about the corporation that had allegedly allowed employees to become contaminated with radioactive plutonium, and they found the company liable for $10 million in punitive damages. . . . Another famous trial attorney, with the colorful nickname "Racehorse" Haynes, was quoted as saying, "The lawyer with the best story wins." He went on to advise (defense) attorneys, "The surest way to win a murder case is to convince the jury that the best ending for the story told by the evidence is that the decedent deserved to die." Anthony Amsterdam, another legendary attorney, has analyzed transcripts of attorney's arguments to the jury to demonstrate that they often tell two kinds of stories: First are stories about the evidence, the "what happened" at the crime scene, and second are stories about the trial, with careful attention to the role that the attorney wants the jurors to play in that narrative (Amsterdam & Hertz, 1992). In the O.J. Simpson murder trial, Marcia Clark's closing argument as prosecutor included a detailed summary of the prosecution crime story, complete with a timeline; in contrast, the defense attorney, Johnnie Cochran, concluded by exhorting the jurors to accept the role, at trial, of protector, even avenger, of oppressed minority defendants (Hastie & Pennington, 1996). . . . Many African Americans and members of their immediate families have had negative, probably racist, encounters with justice system authorities. African Americans know of many

> more stories of police racism and police brutality directed against members of their race than do European Americans. This background of experience, beliefs, and relevant stories made it easy for African Americans to construct and believe a story in which a police officer manufactured and planted key incriminating evidence.
>
> (Hastie & Dawes, 2010, p. 123, p. 125)

As Jackson, Rogers, and Shuman (2004) demonstrated experimentally, "certain types of information, such as emotionally-evocative victim statements, can bias the professional conducting the forensic evaluation" (p. 125). Focusing on highly evocative, vivid information can lead to an overestimation of predictive efficacy and erroneous judgments. Vivid information is more persuasive than "pallid" information, because vivid information is more "available," easier to retrieve, and presumably lingers more in the memory. Vividness is a first indicator of availability, and frequently an important red flag of a lurking heuristic. Our good friend and colleague, Dr. Barbara Schwartz, who has evaluated "thousands" of sex offenders over the past 40+ years, is famously quoted as saying, "The visuals can kill you." Barbara's simple, pithy expression captures the perils of vividness for forensic examiners.

Illusory Correlations

Tversky and Kahneman (1974) described the illusory correlation effect, noting that it was a natural byproduct of the *availability heuristic*. The *representative heuristic* may also explain some illusory correlations (e.g., when one event appears to be typical or representative of another event). Our judgments of how often two "events" co-occur (e.g., substance abuse and recidivism) can be explained by the perceived strength of the association between them. When the association is perceived to be strong (substance abuse frequently contributes to recidivism), the judge/expert is likely to conclude that the two frequently co-occur. The strength of the association may be understood as a function of its *availability*. These *apparent* correlations (illusory, imaginary, unreal), referred to by Fiedler (2011) as voodoo correlations, can be irresistible and ubiquitous.

Tversky and Kahneman (1974) reported a study by Chapman and Chapman (1969) in which naïve judges were given information about hypothetical mental patients. The information consisted of a clinical diagnosis and drawing supposedly made by the patient. The judges were asked to estimate the frequency with which the diagnosis was accompanied by features of the drawing. The judges "markedly overestimated the frequency of co-occurrence of natural associates, such as suspiciousness [an aspect of the clinical diagnosis] and peculiar eyes [a feature of the drawing]" (Tversky & Kahneman, 1974). Chapman and Chapman (1969), referring to this effect as an "illusory correlation," noted that

> in clinical practice the observer is reinforced in his observation of illusory correlations by the reports of his fellow clinicians, who themselves are subject to the same illusions. Such agreement among experts is, unfortunately, often mistaken as evidence for the truth of the observation.

The Chapmans concluded that "the clinician's cognitive task may exceed the capacity of the human intellect. They suggested that subjective intuition may need to be replaced, at least partly, by statistical methods of prediction" (Slovic, Kunreuther, & White, 2000, p. 12). Similarly, Tversky and Kahneman (1974) noted that, "The illusory correlation effect was extremely resistant to contradictory data. It persisted even when the correlation between symptom and diagnosis was actually negative, and it prevented the judges from detecting relationships that were in fact present." In the first paper by Loren Chapman (1967) on the illusory correlation, he noted that this effect was not solely an attribute of clinicians. Indeed, the effect of illusory correlation paints a very wide brush stroke across human beliefs that are empirically unfounded and often associated with severely adverse outcomes, including most racial, ethnic, and religious stereotypes (Jennings, Amabile, & Ross, 1982). Clearly, within the "realm of covariation assessment, the contest between expectations and evidence is apt to be an unequal one" (Jennings, Amabile, & Ross, 1982, p. 215).

A variation of the illusory correlation might be Felson's (1998) "pestilence fallacy." Felson used the term "pestilence fallacy" to refer to the tendency to think of crime "as one of many evils that comes from other evils in society" (p. 19). As Felson pointed out, bad things often occur together or around the same time, but that doesn't mean that one caused the other. Poverty does not *cause* crime, and crime does not *cause* poverty, but the two are often correlated. A similar example is paternal absence. An absent father does not *cause* crime, but it is often correlated with crime. In these instances, there is a statistical correlation but it is valueless.

The effect of illusory correlations is profoundly important (and equally unacknowledged) in forensic risk assessment. Examples are far too numerous to detail, although several that are more common include the effect of a substance abuse history or a history of childhood sexual abuse on recidivism *among sex offenders*, as well as many clinical variables, such as "denial," and lack of motivation for treatment. In the Hanson and Bussiere (1998) meta-analysis, the Pearson correlation (r value) between being sexually abused as a child and recidivism was .00, and the correlation of having a negative clinical presentation and recidivism was also .00. In the Hanson and Morton-Bourgon (2005) meta-analysis, which used the average Cohen's d value as the effect size indicator, the d value denial and recidivism was .02; the d value for lack of victim empathy and recidivism was –.08, and the d value for low motivation for treatment and recidivism was also –.08. Poor treatment progress/failure to complete treatment, often introduced as aggravating evidence in court, are only weakly associated with recidivism ($r = .17$ in Hanson and Bussiere, 1998; $d = .14$ in Hanson and Morton-Bourgon, 2005). As a rule, d values $\leq .20$ reflect a small effect size; thus, $d = .14$ is clearly in the range of a small effect, and d values of .02 and –.08 reflect no effect. Introducing evidence based on correlations of 0 or d values of –.08 – .14 as probative, or assuming causality based on such evidence, is all too commonplace in the SVP courtroom.

A meta-analysis of 58 studies (64 unique samples) of mentally disordered offenders found similar results (Bonta, Law, & Hanson, 1998). Bonta et al. (1998) used the Pearson correlation coefficient as their effect size indicator, reporting the Z-transformed r. For general recidivism, the correlations were: alcohol use (.06), drug use (.09), and substance abuse of any kind (.11). For violent recidivism, the correlation with substance abuse of any kind was .08. Bonta et al. (1998) also found that the correlation between clinical variables (as a domain) and general recidivism was –.02 (and –.03 for violent recidivism). Clearly, none of these effect sizes justify their use in supporting judgments of risk for recidivism.

Affect Heuristic

We introduced the availability heuristic with Doyle's *The Sign of the Four*, and provided, by way of Watson's initial response to Mary Morstan, an example of availability. As Konnikova (2013) observed, however, "a host of biases are at play" in this mystery. Another prominent heuristic, according to Konnikova (2013), involves Dr. Watson's affect:

> The first thing Watson notices is the lady's appearance. She is, he remarks, a rather attractive woman. Irrelevant, counters Holmes. "It is of the first importance not to allow your judgment to be biased by personal qualities," he explains. "A client is to me a mere unit, a factor in a problem. The emotional qualities are antagonistic to clear reasoning. I assure you that the most winning woman I ever knew was hanged for poisoning three children for their insurance-money, and the most repellent man of my acquaintance is a philanthropist who has spent nearly a quarter of a million upon the London poor." Holmes' point is clear enough. It's not that you won't experience emotion. Nor are you likely to be able to suspend the impressions that form almost automatically in your mind. But you don't have to let those impressions get in the way of objective reasoning.
>
> (p. 40)

Humans, with a few notable exceptions (e.g., psychopaths), are emotional creatures. Emotions color our perceptions and can profoundly affect our judgments of risk (Finucane, Alhakami, Slovic, & Johnson, 2000; Loewenstein, Weber, Hsee, & Welch, 2001; Slovic, Finucane, Peters, & MacGregor, 2002; Slovic, Finucane, Peters, & MacGregor, 2004; Slovic, Peters, Finucane, & MacGregor, 2005). The occasional tension between prudent self-control and wild abandon to the id's self-indulgent wishes is a duality of human nature that can be traced as far back as Plato, who described an otherwise rational charioteer trying to control two horses, one of whom was wild and poorly trained (Hastie & Dawes, 2010, p. 304). Seymour Epstein alluded to this duality in commenting that "there is no dearth of evidence in everyday life that people apprehend reality in two fundamentally different ways, one variously labeled intuitive, automatic, natural non-verbal, narrative and experiential, and the other analytical, deliberative, verbal and rational" (p. 710). The vast majority of us are adequately trained to manage our urges and impulses, if for no other reason than fear of social and/or legal sanction. Those of us with behavior management problems and poorly installed or defective monitoring software who are bent on violating social mores and laws are labeled as "impulsive." This does not mean that the rest of us do not share similarly extravagant, self-indulgent, or even criminal urges. President Jimmy Carter was famously quoted during an interview with Robert Scheer for *Playboy* during the 1976 Presidential Campaign as saying that he had "lust in his heart." However inappropriate his disclosure may have been given his standing and the occasion (cf. Solomon, 1978), he nonetheless reminded us that even he had "impure" thoughts.

One of the most prominent exponents of the importance of emotions in decision-making was Robert Zajonc (1980, 1984), who believed that our affective responses are automatic and influenced subsequent decisions. The affect heuristic, as described by Slovic et al. (2005), is reliance on affective or emotional responses, which may occur rapidly and automatically, in the decision-making process. The characterization of affect as a heuristic can be found in Finucane, Alhakami, Slovic, and Johnson (2000), wherein one's awareness of one's affect provides a cue (a mental shortcut) in arriving at a decision. Reliance—or non-reliance—on affect as part of our decision-making has a long lineage. Risk "analysis" dates back to the Mesopotamian priests (6th millennium BC) who routinely evaluated the impacts of proposed technological projects (Shrader-Frechette, 1991). The *science* of risk analysis, however, emerges only within the past half-century, dating back to the late 1960s. Early studies on perceived risks and perceived benefits revealed an apparent inverse relationship (Alhakami & Slovic, 1994; Slovic et al., 2005). When the perceived risk is low and the perceived benefit is high, the individual is favorably disposed toward a positive judgment or decision. Conversely, when the perceived risk is high and the perceived benefit is low, the individual is favorably disposed toward a negative judgment or decision. The significance of this inverse relationship is quite interesting: we evaluate risk not only by our rational estimation of the quantum of risk present but also by how we *feel* about the risk (Slovic & Peters, 2006).

Ordinarily, risks and benefits are coupled and examined together (e.g., risk of pesticides offset against the benefits of improved crop yield). If pesticide use has a positive valence (has positive affect associated with it), then the judgment of risk and benefit is linked to the strength of the positive affect connected with pesticide use. Placing this lesson in a forensic context is difficult, since forensic evaluations are not conducted under the controlled conditions of a laboratory study. However, we can offer an extrapolation. When we evaluate whether an incarcerated inmate (civilly committed or incarcerated) should be supported for release or parole, we weigh what we believe to be risk-aggravating factors (e.g., a score on a risk scale, extent of criminal history, nature of governing offense, age/gender of victim(s), institutional violations/observation of behavior reports/disciplinary reports, etc.) against what we believe to be risk-mitigating factors (age, length of time in prison, treatment in prison, educational or avocational programs in prison, quality of the discharge plan, etc.).

The "benefit" in this context is not our personal benefit—like weighing the risks of skiing a new black diamond route against the expected benefits of a challenging run. The "benefit" is couched in terms of a personal conviction that (a) most offenders are basically good people that made a mistake and deserve a second chance; prison is costly and provides no meaningful rehabilitation; I was hired by the defense attorney and want to support her/his client, etc., or (b) most offenders are basically unredeemable and don't deserve a second chance; protecting society is more important than giving this guy another chance; I was hired by the prosecutor and want to support her/him, etc. These personal convictions reflect not only values but also real affect. As we discuss later on in the book, biases in both directions lead to increased mistakes: (a) *Reluctance to find someone "dangerous" (high risk)* leads to a potential increase in false negative errors and a decrease in false positive errors, and (b) *Reluctance to find someone not dangerous (low risk)* leads to a potential increase in false positive errors and a decrease in false negative errors.

From a historical perspective, this contrasting stance involving one's feelings about crime and those who perpetrate it was clearly expressed by Sir William Blackstone, whose 18th-century mindset sounds familiar:

> Never was it clearer that "humanity" to Blackstone did not always mean mercy. He insisted that a proper measure of punishment for crime was the "malignity," "heinousness," or "enormity" of an act committed. Hatefulness and disregard for natural feelings, whenever such viciousness appeared in human action, had to be punished; "humanity" itself demanded it. . . . Murder

> demanded capital punishment because it was "a crime at which human nature starts, and which is, I believe, punished almost universally throughout the world with death." The sexual "crime against nature" had to be similarly penalized because "this the voice of nature and of reason, and the express law of God, determined to be capital. . . . For evil, the nearer we approach it, is the more disagreeable and shocking; so that it requires more obstinacy in wickedness to perpetrate an unlawful action, than barely to entertain the thought of it: and it is an encouragement to repentance and remorse, even to the last stage of any crime, that it never is too late to retract."
>
> (Boorstin, 1958, p. 144)

Beginning in the 1990s, evidence accumulated supporting dual-process theories of information processing and the important role of affect in information processing (e.g., Chaiken & Trope, 1999; Epstein, 1994; Sloman, 1996). Slovic et al. (2004) described three such modes of processing information related to risk: *risk as feelings*, *risk as analysis*, and *risk as politics*. Risk as feelings "refers to our fast, instinctive, and intuitive reactions to dangers . . . an important vestige of our evolutionary journey" (p. 1). Risk as analysis "brings logic, reason, and scientific deliberation to bear on hazard management" (p. 1). The "clash" between these two leads to the third, risk as politics. Were rationality absent from risk as feelings, the human species might have gone the way of the dinosaur. As Slovic et al. (2005) note:

> There are strong elements of rationality in both systems. It was our experiential system, after all, that enabled human beings to survive during their long period of evolution. Long before there was probability theory, risk assessment, and decision analysis, there were intuition, instinct, and gut feeling to tell people whether an animal was safe to approach or water was safe to drink. As life became more complex and humans gained more control over their environment, analytic tools were invented to "boost" the rationality of their experiential thinking. Subsequently, analytic thinking was placed on a pedestal and portrayed as the epitome of rationality. Affect and emotions were seen as interfering with reason.
>
> (p. S35–S40)

Earlier we spoke of pervasive fear leading to moral panic, a "social paranoia" as Lancaster (2011) referred to it (p. 281), that led to lynchings, witchcraft trials, and black lists. Clearly, fear plays a central role in risk as feelings, not only for cave dwellers but also for the pilgrims in Salem. This was the *dread* when confronting a saber-tooth tiger or the incarnation of

Satan. This visceral fear is invariably threat-based and subject to clan or group contagion, prompting group or societal panic.

Sandman (1989) developed an "outrage model" in which "dread" was associated with a range of factors, such as lethality, fairness, and controllability. Outrage was, for Sandman, the bright line that separated lay (society's) evaluations of risk from professional (expert) evaluations of risk. Two recent studies by Salerno and Peter-Hagene (2013) found that moral outrage is a combination of anger and disgust. In their first study, anger toward sexual assault and funeral picketing (two moral transgressions) predicted moral outrage only when the anger co-occurred with disgust; conversely, disgust predicted moral outrage only when it co-occurred with anger. In their second study using mock jurors and emotionally disturbing photographs of a murder victim, disgust was a more consistent predictor of moral outrage than anger. Thus, Salerno and Peter-Hagene (2013) provided evidence that moral outrage emerges from a combination of anger *and* disgust—even when the moral transgression was not a "body-disgust violation" (i.e., funeral picketing). Moreover, in their second study, moral outrage mediated the effect of both anger and disgust on the murder verdicts: Anger increased moral outrage, which in turn increased the subject's confidence in a guilty verdict, but only when the anger co-occurred with disgust; disgust predicted confidence in a guilty verdict at all levels of anger.

The role of affect in rational decision-making clearly includes judgments about risk of criminal behavior and is central to rendering reliable opinions. The affect to which we refer, however, is best captured by what Slovic et al. (2005) aptly referred to as a "faint whisper of emotion" (p. S35). As human decision-makers, we do not process information as automatons; we frequently contend, consciously or unconsciously, with a "faint whisper of emotion." As Damasio (1994) demonstrated 20 years ago, affect is integral to rational decision-making. Damasio's well-known somatic-marker hypothesis argued that emotions act as "markers," either overtly (e.g., "gut feelings") or covertly below our conscious radar (e.g., at the level of neurotransmitters). The somatic-marker hypothesis proposes that optimal decisions are aided by emotions, especially when the various pros and cons of decision options—the risks and benefits—are uncertain. The neuroscience of decision-making underscores the complexity of the interplay between two engaged systems, the neural system responsible for eliciting emotions ("gut feelings") and the neural system responsible for influencing decisions (i.e., behavior) in response to the emotions (Naqvi, Shiv, & Bechara, 2006).

Although some (e.g., Camerer & Kunreuther, 1989) long ago described the emotional dimensions of risk, the role of affect in assessing risk has been the subject of much controversy. Those who determined risk solely according to "gut feelings" were derided, as evidence mounted that clinical judgment was inferior to empirically guided judgment. Forensic experts have, for the most part, studiously and conscientiously abided by the lessons of a half-century of research pointing to the superiority of empirically based judgments of risk. The courts, moreover, are so accustomed to hearing testimony supported by one or more risk assessment scales that it has become the norm. Ideally, this is as it should be—adherence to science, proper interpretation of the science, effective communication of the science, and admissibility of the science. It appears, however, that in our due diligence we have lost a potentially critical element—affect.

If risk assessment was little more than the accurate coding of risk factors from archival data, expensive forensic psychologists and psychiatrists would not be needed. Computers could replace humans in the courtroom. Relevant data would be fed in and the computer would spit out, affect-free, a strictly actuarial appraisal of risk with a range of probabilistic estimates based on different conditions and circumstances. Since cross-examining a computer may be unrewarding, yielding suboptimal responses, the court may be forced to call upon our affect-compromised humans. Fortunately for our affect-compromised humans, the latest wave of cognitive neuroscience, and the comparatively new reincarnation of *neurolaw*, may provide the forensic examiner with new tools, less susceptible to emotions, such as functional neuroimaging (Gazzaniga & Steven, 2005). Our experts may one day bring into the SVP hearing a functional magnetic resonance image (fMRI) of the defendant's/respondent's ventromedial hypothalamus.

In the meantime, forensic risk assessors are saddled with making affect-infused, rational decisions. As Gerald Clore implored in his 2013 William James Fellow Award Address to the Association for Psychological Science, our emotions color our cognitive processes, including our capacity for rational decision-making (Merluzzi, 2014). Being blind to our feelings or ignoring our feelings is not an option if reliability is our end goal. Awareness of an emotional response to a client must be "factored out." The affect to which we refer is *not* incapacitating fear or existential threats or moral panic. Rather, the "faint whisper of emotion" that Slovic and Peters (2006) described is more germane. This faint whisper most often takes the form of varying degrees of discomfort in reading discovery, viewing crime scene photographs, watching videotapes of rapes or child pornography, or hearing the client's disclosures, all of which may be sufficiently "dissonant," "foreign" (unfamiliar) or familiar and disturbing that judgments about risk are colored. We try to bring this message closer to home in the next section on familiarity.

Familiarity and Similarity

What is instinctively "safe" is that which evokes similarity to *self*, again undoubtedly a hold-over from pre-historic times when members of other tribes, representing the *unknown*, were feared as potential threats. The Yiddish/Middle High German expression *landsman* captures this universal sense of *familiarity*. When meeting a *landsman*, we are rewarded by an instant feeling of comfort knowing that a stranger is a fellow Jew and hence can be trusted. Whether the fellow traveler can objectively be trusted merely because of religious affiliation is questionable at best. What is relevant, however, is the *gut feeling* that he can be trusted, which is no more than the perception of familiarity or similarity based on religious affiliation. Most of us share that common sense of connection, traveling in a foreign land, stumbling upon a stranger and discovering that she or he hails from the same country or even the same region of our country. Religious affiliation is only one of many identities that may confer this sense of comfort based on something shared, hence familiar. You may hail from Boston and discover another Red Sox fan on the streets of Milan. And of course it's always comforting thousands of miles from Milwaukee finding a Red Dog fan on the streets of Prague, or a Mississippi Mud Black & Tan (NY) fan in Athens, or a Red Brick Beer (Atlanta) fan in Moscow. These similarities, admittedly, are superficial to say the least, but there is an instant sense of familiarity that is comforting and paves the way for further discourse. Noting that the evolutionary biologist Stephen J. Gould once remarked that, "our minds are not built . . . to work by the laws of probability," Hastie and Dawes (2010) went on to say, "What our minds do seem to work by is a basic sense of similarity" (p. 104). As noted, from an evolutionary standpoint, what is similar or familiar is distinctly less threatening than what is experienced as foreign or alien.

The importance of similarity can be traced back at least to Byrne (1961), who introduced the notion of attitude similarity as a method for studying attraction. Byrne (1961) discovered a powerful connection between similarity and attraction. Byrne's research demonstrated that "any time another person offers us validation by indicating that his percepts and concepts are congruent with ours, it constitutes a rewarding interaction and, hence, one element in forming a positive relationship" (p. 713). The opposite is, similarly, the case as well. When attitudes (or percepts and concepts) are incongruent (dissimilar), it introduces dissonance (e.g., Festinger, 1957), and degrades the relationship by invalidating what we believe to be true. Although dissimilarity functions at multiple levels, the net effect is frequently affect (i.e., what is dissimilar can be threatening, prompting reactions ranging from unease, distress, and angst to panic).

The targets for many of those accused of witchcraft were *dis*similar; they were set apart, social outcasts; by virtue of their breeding, class status, skin color, or origin, they were different. Perhaps most importantly, they were different in a way that aroused some discomfort, in a similar way that a homeless beggar on the street arouses discomfort, prompting us, most likely unconsciously, to move several feet away as we pass or to increase the pace of our gait. Although we may feel discomfort, we don't feel threatened. Our "split second" decision to choose engagement reappraisal (drop a few coins into his can) or disengagement distraction (move away, cross the street, pull out your phone and pretend to make a call) depends on the intensity of our negative emotion (Sheppes, Scheibe, Suri, & Gross, 2011). The higher the intensity, the more likely we are to disengage. At some point, the intensity reaches threat-level. We are informed by "reliable" sources, for example, that some street people carry an infectious disease that is highly transmissible and can be fatal! Street people now become pariahs; more than momentary discomfort, they pose a serious threat. Mere discomfort turns to anger and disgust; moral outrage takes over, and we demand that the city "do something." "Witches" were far more than simply dissimilar. Witches posed an existential threat to the lives of the Puritans. True witches were agents of Satan and had to be destroyed. Perhaps most importantly, similarity is not merely appearance; it includes shared moral values and even shared affective norms (Szczurek, Monin, & Gross, 2012). Szczurek and her colleagues (2012) reported that their subjects had "moral outrage" at those who violated affective norms.

Hastie and Dawes (2010) noted the importance of similarity:

> As in the case of availability-based judgments, similarity slips into the judgment process automatically and dominates spontaneous judgments of category membership. The primary behavioral "signature" of relying on similarity is that people miss important statistical or logical structure in the situation and ignore relevant information.
>
> (p. 102)

On a pedestrian note, I (RAP) recently visited a moderate-size mid-Western city with my wife. It was a beautiful fall weekend, and we were there for a wedding. On Sunday morning we drove to a fancy downtown hotel for a brunch/reception. It was warm, the sky was blue, and downtown was deserted. We parked on the street three blocks from the hotel. As we were leaving the car, my wife admonished me to empty the back seat. There were several coats and miscellaneous papers. I protested, and it ended in a squabble. Insensitively, I pointed out that her fear of someone breaking into the car under existing conditions exemplified base rate neglect, which, of course, did not ameliorate matters. As we discussed it later on, she reminded me that she, not I, spent most of her young adult years living in downtown Philadelphia where she, not I, had been twice assaulted at knifepoint on the street and had her car broken into. If we applied the availability heuristic, it is obvious that far more examples of risky outcomes leap to her mind than to mine; moreover, these examples were far more salient for her than anything remotely comparable were for me. Although my car was twice vandalized in NYC, these incidents constituted more of a nuisance involving police reports and dealing with the insurance company. Thus, my *familiarity* with this sort of outcome was vastly different from hers. In sum, we arrived at very different conclusions about the risk posed to our vehicle.

A familiar example of the availability heuristic and familiarity was provided by Silver (2012), who related comments from Secretary Donald Rumsfeld at a U.S. Department of Defense News Briefing in February 2002 about the lack of evidence of weapons of mass destruction in Iraq and hence the lack of evidence of a supply chain to terrorists:

> You can reasonably predict behavior if people would prefer not to die. But if people are just as happy dying, or feel that it's a privilege or that it achieves their goal, then they're going to behave in a very different way.
>
> (p. 424)

Stated otherwise, the behavior of the Al Qaeda terrorists was wholly *unfamiliar* to us. Rumsfeld has been more famously quoted as saying at that News Briefing:

> As we know, there are known knowns; there are things that we know that we know. We also know there are known unknowns; that is to say we know there are some things we do not know. But there are also unknown unknowns, the ones we don't know we don't know.

Translated, Al Qaeda was "known" as an entity but for all intents and purposes "unknown" at that time in terms of an instinctual understanding of motivation, as well as operational capacity. Thus, *prior* to September 11, the devastation wrought by the terrorists was under-predicted, because it was "unavailable" (nothing like it had ever happened on American soil) and "unfamiliar."

Familiarity and Sexual Crimes

Sexual interest in children and sexual crimes committed against children are as disturbing and as cognitively dissonant to forensic mental health professionals as they are to everyone else. We are not immune to feelings of repugnance. When conducting an interview, listening to a child molester recount the details of his offenses, there is a homunculus in our brain that occasionally whispers, "You did what!?!" Hopefully, we are trained to ignore the homunculus and get on with the interview. The presence of that "inner voice" is a sign of *un*familiarity or *dis*similarity—in this case, inability to comprehend at some human level the behavior of the defendant. If the reason for unfamiliarity is cognitive, evoking no particular emotional response (e.g., walking down Fifth Avenue in Manhattan seeing a group of women in burqas), any residual discomfort rarely influences our behavior. As discomfort begins to stoke our emotions, raising fear, revulsion, anxiety, and anger, a behavioral response becomes increasingly likely (e.g., extricating ourselves from the circumstances or stimuli evoking the negative feelings). Since our emotions appear to affect our perception of risk in different ways (Slovic & Peters, 2006) (e.g., fear exacerbates our estimation of risk, while anger seems to mitigate our sense of risk), our behavioral response is highly likely to be influenced by our emotional state. Walking down Fifth Avenue in Manhattan seeing a disheveled street barker cloaked in large black trash bags holding a placard and railing about the end of days, we might be inclined to give the gentleman a wide berth. Removing ourselves is not an option when seated in front of a defendant conducting a forensic interview.

Our capacity for holding at bay our emotional responses to clients is instrumental to conducting an unbiased, objective evaluation. Sex offenders often challenge our capacity for unwarped judgment. The more that a client's sexually deviant and offense-related behavior violates the "norm" and magnifies feelings of unfamiliarity and hence discomfort, the more challenging is the task of remaining objective. Although what pushes our proverbial "buttons" varies by life experience, it is reasonable to surmise that gratuitous or expressive aggression, wanton or cruel physical injury, sadism and related paraphilias, and offenses involving children tax us the most. Part of our job is learning to maintain a guard, an impermeable membrane that *modulates* emotional responses to defendants. No matter how many years of experience we have under our belts, we are never immune to being caught "off guard" if the membrane leaks.

Many years ago, one of us (RAP) was asked to evaluate several individuals within a space of two weeks who had been picked up by the police for being sexual with animals. Not surprisingly, the police were at a loss what to do with them (the offenders, not the animals). The second of these clients was a young woman who was engaging in intercourse with a German Shepherd while her boyfriend videotaped the encounter. A good samaritan neighbor, reportedly just happening to be walking by and glancing in the window of a residential home, saw the encounter unfolding. He called the police. I set out to conduct a standard interview, admittedly unsure at the outset what the police wanted to know or what exactly I was looking for. Nevertheless, I proceeded to walk through a more or less typical history (e.g., details of relationship with boyfriend, full sexual history with boyfriend, history of engaging in similar acts with animals before, and of course the purpose or intention of videotaping it). At some point, when asking the client about the "mechanics" of the act, I asked her how the dog got aroused. As if it was the dumbest question, she looked at me with disbelief and responded "Obviously, I came down on him." I was completely caught off guard by the visual image, and it took me a minute or two to re-group.

That incident has stayed with me all these years, not because of the image, which admittedly I found a bit repulsive, but because of how I allowed myself to be caught off guard. Somehow the act of "intercourse," although straining the boundaries of what I recognized as "familiar," was more acceptable than putting her mouth on a dog's penis, which was utterly unfamiliar and highly discomforting. Although this example is trivial in its import, it illustrates, at the lowest end of a continuum of gravity, the sort of "atypical" (and unfamiliar) behaviors that we are exposed to as forensic examiners and, most importantly, how our visceral responses to those behaviors can affect our judgment. Other clients that I have evaluated engaged in vastly more violent acts—such as a sexual homicide of a young girl by a man widely reported by the media to be a "cannibal," and three strangulations of women by a woman widely reported to be a "multiple" and a "vampire"—requiring emotional distance from these high-voltage reports and an objective (i.e., "rational") analysis of the risk-relevance of cannabilistic fantasies or vampyrism. As forensic examiners evaluating criminals, we have all been exposed, to one degree or another, to behavior that is repugnant and elicits disgust. At some point, we become inured to such behavior. Even then, however, the most case-hardened forensic examiner remains susceptible to that *faint whisper* of the homunculus that says "yuck."

Other Sources of Bias

Overconfidence: The Illusion of Certitude

Hubris is the *tragic flaw* afflicting the character of mortals and immortals alike, *hamartia* to the Ancient Greeks, a condition that today suggests overweening pride, arrogance, or pomposity. Self-importance, perhaps a somewhat less pejorative way of describing it, has one remarkably important attribute—overconfidence. Optimal confidence, healthy and inspiring, becomes a potential tragic flaw when excessive. As Plous (1993), stated, "No problem in judgment and decision-making is more prevalent and more potentially catastrophic than overconfidence" (p. 217), and Slovic, Fischhoff, and Lichtenstein (1982) referred to overconfidence as "A particularly pernicious aspect of heuristics" (p. 472). Similarly, Hastie and Dawes noted that, "Our judgment faculties are subject to certain systematic flaws, perhaps the most prominent of which is simple overconfidence" (p. 46).

Even the iconic sleuth Sherlock Holmes occasionally had overconfident days. As Konnikova (2013) observed,

> We run the risk of falling prey to those two great slayers of success: complacency and overconfidence. These are powerful enemies indeed. Even to someone like Sherlock Holmes. Consider for a moment "The Yellow Face," one of the rare cases where Holmes' theories turn out to be completely wrong. . . . As "The Yellow Face" draws to a close, Holmes has one final message for his companion. "Watson, if it should ever strike you that I am getting a little overconfident in my powers, or giving less pains to a case than it deserves, kindly whisper 'Norbury' in my ear, and I shall be infinitely obliged to you." [Norbury is a town in a borough of London where the story took place.]
>
> (p. 197, p. 205)

The import of overconfidence struck Daniel Kahneman at a young age during the time that he was satisfying his national service requirement in the Israeli Army, an experience recounted in some detail in his New York Times article "The Surety of Fools" (Kahneman, 2011a) and mentioned in his book *Thinking, Fast and Slow* (Kahneman, 2011b). As a 21-year-old lieutenant, Kahneman was tasked with developing an interview system to select candidates for officer training school. Kahneman observes in retrospect,

> Despite our certainty about the potential of individual candidates, our forecasts were largely useless. The evidence was overwhelming . . . The story was always the same: our ability to predict performance at the school was negligible. Our forecasts were better than blind guesses, but not by much. . . . The dismal truth about the quality of our predictions had no effect whatsoever on how we evaluated new candidates and very little effect on the confidence we had in our judgments and predictions.
>
> (2011a, pp. 31–32)

Kahneman also notes,

> I thought that what was happening to us was remarkable. The statistical evidence of our failure should have shaken our confidence in our judgments of particular candidates, but it did not. It should also have caused us to moderate our predictions, but it did not. We knew as a general fact that our predictions were little better than random guesses, but we continued to feel and act as if each particular prediction was valid. I was reminded of

> visual illusions, which remain compelling even when you know that what you see is false. I was so struck by the analogy that I coined a term for our experience: the illusion of validity. I had discovered my first cognitive fallacy.
>
> (Kahneman, 2011a, p. 32)

As Kahneman (2011b) asserted,

> The clinical psychologist, the stock picker, and the pundit do have intuitive skills in some of their tasks, but they have not learned to identify the situations and the tasks in which intuition will betray them. The unrecognized limits of professional skill help explain why experts are often overconfident.
>
> (p. 242)

Absence of any appreciation for the limitations of our skills, no matter how seasoned we are, leads unfailingly to hubris. High-stakes legal decision-making, however, encourages overconfidence. It is a rare (successful) expert that takes the stand and wavers or is irresolute. It would be unacceptable to retaining counsel, to put it mildly, if you acknowledged on cross-examination that you were less than confident in your opinion. Indeed, the hallmark of a prized expert is a steadfast defense of one's opinions and adroit parrying with opposing counsel. All lessons learned about maximally effective expert testimony reinforce hubris and undercut any acknowledgement of personal limitations. As Konnikova (2013) observed, "success breeds overconfidence" (p. 199), and Holmes had every reason to be overconfident, since he was (almost) always right. Sherlock Holmes had the great fortune, however, of being a fictional character; Sir Arthur Conan Doyle made him right almost all the time. By stark contrast, "success" means something quite different for forensic experts. Success means being congratulated by retaining counsel for your masterful testimony, hearing from counsel that "you won," receiving kudos from your colleagues for your nimble jockeying on the stand, and, of course, being hired again by admiring lawyers. Success does *not* mean being right. You may have been right, but it is unlikely that you will ever know it. Feedback about actual "outcomes" is something we rarely receive.

Needless to say, success is not only the pitfall of unwary forensic examiners. Posner (2010) points to its potent effect on Wall Street, citing the research of psychologists working with traders who reported that confidence levels were overly affected by the success of recent trades (Steenbarger, 2002). This is Silver's (2012) winner's curse, placing excessive confidence in forecasting ability—based in good measure on past success. In a marvelous example of unadulterated hubris, Silver (2012) brings us into the world of "Poker Delusions," quoting an accomplished poker player, Darse

Billings, "who developed a computer program that competed successfully against some of the world's best limit hold 'em players" (p. 324):

> There is no other game that I know of where humans are so smug, and think that they just play like wizards, and then play so badly. Basically it's because they don't know anything, and they think they must be God-like, and the truth is that they aren't. If computer programs feed on human hubris, then in poker they will eat like kings. (p. 324)

In the realm of human judgment, the effect of overconfidence is more than merely a nuisance. It is generally regarded as the single most pervasive and potent bias in human judgment (Mannes & Moore, 2013). It was similarly regarded by DeBondt and Thaler (1995), Plous (1993), and Freudenburg (1988), and underscored by Kahneman (2011b). And parenthetically, we might note, by the eminent Scottish philosopher David Hume, who observed that "there is a degree of doubt, caution, and modesty, which, in all kinds of scrutiny and decision, ought for ever to accompany a just reasoner" (cf. Hume, 2001). A variant of overconfidence, referred to as over-precision by Moore and Healy (2008), was examined recently in three experiments by Mannes and Moore (2013). The effect of over-precision, defined as excessive confidence that one knows the truth, was deemed "profound." Participants in the studies "adjusted their estimates less than they should have given their actual knowledge, and this effect was driven by their subjective confidence" (p. 1190). Mannes and Moore (2013) concluded that, "People cling too fervently to beliefs that are poorly supported by evidence, adjusting their beliefs too little in light of the evidence or the consequences of being wrong" (p. 1196).

A related flaw, the hindsight bias, "plays an insidious role in generating unwarranted overconfidence" (Arkes, 2013, p. 357). The hindsight bias is the tendency to exaggerate one's ability to have predicted a past event before it occurred. With the *benefit* of hindsight, our predictive accuracy improves considerably. To assert such accuracy *without* the benefit of hindsight ("Monday morning quarterbacking") may necessitate a bit of clairvoyance—or supreme overconfidence. Testimony from forensic examiners that the governing offense was anticipatable and indeed could have been predicted based on the extant information known before the offense occurred verges on hindsight bias.

The "Winner's Curse" of overconfidence was described by Nate Silver (2012) as the "most pernicious" cognitive bias "that investors suffer from" (p. 359). Silver (2012) was kind enough, however, to assure us that this pernicious cognitive bias was spread democratically across disciplines, effecting medical researchers, political scientists, and psychologists, as well as those in finance (p. 183). Mannes and Moore (2013) also pointed to the effect of overconfidence (or over-precision) on physicians, as well as the broader influence of decreasing tolerance for dissenting points of view.

Perhaps most distressing is the immutability (or recalcitrance) of overconfidence. Dunning, Griffin, Milojkovic, and Ross (1990) noted, almost a quarter century ago, that

> There is reason to believe that highly confident judgments, predictions, or beliefs are apt to persevere even in the face of objective evidence that dispassionate observers would regard as disconfirmatory. By taking at face value information congruent with strong expectations, by "explaining away" apparent failures, and by assimilating mixed or ambiguous evidence with a confirmatory bias, we may multiply the costs of our folly by persisting both in particular judgments and judgmental strategies and in the broader theories or beliefs that underlie them.
>
> (p. 568)

The consistent finding, however, that lay people as well as experts overestimate the accuracy of their judgments (Dunning et al., 1990) would seem to be evolutionarily maladaptive (Posner, 2010). Posner (2010) regards it as *odd*, noting,

> Presumably the human species would not have survived if our sense of confidence was dramatically miscalibrated. If our ancestors had been overconfident, they might have perished picking fights with saber-tooth cats. If they had been underconfident, they might have starved, too fearful of predators to venture from their caves in search of food.
>
> (p. 60)

Presumably, there is a reasonable Darwinian explanation (e.g., overconfidence combined with ineptitude increases the risk of being gobbled up, leaving the overconfident, sly, and deliberate cave dweller to reproduce).

Whatever the actual explanation, there is a clear association between intuitive recognition of "patterns" and feeling confident (Posner, 2010). Premature or erroneous pattern recognition in the presence of (unwarranted) increased confidence is a recipe for defective judgment. Oskamp's (1982) wry conclusion was that,

> It can clearly be concluded that a psychologist's increasing feelings of confidence as he works through a case are *not* a sure sign of increasing accuracy for his conclusions. So-called clinical validation, based on the personal feelings of confidence of the clinician, is not adequate evidence for the validity of clinical judgment in diagnosing or predicting human behavior.
>
> (p. 293)

The potentially "catastrophic" nature of overconfidence was exemplified in a study by Bedau and Radelet (1987) on 350 cases of *wrongful* convictions of capital crimes in the US. Among these 350 cases, 5 were satisfactorily resolved, and all others were sentenced to prison: either terms up to 25 years (n = 67), life (n = 139), or death (n = 139), and 23 had been executed (cf., Radelet, Bedau, & Putnam, 1992). Bedau and Radelet (1987) concluded in their *Stanford Law Review* article:

> We agree with the observation of a supporter of the death penalty who writes: "[T]o say that someone deserves to be executed is to make a godlike judgment with no assurance that it can be made with anything resembling godlike perspicacity." The research presented in this article underscores the all-too-human errors that afflict the actual attempt to render such judgments.
>
> (p. 90)

Feedback

We have mentioned on several occasions failure to receive feedback as a critical flaw in the learning process of forensic examiners. Feedback, or lack of it, is a major cause of expert error, especially in the presence of overconfidence. Feedback can have an appreciable attenuating effect on overconfidence. In all domains of learning, the contours of knowledge are shaped and modified by feedback. Einhorn (1982) discussed the role of feedback in heuristics, "A major variable in understanding heuristics is outcome feedback . . . outcome feedback is the main source of information for evaluating the quality of our decision/judgment rules" (p. 269). Learning from experience is inductive. We learn that general conclusions may be drawn from particular examples. Without feedback, we have no way of knowing that those inductive associations may be weak or erroneous under a different set of circumstances. In a word, feedback is self-correcting. Through no fault of their own, experts work under a particular set of difficult conditions. Not only is there no systematic or built-in procedure for providing feedback about outcome, frequently there is no opportunity for assessing outcome (and thus providing feedback) for many years (i.e., defendants assigned long prison terms or civilly committed for lengthy periods of time). Even when a short-term outcome is known, communicated directly by the attorney or spread virally on one of the forensic blogs, it is typically impossible to reconstruct from the scant "facts" why your judgment may have been wrong (or right). Unfortunately, the only feedback that experts more reliably receive is from retaining counsel, and that feedback is about how the expert "performed" on the stand. When the expert *performs* well, it is in skillful defense of counsel's client. When the expert *performs* poorly, it often reflects a less than artful duel with opposing counsel. In either case, the feedback has nothing at all to do with the expert's acuity of judgment.

Hastie and Dawes (2010) summed up "the biased availability of feedback" thusly:

> When we construct a linear model in a prediction situation, we know exactly how poorly it predicts. In contrast, our feedback about our own intuitive judgments is flawed. Not only do we selectively remember our successes, we often have no knowledge of our failures—and any knowledge we do have may serve to "explain" them (away).
>
> (p. 63)

To make matters even worse, as noted above, forensic experts rarely know about their successes, let alone their failures. Again, as noted, "feedback" typically is from the attorney about "performance" when testifying; invariably such feedback will range from positive to glowing. If the expert's performance was poor, the attorney would likely say nothing and think twice about retaining that expert again. As Einhorn (1982) pointed out, "large amounts of positive feedback can lead to reinforcement of a non-valid rule" (p. 279).

Feedback, it should be noted, is by no means a simple recipe for correcting overconfident, hasty, or biased judgments. As Lichtenstein and Fischhoff (1980) found, their subjects did learn to improve but *only after making 200 judgments and getting intensive performance feedback*. It is highly unlikely that forensic examiners could ever receive "intensive performance feedback" on real as opposed to mock cases. The only remedy would seem to be intensive training on mock cases prior to exposure to real cases.

Regression Toward the Mean

Regression toward the mean, first reported by Sir Francis Galton in 1886, making reference to "filial regression toward mediocrity" (p. 246), is a ubiquitous phenomenon. Simply put, it refers to the statistical probability that extreme scores—unusually low or unusually high—will be followed by more average scores. A more technical definition is the difference between a perfect correlation (+/– 1.00) and the linear correlation.

As Kahneman and Tversky (1982) quipped, "In our experience, most outstanding fathers have somewhat disappointing sons, brilliant wives have duller husbands, the ill-adjusted tend to adjust and the fortunate are eventually stricken by ill luck" (p. 66). Regression toward the mean explains why exceptional performance in the stock market is often followed by a slump, why a Tony, Emmy, or Grammy award-winning performance is likely to be followed by less exceptional achievement, and even why superstar athletes and winning teams see a drop in performance right after appearing on the cover of *Sports Illustrated* (Hastie & Dawes, 2010; Plous, 1993). The latter phenomenon is sufficiently well known that it is referred to as the "Sports Illustrated Jinx." As Yogi Berra wisely observed, "Slump? I ain't in no slump. . . . I just ain't hitting."

Somewhat more practically, regression toward the mean explains why tall parents are likely to have shorter children and short parents will have taller children. Similarly, parents with exceptionally high IQs will have children with somewhat lower IQs, while parents with low IQs will have children with higher IQs. On a considerably more somber note, Jaffe (2006) explored whether regression toward the mean could account for the origins of human cruelty.

Failing to consider regression toward the mean can lead to erroneous decisions. As Nisbett and Ross (1980) pointed out over 30 years ago, "mislabeling of simple regression phenomena" can have "disconcerting implications" (p. 163). When witnessing crises, such as "a sudden increase in crime, disease, or bankruptcies," our responses to these crises will appear to have a greater effect than there has been. This result was stated in starker terms by Hastie and Dawes (2010):

> Regression toward the mean is particularly insidious when we are trying to assess the success of some kind of intervention designed to improve the state of affairs. . . . The worst case scenarios for understanding the effects of interventions occur when the intervention is introduced because "we've got a problem". For instance, it is almost impossible to accurately assess the causal effects of the introduction of a strict traffic enforcement program *after* a flurry of tragic traffic accidents. . . . The chances are, the interventions are going to show improvements, and it is almost certain that some or most of the effect will be due to regression toward the mean.
>
> (pp. 154–155)

Kahneman and Tversky (1973) query,

> What is it that makes the concept of regression counterintuitive and difficult to acquire and apply? We suggest that a major source of difficulty is that regression effects typically violate the intuition that the predicted outcome should be maximally representative of the input information.
>
> (p. 250)

The import of this caveat is obvious. Crime-related "crises" seem to occur as a common part of our lives, and these crises invariably are responded to quickly, in the aftermath of a wave of crimes. We discussed in Chapter 1 this reactive response to legislation in the wake of particularly heinous crimes. These nonregressive shortcuts at best soothe frayed emotions. At worst, they offer a false sense of security. A short-term decrease in crime will likely be attributed to the new law (or change in existing law), when the greater likelihood is that the incidence of such crimes would have dropped simply due to regression toward the mean.

Clearly, this does *not* mean that we should throw up our hands in despair and do nothing. It does mean that we should: (1) Avoid nonregressive prediction, (2) Avoid hasty, ill-informed recommendations, (3) Avoid hasty policy changes and drafting new laws based on ill-informed recommendations, and (4) Avoid hasty conclusions that short-term changes are directly attributable to these interventions.

With respect to (1), we place ourselves at "high risk" to make nonregressive predictions when we neglect relevant base rates. Nonregressive predictions typically come about when predictions are based on a match of attributes or characteristics that are statistical outliers.

Groupthink and Herding

As Posner (2010) points out, many animals travel in herds, principally for protection from predators, and even many predators hunt in "herds" (packs). Herding is an adaptive strategy for both the predators and the prey. Our paleolithic ancestors, denizens of caves, undoubtedly also found groups to be adaptive for hunting, as well as for protection. Groups still serve an important role for modern "cave dwellers." In his classic book *Groupthink*, Irving Janis (1982) described a way of thinking among people deeply entrenched in a cohesive in-group. Perhaps borrowed from George Orwell's (1949) *1984* newspeak with terms like "doublethink" and "crimethink," groupthink "refers to a deterioration of mental efficiency, reality testing, and moral judgment that results from group pressures" (Janis, 1982, p. 9). Janis (1982) recounted eight symptoms of groupthink, partitioned into three types of groupthink: Type I—Overestimation of the power and morality of the group (Symptom 1—An illusion of invulnerability, excessive optimism, leading to extreme risk-taking and Symptom 2—An unquestioned belief in the group's morality), Type II—Close-mindedness (Symptom 3—Discounting all information that might lead members to reconsider their beliefs and Symptom 4—Stereotyped views of enemy leaders as evil or weak or stupid], and Type III—Pressure toward uniformity (Symptom 5—Self-censorship of deviations from consensus thinking; Symptom 6—Shared illusion of unanimity; Symptom 7—Direct pressure on those who express alternative views; and Symptom 8—Emergence of self-appointed mindguards). The illusions of unanimity and invulnerability seem to be particularly critical features of groupthink.

Myers and Lamm (1976) pointed out that, "Experiments exploring the effects of group discussion on attitudes, jury decisions, ethical decisions, judgments, person perceptions, negotiations, and risk taking are generally consistent with a 'group polarization' hypothesis, derived from the risky-shift literature" (p. 602). Myers (2002) and Myers and Lamm (1975) further explored the polarizing effects of groups, while Myers and Kaplan (1976) demonstrated the presence of group-induced polarization in simulated juries. Esser and Lindoerfer (1989) analyzed the Space Shuttle Challenger explosion, finding that the decision to launch the Challenger was consistent with groupthink.

The risky shift, which, as noted above, inspired the research on group polarization, reflects a well-documented phenomenon that people tend to make riskier decisions in groups. In fact, group polarization seems to strengthen whatever point of view is dominant within the group, whether risky or conservative. The group confers, as Janis described, "cover" (i.e., a sense of invulnerability). The joint "wisdom" of the group often works. As Nate Silver (2012) put it: "The heuristic of 'follow the crowd, especially when you don't know any better' usually works pretty well" (p. 358). Like most heuristics that serve us well most of the time, groupthink can occasionally be catastrophic. As Silver (2012) further noted, on occasion, "The blind lead the blind and everyone falls off a cliff. This phenomenon occurs rarely, but it can be quite disastrous when it does" (p. 358). At its worst, groupthink paved the way for, and insured the life span of, morally bankrupt social institutions, such as slavery and McCarthyism.

Application of the groupthink phenomenon to the realm of sex offender law and assessment may express itself in two ways. The more obvious application is the process of enactment of law as discussed in Chapter 1. Once fear has been aroused by media reports, blogs, and special interest groups, we gravitate toward an amorphous group of similarly alarmed citizens. Initially, other voices of concern provide assurance that we are not alone. As with most groups, a few dominant spokespersons begin to emerge. Their rousing chatter is persuasive, and we are increasingly drawn into the fold as we follow the crowd in decrying the failures of those who permitted the threat to reach this "tipping point." Along with everyone else, we buy into the remedies that the spokespersons have deemed necessary. It takes remarkable forbearance and independence to question the wisdom of the group. Although membership in the group feels emboldening and protective, it produces, as Janis described, insularity and a false sense of authority and invulnerability.

A second less clear application is the ill-defined relationship between forensic examiners who offer opinions for the court on the risk posed by sex offenders and the attorneys that retain them. Attorneys hire experts with an implicit understanding that the expert will assist the attorneys win their case. Although there is an understood obligation of objectivity, there is no bright line between objectivity and advocacy. Grisso and Steinberg (2005) lamented that, "Scientific credibility demands impartiality, whereas advocacy is never impartial" (p. 619). Some degree of advocacy, however, is unavoidable. When retained, there is a reasonable expectation of the expert that she/he will support the attorney. Support is a slippery slope, however, and can easily morph into advocacy. As Grisso and Steinberg noted, advocacy comes at a price—sacrificing objectivity. At its worst, advocacy can lead to blind faith, or, stated otherwise, Janis' groupthink.

Most troubling, *evidence*, the indispensable gruel of any forensic evaluation, can become a casualty of blind faith. Information that is supportive of the attorney's client—either finding the client low risk/not "SVP" or finding the client high risk/"SVP"—is likely to be emphasized, while unsupportive information is likely to be ignored or downplayed. The potential casualty of overlooked, unacknowledged, overemphasized, or improperly interpreted information is incalculable. This is all the more problematic given the limited relevant information, and variable quality of relevant information, that the expert must frequently rely upon.

Forensic experts that work predominantly for the defense or for the prosecution can be invaluable with respect to strategizing about how to handle evidence, communicating tips for both direct and crossing opposing experts, recommending responses for anticipated questions, circulating supportive articles among the team, and supportive networking, blogging, and emailing. Legitimate scientific questions having case-specific merit, such as the empirical basis of novel paraphilia diagnoses (Paraphilia NOS: Nonconsent, Paraphilic Coercive Disorder, Hebephilia, Ephebophilia), estimated base rates, how the prior probability changes as a function of new evidence, and the risk-mitigating influence of advanced age or treatment, may be substituted with canned or formulaic arguments and highly selected (biased) literature.

For lack of any clear guidance or canon of professional ethics that draws the proverbial line in the sand, we can at the least describe a continuum of adherence to objectivity: at one end, rigorously protected impartiality to impartiality colored by varying degrees of advocacy, to advocacy, at the other end, that is cloaked with a veneer of impartiality. The more that we move toward the end of the continuum that is dominated by advocacy, the more we abandon our primary obligation to conduct a competent, thorough, objective evaluation of the attorney's client. Although we all regard ourselves as principled professionals, the insidious nature of groupthink can go a long way toward compromising our objectivity.

9

POLICY, LAW, AND COST BENEFITS OF MANAGEMENT

Public Policy

> Public policy is the overarching umbrella that covers all aspects of treatment, management, and research on sexual coercion. Public policy is also the principal driving force that influences the enactment of laws, authorizes state-sponsored treatment programs, influences the amount and direction of funding for federally sponsored research, and affects most management and discretionary decisions.
>
> (Prentky, 2003, p. 27)

The pivotal role of public opinion in triggering policy that leads to sex offender laws was introduced in Chapter 1 as a *cycle of events*, beginning with a state of fear generated by a high-profile, well-publicized sexual crime, leading to a drumbeat of calls for action by citizens, prompting politicians to create committees "to study the problem," or simply bypassing the committees and enacting legislation directly. A number of horrific sexual crimes led to the first wave of sexual offender civil commitment laws (sexually dangerous persons), beginning in the late 1930s and extending to the mid-1970s. By the mid-1970s, well over half of the states in the US had sexually dangerous person or sexual psychopath laws. The tide of public opinion began to change in the mid-1970s and with it, public policy. The forces leading to changes in policy—and with it the repeal (or disuse) of these laws in almost all of the states (by 1985, these laws were being regularly enforced in only six states)—were described in Prentky and Burgess (2000). These forces included:

1 The growing authority and influence of the feminist movement, which held that rape was a crime of violence and should be treated

no differently from all other violent battery offenses; since civil commitment required a finding of "mental disturbance," the medicalization of rape might provide an exculpation, an "out," thereby diminishing the offender's responsibility.

2 The mental health professionals, primarily psychiatrists at that time, were becoming increasingly disenchanted with the law and their role in executing the law; the two Group for the Advancement of Psychiatry (GAP) reports (1950, 1977) did not mince words, famously stating that these laws were "social experiments that have failed and that lack redeeming social value" (1977, p. 840), the term sexual psychopath has "no precise clinical meaning" (1977, p. 840), "predictions about sexual dangerousness are unreliable" (1977, p. 939), "constitutional questions are involved on many levels" (1977, p. 937), and finally "sex psychopath statutes should be repealed . . . when an experiment has failed, it is time to say so rather than continue an exercise in futility" (1977, p. 942).

The 10 specific conclusions from the second GAP (1977) report were: (1) "First and foremost, sex psychopath and sexual offender statutes can best be described as approaches that have failed," (2) "The categorization process projected by sexual psychopath statutes lacks clinical validity," (3) "The ambivalence of the public about sexual deviance and sex crimes has never been resolved," (4) "Constitutional questions are involved on many levels," (5) "The proper role of the psychiatrist when dealing with sex offenders is first and foremost that of a clinician," (6) "Predictions about 'sexual dangerousness' are unreliable," (7) "Possibilities for carrying out certain treatment programs or research have always existed," (8) "Community pressure to 'do something' poses special dangers," (9) "Courts need a variety of meaningful options," and (10) "Sex psychopath statutes should be repealed" (pp. 935–942).

3 This same time period has been referred to as the "due process revolution," which brought many lawsuits filed on behalf of civilly committed mental patients, raising both procedural and substantive due process issues, including those who were civilly committed under the prevailing sexually violent predator (SVP) or sexual psychopath statutes.

4 A fourth factor was ever-increasing social disapprobation with the treatment of sex offenders; citizens were growing increasingly disgruntled over the mounting costs of treating sex offenders, who were seen as deserving punishment more than treatment; as treatment programs were drawn down, the core element of the constitutionality of the statutes (mentally disturbed individuals in need of treatment) was compromised, rendering the laws more vulnerable in court.

Violence as a Public Health Problem

Casting violence as a public health problem dates back at least 25 years. In 1988, Mercy and O'Carroll placed interpersonal violence in a public health context, highlighting four priorities: (1) develop surveillance systems for morbidity associated with interpersonal violence, (2) identify risk groups for nonfatal violent events, (3) apply case-control methods for examining modifiable risk factors for violent behavior, and (4) rigorously evaluate programs that are intended to prevent interpersonal violence or mitigate suspected risk factors. The applicability of the public health model to sexual violence has long been advocated (Basile, 2003; Laws, 2000; Mercy, 1999; McMahon, 2000; McMahon & Puett, 1999; Post, Mezey, Maxwell, & Wibert, 2002; Prentky, 2003; Prentky & Burgess, 2000; Saltzman, Green, Marks, & Thacker, 2000).

The *life and death* of these sex offender management statutes hinges on public opinion and with it, public policy. In designing a public health agenda for sexual violence, the first task is to craft a policy that all principal stakeholders agree upon. Although the ultimate goal, reducing sexual violence, is universally accepted, the paths to reaching that goal are not. In her opening remarks at the meeting of the New York Academy of Sciences on "Sexually Coercive Behavior," Laurie O. Robinson (2003), former Assistant Attorney General for the U.S. Department of Justice Programs in both the Clinton and Obama Administrations, focused on six key public policy challenges:

1 "First, and perhaps most centrally, is the issue of education, communication, and translation. Despite the fact that research knowledge about sexually coercive behavior and treatment approaches has grown tremendously over the past decade, the fact remains that policymakers, elected officials, the media, and criminal justice practitioners still know relatively little about sex offending and how to deal with it. In fact, the response by government officials is still too often driven by anecdote and rhetoric rather than by facts, research, and successful practice" (p. 3).
2 "A second public policy challenge is the need for greater cross-disciplinary collaboration" (p. 4).
3 "A third public policy challenge is that of ensuring a strong federal leadership role on this issue . . . attention to the problem of sex offending should not be a political issue. At base, it is a 'public safety for communities' issue. All appropriate federal agencies should thus be encouraged . . . to place the subject of sexually coercive behavior high on their agendas" (p. 5).
4 With regard to prisoner reentry, "it is important that emerging initiatives in this area do not overlook the special challenges presented in

dealing with the sex offender population as it returns postprison to the community" (p. 5).

5 "A fifth public policy challenge is the importance of ensuring that victim groups are part of the policy development process. Because of their powerful voice in helping shape crime policy in this country, victims should be drawn into both policy formulation and planning for programs and research" (p. 5).

6 "Finally, it is crucial, as new policies are considered, that the potential for unintended consequences be examined. When the Clinton Administration and Congress in the 1990s rushed to pass Megan's Law (1996) and similar statutes, it reflected the familiar Washington race to see who can be tougher on crime. While definitive research is still lacking on whether these laws have increased public safety, there are incidents of vigilantism and harassment reported in almost every state (Matson, 2001), and anecdotal reports that, following the implementation of community notification requirements, some sex offenders may have gone 'underground' (Matson, 2001). . . . Steps of this kind, like any other single response, are not a successful 'quick fix.' Instead, comprehensive, multidisciplinary approaches are needed" (p. 6).

At the same meeting of the New York Academy of Sciences, Kathleen Basile (2003), from the Division of Violence Prevention at the Center for Disease Control and Prevention, spoke in detail about why "Sexual Violence is a Public Health Issue," noting that

> Sexual violence can be treated as a public health problem for a variety of reasons. First, sexual violence should be a public health concern due to the magnitude of the problem. . . . Second, sexual violence should be considered a public health concern because many of the consequences of sexual violence are health related. . . . Third, implicit in the public health focus are the ideas that public health problems are preventable and that more emphasis should be placed on the front end before a problem begins or becomes widespread. Sexual violence is amenable to prevention. Public health underscores the importance of *primary prevention.*
>
> (p. 447)

Basile (2003) described the four steps in a public health approach: (1) *Surveillance*—"Traditionally, public health surveillance is the ongoing systematic collection, analysis, and interpretation of data on the incidence, prevalence, and risk factors of a public health problem," (2) *Identifying Causes*—Identifying causes "is accomplished through research to better identify persons at risk in order to inform preventive efforts," (3) *Development and Evaluation*—"Development and evaluation of programs is a very important step in public health, because it is where preventive efforts begin. At this step, surveillance and research are used to develop and test programs aimed at prevention," and (4) *Dissemination and Implementation*—Dissemination and implementation "involving communicating which preventive programs work based on evaluation of data and putting these programs into practice" (pp. 448–449).

The *context* of policy development is critical. It must *not* be forged in a state of passion prompted by the latest horrific crime. Since policy will often point to management strategies, *all* stakeholders must be contributing members to the process. All agreed-upon strategies must be empirically informed, operationalized for implementation, and designed for ongoing review of effectiveness. Equal participation of all stakeholders has the advantage of "buy in"; all parties at the table have a vested interest in optimizing the results of the agreed-upon strategies. Couching sexual violence in a public health context has the *very* distinct advantage of confronting *all* manifestations of sexual violence in society, no matter how disconcerting or embarrassing—e.g., in high school among our most esteemed athletes, on college and university campuses among the ranks of fraternities and highly prized athletes, professional athletes, soldiers, among professionals—physicians, therapists, teachers, clergy, police, politicians—who exploit an authoritative relationship, and between partners in relationships. The "instinctive" organizational response—e.g., at colleges and universities, the church, professional sports teams, the army—is denial or minimization and damage control. When a problem is recognized as endangering public health, it does not matter *where* the problem arises; it must be addressed forthrightly—directly and without evasion.

If an anti-sexual violence campaign were half as aggressive as the anti-smoking campaign, the level of sexual violence in this country would diminish considerably. We learned from the anti-smoking campaign that the cumulative effect of persistent publicity and taxation, supported by public policies (e.g., designating smoke-free zones/no-smoking areas), was substantial in reducing cigarette use. Similarly, adopting a zero-tolerance policy for sexual violence supported by persistent and widespread publicity, mandatory trainings for *all* high school students, *all* college freshmen, and *all* soldiers at boot camp is a start. For every category of unwanted sexual behavior, bright lines must be adopted with appropriate sanctions for crossing the line. Matching the powerful graphics of the anti-smoking ads with anti-sexual violence ads would go a long way toward off-setting the damage done by the perfusion of advertising and marketing that relies on the use of highly sexualized, if not erotic, images of women to sell products. The message is simple—women are sexual objects for men's pleasure, much like the latest crop of sleek, high-performance coupes are virility objects for men's pleasure. Banning such ads as a matter of policy would eliminate the "mixed message." This is not the forum for developing a comprehensive public health model. The message that we wish to convey is that focusing all of our time, effort, and money on incarcerating day-to-life a small proportion of the known sexual offenders will *never* reduce—in any meaningful way—the level of sexual violence in our society.

Prentky and Burgess commented 15 years ago that,

> The *totality* of the problem of sexual coercion in our society is incalculable. In its *larger* context, sexual coercion permeates all of society, affects hundreds of thousands of people each year, places an astronomical financial burden on society, and makes vast demands on system resources. Society now spends hundreds of millions of dollars each year to cope with the direct and indirect effects of the problem. A complex system of laws, state and federal, attempt to contain the problem. *Clearly, by any definition, sexual coercion must be regarded as a public health problem.*
> (2000, p. 237)

Rather than accepting that sexual violence is a legitimate public health problem, quite the opposite applies. We evidence a rather profound ambivalence, at least with regard to sexual assault of adult women. Two very different stories serve as examples. With regard to the sexual assault of U.S. soldiers by U.S. soldiers, White (2012) wrote,

> When Fox News commentator Liz Trotta addressed the topic of sexual assault in the military this past February, telling her audience that women who serve should "expect" to get raped, she seemed barely able to conceal her contempt for U.S. servicewomen—at least those who are speaking out against sexual violence.

More recently, Vaughan (2014) reported on collusion between the police and a university to cover up crime, including allegations of rape. Vaughan stated,

> Florida State University administrators and Tallahassee police took steps to both hide and then hinder the criminal investigation of the school's Heisman Trophy winning quarterback Jameis Winston last fall. . . . Winston was not charged with a crime in the case, but FOX found that the criminal investigation was hampered, in part, as a result of the actions of university administrators along with campus and city police. After learning in December 2013 that charges wouldn't be filed, FOX Sports

> examined thousands of pages of documents. Among those findings, it was revealed that when Tallahassee police caught wind that a reporter was looking into the alleged rape, they turned reports in the case over to Florida State administrators. By November of 2013, nearly a year after a woman alleged that Winston raped her and nine months after Tallahassee police shelved the case, the Florida State administrators had those documents.

In both instances, the alleged crimes of rape are trivialized and subordinated in importance to the loftier goals of preserving esprit de corps and comradeship in the military and premium athletic "assets" on the field along with the trove of monetary assets that accompany victory, while making any adverse publicity evaporate. There remains, deeply embedded in the male psyche (and apparently the occasional female psyche as well), confusion as to whether unwanted sex is really a crime. Unwanted non-sexual battery appears to raise no such confusion. Had a woman in the military been physically assaulted by another soldier and left with a black eye or a broken nose or severe contusions, it is unlikely that Liz Trotta would have said that she should have expected it. Similarly, if Winston was not a football player, there is a high likelihood that the allegations of rape would have been investigated. These two stories are emblematic of a far more deeply rooted problem; it is this pervasive, insidious problem that defines sexual violence as a public health issue.

Assessing "Interventions" as a Matter of Policy

In one of the earlier expositions of "dangerousness" and public policy, Saleem Shah (1975) offered a panoply of troubling implications of the involuntary civil commitment of those deemed dangerous by virtue of mental illness. One of Shah's more disconcerting conclusions was that,

> One might well wonder whether, in the various civil and *parens patriae* proceedings in which psychiatric concepts are invoked and mental health professionals are involved, the societal practices seem to be more concerned with using these professionals as agents of social control rather than as individuals functioning in their usual and traditional therapeutic roles.
>
> (p. 505)

A similar point was made by Monahan (1984), observing that one of the generic attacks on professionals who offer predictions about violent behavior is "that predicting dangerousness destroys the essential 'helping role' of the mental health professions and turns psychiatrists and psychologists from healers of psychic pain into agents of social control" (p. 14).

Perhaps in the broadest sense, our book has the principal mission of helping to reinforce our mental health professionals as agents of social justice, rather than as agents of social control. This task is made all the more difficult, however, given the image of the court as a bastion of rectitude set against a praxis of gladiatorial combat. The adversarial climate of an American courtroom, reaching high voltage in *hot* cases, with winning at (*almost*) any cost being the goal, can easily subvert the mental health professional's principal mission of objectivity. The challenge confronting forensic experts was captured by Laurence Steinberg and his colleagues as something of a precarious balancing act:

> When psychologists agree to provide guidance on matters of law, they must be able and willing to simultaneously plant their feet in two worlds—that of social science and that of legal policy and practice. These worlds operate on different principles and with different expectations. Social scientists are accustomed to providing complicated answers to seemingly simple questions, whereas legal professionals typically want simple answers to complicated ones. Social scientists avoid casting things in black and white, whereas legal professionals are often forced to do so.
>
> (Steinberg, Cauffman, Woolard, Graham, & Banich, 2014, p. 601)

The rules of court prevail, and expert testimony is often shaved down to black and white morsels tailored precisely to the "legal policy" objectives of the retaining attorney. Again, the rules prevail on cross-examination, when the expert is asked to respond *only* in black or white (yes or no); the tactic of course is a ploy to force a response that detracts from or contradicts the expert's stated opinion. More importantly, a "yes or no" response rarely is adequate to convey the extraordinary complexity and subtlety of the proffered opinion. Occasionally, experts have the temerity to say, "I'm sorry counselor, but I cannot answer your question in terms of yes or no."

A secondary effect of the sex offender laws has been a cottage industry of developing, testing, revising, and promoting risk assessment scales for use with sex offenders. Without numerous laws that implicitly require assessments of risk, the demand for experts with presumptive skills in evaluating sex offender risk would be diminished considerably. Again, although not a focal mission of this book, examining the relative costs and benefits of these legal remedies is so fundamental to addressing the larger fix of sex offender management that we will briefly discuss it.

Close to half a century ago, the President's Commission on Law Enforcement and Administration of Justice, established by President Johnson in 1965, submitted their final report (1967), which stated,

> The Commission believes that there is a clear public responsibility to keep citizens fully informed of the facts about crime so that they will have facts to go on when they decide what the risks are and what kinds and amounts of precautionary measures they should take. Furthermore, without an accurate understanding of the facts, they cannot judge whether the interference with individual liberties which strong crime control measures may involve is a price worth paying.
>
> (pp. 52–53)

Not long after this report was issued, Monahan and Cummings (1975) reminded us that the price of these crime control measures can be exorbitant, and the measures themselves manifestly indefensible. Monahan and Cummings (1975) recounted the occasion, etched in the annals of psychiatric lore, when President Nixon called upon his Department of Health, Education, and Welfare in 1970 to examine the proposal of Dr. Arnold A. Hutschnecker, a psychiatric consultant to the National Commission on the Causes and Prevention of Violence (NCCPV) and President Nixon's personal therapist since 1952 (Goode, 2001; Robb, 2012). NCCPV had been established by President Johnson in 1968 after the assassinations of Martin Luther King, Jr. and Robert Kennedy. President Nixon extended NCCPV until 1969 (or the submission of its final report).

Dr. Hutschnecker recommended that psychological tests such as the Rorschach be given to all young children in America (age range of 6–8) to determine their potential for criminality. Those children considered criminally inclined would receive "massive psychological and psychiatric treatment" (Hutschnecker, 1973, p. E-15). Dr. Hutschnecker's intervention, according to Maynard (1970), was "a better short-term solution to the crime problem than urban reconstruction. Teenage boys later found to be persisting in incorrigible behavior would be remanded to camps" (p. 9). Dr. Hutschnecker's confidential report on crime prevention, intended for President Nixon, found its way into the news media, prompting Hutschnecker to write a letter to the *New York Times*, saying that his report had been subjected to "malevolent distortion" by the media (Goode, 2001). As it turned out, it appears that the only distortion was in the intended meaning of the word "camp." Hutschnecker noted that,

> My use of it dates back to when I came to the United States in 1936 and spent the summer as a doctor in a children's camp. It was that experience and the pastoral setting, as well as the activities, that prompted my use of the word "camp."
>
> (Goode, 2001)

Fellow psychiatrist Dr. Leopold Bellak (1971) essentially concurred, recommending:

> A psychiatric examination of children at school entrance time should be required, like vaccination. If a child is found to be in a markedly disturbed environment, school attendance should be denied unless parents are willing to have the child or themselves treated or advised. . . . In those who are already dangerously disturbed, enforced treatment might prevent many future Oswalds [whose mother was able to remove him from treatment].
>
> (p. 120)

For those who find these recommendations abhorrent, Dr. Hutschnecker's suggestion that teenage boys with incorrigible behavior be remanded to camps has been duly instituted, arguably in a more draconian way than even Dr. Hutschnecker envisioned. The camps of today are prisons, not children's camps in pastoral settings. Teenagers who commit a sex offense may be civilly committed for an indeterminate period when they age out (turn 20 or 21) in 14 states (13 of the 21 states with civil commitment laws for adult sex offenders plus Pennsylvania), and are subject to public notification in 24 states (Pittman & Nugent, 2011; Pittman, 2014).

The greater problem is *not* the radicalness of any recommended interventions, including those of Dr. Hutschnecker or Dr. Bellak. The problem is *instituting* recommendations as a matter of public policy without any empirical grounding, failing to evaluate rigorously the outcomes of those interventions, and then failing to act in accordance with the findings from those program evaluations. Over a quarter of a century ago, the doyen of American criminology, Marvin Wolfgang, remarked that "The empty cup of our ignorance has often been filled not with facts and knowledge but with good intentions" (p. 120). We need more than good intentions. As Rice (1997) concluded, "As a matter of public policy, any interventions designed to reduce the likelihood of violence should be required to include an empirical evaluation of outcomes" (p. 421). We would take Marnie Rice's admonition one step further—the most sophisticated empirical evaluations of intervention effectiveness will serve little purpose if they are ignored by the authors of the intervention. Results from outcome studies must be integrated into ongoing analysis of the intervention, revisions made if called for, and the intervention terminated if deemed necessary.

Cost-Benefit Analysis

In the late 1980s, concerns about the causes and consequences of health care practices brought about the "Era of Assessment and Accountability," dubbed the third revolution in U.S. health care after World War II (Lezzoni, 1994). Unlike the second revolution of "Cost Containment" during the 1970s to the early 1980s, the Era of Assessment and Accountability emphasized not only costs but also clinical outcomes. Outcomes were essentially report cards on the degree of success or failure of the program. Since all programs come with a price tag, it was argued that those who create and implement new programs should be held accountable to those who pay for the programs—the taxpayers. Thus, it should be left to the taxpayers to decide whether the effectiveness of the programs warranted the cost.

A principal vehicle for assisting with that determination is cost-benefit analysis (CBA), long adopted as an invaluable asset and integral part of public policy for evaluating healthcare programs, environmental programs, tax programs, and transportation programs, to name just a few. CBA is essentially: incremental costs($)/health consequences($). By contrast, a cost-effectiveness analysis (CEA) asks a slightly different question: Incremental costs($)/health benefits($). CEA estimates the cost of producing a health effect (e.g., the cost of reducing the incidence of sexual violence). CEA is sometimes viewed as a subset of CBA. Johannesson (1995) demonstrated that CEA "can be interpreted as a cost-benefit analysis where the willingness to pay per effectiveness unit is assumed to be constant and the same for everyone" (p. 483), a condition highly unlikely to be met in the case of sexual violence. Johannesson (1995) concluded that "to interpret and use cost-effectiveness analysis as a tool to maximize the health effects for one specified real-world budget will be inconsistent with a societal perspective and is likely to lead to major problems of suboptimization" (p. 483). For present purposes, our focus has been on CBA.

The major drawback—or challenge—to CBA, however, is the need to assign monetary values to all costs and consequences. Numerous costs and consequences are intangible and therefore very difficult to monetize. In sum, the complexity of estimating costs and consequences *in practice* can be challenging, controversial, and heated, especially when there are competing interests. The proposed Keystone Oil Pipeline, running for over 2,000 miles from Alberta, Canada, through Nebraska, Illinois, and down to the Gulf Coast of Texas, is a current, much-debated example, with environmentalists raising many concerns about the environmental "costs" of the project. In a recent article in the *New York Times*, titled "Frack Quietly, Please: Sage Grouse Is Nesting," Cardwell and Krauss (2014) began by noting that

> In a new oil field among the rolling hills near here [Casper, Wyoming], Chesapeake Energy limits truck traffic to avoid disturbing the breeding and nesting of a finicky bird called the greater sage grouse. To the west, on a gas field near Yellowstone National Park, Shell Oil is sowing its own special seed mix to grow plants that nourish the birds and hide their chicks from predators.

The article proceeds to point out the opposing concern of Representative Cory Gardner, Republican of Colorado:

> "The sage grouse has seven times the acreage of the spotted owl. You are looking at billions of dollars in lost economic activity, millions of dollars in lost state and local revenues and tens of thousands of jobs being lost" . . . Gov. Matt Mead of Wyoming expressed frustration with that prospect, given his state's preservation of 15 million acres of land at a cost of $32 million and millions of dollars more from the private sector. He suggested that a listing could jeopardize conservation efforts in the state.

CBA has now been adopted in most areas of criminal justice reform as well. The book by Mark Cohen (2005) is an obvious source. In a report for the Urban Institute on Cost-Benefit Analysis and Crime Control, Roman, Dunworth, and Marsh (2010) observed that criminal justice programs must demonstrate effectiveness as well as a clear return on the tax dollars that paid for the program. As the literature on the costs of criminal justice programs suggests, the most difficult—and controversial—areas of cost estimation are victim-related *intangibles* (e.g., fear, pain and suffering, and diminished quality of life, including impact on relationships) (Cohen, 2000, 2008; Cohen & Bowles, 2014). Although there have been no systematic attempts to estimate the costs of rape and sexual assault, cost estimates of sexual assault have typically been included in most studies of crime in general (e.g., Cohen, Rust, Steen, & Tidd, 2004). As one would imagine, the intangible costs associated with fear, lost quality of life, impaired relationships, lost work productivity, and long-term symptoms associated with post-traumatic stress disorder (PTSD) account for the most significant part of the costs to victims. Although such intangibles are extraordinarily difficult to assign a dollar figure to, several studies have attempted to "quantify" in dollars the fear of rape by examining the impact on housing prices in communities where registered sex offenders are living (Linden & Rockoff, 2006; Pope, 2008). Pope (2008) reported, for example, that after a sex offender moves into a community, the prices of homes nearby drop by 2.3% (translating to an average of $3,500). This study, however, looked only at one county in Florida.

When it comes to *sexual* crime, the maxims mentioned above justifying the need to demonstrate the merit of a program by examining costs relative to consequences make rational sense but tend to be lost in the torrent of strong emotions that cloud otherwise objective decisions. If *no* program is instituted, or if the program is inappropriate or suboptimal, or carelessly implemented, the result may be an increase in victims. Thus, society is likely to argue, and policy-makers are likely to follow suit, any face valid program is better than none at all. However meritorious that argument, it may not pass muster in a healthcare climate of accountability and cost containment. Sexual crime, however, appears to be a stark exception to this last statement. Accountability and cost containment do not appear to be relevant considerations for either society or policymakers when it comes to sexual crime.

The two primary areas in which the *costs* of rape and sexual assault must be gauged are (1) the costs to the victims and (2) the costs to society to implement the program created by law for managing sex offenders. The preponderance of documentation of costs has been in the latter area (i.e., how much does it cost to warehouse, feed, care for, and treat SVPs). Costs have been estimated generally in four categories: (a) costs related to capital expenses for building new prisons, (b) costs for legal proceedings associated with civil commitment, (c) costs for maintaining each offender in the facility for one year, and (d) costs associated with community release, monitoring, and supervision.

In one of the earliest detailed enumerations of costs associated with sexual predator laws, LaFond (1998) reported that,

> More recent budgets are available for the 1998 and 1999 fiscal years. They project a total cost of $5,411,000 for 55 residents at the SCC [Special Commitment Center at Monroe Penitentiary in Monroe, WA] in 1998 and $6,070,000 for 66 residents in 1999. These projections seem low in light of more recent projections that the population will increase to 150–200 residents over a 4-year period. These costs include the following categories: treatment staff, evaluation team, support and superintendent's office, other costs (goods and services), and court costs.
>
> (p. 478)

Post, Mezey, Maxwell, and Wibert (2002) estimated that the combined tangible and intangible costs of sexual violence in the state of Michigan for 1996 were $6.5 billion. Post and her colleagues further noted that if the $6.5 billion was divided equally among all residents of the state as a "rape tax," each resident would have paid close to $700 in 1996. Post et al. (2002) draw the implication that prevention is the only way to reduce this extraordinary financial burden *and* that sexual violence must be considered a public health issue. As of 2003,

> States reported per capita treatment costs ranging from $47,555 in Florida to $138,841 in North Dakota. A good rule of thumb is that it costs about $100,000 per person to keep someone committed in an institution for a year as an SVP. These costs do not include the capital expense of building or renovating facilities to house SVPs.
>
> (LaFond, 2005, p. 150)

In Virginia, it is estimated to cost $140,000 per resident per year to stay at the newly constructed prison for SVPs; this cost is six times higher than the cost per inmate per year at the other Virginia prisons (Geissenhainer, 2008).

Ewing (2011) provided the annual budgetary allowances for the SVP programs in 18 states and compared the average cost per SVP resident with the average cost per prison inmate. Ewing (2011) summarized his findings:

> In total, these states spent $454.7 million, nearly half a billion dollars, in one year simply providing secure confinement (or, in the case of Texas, supervision) and treatment. Aside from Texas and Pennsylvania, states spent between $2.9 million and $147.3 million in one year on this aspect of their SVP programs alone. Moreover, these states spent an average of more than $94,000 per offender simply providing secure confinement, care, and treatment. The comparable annual cost of confining these individuals in prisons would have averaged about $26,000.
>
> (p. 57)

Ewing (2011) then proceeds to point out that these figures are outdated and "do not come even close to fully detailing the economic costs of SVP laws" (p. 57). New York, for instance, "is currently spending approximately $175,000 per year per offender for these purposes" (Ewing, 2011, p. 57).

In Illinois, it was estimated that the sexual predator law would,

> increase its prison population by 7,650 inmates over ten years at a cost of $1,007,719,300. Operating costs during this period were projected to increase by $703,073,300; four new medium-security correctional facilities would have to be built at a cost of $304,646,000.
>
> (LaFond, 1998, p. 500)

Washington State estimated that the cost of building a new prison for 400 SVPs would be $81,000,000 (LaFond, 2005). On February 28, 2008, Virginia opened its new $62,000,000 facility to accommodate 60 SVPs (Geissenhainer, 2008). Ironically, Virginia, which is the only state that explicitly mandates the use of a particular risk assessment scale (Static-99), built a much larger (300-bed) facility, because the smaller 100-bed facility was considered insufficient to accommodate the number of offenders eligible for commitment using the Static-99; with only 60 men placed at the facility when it opened, and a projection of only 113, the prison was far under capacity and losing money (Geissenhainer, 2008). Minnesota spent $45 million on an SVP facility and then budgeted for a second facility, estimated to cost between $45 million and $89 million (Ewing, 2011). New York spent $30 million renovating an existing state hospital (Ewing, 2011).

In California, the costs are even higher. LaFond (1998) reported that,

> The fiscal budget for the California program for the fiscal year 1996–1997 was $10.8 million. Governor Wilson requested $16.6 million for the program for 1997–1998, an increase in 1 year of almost 54%. This figure, reported by the media, may actually understate the funds allocated to implement the law. It is estimated that it will cost about $107,000.00 a year to house and treat each person committed under the California law.
>
> (p. 482)

Since space at the existing facility in California (Atascadero State Hospital) could not accommodate the additional 400–500 beds needed by the end of 1999, $36 million was needed to expand Atascadero or $106 million would be required to build a new facility (LaFond, 1998). California opted for a new 1,500-bed state hospital in Coalinga, which opened in August 2005 at a cost of $388 million (Wilkens, 2010). Wilkens (2010) pointed out that at $185,000 a year per resident, it is almost four times as expensive as attending Stanford University.

Once again, Ewing (2011) has emphasized that these are 2006 figures:

> The costs of these programs have risen steadily over the years, partly due to the influx of newly committed offenders and the extremely low rate of release from SVP commitment facilities. Thus, it seems reasonable to estimate that current costs of maintaining SVP programs in 20 states, now including New York and New Hampshire as well as the District of Columbia and the federal criminal justice system, are well in excess of a billion dollars a year and rising.
>
> (p. 59)

The cost of a sexual predator commitment trial can run as high as $100,000 (Fitch, 2003). Fitch (2003) reported that officials in Minnesota estimated that each civil commitment trial costs about $100,000 just for attorneys and experts; that figure did not include court costs. According to LaFond (1998), that is what Minnesota officials estimate the cost of conducting a trial to be. In Washington State, attorneys analogized sexual predator commitment trials to death penalty trials in terms of the costs incurred by both the government and the defense (LaFond, 1998).

The fees alone paid to experts hired to evaluate SVPs and testify at the hearings can be extraordinary. Ewing (2011) reported,

> In California, the state has paid such independent evaluators $3,500 for an initial evaluation plus $200 per hour for services

> thereafter. In one recent year, the state utilized the services of 79 psychologists and psychiatrists and paid them a total of $24 million. Fourteen of these doctors billed the state in excess of $500,000 each and two earned more than $1 million each. The top earner, a psychologist, was paid $1.5 million. The second-highest-paid evaluator, a psychologist who earned $1.1 million, billed the state $17,500 for a single day's work. The third-highest-paid evaluator, a psychiatrist who billed the state almost $1 million for a year's worth of SVP evaluations, did so while maintaining a private practice, conducting other forensic evaluations and testifying in court, directing a laboratory, and supervising medical residents. The Los Angeles Times reported that this doctor conducted as many as 20 SVP evaluations a month and concluded that "even at 100 hours per week, he would have had no more than six hours to complete each of five evaluations."
>
> (p. 60)

A further cost is probation, often lifetime probation. In Maricopa County, Arizona, for example, 13 probation officers track 600 sex offenders at a cost estimated at $840,000 per year (600 x $1,400/offender) (LaFond, 1998). The State of Washington has a Least Restrictive Alternative (LRA) component in its statute. LaFond (2005) reported,

> The costs of placing an individual in a community LRA vary widely. In 2003, reported costs in Washington State generally ranged from $25,000 to $400,000, though individual costs can be astronomical. Washington, reportedly, spent $740,000 on placing one SVP on conditional release for 1 year in 2003. . . . Most SVPs on conditional release, though not all, are also taking drugs designed to reduce their sexual drive. These drugs are expensive. Kansas reported that it spends $100,000 annually for "transitional services" for SVPs in the community. Illinois reported an average of $80,000 for each of its five patients in the community. California expects to spend $180,000 per year on placing its first SVP in the community; this compares with $28,500 for the average prison inmate.
>
> (pp. 152–153)

As astronomical as these figures appear, they only represent offender-related estimated costs (capital expenses for prisons, legal proceedings, housing/program costs, conditional release), *not* victim-related costs. As noted above, victim costs are largely intangible and very difficult to monetize, essentially falling under two umbrellas—quality of life and impact on society, both of which may be intertwined (e.g., long-term emotional impact, including depression, anxiety, fear, and symptoms of PTSD, will affect work productivity as well as relationships). To the best of our knowledge, there are no reliable replicated estimates of victim-related costs. A National Institute of Justice Research Report concluded that when only tangible (out-of-pocket) expenses are considered, the average rape or attempted rape costs $5,100, but when the intangible quality of life costs are quantified, the average rape costs $87,000 (Miller, Cohen, & Wiersema, 1996). Miller et al. (1996) point out,

> Unlike tangible losses such as medical expenses or lost wages, pain, suffering, and reduced quality of life do not have a market price and cannot be bought and sold. Nevertheless, these losses are real. Victims would pay dearly to avoid them.
>
> (p. 14)

Miller et al. (1996) quantified lost or diminished quality of life using jury awards in rape cases. Using this measure of quantifying intangible costs, the aggregate cost of rape, based on 1,467,000 victimizations at a cost per victimization of $87,000, was estimated to be $127 billion (in 1993 dollars) (Miller et al., 1996). Using a consumer price index inflation calculator, this would be roughly $209 billion in 2014 dollars. Notably, however, that cost per victimization may be low. As Miller et al. (1996) noted,

> Researchers estimated that the 1.1 million rape victims suffer 1.45 million rape victimizations annually. That means annual rape victimizations average 1.27 per victim. Multiplying 1.27 by the $81,400 quality of life loss per rape victimization yielded estimated quality of life losses of $103,400 per rape victim.
>
> (p. 15)

Whatever the current estimates are in today's dollars, the amount is astronomical, somewhere in the neighborhood of $200–$250 billion annually.

In what may be one of the only attempts at a more comprehensive CBA with sex offenders, a study examined 129 child molesters released from the Massachusetts Treatment Center, detailing offender-related costs (pretrial investigation, trial costs, incarceration, and parole) and estimating victim-related costs (Department of Social Services, hospital and medical expenses, victim evaluation, witness services, and treatment) (Prentky & Burgess, 1990). The Prentky and Burgess study concluded that the expenses per offense totaled $183,333. Assuming risk of re-offense is .40 for untreated child molesters and .25 for treated child molesters, the expected cost of re-offense for the untreated offenders was $231,968, and the expected cost of re-offense for the treated offenders was $163,979, yielding a cost saving of $67,989 with treatment. There are, of course, many current limitations to that study: (a) the cost estimates were derived 25 years ago and are now obsolete; (b) the study focused only on child molesters; (c) the expected cost of re-offense hinges on the estimated base rates for treated and untreated child molesters, which used a 15% treatment effect, and that may well be spurious in the context of current findings (e.g., there was no treatment effect in the Marques et al. study, 2005); and (d) the offenders were committed under the old version of the current SVP law, which meant that offenders were civilly committed at the time of sentencing and served their determinate sentence in a prison facility with a treatment program and most were released on parole at the expiration of their sentence.

On the benefits side, we have two inter-linked factors: the estimated reduction of sexual crimes as a result of the program (in the above cost-detailed case, SVP civil commitment) and the estimated victim costs (monetary savings as a result of fewer victims). Estimating the reduction in sexual re-offenses is fraught with methodological challenges, most notably the large portion of sexual assaults that go unreported. Adult victims that know the offender (marital rape, college campus rape, date rape, social acquaintance rape) are less likely to report than victims of unknown (stranger) sexual assault. Among child victims, once again children that know the offender are less likely to report. In both instances, for both child and adult victims, assaults by known offenders account for the distinct majority of sexual crimes. Thus, we can reasonably conclude that a considerable proportion of all sexual assaults are unreported and hence are unknown.

Treatment Impact: What is Known of Those Who are Known?

In an early meta-analytic study, Hall (1995) combined 12 studies of treated sex offenders for a total sample of 1,313 men. Hall found a small but significant overall decrease in sexual recidivism as a function of treatment. The recidivism rate for treated sex offenders was 19%, compared with the recidivism rate of 27% for untreated sex offenders. For those studies that used cognitive-behavior therapy or anti-androgen medication (drugs that lower the level of testosterone, reducing the frequency and intensity of sexual urges), the decrease resulting from treatment was greater than 8%.

A Canadian study followed 296 treated and 283 untreated offenders for an average of six years (Nicholaichuk, Gordon, Gu, & Wong, 2000). This study provided the most convincing evidence for the efficacy of treatment, with conviction rates of 15% for treated sex offenders and 33% for untreated sex offenders. Nicholaichuk and his colleagues noted the obvious fact that the statistical difference between the two groups was attributable to the unusually high sexual recidivism rate for the matched comparison group of untreated offenders, *not* the lower recidivism rate for the treated offenders.

The Collaborative Outcome Data Project on the Effectiveness of Psychological Treatment for Sex Offenders (Hanson et al., 2002) meta-analyzed 43 studies with a total of 9,454 sex offenders (5,078 offenders had received some form of treatment and 4,376 offenders received none). Averaged across all studies, the percentage of offenders who re-offended was approximately 12% for those who were treated and 17% for those who received no treatment, yielding a 5% treatment effect. When Hanson and his colleagues (2002) included only those studies that examined treatments in effect after 1980 (presumably those that used the relapse prevention model), the sexual recidivism rate for those who were treated dropped to 10%, increasing the treatment effect to 7%. The largest meta-analysis to date collapsed 69 studies with a total sample size of 22,181 sex offenders (Losel & Schmucker, 2005), finding a 6% reduction in sexual recidivism with treatment.

The gold standard for program evaluation is the randomized clinical trial (RCT), which involves the random assignment of study participants to different conditions. The only study of treatment efficacy with sex offenders that incorporated RCT into the design was California's Sex Offender Treatment and Evaluation Project (SOTEP) (Marques, Day, Nelson, & West, 1993; Marques, Nelson, Alarcon, & Day, 2000). SOTEP included three groups. Volunteers were randomly assigned to either the treatment condition or the no-treatment condition (no-treatment volunteer control group). The third group was a randomly selected sample of sex offenders who had *not* volunteered (no-treatment, non-volunteer control group). At the end of the 10-year study (1985–1995), with follow-up ranging from 5 to 14 years, the sexual re-offense rates were: 22% for the treatment group, 20% for the no-treatment, volunteer control group, and 19% for the no-treatment, non-volunteer control group (Marques, Wiederanders, Day, Nelson, & van Ommeren, 2005).

In essence, those who did not volunteer and received no treatment had a 3% lower sexual recidivism rate than those who volunteered and received treatment. These rates, however, were not significantly different. All three groups re-committed sexual offenses at roughly the same rate, providing no evidence of a treatment effect. This was also true when rapists and child molesters were examined separately (i.e., there were no significant group differences for either rapists or child molesters). Despite the disappointing outcome of this study, there was a very interesting highlight. Marques et al. (1993, 2000) found that those individuals who met the program's treatment goals (who were judged by the research team to have "got it") had substantially lower re-offense rates (10%) than those who did not (50%). We may speculate that reduced recidivism related to treatment effects for those who "got it" is the consequence of an ability to apply the principles of relapse prevention to real-life situations. It is reasonable to conclude, however, that "got it" reflects not merely a superior cognitive understanding of the principles but a stronger desire to apply them.

A somewhat more complex methodological issue related to the SOTEP study concerns the number of "dropouts" in the treatment condition, who predominantly had high recidivism rates. This "phenomenon" is common (i.e., dropouts from treatment often evidence higher relapse rates), and the fact that these dropouts were included as "treated" in the data analysis is what statisticians might well recommend. Nevertheless, including these dropouts in the treatment condition most certainly suppresses the treatment effect.

All three meta-analytic studies yielded similar results: a treatment benefit of approximately a 6% to 8% reduction in sexual re-offending. Given the consistency of these findings, it is tempting to conclude that treatment can reduce sexual recidivism by roughly 6% to 8%. By doing so, however, we ignore the results of SOTEP, California's state-of-the-art study employing RCT. How to place the findings from SOTEP in perspective has itself become a matter of some controversy (Marshall & Marshall, 2007, 2008; Seto et al., 2008).

Ignoring what is generally regarded as the methodological gold standard is obviously risky. Janice Marques and her colleagues (2005) pointed out, "The most important safeguard against misleading results . . . remains a randomized design" (p. 103). Although we would certainly agree, we have gone a step further, arguing that the most well-controlled program employing all of the bells and whistles of best practice treatment may prove suboptimal in prison-based sex offender treatment, compromised by innumerable violations of best practice assumptions regarding treatment efficacy (Prentky, Gabriel, & Coward, 2011). Marshall and Marshall (2008) appear to make this point when they refer to "the very important process issues of how treatment is delivered" (p. 257).

The taxpayers that underwrite these treatment programs for sex offenders deserve to know whether treatment "works," or at least works well enough to justify the cost. Most of the treatment outcome studies with sex offenders suggest a weak to no treatment effect. A partial explanation may be deceptively simple, having nothing to do with the clinical integrity of the treatment model—or the fidelity of its application. As Prentky, Gabriel, and Coward (2011) suggest, best practice methodology requires more than just a sound clinical model. Best practice includes, among other things, certain underlying conditions that facilitate the process of treatment. We will discuss three such conditions and how these conditions are met in prison-based treatment: (a) voluntariness, (b) confidentiality, and (c) dual roles. These conditions are discussed in greater detail in Prentky et al., 2011.

A. Voluntariness. A rudimentary assumption of therapy is that the client has voluntarily chosen to be in therapy rather than being coerced to be in therapy. In other words, internal motivation is, at least to some degree, assumed. Much emphasis has been placed on this aspect of the therapeutic process, since "the patient's capacity and willingness to participate in the therapy interaction are among the most important determinants of improvement" (Gomes-Schwartz, 1978). Patient involvement correlates significantly with outcome (Windholz & Silberschatz, 1988) and predicts overall improvement (O'Malley, Suh, & Strupp, 1983). It may be assumed that for many of those who have minimal or no desire to be in treatment, motivation to engage in the process is minimal and commitment to change their behavior is similarly minimal. The studies that have looked at this seem to support this assumption. Compliance with treatment (e.g., consistent attendance at treatment groups, active participation in treatment groups, and willingness to disclose personal and offense-related information during sessions) tends to be poor, ranging from approximately 46% (Miner & Dwyer, 1995) to 53% (Geer, Becker, Gray, & Krauss, 2001).

The question of voluntariness of treatment in a forensic context was specifically addressed as early as 1978 in the Report of the Task Force on the Role of Psychology in the Criminal Justice System (Report of the Task Force, 1978):

> In the role of a therapist providing treatment for an offender . . . the psychologist, we believe, primarily must be the agent of an individual. This would mean that therapy should only be given on a truly voluntary basis and that it should not be used as a means to pursue administrative ends, such as release or promotion decisions. (p. 1103)

The condition that treatment should be voluntary and elective is not met in most, if not all, civil commitment treatment programs. Residents are placed in the classic catch-22—if they opt out of treatment (i.e., refuse), they will surely undermine their own chances of ever being cleared and released; if they participate in treatment, they do so with the understanding that whatever they disclose in treatment may be used against them when they petition for release.

This issue has not been lost on the courts (Myers, 2002). In McKune v. Lile, 122 S.Ct. 2017 (2002), the respondent Robert Lile, an inmate in Kansas convicted of the rape, aggravated sodomy, and aggravated kidnapping of a female high school student, was ordered to participate in the Sexual Abuse Treatment Program (SATP). As Attorney Myers reported,

> The SATP required inmates to admit responsibility for the crimes for which they had been sentenced and provide an extensive

> sexual history detailing all prior sexual activities, regardless of whether the activities constitute uncharged criminal offenses. A polygraph examination was used to verify the accuracy and completeness of the offender's sexual history . . . inmates are not granted immunity from future criminal proceedings based on these admissions. Also, Kansas law required SATP staff members to report any uncharged sexual offenses involving minors to law enforcement authorities.
>
> (p. 67)

Inmate Lile refused to participate in SATP on the ground that compelled disclosures of his criminal history violated his Fifth Amendment right against self-incrimination. The District Court granted Lile summary judgment on his action for injunctive relief under 42 U.S.C. §1983. The Court of Appeals for the Tenth Circuit affirmed, "holding that the consequences Lile faced if he refused to participate in the program constituted coercion in violation of the Fifth Amendment" (p. 67).

The U.S. Supreme Court, in a 5–4 opinion, held that "minimal incentives" did not constitute "compulsion." The majority opinion was handed down by Justice Kennedy, who "concluded that the SATP serves a vital penological purpose, and that offering inmates minimal incentives to participate does not amount to *compelled* self-incrimination prohibited by the Fifth Amendment" (McKune v. Lile (00-1187) 536 U.S. 24 (2002) 224 F.3d 1175). Kennedy was joined by Chief Justice Rehnquist, Justice Scalia, Justice Thomas, and Justice O'Connor, although O'Connor disagreed with the rationale of the majority opinion in her concurrence. Justice Stevens, Justice Souter, Justice Ginsburg, and Justice Breyer dissented. In dissent, Justice Stevens found that "the plurality's policy judgment does not justify the evisceration of a constitutional right."

Although the Supreme Court underscored the rehabilitative goals of SATP, the principal legal arguments centered on the nature of compulsion (self-incrimination must be *compelled*). Although the rehabilitative goals of SATP are admirable, they are not the subject of legal scrutiny. From a strictly *clinical* perspective, the critical issue is effectiveness of coerced treatment, or, to use a less pejorative term, required, mandated, or compelled treatment. Beyond the obvious concern of begrudging or half-hearted participation in treatment is the even more serious problem of prevarication—deception, evasion, misrepresentation, distortion, outright fabrication, and myriad levels of denial—all features that sex offenders may excel at. Moreover, we may reasonably assume that those sex offenders who excel the most are the most dangerous (i.e., psychopaths). We need not assume pathological lying, however. Most sex offenders are not psychopaths and are not pathological liars. Most sex offenders will find the need, however, to navigate a course that is perceived as hazardous (defined as posing a risk or hazard to their eventual release). The not unreasonable course to take will be to engage in the process but to be very careful not to say anything that is detrimental to the goal of release. The smarter the offender, the more savvy the offender, the more charismatic the offender, the better he can accomplish his goal of sliding through treatment, appearing to earnestly engage in the process by forcefully confronting other group members about their distortions, and never revealing any "secrets."

Yes, this problem will, to some extent, be checked by the use of full disclosure or sexual history polygraphy, used in the United States with adult sex offenders in 53% of residential/prison programs and 67% of community programs (McGrath, Cumming, Burchard, Zeoli, & Ellerby, 2010). Disclosure polygraphs are not used in residential programs in Canada and only in about 5% of community programs in Canada (McGrath et al., 2010). Thus, roughly half of the prison-based treatment programs in the US do not include polygraphy, and of those that do, an unknown number of cases will be false negatives. Last, of all the true positives, some offenders may indeed be "incentivized" to "come clean" about some incident that the polygrapher says he responded to. There is no way of knowing, however, the truthfulness of the narrative about the incident, whether it was an isolated incident, the gravity of the incident, etc. Simply knowing that he revealed this incident, even if facts were blurred a little, may be enough to pass the polygraph the next time around.

There is a substantive gap between self-incrimination in a legal context and "self-incrimination" in a psychotherapeutic context. In the former—legal—case, we cannot be *compelled* to provide evidence against ourselves. Although what constitutes compulsion, as we see in McKune v. Lile (2002), may not be agreed upon, the essence of the Fifth Amendment is crystal clear. The more or less equivalent of self-incrimination in a therapeutic context, if we can apply the term loosely, might refer to the multitude of defense mechanisms that we use to protect ourselves. The mission of therapy is *not* to encourage the use of these "defense mechanisms." The mission is the opposite—to drop the protective armor. What happens in mandatory prison-based treatment is rather oxymoronic. The message seems to be "come clean or else." The "or else" is claimed by the majority in McKune v. Lile (2002) not to rise to a level of compulsion. In the majority opinion, "or else" is referred to as consequences:

> The consequences here—a transfer to another prison where television sets are not placed in each inmate's cell, where exercise facilities are not readily available, and where work and wage opportunities are more limited—are not ones that compel a prisoner to speak about his past crimes despite a desire to remain silent.
>
> (Id. at 2026)

Consequences are trivialized when reduced to access to exercise, work, or wage opportunities, not to mention having your own TV. In the minds of the vast majority of sex offenders, "or else" refers directly to their liberty interests. When liberty is at stake, the incentive to game the system is very high (i.e., to do whatever you think you must do to minimize harming your chance to be released). The majority in McKune v. Lile (2002) held that "minimal incentives" do not equate to "compulsion." The error in reasoning is that liberty is not a "minimal" incentive. Sex offenders that are "gaming the system" in therapy groups are sex offenders who are unlikely to benefit.

B. Confidentiality. Psychotherapy places the highest premium on confidentiality, regarding it as an indispensable element of the therapeutic process. Even assurances of *partial* confidentiality have been found inadequate. That is, individuals are less willing to disclose personal information when they are promised only limited confidentiality (Haul & Muehleman, 1986; Marsh, 2003; Nowell & Spruill, 1993; Woods & McNamara, 1980). Not surprisingly, the type of information individuals are willing to disclose is also affected by limits on confidentiality. Individuals report being more willing to disclose highly sensitive information when they are assured complete confidentiality than when they are given only limited confidentiality (Nowell & Spruill, 1993; Taube & Elwork, 1990).

The issue of confidentiality is, admittedly, a complex one with a range of strongly held views. The Task Force Report (1978) clearly reflected the variance of opinion, from Siegel (1977), who "argued that there are no circumstances that ethically can justify the breaking of confidentiality" to Shah (1977), who argued that exceptions of confidentiality are not "lethal" to the practice of psychology (p. 1103). The Task Force Report (1978) goes on to state that its view "is closer to that of Shah (1977) than to that of Siegel (1977)," noting that:

> In the case of psychological treatment undertaken in criminal justice contexts (whether with prisoner or staff), we would take as a goal that the same standards of confidentiality should apply in criminal justice settings as apply in "free-world," privately contracted therapy—no less, but no more. This would mean that information obtained in treatment not be released with client consent . . . it would also mean that the same specific exceptions to confidentiality in "free-world" settings can apply to confidentiality in criminal justice settings, namely, when knowledge of a "clear and imminent danger" (e.g., a prison riot) is volunteered.
> (pp. 1103–1104)

It might be noted that the Task Force Report was issued shortly after Tarasoff v. Regents of the University of California (1976) and undoubtedly was influenced by what the Report itself referred to as a "far-reaching and bitterly contested decision" (p. 1103).

Three levels of confidentiality theoretically exist in a prison setting: (1) between the therapist and inmate, (2) between the therapist and the institution, and (3) among inmates. Therapists' files can be read by prison staff at any time, and the prison has the authority to release records to the courts, to the prosecuting attorney's office, or to other interested parties whenever it is deemed necessary, effectively destroying both therapist/inmate and therapist/institution privileges (Schlesinger, 1979). Sex offenders typically are required to sign an informed consent statement acknowledging the potential release of such disclosures to the criminal justice system. If treatment disclosures are deemed partial or incomplete, the offender may be classified non-compliant by the therapist. If disclosures include previously unknown victims or unknown inappropriate or coercive sexual behavior, those disclosures will be documented in the progress notes and thus become part of the permanent institutional record that will weigh heavily in future determinations of risk.

Once again, the importance of confidentiality has not been lost on the courts. In Jaffee v. Redmond, 518 U.S. 1 (1996), the United States Supreme Court proposed a therapist–patient privilege in the Federal Rules of Evidence. Redmond was the first responding police officer to a fight. When she arrived, she observed Allen chasing another man with a butcher's knife. Allen ignored Redmond's repeated orders to drop the knife. When it appeared that Allen was about to stab the other man, Redmond shot and killed Allen. Jaffee, acting as the representative of Allen's estate, filed suit under 42 U.S.C. § 1983, claiming that Redmond had used excessive force. When it was revealed during discovery that Redmond had been in therapy, Jaffee sought the therapist's notes. Redmond opposed the request, claiming therapist–client privilege. The trial judge rejected Redmond's argument, and the jury subsequently awarded Allen's estate $545,000 in damages. Redmond appealed to the Seventh Circuit, which vacated the trial court's decision and remanded. In the opinion of the Seventh Circuit, the privilege that Redmond sought did exist in federal law. Jaffee petitioned Supreme Court, and USSC granted certiorari. The relevant law in the case was FRE 501. The majority opinion by Justice Stevens, joined by Justices O'Connor, Kennedy, Souter, Thomas, Ginsburg, and Breyer (Justices Scalia and Rehnquist dissenting):

> *Held:* The conversations between Redmond and her therapist and the notes taken during their counseling sessions are protected from compelled disclosure under Rule 501. Pp. 5–17.
>
> a Rule 501 authorizes federal courts to define new privileges by interpreting "the principles of the common law . . . in the light of reason and experience." Pp. 5–7.

b Significant private interests support recognition of a psychotherapist privilege. Effective psychotherapy depends upon an atmosphere of confidence and trust, and therefore the mere possibility of disclosure of confidential communications may impede development of the relationship necessary for successful treatment. The privilege also serves the public interest, since the mental health of the Nation's citizenry, no less than its physical health, is a public good of transcendent importance. Pp. 7–13.

c The federal privilege, which clearly applies to psychiatrists and psychologists, also extends to confidential communications made to licensed social workers in the course of psychotherapy. The reasons for recognizing the privilege for treatment by psychiatrists and psychologists apply with equal force to clinical social workers, and the vast majority of States explicitly extend a testimonial privilege to them. Pp. 13–16.

When the guarantee of confidentiality is broken or understood to be partial, trust is undermined and with it the assumption of complete and veridical disclosure. Yet confidentiality is fully understood to be, at best, partial in the prison-based treatment programs for sex offenders. As a result, inmates are less likely to disclose in treatment and often do not trust prison therapists, since they are seen as members of the prison staff (Goffman, 1961) rather than individuals whose only consideration is what is in the inmate's best interests. Although approximately 90% of inmates receiving treatment in the 1960s admitted to their therapists that they had committed the offenses for which they had been incarcerated, this rate declined steadily beginning in the 1980s and dropped to only 50% by the 2000s (Langevin, 2006). The less an inmate reveals in therapy about his history of sexual crimes, the less likely that incriminating information will become public and used against him. Inmate subculture, moreover, derives its structure from identifying weaknesses in other inmates and exploiting those weaknesses (Schrag, 1973); the less an individual's fellow inmates know, the safer he is likely to be.

C. Dual roles. The APA Code of Ethics (2002) protects clients by prohibiting therapists from engaging in dual-role relationships. No such protection applies to prisoners. In the criminal justice system, therapists often perceive that they have multiple responsibilities. They are not only responsible to their client/inmate, they are also responsible to the prison in which they work. As a result, therapists may find themselves acting as *de facto* informants. Their duty to the prison is to help ensure the safety of the custodial environment by alerting custody staff about potentially volatile situations. Moreover, due to the nature of the "operating environment," therapists often spend "down time" with inmates, talking informally on living units, particularly on units intended to be therapeutic communities. Coupled with the presumptive training that therapists receive in identifying warning signs of potential custodial disruption, including drugs and inmate-on-inmate violence, therapists are frequently seen as allies of the custody staff. Therapists may also have a perceived duty to protect society by testifying in court about the lack of progress in treatment of an inmate who has petitioned for release. Since the petitioning inmate is sitting in the courtroom, he hears firsthand what his therapist is saying about him. Given the adversarial nature of the proceeding, what the therapist says may not be flattering and may contribute to a finding that the inmate has not made sufficient progress in treatment, remains at high risk, and must remain at the prison. It is clear that the duties and responsibilities of a therapist working in a prison environment are more complex than the duties and responsibilities of a therapist working in the community with outpatients who are not in the criminal justice system. Conflicting responsibilities and blurred roles are "part of the territory" for many prison-based therapists.

In summary, we have argued that the effectiveness of treatment provided to sex offenders in a prison environment is undermined by the following factors (Prentky et al., 2011):

a treatment is subordinated to security, with the inevitable consequence that institutional priorities will always place security above therapy;
b conditions for therapy are suboptimal (e.g., severe space limitations often require relying on part-time staff, limited scheduling options, adapting to the ever-changing conditions of a prison environment, which may require canceling groups or other treatment activities on a moment's notice, maintaining staff morale in an environment that is often unsupportive of, or even hostile to treatment);
c physical safety of prisoners is threatened when they are known in population as sex offenders, which places therapy goals dependent on disclosure at odds with physical survival; this may apply even in prisons that only have sex offenders (e.g., rapists are not above assaulting child molesters, whose crimes they find particularly odious);
d confidentiality cannot be assumed or assured;
e offenders are typically mandated or required to be treated and are reluctant customers;
f therapists often are inadequately trained and supervised;
g program-related resources are limited and often restricted (e.g., inability to provide desired interventions or assessments, such as ammonia often used with covert sensitization, anti-androgen medication, and penile plethysmography);
h the environment *after* release is determined not by individualized considerations but by a complex legal process that typically

> imposes control sanctions, such as sex offender registration and restrictions on residency, work and leisure activities, making the task of examining the effectiveness of treatment exceedingly difficult. Such control strategies, moreover, may have the reverse effect of aggravating re-offense risk by imposing insurmountable obstacles to normal re-integration through forced social isolation, unemployment or underemployment, harassment and social ostracism, and adverse stress and negative effects on whatever social and familial supports may exist (e.g., Kruttschnitt, Uggen, & Shelton, 2000; Lasher & McGrath, 2012; Logan, 2003; Whitting, Day, & Powell, 2014). The Wisconsin study is a noteworthy example of such problems.
>
> (Zevitz & Farkas, 2000a,b,c)

Under these conditions it would be a mistake to conclude that prison-based or community-based sex offender treatment is ineffective, or insufficiently effective to warrant the cost. We hasten to add that there are many other outcomes of treatment, or secondary effects, that merit consideration and may warrant the cost, such as increasing awareness and accountability among the offenders, validating the wrongfulness of their behavior, increasing their vigilance around warning signs and lapses, and encouraging those who have yet to offend or who have offended but are not registered to seek therapy to avoid the consequences of registration (Finn, 1997).

Registration "enjoys enormous popular support" (Logan, 2003, p. 344) in the community among residents and generally among law enforcement. Popular support, however, seems inconclusive. Zevitz and Farkas (2000a) found that two-thirds of the residents felt more uncomfortable or less safe *after* the community informational meeting than before. In addition, there is the uncertain question of the impact of registration on those offenders, arguably most, who deem these requirements unjust and arbitrary. Taken alone, an offender's feelings of unfairness would attract little sympathy. It has been pointed out, however, that these feelings reduce offender compliance (Tyler, 2001) and may well contribute to offenders going "underground," thereby short-circuiting the law entirely. According to an article in the *Huffington Post* (2014), "Roughly one in six sex offenders uses techniques pioneered by identity thieves to fly under the radar and avoid registering their addresses and work places." The news report cited a Utica College study, supported by the Department of Justice, finding that 92,000 out of 570,000 registered sex offenders throughout the United States have changed their personal identities. An article by Davey (2006) in the *New York Times* proclaimed "Iowa's Residency Rules Drive Sex Offenders Underground," noting that 400 of the 6,000+ sex offenders on Iowa's registry are listed as "whereabouts unconfirmed" or living in "non-structure locations." An Associated Press article proclaimed that "California 'loses' 33,000 sex offenders" (Curtis, 2003). This common theme in the media about "missing" sex offenders may be alarmist (Levenson & Harris, 2012), reflect some truth, or pose a real (and serious) problem. Ackerman et al. (2012) reported that 43% of the registered sex offenders in the five states examined, ranging from 25% in Texas to 60% in Florida, were not living in the community.

Whatever the answer, there clearly are some absconders, and those that cannot be tracked are missing from any systematic analysis of re-offense, affecting the reliability of all studies looking at the accuracy of risk scales, effectiveness of treatment, reintegration problems, and, of course, any attempt to assess the efficacy of these judicial interventions by examining costs and benefits. The most sophisticated, large-scale study of registration/notification efficacy was conducted by Prescott and Rockoff (2008) for the National Bureau of Economic Research using data from the National Incident Based Reporting System (NIBRS). NIBRS is a system for gathering data on each incident and arrest for all 46 Group A offenses and reporting those data to the FBI's Uniform Crime Reporting (UCR) Program. NIBRS has the advantage of linking information on victims, offenders, and arrestees for each incident in the dataset. Prescott and Rockoff (2008) examined data from 15 states (Colorado, Connecticut, Idaho, Iowa, Kentucky, Massachusetts, Michigan, Nebraska, North Dakota, Ohio, South Carolina, Texas, Utah, Vermont, and Virginia). The dataset included 4,757,118 assaults, including 328,260 sexual offenses. Prescott and Rockoff (2008) concluded,

> We find evidence suggested that registration laws reduce the frequency of sex offenses, particularly for local victims, by providing information on convicted sex offenders to local authorities. Our results also suggest that the reduction in crime was locally concentrated, in line with policymakers' intentions, with reductions generally greater among victims with a personal connection to offenders. We did not find evidence of any crime displacement that would increase victimizations of strangers. We also find evidence that notification laws reduce crime, but do so by deterring potential criminals, not necessarily recidivists. In fact, our results suggest that registered offenders might be more likely to commit crime in a state that imposes a set of notification requirements, perhaps because of heavy social and financial costs associated with the public release of their information.
>
> (pp. 33–34)

In sum, registration/notification was found to reduce the frequency of sexual offenses, especially with known friends (family, friends, acquaintances, neighbors); however, there was little evidence of a decrease in frequency of sexual offenses against strangers. The investigators further observed that community notification functions as a deterrent in a *different* way from what the legislators anticipated—first-time sex offenders are deterred, while registered sex offenders are not. This finding, the investigators argue, is quite consistent with the criminological model predicting that notification would increase recidivism among those who are registered by making law-abiding activity less attractive due to the social and financial costs of notification. The Prescott and Rockoff (2008) study reveals the easily predicted complexity of the impact of registration and notification, further underscoring the *critical importance* of fine-tuning the implementation of these programs by incorporating findings from rigorously conducted studies, such as this one. Finding ways to maintain adequate surveillance while easing the social and financial burden might turn the registration/notification program into a more effective risk-mitigating intervention.

Community notification, at best, restores a feeling of control over the threat posed by sex offenders. Community notification makes the invisible visible. When we know "who" poses the threat, we can avoid (or counter) the threat. Community notification has more to do with assuaging fear by bolstering feelings of control than reducing risk of re-offense. For those who exercise their privilege of learning the identity and address of nearby sex offenders, they can employ avoidance strategies, reducing the likelihood of their children crossing paths with those individuals. Community notification may not deter those same offenders, however, from re-offending in other communities. Like the rest of us, sex offenders are not restricted to huffing it on foot. They have access to cars, motorcycles, bicycles, and public transportation. For a sex offender who is motivated to offend, community notification merely increases the likelihood that he will travel outside the community in which he lives.

The same logic applies to residency restrictions. By prohibiting sex offenders from establishing a residence living within 1,000 yards of a school or daycare center, we seem to be suggesting that the individual will not travel to a school or daycare center 2,000 yards away, or 10 miles away, or find a child at some location other than a school or daycare center, such as a shopping mall or a town park. Building a "statutory fence" around schools and daycare centers does not prevent sex offenders from offending, if they are highly motivated to do so. These comments should not be taken as nihilistic, just common (and empirical) sense. Managing sex offenders in the community should fall squarely on the shoulders of those who are properly trained—probation and parole officers and police—not the neighbors. Reducing the likelihood of re-offense does not benefit from a handful of neighbors avoiding the sex offender; it requires a trained, multidisciplinary team of professionals providing offender-specific interventions ranging from unannounced, periodic visits by probation officers,

GPS surveillance, polygraphy, and periodic dynamic risk analysis by a forensic mental health professional to job training, random drug screens, medication, and treatment. These interventions, in the spirit of risk-need-responsivity (RNR), should be tailored to the "needs" of the individual.

The bottom line is that these questions are complex and demand *objective* answers if we are to reduce the likelihood that known sex offenders who are returned to the community re-offend. Feel-good legislation is unlikely to reduce recidivism, and may not even make us feel better. Research alone cannot solve the problems enumerated above. Those problems can only be addressed through policy changes that re-structure and re-prioritize the demonstrated effectiveness of our interventions, be they treatment in prison or registration/notification in the community. Only then will these interventions serve the implicit purpose of civil commitment and the explicit purpose of public safety. As it stands, ineffective or suboptimal interventions serve neither.

As stated earlier, sex offender *treatment alone* is *not* a panacea. Treatment alone can *never* effectively mitigate sexual violence in our society. Treatment is a secondary intervention only for those who have been caught and subjected to treatment. Even among that small group, the effectiveness of treatment in reducing re-offense is uncertain. As we have elsewhere noted,

> The branches of this pervasive problem insinuate themselves into, and directly affect, all aspects of society. The problem is not confined to the handful of offenders who spend time in prison and are offered some limited exposure to treatment. By merely reducing the risk of those who have already turned to sexual violence, we will never achieve the ultimate aim of making society a safer place.
> (Prentky & Schwartz, 2006, p. 6)

Primary prevention is the only effective remedy for reducing the incidence of sexual violence. Restoration of the rights to sexual autonomy for women and children requires a public health policy that drives a comprehensive public health plan to address *all* factors that promote *all* expressions of unwanted sexual behavior. Thus far, we appear to be quite content to focus only on the few bad actors that are caught. We seem remarkably resistant to primary prevention strategies that alter the calculus of sexually violent behavior *before* it occurs. The organizational propensity is to cover up and thus ignore incidents of sexual violence. Such was the case with clergy sexual abuse, until lawsuits and adverse publicity forced change. Such is presently the case with sexual assault in high schools and on college campuses all over the country. Colleges, it would seem, prefer to dismiss the problem as an occasional annoyance than to deal with it head-on. Dealing with the problem head-on requires acknowledgement of the problem—and coping with the inevitable adverse publicity. Such is presently the case with sexual assault in the military. The same response—damage control. The *only* impediment to a direct, clear, forthright response to sexual violence is *accepting* the problem. The instinctive institutional response is *denial*, ironically precisely the same problem that sex offenders are treated for. If society had the same investment in tackling sexual violence as it has in tackling cigarette smoking, the incidence of sexual violence would drop dramatically.

A Path Not (Yet) Taken

Some 15 years ago, we made the following plea:

> The path into the 21st century must move us beyond the "high drama" of sexual assault that is fueled by the media and responded to by politicians who draft myopic, reactive laws. The model that we propose treats sexual assault as a public health problem, indeed a very serious public health problem. Despite the hypervigilant attention to sexual crimes by the media and the draconian responses to those crimes by many politicians, our legal and social remedies are woefully inadequate and fail to address the preponderance of individuals who violate the sexual autonomy of others. By and large, those who sexually intimidate and sexually coerce others do so with impunity. Even clear instances of aggravated sexual assault may be treated as normative behavior. In sum, the number of individuals who are apprehended, charged and convicted of their sexual crimes is greatly eclipsed by the total number of men who engage in the full gamut of sexually coercive and abusive behavior.
>
> (Prentky & Burgess, 2000, p. 237)

At this point it is only fair to say that the above statement, "Despite the hypervigilant attention to sexual crimes by the media and the draconian responses to those crimes by many politicians," is incomplete. Responses by politicians and political commentators often are highly polarized, either myopic and draconian or unabashedly ignorant and dismissive. As best as we can tell, it seems that the former response is much more likely when the victims are children, and the latter response is much more likely when the victims are adults.

10

SCIENCE AND FORENSIC PRACTICE

Recommendations

Issues in Risk Communication

Close to three decades ago, *American Psychologist* published in its September 1996 issue three articles on risk communication. One of the three, by Monahan and Steadman (1996) on "Violent Storms and Violent People," introduced, by way of analogy, weather forecasting to the center-stage of discourse on behavioral risk assessment. In their oft-cited paper, Monahan and Steadman began by querying why weather forecasters do such a good job. They cited the report of the National Research Council's Committee on Risk Perception and Communication (Improving Risk Communication, 1989) as identifying five chief reasons for the success of weather forecasters: (1) frequent practice, (2) base rate information, (3) actuarial support, (4) availability of feedback, and (5) educational programs/training programs. Although the theme of their article is how behavioral risk prediction can benefit from lessons learned from meteorologists, the substance of the article explored risk communication. Monahan and Steadman note that the National Weather Service (NWS) went through three iterations, from deterministic predictions prior to 1965 ("It will/will not rain today") to probabilistic pronouncements ("There is a 40% chance of rain today") to categorical messages, reserved primarily for severe weather (e.g., tornado or hurricane "watches" and "warnings"). The NWS apparently still uses probabilistic statements when it comes to common weather events and categorical messages only for severe events. Why the NWS shifts to categorical messages for severe (rare) events lies in the NWS's "skepticism about the competence of users—particularly the general public—to optimally process information about low probability events (Hughes, 1980)" (Monahan & Steadman, 1996, p. 934). A more generalized problem of innumeracy (a relative incapacity or difficulty with numbers) was described more recently by Scurich, Monahan, and John

(2012). Scurich et al. (2012) noted, "almost half the population has trouble with mundane, simple numeric tasks, such as estimating a price per ounce at a grocery store" (p. 549).

The implication of innumeracy for risk communication would seem evident. Monahan (2008) similarly observed, "Innumeracy, as this monograph makes abundantly clear, is an enormous societal problem" (p. 15). If estimating a price per ounce at a grocery store proves challenging, comprehending the rudiments of probability is daunting. In fact, we rarely contemplate the probability of risky outcomes that we are confronted with. The natural tendency to eschew probabilistic thinking is referred to as "probability neglect." Seasoned defense attorneys (and their seasoned defense experts), for example, will always use a probability format: "Individuals like Mr. Smith are estimated to have a 20% probability of re-offending during the next three years." The statement is bland, mundane, humdrum. The statement is unlikely to engage (or even interest) the jury. By contrast, seasoned prosecutors (and their seasoned experts) will likely rely on a frequency format: "Of every 100 individuals similar to Mr. Smith, 20 are estimated to commit another sexual offense." That statement is far more impactful. The "20" is now etched in the minds of jurors as *real victims*, not an obscure probability.

This is precisely what Monahan, Heilbrun, Silver, Nabors, Bone, and Slovic (2002) found. Monahan et al. (2002) surveyed 226 clinical psychologists with an expressed interest in forensic work. Both formats (probability vs. frequency) and vividness (pallid vs. vivid) were manipulated in a brief scenario, and participants were randomly assigned to one of four conditions. Among those psychologists who reported working full or part-time in a forensic facility, 73.9% of those receiving the frequency format ("of every 100 patients similar to Mr. Jones, 20 are estimated to commit an act of violence") and 53.6% of those receiving the probability format ("patients similar to Mr. Jones are estimated to have a 20% probability of committing an act of violence") would *not* discharge the patient in the scenario. The proportional difference was significant ($p = .03$). This effect was only found among those who worked in forensic facilities. Moreover, when the depiction was vivid, 80% of those receiving the frequency format compared with 60.7% of those receiving the probability format said they would *not* discharge the patient. The lowest proportion of respondents (46.4%) recommending no discharge were those in the pallid depiction/probability format condition. In sum, the most conservative decisions were from those in the frequency/vivid condition. Once again, these findings were specific to those psychologists that reported working in forensic facilities.

In a different example, a seasoned defense attorney may wish to cast doubt on the reliability of DNA evidence against her client. She is likely to say something along the lines of: "A false match occurs in 1 out of every 1,000 capital cases." The prosecutor, with a very bored expression, will retort: "The chance of a false match is 0.1%." The jurors will likely pay little attention to the prosecutor's retort, and disregard the chance of a false match. By contrast, however, the defense attorney introduced the human element by directing the jurors to think about a falsely convicted defendant—even if it is only one person out of a thousand. Indeed, that one falsely convicted defendant may be enough in the minds of some jurors to reach the threshold of "reasonable doubt." How concepts are communicated affects our judgments.

In an interesting test of our aforementioned experiential observation of how seasoned experts opine, Scurich and John (2011) examined the role of framing risk estimates in "commitment decisions" by mock judges (college students). In this test, Scurich and John manipulated the percent probability of those estimated to re-offend versus the percent probability of those estimated to not re-offend. As expected, "risk framed as 26% probability of violence generally led decision-makers to authorize commitment, whereas the same risk framed in the complement, a 74% probability of no violence, generally led decision-makers to release" (p. 83). Although the Scurich and John study was certainly more subtle than our comparison of two different communication formats, they still found that the negative frame—attaching the 26% to real violence—was more impactful in swaying decisions toward commitment than the positive frame of no violence among 74%. As Scurich and John (2011) pointed out, "By emphasizing different aspects of the same risk estimate, the balance can be inappropriately skewed" (p. 88).

A further clear implication for risk communication comes from the study by Scurich, Monahan, and John (2012) on "unpacking" risk factors (i.e., rather than simply reporting a risk estimate derived from a scale, the investigators unpacked the estimate by delineating the risk factors that went into the estimate). They compared no unpacking (just the risk estimate) with three risk factors and six risk factors. The degree of unpacking *increased* the likelihood that 380 jury-eligible citizens recommended the commitment of higher-risk respondents and *decreased* the likelihood that citizens would recommend the commitment of lower-risk respondents. As Scurich et al. (2012) pointed out, unpacking "increased the perceived relevance of the group-level risk estimate to the individual case" (p. 551). The investigators further found that by disaggregating the sample based on self-reported numeracy (facility with numbers), numeracy moderated the effect of "unpacking" risk factors (i.e., the unpacking effect remained for the innumerate subjects but not for the numerate subjects).

Scurich et al. (2012) used a median split on the distribution of scores from their numeracy scale, resulting in two more or less equivalently sized subgroups (only slightly more innumerate subjects). Although it is not known how this proportional distribution of numerates and innumerates generalizes to the population at large, the takeaway message from these findings was clear: Prosecutors (and their experts) should unpack *high*—but *not* low—risk estimates. Defense attorneys (and their experts) should unpack *low*—but *not* high—risk estimates. Scurich et al. (2012) were quick to clarify that they were not advocating unpacking as a strategy for manipulating the system. Unpacking (although it had not occurred to us to use that word) is not only something that we *strongly* recommend for *all* sexually violent predator (SVP) evaluations (not just when it benefits the petitioner or the respondent); it is fundamental to risk-need-responsivity (RNR) and fundamental for honesty and transparency. By requiring the expert to "unpack" her/his opinion, we are making the preeminently reasonable assumption that the court should *fully* understand the reasoning behind, and evidence for, the expert's opinion. Parenthetically, in illustrating how prosecution and defense attorneys (and their experts) might "unpack" as a trial strategy, we are not endorsing or recommending this. Unpacking should facilitate transparency, not winning.

Providing Testimony in Highly Charged, Adversarial Cases

Litigation involving sex offenders, although not uniquely so, is often characterized by a high level of contentiousness. An unfortunate, and perhaps inevitable, outcome is the sacrifice of objectivity and transparency as adversaries place "winning" over "the whole truth." This point is illustrated by Woodworth and Kadane (2004), who examined whether expert testimony in SVP trials met Daubert and Frye's admissibility standards. Woodworth and Kadane (2004) concluded:

> It goes almost without saying that sexual violence against children is viewed as one of the most despicable crimes imaginable. Thus elected judges and prosecutors seem caught between the proverbial rock and a hard place—the consequences of participating in the release of a sex offender who ultimately re-offends (a Type I error) or of participating in the long-term confinement of a harmless individual (a Type II error) are unbalanced. Long-term confinement of a non-recidivist is unjust to the respondent but doesn't produce the public opprobrium and career-ending potential of being associated with the release of a sexually violent re-offender. Prosecution experts, who are often state employees, may well feel similar pressures. On the defense side, failure to win a release in a civil commitment hearing does not on its face seem to carry the same kind of personal risks. [The authors fail to point out the equally profound negative consequences of helping to win the release of a sexually violent re-offender.]
>
> We suggest that these unbalanced consequences combined with the comparatively relaxed rules of evidence in a civil hearing

> both skew the incentives of the actors in the system and provide an opportunity to skew the presentation of evidence in ways that might not be transparent. In statistical terms, this imposes on the fact-finder the burden of modelling the behavior of the expert witnesses, particularly experts who are state employees. We argue that requiring strong standards of statistical and scientific evidence will make the weighing of evidence more transparent for the fact-finder.
>
> (p. 239)

The most remarkable paradox of expert testimony is hubris. The clear downside of overweening self-confidence, if not arrogance, is relative absence of judicious introspection and discriminating judgment born of humility. The task of accurate risk prediction of violent behavior under conditions of uncertainty is challenging enough. Over-regard for one's self as an "expert" and one's expert opinion, however, will further undermine any semblance of objectivity and increase false positivity. Indeed, one's confidence in the accuracy of one's opinion is likely to be inversely correlated with accuracy (Silver, 2012).

Coates (2012) provided a vivid image of the over-inflated Wall Street trader:

> As a bull market starts to validate investors' beliefs, the profits they make translate into a lot more than mere greed: they bring on powerful feelings of euphoria and omnipotence. It is at this point that traders and investors feel the bonds of terrestrial life slip from their shoulders and they begin to flex their muscles like a newborn superhero. Assessment of risk is replaced by judgments of certainty—they just *know* what is going to happen: extreme sports seem like child's play, sex becomes a competitive activity. They even walk differently: more erect, more purposeful, their very bearing carrying a hint of danger: "Don't mess with me," their bodies seem to say. "I can handle anything." Tom Wolfe nailed this delusional behavior when he described the stars of Wall Street as "Masters of the Universe."
>
> (pp. 18–19)

By marked contrast, however, the equally clear *upside* to hubris is its effectiveness on the witness stand. Jurors tend to be persuaded by testimony that is unwavering, as long as there is not a glint of arrogance. Jurors are as likely to be turned off by cockiness or pretentiousness. A poised, self-assured presentation of a tightly constructed story that weaves together and appears to explain all of the facts can be highly persuasive. For jurors, such a compact narrative "explains" the case in a more logical, comprehendible, easily digestible fashion than a dissection of risk factors. The strength of such testimony derives from two factors—the self-confidence and self-assuredness conveyed by the witness, and the coherence of the explanation. The narrative could be a "bill of goods," but it is likely to be more effective than a modest, reserved witness who is more faithful to the science and to all of the known facts of the case. The modest, demure, or unassuming witness may come across as unassured and lacking conviction. Faithfulness to science and to "facts" may not come across as coherence, especially when the facts and/or the science do not blend into a coherent narrative. The danger is that "if such 'experts' are consulted (and paid) as a function of the confidence they inspire, they may be tempted to misrepresent how much they know" (Fischhoff, 1982, p. 439). Stated more precisely, the likely outcome will be a selective presentation of the evidence, excluding whatever fails to support the narrative.

Hastie and Dawes (2010) noted that, "The central cognitive process in juror decision-making is *story construction*—the creation of a narrative summary of the events under dispute" (p. 123). Hastie and Dawes hypothesized that "the story the juror constructs, often quite deliberately to 'piece together the puzzle of historical truth,' determines the juror's verdict" (p. 123). As we noted in Chapter 3, Hastie and Dawes illustrated the point with three examples of famous (i.e., highly successful) attorneys who won by weaving the best story. To re-state their last example of O. J. Simpson:

> In the O. J. Simpson murder trial, Marcia Clark's closing argument as prosecutor included a detailed summary of the prosecution crime story, complete with a timeline; in contrast, the defense attorney, Johnnie Cochran, concluded by exhorting the jurors to accept the role, at trial, of protector, even avenger, of oppressed minority defendants (Hastie & Pennington, 1996).
>
> (Hastie & Dawes, 2010, p. 123)

Hastie and Dawes advised attorneys "to tell good stories, when they can" (p. 127). Although that is the role of the attorney—to provide the best possible representation for their client—it is *not* the role of the expert, and we do *not* support storytelling on the stand, unless, of course, the story happens to narrate all of the facts of the case, leading to fully defensible opinions.

Most forensic examiners do possess skills unique to their trade. Acquisition of skills tends to be nonlinear, however, conforming more to what Silver (2012) referred to as the Pareto Principle of Prediction. In other words, the greatest initial expenditure of effort (or practice) translates to the greatest amount of progress. Using Silver's principle, the first 20% of effort (experience doing forensic work) equates to roughly 80%

of one's accuracy in prediction. Thereafter, improvements in accuracy come slowly and in small increments. This steep distributional skew of skill acquisition, assuming it applies to those who evaluate sex offenders, reflects relative dormancy after a sharp but brief initial learning period. If it does apply, either these practitioners are quick learners and achieve a high level of accuracy quickly, or a high level of self-confidence assumes accuracy, or accuracy is not mindfully considered.

The challenge is knowing (and accounting for) the *limitations* of one's skills. Forensic practice can easily breed overconfidence, in some cases exaggerating an existing sense of self-importance or creating an artificial aura of self-importance among those who tend, by their nature, to be more humble. Anointed by the court as "experts" and referred to only by the generic dignified title of "Dr.," the psychologist or psychiatrist dutifully assumes the role. "Experts have been revered—and well paid—for years for their 'It is my opinion that . . . ' judgments" (Hastie & Dawes, 2010, p. 63). Cohen, Groth, and Siegel (1978) pointed out long ago that "courts too often simply rubber stamp the opinion of the psychiatrist or the psychologist" (p. 38).

The well-prepared expert takes the stand holding a significant "hand." The expert has been anointed an "expert" by the court, often after the ritual recital of the CV. Most importantly, however, jurors typically begin by wanting to hear the opinion of "this expert." The expert is, at least at first, the trail guide who will lead us through this mélange of evidence. Perhaps even more to the point, lay jurors are likely to believe in the power of the expert to *predict*. As Harcourt (2007) noted, "The fact that we *do* believe [in prediction] tells us about our *desire* to believe, our *desire* to predict, our *desire* to know the recidivist. We are, it seems, predisposed to wanting the actuarial model to be right" (p. 144). Experts clearly have their Achilles' heel, however. Lack of preparation and/or arrogance are their undoing.

The crackerjack powers of the forensic investigator/examiner are trumpeted in umpteen forensic crime TV shows (e.g., *Law & Order, CSI, Criminal Minds, NCIS, Blue Bloods, Hawaii Five-0, Sherlock Holmes*) and legal TV shows (e.g., *Law & Order, JAG, L.A. Law, Damages, The Defenders, Boston Legal, Shark, Matlock*). Among the lay public, there is indeed something magical about the attributed ability to "read criminal minds." And so it is that we have a generation of young women who apply to graduate programs in forensic psychology with the expressed wish to be the next Clarice Starling, rated by the American Film Institute as the sixth greatest protagonist in film history *and* the highest-ranking heroine in film history (American Film Institute, 2003). It is a notable commentary that the foremost female protagonist in film history is a fictional FBI agent who matches her wits with Dr. Lecter, a brilliant psychiatrist (and cannibalistic serial killer).

Although forensic experts legitimately possess training and (hopefully) a modicum of experience and wisdom not possessed by other professionals, the boundaries of expertise are delimited by the inherent fallibility of human judgment. Moreover, when forensic experts move away from or ignore their data and rely principally on instinctive judgment, they are as prone to overconfidence as lay people (Oskamp, 1982). As noted, the conundrum is that instinctive judgment and overconfidence "works" (i.e., it is most persuasive) in court, while a tedious recitation about the virtues of probabilistic judgment does not. "An expert who constructs a linear model is not as impressive as one who gives advice in a 'burst' of intuition derived from 'years of experience'," (Hastie & Dawes, 2010, p. 63). As we discussed above, "a linear model" is far more likely to lose jurors than an impassioned story that appears to explain the respondent's behavior. Unpacking, as described earlier, can theoretically occur in either case, but the principle holds. Unpacking risk factors can be dreary and "scientific," or it can be a highly compelling part of the story that draws jurors in.

For most seasoned professional expert witnesses, and certainly for nonprofessional expert witnesses (those who do not routinely work as expert witnesses), the "cross-exam" is anticipated as stressful and characterized both by uncertainty and uncontrollability. A common response is to reframe the cross-examination—You are in control, because you are the "expert." You are the fount of wisdom, at least regarding the matters of your testimony. Since you are the expert, you are *certain* of your opinion. Since you are the expert, you are in *control.* Since the Court has agreed that you are an expert, you assume your role with *confidence.* Some professional experts quaff prodigious quantities of the Kool-Aid and come to believe that their opinions are indeed gospel. They have arrived at that magic place of supreme overconfidence, a very dangerous place to be from the standpoint of objectivity and accuracy. For most other experts, who own the mantle of authority and testify firmly in black and white terms but retain a semblance of humility, overconfidence is still a helpful defense against uncertainty.

The courtroom, counterproductively, breeds—perhaps demands—overconfidence. For most of us, overconfidence is an appearance, an invisible cloak that we wrap around ourselves as we take our oath to speak only the truth. For some of us, the cloak never comes off. In either case, we find ourselves in a paradoxical situation, sworn to tell the truth about matters that are inherently uncertain, and to do so with conviction, persuasion, even passion. The most persuasive experts are steadfast and indefatigable, traits that are incompatible with uncertainty and inconsistent with our implied obligation to "tell the truth, the whole truth, and nothing but the truth." Although we swear to tell the truth, our testimony frequently is *not* the *whole* truth, since the whole truth might include evidence that is disconfirmatory of our opinion. The flip side of this conundrum is that by omitting disconfirmatory evidence, the expert witness undercuts her coherence and exposes herself to impeachment on cross-examination.

Throughout this book we have discussed the countervailing forces that undermine objectivity—biases and heuristics in their many incarnations. We have not thus far entertained the possibility of empathy as such a force to be reckoned with. Shuman and Zervopoulos (2010) address what they refer to as the forensic examiner's dilemma—empathy vs. objectivity. The message is that "forensic mental health examiners must put aside . . . empathy and conduct their work . . . objectively" (p. 590); "can examiners adequately monitor and govern their personal views about cases to ensure that bias does not improperly influence their expert opinions" (p. 591). Although empathy might intervene as a form of bias in child custody cases, we would speculate that empathy, defined by the authors as identification with another (presumably the defendant/respondent), is not the norm among examiners who evaluate adult male sex offenders. Identification with the retaining attorney, and feeling the need to help the attorney, is more likely, although even here it is unlikely that this qualifies as empathy. Empathic over-identification with the defendant/respondent is more likely when the sex offender is young (pre-adolescent or adolescent). Cases involving juveniles, especially those involving civil commitment and lengthy periods of registration/community notification may indeed challenge one's capacity for objective judgment.

Shuman and Zervopoulos (2010) provide a model to minimize empathy-bias: Step One—Generate plausible alternative hypotheses; Step Two—Actively challenge plausible alternative explanations. Step One introduces *inference to the best explanation*, or what used to be commonly referred to as abduction. Abduction, the third leg of the inferential triad (induction and deduction), is generally understood by philosophers and psychologists alike to be ubiquitous in common everyday reasoning. For present purposes, it should simply be noted that abduction is not only seen as compatible with Bayesian confirmation theory (Weisberg, 2009), but some argue that it is an important supplement to Bayesianism (cf. Lipton, 2004). Step Two requires the examiner to "actively challenge how each plausible explanation squares with the data until an explanation emerges that best 'fits' the data" (Shuman & Zervopoulos, 2010, p. 597). Although both steps are excellent recommendations, they are more easily suggested than accomplished. To challenge bias, bias must first be identified. Recognizing our own sources of bias is the first challenge, since our biases are often unconscious. Goldyne (2007) recommended that forensic experts *proactively* challenge their biases as a way to minimize "unconscious bias." We do not underestimate the difficulty of "second guessing" ourselves, especially when we are inclined to think of ourselves as "experts." Second guessing our *opinions*, however, should be adopted as standard practice. Not only will it enhance our accuracy, it will serve the not inconsequential goal of enhancing our preparedness for cross-examination. Critical thinking is a refined skill that comes only with awareness and single-minded, diligent effort. Sharon Begley (2006), a science columnist for *The Wall Street Journal*, wrote, "You have to want to think critically. If you have good critical-thinking skills but for some reason are not motivated to deploy them, you will reach conclusions and make decisions no more rationally than someone without those skills" (p. B1).

Issues in Risk Determination

Moving Beyond the Twin Great Debates

Although we cannot resolve the seemingly interminable, occasionally raucous, debates over (1) application of group-level data to individuals and (2) probabilistic versus categorical expressions of risk, we strive to offer parsimonious answers.

Application of Group-Level Data to Individuals

Heilbrun, Douglas, and Yasuhara (2009) refer to this debate as a "core controversy." It strikes us, however, as the more easily addressed of the two. *All* psychological testing yields group-level data (Heilbrun, 1992). Heilbrun (1992) long ago advised, moreover, that

> Because of this premium on the accuracy of information provided to the factfinder, the *results of psychological tests should not be used in isolation* from history, medical findings, and observations of behavior made by others. . . . This point . . . has also been made by others (e.g., Heilbrun, 1988; Melton et al., 1987; Rogers, 1986; Shapiro, 1984, 1991).
>
> (p. 263)

Heilbrun (1992) goes on to say,

> Psychological testing can serve as one source of information that can both formulate and confirm or disconfirm hypotheses about psychological constructs relevant to the legal issue, but there are others as well: history, medical testing, interview data, and third-party observations of behavior can all be used for these purposes. Once hypotheses are formulated, they must then be translated into falsifiable terms, subject to verification, disconfirmation, or mixed support. It is noteworthy that such translation should not encompass the ultimate legal issue.
>
> (p. 268)

If we banned the application of group-level data to individuals, we would be barring most personality testing (e.g., MMPI or MCMI), most cognitive testing (e.g., WAIS), and all actuarial risk assessment scales (e.g., VRAG, SORAG, PCL-R, Static-99/Static-99R/Static-2002/Static-2002R), along with many other tests that yield norm-referenced results. The relatively simple, straightforward resolution of this "core controversy" would seem to be obvious: group-level data (including the results from actuarial risk assessment scales) are commonly gathered in the course of doing an SVP evaluation but those data should *never be used in isolation* to forecast outcomes or to reach conclusory opinions. The controversy, as Heilbrun et al. (2009) referred to it, seems less to do with this logical resolution and more to do with the tendency for group-level data (to wit, a Static-99 score) to *drive* the opinion about the ultimate 3rd prong question of risk. Testimony often will center wholly, if not entirely, around the Static-99 score. In this instance, the *individual* (respondent/defendant) is, in fact, reduced to one piece of group-level data, and we would agree emphatically that this is not appropriate. This will not be an issue if we abide by Heilbrun's (1992) dictum: *results of psychological tests should not be used in isolation.*

Tom Grisso (1987) pointed out, nearly three decades ago, that the concern registered in United States v. Downing (1985) about "the spectre of the creation of a cottage industry of forensic psychologists" was belated—it had already arrived (p. 831). Grisso's article in *American Psychologist* dealt with the future of forensic *assessment*. Psychological testing is potentially contributory to most areas of forensic assessment and is commonly relied upon in most forensic evaluations. The 15-year follow-up in *American Psychologist* by Randy Otto and Kirk Heilbrun (2002) addressed "The explosion of forensic assessment instruments and forensically relevant instruments" (p. 9). The Specialty Guidelines for Forensic Psychology (2013) specifically address the use of "assessment instruments" (10. Assessment, p. 15).

Buchanan (2013) raised yet a different issue, arguing that our concern is misplaced. The issue, according to Buchanan, is not whether violence risk assessment is epistemic ("degree of confirmation"), as it is typically treated, or whether it is aleatory ("statistical"). The issue, simply stated, should not be couched in terms of whether group-based estimates generated by risk assessment scales can be applied to individuals. The relevance of group-based estimates for Buchanan lies in non-statistical matters, such as whether it makes sense to consider a particular individual as being similar enough to the reference group used to develop the scale's estimates and whether the criterion of interest in developing the scale is exactly the same as the criterion of interest for the individual being evaluated.

To question the use of test or instrument-derived scores, all group-based information, in conducting forensic psychological assessments makes little sense. The potentially vital role of nomothetic data in forensic evaluations is, in our opinion, indisputable. A similar opinion was expressed by Skeem and Monahan (2011), who noted that "group data theoretically can be, and in many areas empirically are, highly informative when making decisions about individual cases" (p. 40). We should point out the seemingly obvious: In general clinical (non-forensic) practice, it is commonplace to integrate nomothetic data (e.g., a WAIS, an MMPI) into an idiographic report. All elements of the report are considered, weighted in import, and presented. Unless one particular element stands out as unusually important, all of the findings are presented, integrated, and summarized in some more or less equally weighted fashion. Forensic reports, however, are frequently quite different in terms of balance. As noted, the crux of the report is frequently one piece of nomothetic data—the score on a structured risk assessment scale—or scores when multiple scales are used. All other data orbit around the results of the risk assessment scale, presumably supporting it. Data that fail to support the findings from the risk assessment scale don't make it into the orbit, or are used to "adjust" the findings. Although the evaluation and the report are presented as idiographic, the result is a vitiation of an idiographic analysis.

What differentiates a forensic report from a general clinical report is the psycholegal opinion in the former case. The interest of the court, at least in the case of SVP litigation, is laser-focused on only two issues—mental abnormality and likelihood of re-offending. Generally, the 2nd prong issue of mental abnormality is rubber stamped, leaving testimony focused almost entirely on the 3rd prong question of likelihood. Although the court *assumes* that the analysis underlying the opinion was idiographic, direct and cross-examination rarely probe the basis of the opinion beyond the routine defense of how or why particular scale items were scored as they were, or more esoteric questions about choice of life tables (in the case of the Static-99), studies reporting area under the curve (AUC) values on the scale that was used, confidence intervals for the life table estimate that was used, how to "adjust" or mitigate risk for treatment in prison, and so forth.

In no area of psychological assessment is a score used in isolation to determine a finding. This would most certainly be egregious in *forensic* psychological assessment, wherein a *full* assessment of risk would almost certainly include factors not represented on any one risk assessment scale. Although our response to this "core controversy" is admittedly imperfect, it partially addresses the criticism of Hart, Michie, and Cooke (2007), who stirred a hornet's nest by arguing that the margins of error in individual risk assessments of violence are so wide that the resulting predictions are "virtually meaningless" (p. 263). There is ample room for fault-finding with present practice. One might note, for example, that margins of error (or confidence intervals) assume that the sample has been randomly drawn from the population, a condition not easily met by most follow-up studies. The only reasonable response, from our perspective, given that the demand for risk assessments will continue unabated and that humans are unlikely to be replaced by a software program anytime soon, is to improve best practice methods. As stated, forensic evaluations rely for their accuracy on a synthesis of data from multiple sources, including group-based data. The examiner's opinion is defended by the weight of the evidence; the opinion, ultimately, is professional judgment. As Steve Hart (and numerous others) would undoubtedly attest, human judgment is fallible, indeed highly fallible about judgments of future violence. Error is a given. For the time being, however, the integration of nomothetic data into a comprehensive, idiographic evaluation approximates *best practice*. Best practice will only be realized in the courtroom, however, when the court demands it (i.e., when the judge expects a full, detailed explication of the expert's findings leading to, and supporting, her/his opinion). Then, and only then, will examination bring out *all* of the data (historical, clinical, and nomothetic) that the expert took into consideration, what data were deemed germane, what data were *not* considered and why, and what data were relied upon to support the expert's ultimate opinions.

Probabilistic Versus Categorical Expressions of Risk

As for the second debate (#2), probabilistic versus categorical expressions of risk, Monahan and Steadman (1996) acknowledged:

> We have long recommended that mental health professionals communicate risk assessments of violence in probabilistic terms . . . but the meteorological analogy forces us to rethink this long-held and taken-for-granted assumption and to ask the following question: Is communicating a risk estimate of a rare and severe behavioral event such as violence sufficiently analogous to communicating a risk estimate of a rare and severe weather event . . . that categorical rather than probabilistic risk messages should be preferred?
>
> (p. 935)

Monahan and Steadman (1996) offered the following hypothetical example of categorical risk messages:

Category 1: Low violence risk. Few risk factors are present.
Category 2: Moderate violence risk. Several risk factors are present.
Category 3: High violence risk. A number of key risk factors are present.
Category 4: Very high violence risk. Many key risk factors are present.

In his response to Monahan and Steadman (1996), Schopp (1996) took issue with the proposed categorical structure above, noting that,

> They extend the risk assessment roles of the psychologist from those of description and explanation to those of evaluation and prescription. Thus, this form of communication system entails an extension of the scope of psychologists' responsibilities from describing and explaining risk to interpreting and applying social values and priorities.
>
> (p. 941)

Schopp (1996) offered the example of risk assessment communication in categorical terms that applies to maximum-security forensic residents, the closest example to SVP civil committees. In this case, the evaluators are not the decision-makers. Descriptive categorical risk-related information is communicated "in combination with statements of absolute and relative probability" (p. 943). In this example, as noted, the process of assessing and communicating risk remains independent of the process of decision-making.

In the context of an SVP hearing, using the Static-99 as an example, if the defendant/respondent falls into Category 1 or 2, no probabilistic estimate should be necessary, since civil commitment is, at least in theory, intended only for the "most dangerous." For Categories 3 and 4, a probabilistic estimate would be included. If a categorical label is included, it should be a rationally derived one such as those illustrated above, not the cutoff-derived category that links the label directly to the probabilistic estimate. As we have stressed elsewhere, a categorical label, for whatever purpose it serves in furthering clarity, should be inclusive of *all* data gathered in the evaluation, not just the score on the risk assessment scale (i.e., the weight of all of the data should point to and support the label, not just the scale score).

The issue, of course, is more complicated than what was stated above. The court, ultimately, must make a binary risk "management" decision (SVP/not SVP). For the expert, the challenge is assimilating all of the risk-relevant evidence gathered in an evaluation and converting it into an estimation of the *degree* of risk posed. To reach a final conclusion, however, some decision threshold *must* be articulated (cf. Swets, 1992; Swets, Dawes, & Monahan, 2000). If the examiner's risk estimate falls at or above the decision threshold, appropriateness for civil commitment will be the probable finding. Where we set the decision threshold is, in and of itself, a decision that should be made by policy-makers (Monahan & Silver, 2003), not by the examiner. In reality, this is not the case. There is no consensus as to where the threshold should be for SVP civil commitment. Monahan and Silver (2003) surveyed 26 judges, inquiring "what is the lowest likelihood of violence to others that you would accept as fulfilling the dangerousness criterion for authorizing short-term civil commitment?" Five options were presented both in frequency and probability formats (1%, 8%, 26%, 56%, 76%, or the equivalency in frequency format). The mean and median response in probability format were 2.9 and 3.0, respectively (i.e., 26%). The mean and median response in frequency format were 2.4 and 2.0, respectively (i.e., around 8%).

Establishing an Optimal Positivity Criterion

The positivity criterion, as used in the present context, is a cutoff value on a risk scale that separates low (or tolerable) risk from high (or intolerable) risk. Stated otherwise, the positivity criterion determines the numerical value on the risk scale that is considered positive ("high" risk) and the value that would be considered negative ("low" risk). "Optimal" simply "means the best threshold [cutoff] for a given, well-defined, decision goal" (Swets, Dawes, & Monahan, 2000, p. 9). Swets et al. (2000) state that,

> The formula to specify the optimal decision threshold for this general goal of maximizing expected value was derived in the context of signal detection theory by Peterson, Birdsall, and Fox (1954). They showed . . . that the value of S [optimal] that maximizes expected value is expressed as the product of (1) the ratio of prior probabilities and (2) a ratio of benefits and costs.
>
> (p. 9)

Although establishing optimality may be neither difficult nor esoteric when used by physicians or aircraft manufacturers (Swets, 1992, p. 531), it is highly unlikely that *policy-makers* will deliberate the costs (of long-term imprisonment and Type II errors) and benefits (of guaranteeing no further victimization and Type I errors). Slovic, Fischhoff, and Lichtenstein (2000) posed the question "How safe is safe enough?" (p. 45). Slovic et al. (2000) point out that whatever approach to a risk-benefit analysis is taken, it must assume "that past behavior is a valid indicator of present preferences" (p. 45), which certainly holds true for all criminal defendants. Slovic et al. (2000) further point out, however, that the chosen approach must factor in "psychological research revealing systematic biases that may prevent an individual from making decisions that accurately reflect his or her 'true preferences'" (p. 45). We devoted most of Chapter 8 to discussing these systematic biases. Finally, Slovic et al. (2000) noted that the approach must not take for granted that the public has a variety of options from which to choose (e.g., unless children are forbade from leaving their home unless accompanied by an adult, it is impossible to achieve *zero* risk that the child will encounter a sex offender at daycare, at school, at the mall, at the movie theater, etc.). Slovic et al. (2000) recommended "risk-benefit trade-offs via judgmental techniques" (p. 46). Stated otherwise, we must develop measures of perceived risk and perceived benefit counterbalanced by desired risk and actual risk. In other words, our perceived risk and benefit should, ideally, be in sync with, or at least approximate, empirical determinations of risk and benefit. Parents routinely, if not unconsciously, make the decision that the perceived benefit of going to school well outweighs the perceived risk of encountering a sex offender. Other decisions are more difficult (e.g., allowing my child to go to the mall with friends, allowing my child to walk to the mall or to a friend's house), because the perceived benefit is far less clear relative to the perceived risk. In a forensic context, these decisions rest with the judge (i.e., deliberation over balancing Type I and Type II errors is up to the judge).

We must point out the obvious "gray zone" problem with establishing a positivity criterion for SVP risk scales. Given the natural continuum of risk, all risk scales will have reasonably well-defined cutoffs for positivity (e.g., a Static-99 score of 6 or more) and negativity (perhaps a Static-99 score of 2 or less). Numerical values that lie in between fall in the gray zone. There must be a translatable connection between the probabilistic estimate and the decision threshold. Since the legal criterion is binary, a cutoff value for the decision threshold must be adopted and that value, in practice, may move up or down, exposing increased error in either direction. As the cutoff value moves down (e.g., from a score of 6 to a score of 5 or 4), the false positive error rate goes up. As the cutoff moves up (e.g., to a score above 6), the false negative error rate goes up. Moving the threshold up rarely happens, but moving it down is common. Changing the criterion for a "positive" (high-risk) result will always affect both sensitivity and specificity. This trade-off is illustrated in Table 10.1 below.

The table is from a study that examined risk factors associated with recidivism among extra-familial child molesters (Prentky, Knight, & Lee, 1997). The table includes a range of prior probabilities with associated sensitivity and specificity values for each. As the prior probability changes, so does sensitivity and specificity. The optimal prior probability for predicting sexual re-offense in this sample using this composite of risk predictors was .30 (sensitivity = .78; specificity = .67). As the prior probability decreases, sensitivity goes up and specificity goes down. As the prior probability increases, sensitivity goes down and specificity goes up. Logically, this makes sense. Sensitivity (TP / TP+FN × 100%) or *hit rate* is the proportion of recidivists that are correctly predicted. When the prior probability is quite low, most of the truly dangerous offenders will be correctly classified (true positive) since there are very few of them. If the estimated prior probability, for example, is 5%, most of the five truly dangerous offenders in a hypothetical sample of 100 are likely to be

Table 10.1 Sensitivity and specificity values for different prior probabilities

Prior probability	*Sexual offense (C statistic = 0.778)*		*Nonsexual victim-involved offense (C statistic = 0.787)*		*Violent offense (C statistic = 0.787)*	
	Sensitivity	*Specificity*	*Sensitivity*	*Specificity*	*Sensitivity*	*Specificity*
0.05	1.00	0.03	0.90	0.33	1.00	0.15
0.10	1.00	0.11	0.84	0.52	0.82	0.47
0.15	0.98	0.19	0.68	0.70	0.59	0.69
0.20	0.90	0.36	0.68	0.80	0.47	0.81
0.25	0.83	0.52	0.58	0.86	0.41	0.90
0.30	0.78	0.67	0.53	0.88	0.35	0.95
0.40	0.60	0.82	0.42	0.95	0.12	0.97
0.45	0.50	0.86	0.26	0.95	0.12	0.98
0.50	0.45	0.93	0.21	0.99	0.06	0.99
0.60	0.30	0.95	0.11	1.00	0.06	1.00
0.70	0.25	0.96	0.05	1.00	0.06	1.00
0.80	0.13	0.97	0.05	1.00	0.06	1.00
0.90	0.08	0.99	0.05	1.00	0.06	1.00

Notes
Sensitivity = TP/(TP + FP); Specificity = TN/(TN + FN). TP = true positive; FP = false positive; TN = true negative; FN = false negative (Prentky, Knight, & Lee, 1997).

classified correctly as dangerous. In a sample with so few *truly* dangerous offenders, it is far more likely that we will err in the direction of classifying many of the *not* dangerous offenders as dangerous (false positive).

By contrast, when the prior probability is high, specificity will be high (and sensitivity low). In our hypothetical sample of 100, instead of 5 truly dangerous offenders, we estimate there will be 80 truly dangerous offenders. When a large proportion of the offenders are estimated to be dangerous (i.e., a high prior probability), the risk scale will likely classify most of the 20 non-dangerous offenders correctly and misclassify a large proportion of the 80 truly dangerous offenders as *not* dangerous.

Risk scales with good discrimination have high true positive rates and relatively low false positive rates (i.e., high sensitivity).

As Swets (1992), pointed out, the positivity criterion can be set anywhere along the scale, thereby allowing the user "to choose the particular criterion that is best for a given purpose and best for the specific situation at hand" (p. 522). Not surprisingly, this is what experts tend to do. SVP litigation often rests on arbitrarily selected cutoff scores used by each examiner, influenced, of course, by the side they are on. When experts render findings using different thresholds, it is most likely to occur with gray zone values (e.g., Static-99 scores of 4 or 5), wherein the potential for error is increased. Moreover, we would speculate that the nature of the error will differ for defense and prosecution experts when they adopt a different criterion. For example, if the respondent's score is 5, the prosecution expert is likely to use 5 as the criterion, while the defense expert is likely to use 6 as the criterion.

For these gray zone values, reporting the stratum-specific likelihood ratio (SSLR) is recommended. We calculate the likelihood ratio (LR) for particular test results (i.e., strata) without aggregating the results of one stratum with those of another. Calculating an LR is quite simple: LR = P(A | Trait) / P(A | No trait). In the present context, "A" is a score on a risk assessment scale, and the "trait" is high risk or *dangerousness*. We simply divide the probability of a score on a risk scale given the condition of high risk by the probability of that same score given a condition of not high risk. Using, as an example, a Static-99 score of 4:

$$\text{SSLR} = \frac{\text{Probability of a score of 4 given High Risk}}{\text{Probability of a score of 4 given Not High Risk}}$$

For a given sample, this translates to: [Proportion of the sample with a Static-99 score of 4 | R+] / [Proportion of the sample with a Static-99 score of 4 | R–], with R+ and R– being high or low risk. The SSLR can be reported for each of the categories or bins in a life table. The SSLR can inform users to what degree falling into a particular category alters the odds of re-offending. As noted, the LR is stratum-specific (i.e., specific to the category or bin that the defendant/respondent is in) and specific to the reference sample used in establishing probability estimates for each of the categories.

In discussing sources of potential estimation error, most obviously variable sample base rates, Mossman (2006) described another

> potential source of estimation error by showing that a risk scale known to be "valid" in several populations can have varying interpretations—that is, can have different probabilities of recidivism associated with each particular score—because the scale behaves inconsistently across these populations.
>
> (p. 60)

It should be pointed out that Mossman (2006) gave examples of how LRs associated with specific scores on risk scales may not be "stable" across populations. Mossman noted that "this phenomenon can occur even when the scales appear to have similar accuracies (as measured using the ROC index AUC) and retain their capacity to rank participants' relative risks of recidivism" (p. 60).

Mossman advised that,

> a score on an actuarial scale should alter an evaluator's belief about an evaluee's odds of recidivism from what the evaluator would believe without having the score. But without knowing the base rate of recidivism or the scale's properties in the population from which the evaluee is drawn, a score on an actuarial instrument only tells us where an evaluee ranks within his population (e.g., his rank among individuals released from a particular prison)—assuming that the scale possesses discriminative capacity for that evaluee's population.
>
> (pp. 60–61)

Importantly, Mossman (2006) went on to recommend that,

> Researchers should consider amplifying their reports on the performance of risk assessment instruments to include not only overall descriptions of accuracy (e.g., correlations and ROC areas), but statistics that characterize levels of discriminative capacity associated with specific test scores (e.g., likelihood ratios as in this article, or other statistics with similar functions) without conflating test performance and base rates.
>
> (p. 61)

The advantages of doing so, Mossman concluded, are at least twofold: (1) dissuading forensic practitioners from assuming that the estimated probabilities of re-offense associated with risk scores derived from one population apply to other populations that may have different base rates and different risk-relevant characteristics, and (2) encouraging forensic practitioners to be mindful that sample base rates and discriminative properties of risk scales are *not equivalent*.

It seems likely that, for the fact-finder, there is no meaningful empirical distinction between gray zone categories carrying labels such as "low moderate" versus "moderate" or "moderate" versus "high moderate." It is clear, however, that labels frequently provide a conveyance of information to jurors and to the court that is quite independent of probabilistic estimates, which, as we have already suggested, may obfuscate more than elucidate. The words "high moderate," for instance, are likely to be far more influential to most jurors than a probabilistic estimate of "35%."

When conveying conclusions, we recommend that practitioners be cautious about applying risk-level labels and refrain from using any labels that cannot be supported by the data (e.g., translating precisely what "high moderate" means in terms of the actual risk factors for a given individual—i.e., "unpacking"). For the sake of transparency, we recommend *never* affixing a label based *solely* on the cutoff score of a risk scale. If a label is used, most of the evidence gathered in an evaluation should support the label (i.e., the full evidentiary weight from the evaluation defines and explains the label, *not* just the scale score).

Application to Juveniles

The most problematic concern with individual-specific risk-level labels in juveniles is the temporal stability of the label. The label may define the youth long after it is no longer valid. Since risk assessments should be revisited as frequently as every two to three months, and certainly every six months, the label may well change; the original label, however, remains on the record forever, effectively carved in stone. Stated otherwise, normative data do not account for the fluidity of adolescent development and environmental flux. Furthermore, labels increase error. Since we are placing all youth into one of three or four bins (e.g., low, medium, or high), the inevitable result is a large number of youth classified as *high* when they are not, resulting in false positive judgment errors and the attendant serious unintended, negative consequences of such a classification. False negative errors may also occur when the label, derived from the results of completing a risk scale, reflects a "low" classification but a careful, idiographic analysis of risk reveals greater risk to re-offend.

Similarly, a score derived from a risk scale, or the labeled bin that the score falls into, should never be used in isolation to support or justify subjecting a youth to long-term statutory requirements, such as registration or community notification (ATSA, 2012). At the present time, Monahan and Steadman's (1996) suggestion of translating categorical labels in terms of the number of risk factors observed to be present would seem to be a reasonable, though not optimal, method for communicating magnitude of risk. The assumption that the more risk factors rated as present equates to greater risk is accurate most of the time but treats all risk factors as equally weighted in predictive importance. A risk factor such as prior nonsexual hands-on criminal offenses or prior sexual hands-on criminal offenses will carry different predictive weight if the known history is "1" or "5."

A troubling concern is raised with the introduction of life tables with probabilistic estimates of re-offense. These life tables, derived from reference groups or development samples of actuarial risk scales, place the individual into a bin based on the scale score. As we noted earlier, these scores are particularly subject to change in adolescents. Unlike the adult actuarial risk assessment tables, which reflect estimates going over many years, juveniles must be re-assessed frequently and any meaningful "prediction" should not be for more than 12 months. What is of greater concern, however, is the potential for misuse or abuse of any estimate derived from a life table. Like a cutoff score with an associated label (low, moderate, high), life table estimates pose a similar, if not greater, danger of becoming an inexpungible, defining feature of the youth, regardless of its accuracy.

Idiographic Versus Nomothetic Evaluations

Although this has not been singled out as another debate or area of controversy, it overlaps considerably with the question of group-level data being applied to individuals. An idiographic approach, both in forensic and clinical practice, focuses on one unique individual. Gathered information focuses on that one individual. A nomothetic approach, both in forensic and clinical practice, is quantitative, comparing the individual to a "class," or group or cohort. Gathered data, typically from tests, questionnaires or scales (including risk assessment scales), provide norms against which the individual is compared. Heilbrun, Nezu, Keeney, Chung, and Wasserman (1998) clearly articulated the need for an individualized, idiographic approach to assessment, intervention, and risk management, employing an "idiographic application of nomothetic principles" (p. 167). As we subsequently discuss, an idiographic approach to conducting an evaluation is both comprehensive in the data gathered from multiple sources and individualized in the sense that it targets key issues or concerns about a particular individual. A critical part of the data gathered is typically nomothetic, or norm-based.

In sex offender evaluations, there is no defensible substitute for an idiographic evaluation that addresses individual, contextual, and situational dynamic needs and protective factors that may exacerbate or mitigate risk, as well as the extent to which these factors are currently present or are likely to be present in the near future, *in combination with nomothetic data*. DeMatteo, Batastini, Foster, and Hunt (2010) provided helpful guidelines for integrating idiographic and nomothetic data, including (1) the use of structured professional judgment measures, (2) a critical evaluation of the risk factors determined to be present, (3) using an anamnestic approach to gather client-specific information relevant to the assessment of risk (Heilbrun et al., 2010; Melton et al., 2007), (4) using a model to guide data collection and interpretation (Heilbrun, 2001), and (5) being aware of heuristics that contribute to bias, including over or under-emphasis of specific risk and/or protective factors.

Kirk Heilbrun and his colleagues (1998) proposed a model for integrating assessment, intervention, and decision-making, noting,

> We cannot simply apply nomothetic principles to every offender; we must use the nomothetic empirical data available for each individual case. As such, each clinician is designing the best

> educated guess for each idiographic risk management plan. It logically follows that the evaluation measures used for assessing progress and prescribing continued management are also individualized. . . . The rationale for idiographic application of nomothetic principles is based on the philosophy that a treatment plan should be tailor-made to fit the dynamic risk factors associated with an individual case.
>
> (p. 167)

By linking assessment, intervention, and decision-making in one model, Heilbrun et al. argued, clinicians can more effectively communicate with decision-makers.

Risk-Need-Responsivity

Although the risk management model that Heilbrun et al. proposed is the one developed by Christine Nezu and Arthur Nezu (Nezu & Nezu, 1989) for clinical decision-making, the underlying principles bear much similarity to the risk-need-responsivity (RNR) model that has been discussed in the criminal justice literature for decades and widely applied to criminal justice populations (cf. Andrews & Bonta, 2010). RNR is an integrative, unifying model that underscores the criticality of *all* phases: comprehensive assessment of needs as well as risk, evaluation-driven treatment plans and all other client-specific interventions, and the "responsivity interface" between "needs" and interventions.

According to the risk principle, the greatest reductions in recidivism will result when individuals who present with the most risk factors associated with re-offending receive the most intensive and relevant interventions. Providing intensive interventions to those with relatively few risks may not only deplete scarce resources but also do more harm than good, particularly when individuals with few risk factors are mixed with those that have substantial risk factors and intervention needs and may model antisocial behaviors or exploit or abuse others.

The need principle asserts that effective interventions are those that target dynamic, risk-relevant factors ("criminogenic" needs). Although some risk factors are historical (static), the need principle directs the focus to factors that can change, and if changed, can decrease risk. Risk reduction requires clinicians to adhere to this principle while facilitating protective factors that increase pro-social behavior.

The responsivity principle emphasizes that interventions are most likely to be effective when they are designed in ways that match individual learning styles, cognitive or developmental challenges, psychological characteristics, motivation to change, and relevant cultural, gender, and other factors, such as individual and family characteristics that affect an adolescent and his/her family's ability to positively engage in and respond to interventions.

Subsequent research has shown that programs that apply these principles of effective intervention have greater reductions in criminal recidivism among both adults (Andrews & Bonta, 2010) and juveniles (e.g., Pealer & Latessa, 2004), including adults and juveniles who have committed sexual offenses (Hanson, Bourgon, Helmus, & Hodgson, 2009).

To be most useful, and consistent with the RNR model, assessments of adolescents who have sexually offended consider factors associated with sexual and nonsexual re-offending by either increasing the likelihood of re-offending (risk factors) or mitigating the risk (protective factors). This consideration focuses not only on individual (ontogenic) factors but also extends to family (microsystemic), community (exosystemic), and cultural (macrosystemic) factors (Bronfrenbrenner, 1979; Belsky, 1980). Additionally, although historical factors that are associated with recidivism or desistence may be useful for assessing risk and understanding needs, identifying dynamic risk and protective factors are essential as they are primary targets for intervention. In addition, assessments that identify traits or characteristics which, if effectively addressed, can enhance treatment responsiveness (i.e., treatment responsivity) are needed as well.

Additionally, there are special issues that may require assessment because they are related to the offending, intervention priorities, or facilitating treatment responsiveness. Such factors may include substance abuse, trauma symptoms, cognitive functioning, and serious mental health issues. Similarly, socioecological factors that can affect service delivery and treatment responsiveness must be considered (e.g., placement stability and support systems if in the community; for juveniles, caregivers' willingness to actively supervise the youth or be involved in his/her treatment; community sentiment and response/community integration problems; integration-related interpersonal problems at school or work; cultural practices and beliefs). By considering these varied factors, assessments that adhere to RNR principles can provide an individualized, and more effective, road map for interventions.

Sifting Through Idiographic and Nomothetic Data to Arrive at Final Opinions

The Hypothesis-Testing Model

We find ourselves facing something of a paradox. After numerous scholarly papers warning that pure clinical judgment of dangerousness was markedly suboptimal, the wave of scholarly opinion swept professional forensic practice to the empirical end of the continuum. By and large, evidence-based forensic practice now prescribes the use of empirically derived risk assessment scales when rendering judgments about dangerousness. The seeming paradox is that having achieved the goal of moving forensic practitioners into the empirical end zone, the net achievement, at least in the adjudication of civil commitment petitions against sex offenders, is naught. That is, the quality of testimonial evidence does not appear to have benefitted substantially from this newfound infusion of empiricism. Rather than science informing and guiding judgment, it provides a patina of legitimacy.

A common approach to evaluating an attorney's client is to begin with the premise that the client is whatever the attorney wants their client to be—guilty or innocent, dangerous or not dangerous, high risk or low risk, etc. We begin not with an open mind to all possibilities, but with an *a priori* belief in only one possibility. The resulting evaluation becomes an exercise in marshaling evidence to support the *a priori* belief. This is a close-minded system that denies the court objectivity, as well as the expert's presumed expertise. We hasten to add that forensic practice is not as infelicitous as we make it sound. Many practitioners will occasionally reach findings contrary to the wishes of the retaining attorney. We offer a simple strategy, however, for insulating the practitioner and making "occasionally" a less than awkward moment.

Law, as a concept, presents with at least two distinct meanings: (1) Society's laws are prescriptive, stating what may or may not be done; these laws must be "breakable." Indeed, if a law could not be broken, there would be little point in having the law, and (2) Nature's laws, which are descriptive. Laws of nature tell us what does or does not happen under certain conditions. As Magee (1975) pointed out, water does not boil at 100°C because it has been ordered to. Natural laws purport to be factual, either supported or not by empirical evidence. For Sir Karl Popper, the answer was clear—falsifiability is the demarcation, the bright line in the sand, between true science and non-science (Popper, 1975). Although scientific theories—say the theory that all swans are white—may never be conclusively or irrefutably verified (all swans observed in Europe were white until black swans were eventually seen in Australia), scientific theories must be falsifiable.

What relevance does this have for forensic practitioners? Courts adjudicate violations of prescriptive laws with clear recognition that the evidence need not be conclusive or irrefutable. The evidence, at least in criminal matters, needs to be *beyond reasonable doubt*. Similarly, the evidence that forensic examiners rely upon in their opinions is never conclusive or irrefutable. In fact, the pool of evidence is often mixed, with facts pointing in both directions, frequently with different probative value. There is a tendency for examiners to overweight facts that support their *a priori* position and underweight, or worse ignore, facts that don't.

We offer a recommendation in the form of an assertion. The "process" of conducting a forensic evaluation should take the form of a critical element of the scientific method: hypothesis-testing. Such a recommendation can be traced for its support to Sir William Blackstone's (1765–1769) 18th-century *Commentaries on the Laws of England*, wherein he urged the prospective lawyer "to lay the foundation of his future labours in a solid scientific method" and reminded him that "the law is to be considered not only as matter of practice, but also as a rational science" (Boorstin, 1958, p. 20). Thus, we strongly endorse the recommendation of Phil Witt and his colleagues (Witt, Dattilio, & Bradford, 2011) that evaluators follow a hypothesis-testing model. The null hypothesis at the outset is that there is no difference in *dangerousness* or *risk* between the client and population from which the client was drawn. We recommend that all forensic evaluations begin with the null hypothesis, whether they are for the prosecution or the defense. Indeed, an examiner who is working for the prosecution will have an even stronger case in terms of credibility when beginning with the null hypothesis. The task going forward in the evaluation is to test a series of alternate hypotheses that are germane to the case with all available data (discovery). These alternate hypotheses might "test" whether the client's:

a Prior history of delinquency and antisocial behavior contributes to a rejection of the null hypothesis (Ho);
b History of prior sexual conduct contributes to a rejection of Ho;
c Governing sexual offense (nature of) contributes to a rejection of Ho;
d Other evidence of sexual preoccupation or sexual deviance contributes to a rejection of Ho.

On a case-by-case basis, these alternate hypotheses are likely to be much more detailed and case-specific. The distinct advantage of a hypothesis-testing approach is that it compels full consideration of all available evidence, and it results in a strong, evidence-linked defense of the expert's findings and opinions. In one word, it will improve *transparency*.

A hypothesis-testing approach will further permit a more conscious deliberation over error. In conventional hypothesis-testing, there are two types of errors. A Type I error (α error) occurs when the null hypothesis is rejected when it is in fact true. In our case, the hypothesis that the client was not different from most other sex offenders with respect to dangerousness (or risk) is rejected in favor of a finding that he *is* more dangerous (or higher risk); that finding is in error (i.e., the examiner was wrong, erring in the direction of finding the client dangerous when the client was not).

A Type II error (β error) occurs when the null hypothesis is *not* rejected when it is in fact false. The hypothesis that the client was not different from most other sex offenders with respect to dangerousness (or risk) is supported when the client was in fact *different* (i.e., the client was more dangerous or at greater risk, and the examiner was wrong).

In practice (statistical hypothesis-testing), Type I and Type II errors are inversely related. The smaller the risk of one, the higher the risk of the other. We would surmise that a similar tendency exists among examiners, namely a greater likelihood of making one type of error or the other. It is, of course, the Type I or alpha error that we would expect to be most common, especially among examiners working for the prosecution, though we would expect it to be common among examiners working for the defense as well. Addressing forthrightly the possibility of error demands greater attention to the full range of possibilities, the full panoply of evidence, and—hopefully—greater rigor in "testing" one's own hypotheses.

A Final Plea for Probabilistic Thinking

> We are capable of sending a spacecraft to Mars, but we are incapable of having criminal trials managed by the basic laws of probability—yet evidence is clearly a probabilistic notion.
>
> (Taleb, 2005, p. 203)

As Taleb reminds us, there is very little about the entire process of adjudication of offenders that escapes probabilistic judgments, including virtually all decisions about the defendant's mental state and behavior.

Silver (2012) noted, in an atypically whimsical fashion, that, "We have big brains, but we live in an incomprehensibly large universe. The virtue in thinking probabilistically is that you will force yourself to stop and smell the data—slow down, and consider the imperfections in your thinking" (p. 450). Having so introduced our plea, we offer three simple points about Bayes, in narrative only for our more innumerate readers, extracted from Silver (2012):

"Bayes's theorem requires us to state—explicitly—how likely we believe an event is to occur *before* we begin to weigh the evidence. It calls this estimate a prior belief" (p. 451). This calls from an estimated base rate, which typically comes from an actuarial or structured professional judgment risk scale.

"Bayes's theorem says we should update our forecasts any time we are presented with new information" (p. 452). Although all "new" information usually comes in roughly the same time frame while conducting the evaluation (all discovery, interview, testing, third-party contacts), additional (new) information may be forthcoming *after* the evaluation is completed, sometimes months afterwards. This new information may be of sufficient importance to change our "forecast."

"Bayes's theorem encourages us to be disciplined about how we weigh new information" (p. 452). New information must be scrutinized critically. Much new information is "noisy" (biased) or illusory (uncorrelated with the criterion). We may be inclined to place undue weight on biased information or to attribute risk-relevance to what is illusory. The opposite bias is perhaps even more serious: being overly invested in an outcome (SVP/not SVP) and failing to recognize or acknowledge that one's opinion must change. Although it can take courage to change one's mind midstream, it is a vital indicator of scientific and professional integrity. As Silver put it, "failing to change our forecast because we risk embarrassment by doing so—that reveals a lack of courage" (p. 66). The principle was cleverly and pithily expressed by the brilliant British economist, Lord J. M. Keynes, who has been variously (and often) quoted as saying: "When the facts change, I change my mind. What do you do sir?"

Posner (2010) discussed "the trouble people sometimes have changing their minds until the evidence is overwhelming—at which point it may be too late to take action" (p. 111). Commonly referred to as *change blindness*, it "happens when we filter out the implications of new information rather than assigning them even partial weight in our thinking" (Posner, 2010, p. 120). When the gravitational pull to support the retaining attorney is strong—as it typically is—we don't "filter out" as much as we "reframe" new *un*supportive evidence, thereby diminishing its importance (i.e., its weight). The same phenomenon has also been referred to as the *boiling frog syndrome*—if you place a frog in a pot of boiling water, it will leap out; if you place a frog in a pot of room temperature water and put the pot on the stove, the frog will remain in the water until it ultimately dies, because "new information" (gradually increasing temperature of the water) is filtered out or ignored.

Posner (2010) pointed out that a phenomenon far better known to psychologists—cognitive dissonance—may manifest itself as change blindness. Change blindness is a metaphor for how humans respond to threats. We have evolved to detect acute changes that pose an imminent threat (the equivalent of being thrown into a pot of boiling water), but not slow, gradual changes. The incremental addition of new information is likely to be ignored in the same way that other gradual changes are ignored. As Posner said, we have trouble changing our minds until the evidence is overwhelming (the water is boiling)—at which point it may be too late to take action (change our opinion). This is a not infrequent occurrence in drawn-out cases with prodigious amounts of discovery and a lengthy interval between the initial review of discovery, the evaluation, and the eventual trial. In the interim, additional evidence may trickle in that supports or undermines our opinion. Unsupportive evidence, especially when it arrives in increments, is likely to be ignored.

One final comment about data concerns its presence. There are times when the *absence* of data is more concerning than the presence of data, much of which may be highly noisy or irrelevant, or unrelated. As we have come to learn in the world of terrorism, the absence of a "signal" may be more worrisome than its presence. In the world of Sherlock Holmes we again learned that it was the absence of evidence, rather than its presence, that was critical (e.g., the case of Silver Blaze). We may overvalue—or overweigh—what is transparently obvious and undervalue, ignore, or worse, be blind to what we don't "see." What we don't see is *not* what we know we would like but don't have access to (e.g., a third party that we would like to speak to but can't be found). What we don't see is far more subtle (e.g., failing to notice important contradictions or inconsistencies in the data). Sifting through mountains of discovery is akin to being a data sleuth, taking copious notes on all seemingly relevant facts and then matching the facts for consistency. Once assembled, the extant data form a partially complete puzzle. The missing pieces of the puzzle are often the questions we overlook or fail to ask, or simply the pieces that will forever be inaccessible. The pieces of the puzzle that don't fit together (because they contradict one another in some fashion) are inconsistencies that we may have failed to follow up on. The task is something like opening a box containing a jigsaw puzzle with 500 pieces. As we begin to assemble the puzzle, we discover that there are only 400 pieces in the box. Some of the pieces don't seem to fit together well, and others seem as though they belong to a different puzzle. We must assemble what we can and "fill in" as best we can what is not in the box to capture as accurate a picture of the defendant as possible.

In one of my most difficult and disturbing cases in recent memory, I (RAP) agreed to evaluate a man who had been petitioned for civil commitment in an eastern state. The man had a single known sexual offense, the index offense. It involved the intoxication-facilitated sexual assault of a young juvenile girl. The assault included several unusual features that ordinarily would raise flags, such as shaving the victim's pubic hair. While the man was serving time in prison for this offense he prepared a "diary." The incident that precipitated the petition for civil commitment was this lengthy (100+ pages) diary of highly explicit narrative and drawings describing and depicting all manner of rather bizarre and sadistic sexual acts. The diary was found by a corrections officer and turned over to the district attorney. The somewhat odd nature of the index offense coupled with the diary caused me considerable concern, raising a number of troubling questions, such as the predictive weight accorded to fantasy and the probative value of the diary. Fantasy alone never appears on risk assessment scales, and generally is only considered when fantasy content is expressed in behavior. It was this latter point, the peculiar nature of some of the sexual acts in the index offense, that worried me. The man's history included a reported year-long relationship with a woman on the west coast. The existence of this woman was confirmed by the prison visitor's log, indicating that this individual had indeed paid one brief visit, lasting only a few hours. I told the attorney that I needed to speak with her. The man signed a release for me, and gave me the woman's address. The attorney retained the services of a private detective who, after considerable effort, was unable to locate her. The absence of what I considered a critical piece of evidence was decisive. I informed the attorney that I could not be a strong witness and should probably not be called to testify.

One final word to the wise from the master of prediction:

> Prediction is difficult for us for the same reason that it so important: it is where objective and subjective reality intersect. Distinguishing the signal from the noise requires both scientific knowledge and self-knowledge: *the serenity to accept the things we cannot predict, the courage to predict the things we can, and the wisdom to know the difference.*
>
> (Silver, 2012, p. 453, adapted by Silver from Reinhold Niebuhr's Serenity Prayer)

Human judgment is inherently subject to bias. On those occasions when human judgment is vitally important and the stakes are high, and the conditions uncertain, routing out bias becomes paramount. In a highly charged, adversarial courtroom, the temptation is to fight to defend one's opinion by digging in one's intellectual heels and refusing to give an inch. There are times when fighting partisan battles to the utmost is heroic and gallant. SVP litigation is not one of them. We have not only a professional but an ethical obligation to the court—and to society—to rise above the clamor and provide the fact-finder with the most objective analysis of risk that the data permit. The "benefit of truthful testimony" was argued persuasively by Mossman (1994). If the data appear unreliable or are inadequate, we may reach the conclusion that *no conclusion* is the most ethical (and truthful) response. A conclusion founded on weak evidence may be worse than no conclusion at all. It would seem that the Hippocratic oath—*Primum non nocere* (First, do no harm)—applies to forensic examiners just as well as physicians.

Recommendations

Reinventing Risk Assessment: A Life-Span Perspective

We would like to end on a final futuristic note. In what must surely be acknowledged an "unnatural" developmental "quadfurcation," there are four wholly independent literatures on assessing the risk of sexually inappropriate, coercive, and aggressive behavior, depending on whether the subject population is children, juveniles, emerging adults (e.g., college students), or adults. Indeed, one might be inclined to conclude that children, juveniles, emerging adults, and adults are unrelated species. How do we conceive understanding adolescence without considering childhood? Similarly, fully understanding adult behavior does not *begin* at age 25. The pioneering research and transformative theoretical contributions of Terrie Moffitt (1993) linking early childhood events to adult criminal outcomes demonstrated the futility of segregating risk assessment into three or four discrete developmental tracks. This same observation was the basis for Sampson and Laub's (2005) critically important life-course perspective on crime, noting that trajectories of criminal behavior—both persistence and desistence—could best be understood from a developmental (age-graded) theoretical perspective. The path that offenders take is *not*, in Sampson and Laub's words, one of unfolding inevitability. Sampson and Laub asserted the importance of human agency, the freedom to make choices and the freedom to "act."

From a psychological perspective, Albert Bandura (2006) posited an "agentic theory of human development, adaptation, and change" in which humans are "unique in their power to shape their life circumstances and the courses their lives take" (p. 164). In Bandura's psychology of human agency, "people are contributors to their life circumstances, not just products of them" (p. 164). Developmental patterns of general (nonsexual) criminal behavior are clear: with the exception of the small number of career criminals and chronic persisters, most offenders initiate delinquent behavior in early to mid-adolescence, persist into late adolescence and their early-20s, and desist by their mid-20s.

The pattern for those with *sexually* problematic and *sexually* aggressive behavior has similar pathways but is more complex. Sexually problematic behaviors first observed in childhood are likely to persist into adolescence if not remediated. Sexually inappropriate and aggressive behaviors with onset in adolescence are more likely to desist by late adolescence. Those that persist into the early-20s are likely to desist by the mid- to late-20s. Although few in number, some individuals will persist into adulthood and are chronic offenders. It is this small group of sex offenders that appear to be disproportionately more likely to engage in coercive and forced sexual behavior (Boutwell, Barnes, & Beaver, 2013). The study by Boutwell et al. (2013) is a particularly interesting one, since it examined three waves of data gathered from the National Longitudinal Study of Adolescent Health, a prospective longitudinal study examining a nationally representative sample of adolescents (Harris, 2009). Fourteen percent of the males in their sample were classified as persistent, more or less consistent with the 10% figure reported by Moffitt (1993) in her original paper.

The only study of which we are aware that begins to address these issues from a longitudinal perspective was retrospective, gathering data on 250 sex offenders who were 36 years old or older at the time of their release from prison (Lussier, Tzoumakis, Cale, & Amirault, 2010). The average age was 45. Data gathered included a semi-structured interview as well as prison files. Lussier et al. (2010) identified four offending trajectories over four age periods: 12–17, 18–23, 24–29, and 30–35. These four age epochs essentially span three of the four major "populations" of sex offenders just alluded to—adolescents, emerging adults, and adults. The investigators found four discrete trajectories: (1) most offenders (56%) fell into the "very low rate" category, with a trajectory that reflected a very low rate of criminal activity over time (i.e., very stable); these offenders committed, on average, less than one offense per age period, (2) the second trajectory accounted for 26% and was referred to as the "low-rate desistors." These offenders increased their offending in early adulthood (18–23) and then gradually decreased their offending to an average of one offense by the last age period (30–35), (3) the third trajectory was referred to as the "late bloomers." These offenders evidenced a very low offense rate during the first two age periods, only to gradually increase to an average of three offenses by the last age period (30–35), and (4) the fourth trajectory was referred to as the "high-rate chronics." The high-rate chronics, as the name implies, was the only group with a high level of offending during the earliest age group (12–17), increasing and peaking in offending frequency during the second age group (average of over five offenses), and beginning a downward linear trend to the final age group (with an average of three offenses by the early 30s). It is this last group that would correspond to the life-course persistent offenders in Moffitt's taxonomy. As Lussier et al. (2010) rightly point out,

> Current actuarial tools aggregate the information characterizing the criminal history of sex offenders. By aggregating the information found in the criminal history of these men, much information is lost about the dynamic aspect of it. This is based on the false assumption that the criminal history is a static, historical risk factor that explains the risk of recidivism. Clearly, past criminal behavior indicates the risk of future criminal involvement; however so do dynamic aspects of offending, a point raised by developmentalists and life-course criminologists.
>
> (p. 163)

It seems ironic that criminologists should have something to tell psychologists about paying attention to the course of human development.

Despite hundreds of scholarly papers over the past half-century, we know remarkably little about the complexly nuanced epigenesis of those who engage in sexually aggressive behaviors. To this day we still speak in simplistic terms about whether the offender was "sexually abused" or "physically abused." Critical determinants of the impact of the abuse—morbidity factors, such as the age of onset of the abuse, the duration of the abuse, the relationship of the offender to the victim, and the seriousness or intrusiveness of the abuse—are infrequently considered. We may take note of "boundary violations" or domestic violence, but the extraordinarily complex interplay of life experiences over time is hopelessly lost. The principles of equifinality and multifinality (Cicchetti & Rogosch, 1996), derived from general systems theory (von Bertalanffy, 1968), clearly apply here. Equifinality implies the existence of a diversity of pathways, including chance events (nonlinear epigenesis), that may lead to the same outcome. Importantly, this assumes an *open system* (Mayr, 1988), "one where there is maintenance in change, dynamic order of processes, organization, self-regulation, etc." (Cicchetti & Rogosch, 1996, p. 597). In closed systems, outcome "is inextricably linked to and determined by the initial conditions; if either the conditions change or the processes are modified, then the end state will also be modified" (Cicchetti & Rogosch, 1996, p. 597). Clearly, we see instances of both, where multiplicity of "input," including chance encounters, define an open system, and where the *initial conditions* of adverse life experiences are so profound and impactful that some adverse outcome is highly predictable. It is the complex chemistry of interactive life events occurring during different developmental epochs that pose the greatest challenges for developmental psychopathologists.

Both equifinality and multifinality are readily demonstrated. In the case of multifinality, similar life events may lead to diverse outcomes. As mentioned above, not all child abuse is "created equal." Morbidity factors, as mentioned above, are highly influential in shaping the proximal and distal responses to the abuse, leading to different internalizing as well as externalizing outcomes. These morbidity factors apply to *all* forms of child abuse, not just sexual abuse. It has become accepted as a truism that the preponderance of child victims of sexual abuse do not go on to become sex offenders, presumably because of the nature of the abuse itself (e.g., the morbidity factors mentioned), as well as critical co-occurring or proximally occurring life events (e.g., the presence (or absence) of supportive, caring adults; the presence (or absence) of treatment, the self-esteem/ego-strength of the child, etc.).

In one of my more memorable cases demonstrating multifinality, one of us (RAP) was asked to evaluate a man with three *nonsexual* homicides of unknown *adult* women. During the course of an eight-hour evaluation, this man spoke candidly about the extreme sadistic abuse that he was subjected to by his mother when he was in the age range of 7 to 10. When he was 12 he ran away from home and was given "shelter" by an accommodating child molester who exchanged the rudiments of a home, support, and even vocational tutelage for sexual favors. When he was 14, he decided to return home. While hitchhiking home, he was picked up by a very large, gruff man who took him to an abandoned hunter's lodge in the woods and brutally raped him over a period of two days. Of all the sexual abuse that he suffered as a child and young adolescent, it was the initial abuse by his mother that was the catalyst for the rage that he unleashed, not at other children but at women. And it was the final rape at age 14 that provided the *method* for murder. He killed using a weapon that penetrated the victim's abdomen. His crystal clear memory of the rape, including olfactory memories of the rapist's sweat, was the searing pain that he felt in his stomach when he tried to stand after being raped. It is unlikely, upon hearing a homogenized summary of his childhood abuse (sexually abused by mother, lived with a child molester for several years, raped by a stranger), that his outcome would ever have been accurately forecast.

In the case of equifinality, diverse pathways may lead to the same or similar outcomes (sexually inappropriate, coercive, or aggressive behaviors). It is abundantly clear that the marked heterogeneity of sexual offenders reflects many different pathways leading to a similar outcome—sexual abuse of others. The heterogeneity of *all* those who engage in sexually problematic behaviors (children) and sexually assaultive behaviors (juveniles, emerging adults, adults) has become a truism in the field. Although we characterize outcomes similarly (e.g., all offenders who molest a child), there are important outcome differences—choosing known (as in the case of exclusive incest) vs. unknown victims, choosing victim gender (males or females) or not (both males and females), and expressing anger and violence toward the child vs. engaging in behaviors that reflect a distorted "love" relationship with the child. If we choose any one of these more differentiated outcomes, however, say an offender with multiple crimes involving the abduction and molestation of unknown boys, the pathways leading to that arguably more homogeneous outcome group will be different, in some cases markedly different.

Explanations for persistent sexually assaultive behavior have traditionally relied on exogenous factors, primarily adverse life experiences (maltreatment) in combination with—or leading to—delinquency, traits of antisociality, criminogenic cognitions, cognitions associated with hostile masculinity, rape myths, and *misogynistic* attitudes, association with *bad* peers, and, in the case of child molesters, immaturity, emotional incongruence, and deficits in social and interpersonal skills. All of these pieces of the puzzle are well known, amply documented, and present in highly varying degrees in different offenders.

A more difficult piece of the puzzle that generally occupies an integral place in the literature for both rapists and child molesters is sexual preoccupation/sexual drive/sexually deviant interests. Our understanding of the role of sexuality in sex offenders, both its normal and abnormal expression, is elusive, despite decades of earnest speculation and countless scholarly articles. A somewhat controversial explanation has been endogenous (biogenetic) factors (e.g., Lalumiere, Harris, Quinsey, & Rice, 2005). Using the same data set as Boutwell et al. (2013), Barnes,

Beaver, and Boutwell (2011) found evidence of a genetic basis for persistent offending; in fact, 80% of the variance in the classification of persistent offenders was attributable to genetic factors. The common traits associated with persistence, however, are many of the same traits associated with psychopathy—high degree of violence, chronic aggression, low or absent empathy and remorse, etc. Thus, persistence of early onset antisocial behavior, however it is expressed, includes traits similar to or the same as *psychopathy* and may have genetic roots. If a biogenetic explanation focuses on traits of psychopathy, we once again are left only speculating as to the role of sexuality—be it an excessive need for gratification (sexual preoccupation or drive), a preference for impersonal sex (without any emotional attachment), or a preference for deviant/atypical objects (children). In the short term, endogenous factors contributing to persistent sexually aggressive behavior are unlikely to replace exogenous factors in psycholegal risk analysis. It is those observable behavioral traits that form different empirically sturdy pathways that must be translated into risk factors for the *full* developmental range of offenders.

As forensic clinicians, we occasionally must confront the role of fantasy in risk analysis. Fantasy, without any known accompanying behavior, tells us relatively little. Fantasy alone is not criminalized, although the line with Internet child pornography is admittedly getting increasingly blurred. We typically anchor our risk assessments with behavior; fantasy *with* behavior can tell us something about what future behavior might "look like." Fantasy without behavior reminds us that if we were all imprisoned for our criminal fantasies, most of us would be in jail. The point here is that our capacity to control our cognitive urges (fantasies), no matter what those urges may be, is critical. From any developmental perspective, behavioral control increases as a function of age. Infants have exceptionally limited control. Tantruming in young children evidences impaired control that is frequently subject to parental "interventions." As we age, we develop ever-increasing hard-wired capacity, as well as learned skills, for monitoring and controlling our urges to engage in unwanted, inappropriate, or destructive behavior. This gradual emergence of control over goal-directed behavior is the hallmark of normal development. Impaired control in adolescence is understood as a normal part of adolescent development. Impaired control in adulthood, however, is a quintessential feature of antisocial behavior. Behavior control is a universally accepted feature both of normal development and of criminal behavior. Indeed, self-control is vitally important across a wide range of outcomes, from criminal behavior and substance abuse to physical health, personal finances, and prosperity (Moffitt et al., 2011; Moffitt, Poulton, & Caspi, 2013).

Although it is well beyond the scope of this book, what is urgently needed, and what we advocate in the strongest terms, is an understanding and perspective on risk that is part of a coherent theoretical model of sexually inappropriate and aggressive behavior, a model that is *developmental* and embraces *all* principal paths from age of onset to desistence. Thus far, the only "call" for a view of the development of sexual aggression through a life-span lens is that of Barbaree, Blanchard, and Langton (2003). The study by Barbaree and his colleagues (2003) demonstrated, as we reported earlier in the book, that risk (i.e., recidivism) declines as a function of age. Thus far, however, this life-span perspective embraces only the full adult range, with the average age being roughly 35. A prospective, life-span approach that we advocate would embrace the full continuum of development. Such a perspective on risk recognizes that constructs vitally important to persistence of criminal behavior, such as impaired self-control, must be viewed developmentally. Such a perspective on risk might add immeasurably to our understanding of the genesis of deviant sexual arousal, a factor in risk assessment regarded as vitally important and yet opaque in origin. Last, and to the mission of this book, such a perspective would add significant transparency to dynamic risk factors (or criminogenic needs) and thus to risk analysis. The discrete paths of a life-span model might further provide the next generation of taxonomic differentiation, potentially yielding distinct paths with known (or knowable) risk profiles. Instead of relying on *one* scale to capture the risk presented by an extraordinarily heterogeneous group of offenders, we might have three or four scales, each defined by omnibus factors, such as age of onset and age disparity. At present, the offenders we evaluate are jigsaw puzzles with many of the pieces missing or inscrutable.

A message that we have sought to convey is that the single most important constraint of risk analysis of sex offenders is the absence of sound theory. Without regard to theory, a cottage industry sprang up to service the new laws of the land. The industry served two purposes—to provide risk assessment scales and to provide a treatment model. The industry—or science—generating and testing risk assessment scales appears to have bumped up against a glass ceiling of accuracy. Mathematics alone will not break the glass ceiling. What is needed is a sound theoretical model to guide risk assessment, and the model that we strongly advocate takes the full life span into consideration.

Recommendations for the Next Generation of Risk Assessment Scales

We have presented findings advancing the notion that a theory of risk forms a sturdier foundation for the further development of actuarial risk assessment instruments (ARAIs) and that this foundation would include, at minimum, risk factors from multiple domains, including: (a) a risk factor representing maturation or aging as indicated by age at release, (b) risk factors representing antisocial orientation that include a measure of the severity of past criminal behavior as well as a measure of a behavioral component representing unstable lifestyle/behavioral dyscontrol, and (c) risk factors representing at least two aspects of sexual deviation, one factor describing the direction of deviant interests, and a second factor describing the impulsivity or force of deviant interests. We are *not* suggesting, however, as noted below, that all seemingly useful risk factors, representing all possible domains, comprise a single scale.

We further promote the now somewhat heretical idea that practitioners play a vital role. Practitioners are not merely "users" of science, applying reflexively what emerges from the "lab." Unlike scientists, practitioners may possess what Michael Polanyi (1958) termed "tacit knowledge," knowledge acquired through practice that may not be explicitly or even coherently expressed. Practice-based *knowledge* is, of course, a razor-thin proposition, which, in the context of sex offender risk assessment, has been dominated by the detractive attributes discussed in Chapter 8—biases and heuristics. Such detractive attributes led to the discrediting and, ultimately, rejection of *pure clinical judgment*. Indeed, Polanyi used the word "intuition" (1964) before reframing it as "the tacit coefficient of a scientific theory" (p. 10). The reconciliation of biased knowledge and tacit knowledge may be understood as the capacity to recognize when our personal judgment conflicts with evidence, thereby invalidating an otherwise sound proposition. Scientists face a similar test, only scientists are trained to adhere to a rigorous set of guidelines for accepting or rejecting evidence.

We would argue that scientists and practitioners can, at least in principle, complement one another. How can scientists benefit? Scientists rarely spend time on the witness stand being examined and cross-examined, and thus rarely appreciate *how* science is used by the legal system. In this book, we have sought to weave a tighter fabric of science and practice, potentially splicing together the complementary objectives of both.

The next generation of sex offender risk assessment scales should:

1 provide estimates of risk with acceptable score-wise error rates;
2 have improved predictive efficacy;
3 allow for the ability to track changes in risk due to treatment or management interventions by embedding dynamic risk factors (as has been demonstrated recently for conceptually based non-actuarial risk instruments (McGrath, Lasher, & Cumming, 2012; Olver, Beggs-Christofferson, Grace, & Wong, 2013); the rationale is clear. At present, scales measuring dynamic risk factors are separate entities and the task of integrating the results with a static scale is essentially a clinical decision with enormous room for bias and thus inter-examiner variability. Standardizing the merger of static and dynamic risk factors

is critical. The dynamic factors that ultimately will be most reliably assessed and arguably most contributory to predictive accuracy are *stable* in nature. At present, those stable dynamic factors that would seem to be likely candidates capture aspects of Facet 1 (Interpersonal: callousness, narcissism, manipulativeness, conning/deceitfulness) and Facet 2 (Affective: unemotional, flat affect, lack of remorse, lack of empathy) of the PCL-R (Hare, 2003), and dysfunctional management of adverse emotional states (e.g., anger);

4 suggest explanations of levels of risk by identification of relevant conceptually meaningful risk factors;

5 provide consistency in risk levels among diverse instruments in the prediction of recidivism risk;

6 address the dysfunctional "quadfurcation" of the science of risk assessment based on the developmental epoch of the target population (children, juveniles, emerging adults (e.g., college students), or adults). As we argued earlier in the chapter, it is illogical to develop and test models of risk like the fabled six blind wise men and the elephant. Analogously, teams of researchers labor over the development and testing of scales intended to assess risk among those roughly 12 to 18 years old, those roughly 18 to 25 years old, and those broadly defined as "adults" (18 or older), effectively "blind" to each other's work, as though these were sovereign, autonomous, unrelated, discrete populations. Not surprisingly, there is "overlap" between all three. Those who work with juveniles will occasionally recommend the use of their scales for those as old as 20 (for youngsters detained until age 21), while those working with emerging adults "overlap" at the lower end as well as the upper end, extending well into the age bracket occupied by those working with adults. Most strikingly, for two completely overlapping populations, emerging adults and adults, the risk factors are almost entirely dissimilar. It would certainly appear that a coherent theoretical model that takes a developmental, life-span perspective is urgently needed;

7 address the obvious, marked clinical, etiological, and risk-related differences between child molesters and rapists. Historically, risk assessment scales have all been "dual-purpose." Every risk scale includes "a few for each." The items targeting rapists have little or no predictive power for child molesters and conversely the items targeting child molesters have little or no predictive power for rapists. These "hybrid" scales that seek to accommodate the risk-relevant demands of both groups are suboptimal and enhance neither the clarity nor the accuracy of either group. In open systems, a diversity of pathways may lead to the same outcome (i.e., equifinality); in the case of sex offenders that outcome is only the same when loosely conceived (i.e., a legally defined sexual offense). Not only are the

> pathways for rapists and child molesters markedly dissimilar, but the "outcomes" are dissimilar (beyond, as stated, the legal definition of a sexual crime). Rapists share many risk characteristics in common with nonsexual offenders. From that vantage, rapists could easily be viewed as a subset of nonsexual criminals. Child molesters, by contrast, are typically viewed as having a focal sexual deviance, an age-inappropriate preference often classified as a paraphilia. In closed systems, as may be more likely with child molesters, outcome is linked inextricably to the *initial* conditions. Combining the two groups in the same risk scale accomplishes little more than obfuscation.

A sound theory of recidivism risk would benefit evaluators as well as clinicians. Assessments grounded in theory and supported by empirical evidence would provide quality information beyond risk level to include the level or severity of specific risk factors. These would inform clinicians using the RNR model (Andrews & Bonta, 2010) by assisting with the identification and evaluation of criminogenic needs. Additionally, such assessments would inform case formulation and treatment planning and provide a baseline for the evaluation of treatment effects.

REFERENCES

Note: * indicates published studies which have utilized the data set we have used here for illustrative purposes.

Abbott, B. R. (2013). The utility of assessing "external risk factors" when selecting Static-99R reference groups. *Journal of Forensic Psychology, 5*, 89–118.

Ackerman, A., Levenson, J., & Harris, A. J. (2012). How many sex offenders really live among us? Adjusted counts and population rates in five U.S. states. *Journal of Crime and Justice, 35*, 464–474. doi:10.1080/0735648X.2012.666-407

Action News Jax. (2013). Donald Smith indicted in killing Cherish Perrywinkle. *Action News Jax*. http://www.news4jax.com/news/donald-smith-indicted-in-killing-of-cherish-perrywinkle/20802192.

Alhakami, A. S., & Slovic, P. (1994). A psychological study of the inverse relationship between perceived risk and perceived benefit. *Risk Analysis, 14*, 1085–1096.

Allan, A., Dawson, D., & Allan, M. (2006). Prediction of the risk of male sexual reoffending in Australia. *Australian Psychologist, 41*, 60–68.

Allan, M., Grace, R. C., Rutherford, A., & Hudson, S. M. (2007). Psychometric assessment of dynamic risk factors for child molesters. *Sexual Abuse: A Journal of Research and Treatment, 19*, 347–367.

American Film Institute. (2003). *AFI's 100 years . . . 100 heroes and villains*. Retrieved from http://www.afi.com/100years/handv.aspx.

American Psychiatric Association. (1974). *Clinical aspects of the violent individual*. Washington, DC: American Psychiatric Association.

American Psychiatric Association. (1980). *Diagnostic and statistical manual of mental disorders* (3rd ed.). Washington, DC: American Psychiatric Association.

American Psychological Association. (1978). Report of the task force on the role of psychology in the criminal justice system. *American Psychologist, 33*, 1099–1113.

American Psychological Association. (1999). *Executive vice president Richard D. Fowler to United States representative Tom Delay*. Retrieved from http://apa.org/delay.html.

American Psychological Association. (2002). *Ethical principles of psychologists and code of conduct*. Washington, DC: American Psychological Association.

American Psychological Association. (2013). Speciality guidelines for forensic psychology. *American Psychologist, 68*, 7–19. doi:10.1037/a0029889

Amsterdam, A. G., & Hertz, R. (1992). An analysis of closing arguments to a jury. *New York Law School Review, 37*, 55–122.

Andrews, D. A., & Bonta, J. (2010). *The psychology of criminal conduct* (5th ed.). New Providence, NJ: LexisNexis/Anderson.

Apfelberg, B., Sugar, C., & Pfeffer, A. Z. (1944). A psychiatric study of 250 sex offenders. *American Journal of Psychiatry, 100*, 762–769.

Arboleda-Florez, J., Holley, H., & Crisanti, A. (1998). Understanding causal paths between mental illness and violence. *Social Psychiatry & Psychiatric Epidemiology, 33*, S38–S46.

Ariely, D. (2008). *Predictably irrational: The hidden forces that shape our decisions*. New York: HarperCollins Publishers.

Arkes, H. R. (2013). The consequences of the hindsight bias in medical decision making. *Current Directions in Psychological Science, 22* (5), 356–360. doi: 10.1177/0963721413489988

Associated Press. (July 12, 1999). House votes 355-0 to condemn findings of child sex abuse study; Journal article concluded that some victims suffer little long-term effects. *Baltimore Sun*, final ed., 6A.

Associated Press. (August 8, 2005). Sex offenders kept from storm shelter. *New York Times*. Retrieved from http://www.nytimes.com/2005/08/08/national/08florida.html?scp=18sq=&st=nyt.

Associated Press. (November 20, 2009). Sex offenders illegally get public housing. *CBS News*. Retrieved from http://www.cbsnews.com/stories/2009/08/20/national/main5236158.shtml.

Association for the Treatment of Sexual Abusers. (October 30, 2012). *Adolescents who have engaged in sexually abusive behavior: Effective policies and practices*. Beaverton, OR: Associate for the Treatment of Sexual Abusers. Retrieved from http://www.atsa.com/adolescents-engaged-in-sexually-abusive-behavior.

Bailar, J. C., & Bailer, A. J. (1999). Risk assessment—the mother of all uncertainties: Disciplinary perspectives on uncertainty in risk assessments. *Annals of the New York Academy of Sciences, 895*, 273–285.

Bandura, A. (June 2006). Toward a psychology of human agency. *Perspectives on Psychological Science, 1* (2), 164–180. doi: 10.1111/j.1745-6916.2006.00011.x

*Barbaree, H. E. (2005). Psychopathy, treatment behavior, and recidivism: An extended follow-up to Seto and Barbaree. *Journal of Interpersonal Violence, 20*, 1115–1131.

*Barbaree, H. E., & Blanchard, R. (2008). Sexual deviance over the lifespan: Reductions in deviant sexual behavior in the aging sex offender. In D. R. Laws & W. O'Donohue (Eds.), *Sexual deviance: Theory, assessment, and treatment* (2nd ed.) (pp. 37–60). New York: Guilford Press.

*Barbaree, H. E., Blanchard, R., & Langton, C. M. (2003). The development of sexual aggression through the life span: The effect of age on sexual arousal and recidivism among sex offenders. In R. A. Prentky, E. Janus, & M. Seto (Eds.), *Sexually coercive behavior: Understanding and management* (pp. 59–71). New York: Annals of the New York Academy of Science.

*Barbaree, H. E., Langton, C. M., & Blanchard, R. (2007). Predicting recidivism in sex offenders using the VRAG and SORAG: The contribution of age-at-release. *International Journal of Forensic Mental Health, 6*, 46.

*Barbaree, H. E., Langton, C. M., Blanchard, R., & Boer, D. (2008). Predicting recidivism in sex offenders using the SVR-20: The contribution of age-at-release. *International Journal of Forensic Mental Health, 7*, 47–64.

*Barbaree, H. E., Langton, C. M., Blanchard, R., & Cantor, J. M. (2009). Aging versus enduring traits as explanatory constructs in sex offender recidivism: Partitioning actuarial prediction into conceptually meaningful components. *Criminal Justice and Behavior, 36*, 443–465.

*Barbaree, H. E., Langton, C. M., & Peacock, E. J. (2006a). The factor structure of actuarial items: Its relation to prediction. *Sexual Abuse: A Journal of Research and Treatment, 18*, 207–226.

*Barbaree, H. E., Langton, C. M., & Peacock, E. J. (2006b). Different actuarial risk measures produce different risk rankings for sex offenders. *Sexual Abuse: A Journal of Research and Treatment, 18*, 423–440.

*Barbaree, H. E., Seto, M., Langton, C. M., & Peacock, E. J. (2001). Evaluating the predictive accuracy of six risk assessment instruments for adult sex offenders. *Criminal Justice and Behavior, 28*, 490–521.

Barbaree, H. E., Langton, C. M., Gopnik-Lewinski, A., & Beach, C. A. (2013). Risk assessment of sex offenders. In H. Bloom & R. D. Schneider (Eds.), *Law and mental disorder: A comprehensive and practical approach* (pp. 783–805). Toronto: Irwin Law, Inc.

Barbaree, H. E., & O'Shaughnessy, R. J. (2013). Adolescent sex offenders. In H. Bloom & R. D. Schneider (Eds.), *Law and Mental Disorder: A Comprehensive and Practical Approach* (pp. 955–976). Toronto: Irwin Law, Inc.

Barefoot v. Estelle, 463 U.S. 880 (1983).

Barnes, J. C., Beaver, K. M., & Boutwell, B. B. (2011). Examining the genetic underpinnings to Moffitt's developmental taxonomy: A behavioral genetic analysis. *Criminology, 49*, 923–954.

Bartosh, D. L., Garby, T., Lewis, D., & Gray, S. (2003). Differences in the predictive validity of actuarial risk assessments in relation to sex offender type. *International Journal of Offender Therapy and Comparative Criminology, 47*, 422–438.

Basile, K. C. (2003). Implications of public health for policy on sexual violence. In R. A. Prentky, E. S. Janus, & M. C. Seto (Eds.), *Sexually coercive behavior: Understanding and management*, Vol. 989 (pp. 446–463). New York: Annals of the New York Academy of Sciences.

Baumeister, R. F., & Tierney, J. (2011). *Willpower*. New York: Penguin Books.

Bayes, T. (1763). An essay towards solving a problem in the doctrine of chances. *Philosophical Transactions of the Royal Society, 53*, 370-418.

Bedau, H. A., & Radelet, M. L. (1987). Miscarriages of justice in potentially capital cases. *Stanford Law Review, 40*, 21–179. Retrieved from http://www.jstor.org/stable/1228828.

Beech, A. R., & Ward, T. (2004). The integration of etiology and risk in sexual offenders: A theoretical framework. *Aggression and Violent Behavior, 10*, 31–63.

Beech, A. R., Friendship, C., Erikson, M., & Hanson, R. H. (2002). The relationship between static and dynamic risk factors and reconviction in a sample of U.K. child abusers. *Sexual Abuse: A Journal of Research and Treatment, 14*, 155–167.

Begley, S. (October 20, 2006). Critical thinking: Part skill, part mindset, and totally up to you. *Wall Street Journal*, p. B1.

Belanger, N., & Earls, C. (1996). Sex offender recidivism prediction. *Forum on Correctional Research, 8*, 22–24.

Bellak, L. (1971). The need for public health laws for psychiatric illness. *American Journal of Public Health, 61* (1), 119–121. doi: 10.2105/AJPH.61.1.119

Belsky, J. (1980). Child maltreatment: An ecological integration. *American Psychologist, 35* (4), 320–335.

Belsky, G., & Gilovich, T. (2000). *Why smart people make big money mistakes and how to correct them: Lessons from the new science of behavioral economics*. New York: Fireside (Simon and Schuster).

Bengtson, S., & Langstrom, N. (2007). Unguided clinical and actuarial assessment of re-offending risk: A direct comparison with sex offenders in Denmark. *Sexual Abuse: A Journal of Research and Treatment, 19*, 135–153.

Ben-Yehuda, N. (2009). Moral panics: 36 years on. *British Journal of Criminology, 49*, 1–3. doi:10.1093/bjc/azn076

Blanchard, R., & Barbaree, H. E. (2005). The strength of sexual arousal as a function of the age of the sex offender: Comparisons among pedophiles, hebephiles, and teliophiles. *Sexual Abuse: A Journal of Research and Treatment, 17*, 441–456.

Blumstein, A., Farrington, D. P., & Moitra, S. (1985). Delinquency careers: Innocents, desisters, and persisters. In M. Tonry & N. Morris (Eds.), *Crime and justice: An annual review of research, Vol. 6* (pp. 187–220). Chicago: University of Chicago Press.

Boccaccini, M. T., Turner, D. B., Murrie, D. C., Henderson, C. E., & Chevalier, C. (2013). Do scores from risk measures matter to jurors? *Psychology, Public Policy, and Law, 19*, 259–269. doi: 10.1037/a0031354

Bochnewich, M. A. (1992). Prediction of dangerousness and Washington's sexually violent predator statute. *California Western Law Review, 29*(1), 277–306.

Bodine, B. G. (1990). Washington's new violent sexual predator commitment system: An unconstitutional law and an unwise policy choice. *University of Puget Sound Law Review, 14* (1), 104–141.

Boer, D., Hart, S. D., Kropp, P. R., & Webster, C. D. (1997). *Manual for the sexual violence risk-20*. Vancouver, BC: British Columbia Institute Against Family Violence.

Bonta, J., Law, M., & Hanson, R. K. (1998). The prediction of criminal and violent recidivism among mentally disordered offenders: A meta-analysis. *Psychological Bulletin, 123*, 123–142.

Boorstin, D. J. (1958). *The mysterious science of the law*. Boston, MA: Beacon Press.

Borum, R. (1996). Improving the clinical practice of violent risk assessment: Technology, guidelines, and training. *American Psychologist, 51*, 945–956.

Borum, R., Otto, R., & Golding, S. (1993). Improving clinical judgment and decision making in forensic evaluation. *Journal of Psychiatry and Law, 21*, 35–76.

Boutwell, B. B., Barnes, J. C., & Beaver, K. M. (2013). Life-course persistent offenders and the propensity to commit sexual assault. *Sexual Abuse: A Journal of Research and Treatment, 25* (1), 69–81.

Brakel, S. J., Parry, J., & Weiner, B. A. (1985). *The mentally disabled and the law* (3rd ed.). Chicago: American Bar Foundation.

Bribiesca, M. (2007). *From the literature* (08(1)).

Bronfrenbrenner, U. (1979). *The ecology of human development: Experiments by nature and design*. Cambridge, MA: Harvard University Press.

Brown, S. (2013a). *How to fill the holes in Florida's sex offender laws*. Retrieved from http://www.wokv.com/news/news/local/critique-sex-offenderpredator-laws-aim-create-chan/nZm4Q.

Brown, S. (2013b). *State rep calls for change in sex offender checks*. Retrieved from http://www.wokv.com/news/news/local/state-rep-calls-change-sex-offender-checks/nYXHn.

Buchanan, A. (2013). Violence risk assessment in clinical settings: Being sure about being sure. *Behavioral Sciences & the Law, 31*(1), 74–80. doi: 10.1002/bsl.2045

Buck v. Bell, 274 U.S. 200 (1927).

Burick, L. T. (1968). An analysis of the Illinois sexually dangerous persons act. *Criminal Law, Criminology, and Police Science, 59* (2), 254–266.

Byrne, D. (1961). Interpersonal attraction and attitude similarity. *The Journal of Abnormal and Social Psychology, 62*, 713–715. doi:10.1037/h0044721

Caldwell, M. F. (2007). Sexual offense adjudication and sexual recidivism among juvenile offenders. *Sexual Abuse: A Journal of Research and Treatment, 19*, 107–113.

Caldwell, M. F. (2010). Study characteristics and recidivism base rates in juvenile sex offender recidivism. *International Journal of Offender Therapy and Comparative Criminology, 54*, 197–212.

California Attorneys for Criminal Justice. (2007). *Statement in opposition to Proposition 83 (Press release)*. Retrieved from http://cacjweb.org/pdf/Prop83.pdf.

Camerer, C. G., & Kunreuther, H. (1989). Decision processes for low probability events: Policy implications. *Journal of Policy Analysis and Management, 8*, 565–592.

Cantor, J. M., Kabani, N., Christensen, B. K., Zipursky, R. B., Barbaree, H. E., et al. (2008). Cerebral white matter deficiencies in pedophilic men. *Journal of Psychiatric Research, 42*, 167–183.

Cardwell, D., & Krauss, C. (July 19, 2014). Frack quietly, please: sage grouse is nesting. *The New York Times*. Retrieved from http://www.nytimes.com/2014/07/20/business/energy-environment/disparate-interests-unite-to-protect-greater-sage-grouse.html?_r=0.

*Carr, C., Schlank, A., Parker, K.C. (2013). Review of Florida's Sexually Violent Predator Program Office. The Florida Department of Children and Families, Substance Abuse and Mental Health (SAMH) Program Office.

Cattell, R. B. (1966). The scree test for the number of factors. *Multivariate Behavioral Research, 1*, 245–276.

Chaffin, M., Levenson, J., Letourneau, E., & Stern, P. (2009). How safe are trick-or-treaters?: An analysis of child sex crime rates on Halloween. *Sexual Abuse: A Journal of Research and Treatment 21* (3), 363–374.

Chaiken, S., & Trope, Y. (1999). *Dual-process theories in social psychology*. New York: Guilford Press.

Chapman, L. J. (1967). Illusory correlation in observational report. *Journal of Verbal Learning and Verbal Behavior, 6*, 151–155.

Chapman, L. J., & Chapman, J. P. (1969). Illusory correlation as an obstacle to the use of valid psychodiagnostic signs. *Journal of Abnormal Psychology, 74*, 271–280. doi:10.1037/h0027592

Cicchetti, D., & Rogosch, F. A. (1996). Equifinality and multifinality in developmental psychopathology. *Development and Psychopathology, 8*, 597–600.

Cipolla, C. (2011). "Preventive corrections": Psychiatric representation and the classification of sexually violent predators. *Journal of Medical Humanities, 32*, 103–113.

Clarke, R. V. (1996). The distribution of deviance and exceeding the speed limit. *The British Journal of Criminology, 36*, 169–181.

Coates, J. (2012). *The hour between dog and wolf: Risk taking, gut feelings and the biology of boom and bust*. New York: Penguin Press.

Cocozza, J. J., & Steadman, H. (1974). Some refinements in the measurement and prediction of dangerous behavior. *American Journal of Psychiatry, 131*, 1012–1014.

Cocozza, J. J., & Steadman, H. (1976). Prediction in psychiatry: An example of misplaced confidence in experts. *Rutgers Law Review, 29*, 1084–1101.

Cohen, J. (1988). *Statistical power analysis for the behavioral sciences* (2nd ed.). Oxford: Lawrence Erlbaum Associates.

Cohen, M. A. (2000). Measuring the costs and benefits of crime and justice. In D. Duffee (Ed.), *Measurement and analysis of crime and justice* (pp. 263–316). Criminal Justice 4. Washington, DC: National Institute of Justice.

Cohen, M. A. (2005). *The costs of crime and justice*. New York: Routledge.

Cohen, M. A. (2008). The effect of crime on life satisfaction. *Journal of Legal Studies, 37* (2), S325–S353.

Cohen, M. A., & Bowles, R. (2010). Estimating costs of crime. In A. R. Piquero & D. Weisburd (Eds.), *Handbook of quantitative criminology*, Part 2 (pp. 143–162). New York: Springer.

Cohen, M. A., Groth, N., & Siegel, R. (1978). The clinical prediction of dangerousness. *Crime and Delinquency, 24*, 28–39.

Cohen, M. A., Rust, R., Steen, S., & Tidd, S. (2004). Willingness-to-pay for crime control programs. *Criminology, 42* (1), 89–110.

Cohen, S. (1972). *Folk devils and moral panics: The creation of the Mods and Rockers*. Oxford: Basil Blackwell.

Cohen, S. (1980). *Folk devils and moral panics* (2nd ed.). New York: St. Martin's Press.

Cole, D. (2014). The difference prevention makes: Regulating preventive justice. *Criminal Law and Philosophy*. doi: 10.1007/s11572-013-9289-7

Colorado Department of Public Safety. (2004). *Report on safety issues raised by living arrangements for and location of sex offenders of the community.* Retrieved from http://dcj.state.co.us/odvsom/Sex_Offender/SO_Pdfs/FullSLAFinal01.pdf.

Com. v. Boucher, 780 N.E.2d 47 (2002).

Cox, D. R. (1972). Regression models and life tables. *Journal of the Royal Statistical Society, 34*, 187–220.

Craig, L. A., Beech, A. R., & Browne, K. D. (2006). Evaluating the predictive accuracy of sex offender risk assessment measures on UK samples: A cross-validation of the Risk Matrix 2000 scales. *Sexual Offender Treatment, 1* (1). Retrieved from www.sexual-offender-treatment.org/19.html.

Craig, L. A., Thornton, D., Beech, A. R., & Browne, K. D. (2007). The relationship of statistical and psychological risk markers to sexual reconviction. *Criminal Justice and Behavior, 28*, 235–251.

Critcher, C. (2003). *Moral panics and the media.* Buckingham: Open University Press.

Cunningham, R. J., Herzog, T. N., & London, R. L. (2011). *Models for quantifying risk* (3rd ed.). Winsted, CT: ACTEX Publications.

Curtis, K. (January, 2003). *California "loses" 33,000 sex offenders.* Retrieved from http://www.cbsnews.com/news/calif-loses-33000-sex-offenders.

Damasio, A. R. (1994). *Descartes' error: Emotion, reason, and the human brain.* New York: Avon.

Davey, M. (March 15, 2006). *Iowa's residency rules drive sex offenders underground.* Retrieved from http://classes.maxwell.syr.edu/psc202_s05/Kristi/sex%20in%20iowa.pdf.

Davis, D., & Follette, W. C. (2002). Rethinking the probative value of evidence: Base rates, intuitive profiling, and the "postdiction" of behavior. *Law and Human Behavior, 26* (2), 133–158.

Dawes, R. M. (1982). The robust beauty of improper linear models in decision making. In D. Kahneman, P. Slovic, & A. Tversky (Eds.), *Judgment under uncertainty: Heuristics and biases* (pp. 351–357). New York: Cambridge University Press.

Dawes, R. M. (2001). *Everyday irrationality: How pseudo-scientists, lunatics, and the rest of us systematically fail to think rationally.* Boulder, CO: Westview Press.

Dawes, R. M., Faust, D., & Meehl, P. E. (1989). Clinical versus actuarial judgment. *Science, 243*, 1668–1674.

Dawes, R. M., Faust, D., & Meehl, P. E. (1992). Statistical prediction versus clinical prediction: Improving what works. In G. Keren & C. Lewis (Eds.), *A handbook for data analysis in the behavioral sciences: Methodological issues* (pp. 351–367). Mahwah, NJ: Erlbaum.

DeBondt, W. F., & Thaler, R. H. (1995). Financial decision-making in markets and firms: A behavioral perspective. In R. Jarrow, V. Maksimovic, & W. T. Ziemba (Eds.), *Handbooks in operations research and management science* (pp. 385–410). Amsterdam: Elsevier.

DeMatteo, D., Batastini, A., Foster, A., & Hunt, E. (2010). Individualizing risk assessment: Balancing idiographic and nomothetic data. *Journal of Forensic Psychology Practice, 10*, 360–371.

DeMatteo, D., Hunt, E., Batastini, A., & LaDuke, C. (2010). The disconnect between assessment and intervention in the risk management of criminal offenders. *Open Access Journal of Forensic Psychology, 2*, 59–74.

D'Emilio, J., & Freedman, E. B. (1997). *Intimate matters: A history of sexuality in America.* Chicago and London: University of Chicago Press.

Dershowitz, A. (1970). The law of dangerousness: Some fictions about predictions. *Journal of Legal Education, 23* (1), 24–47.

Dershowitz, A. (1974a). The origins of preventive confinement in Anglo-American law—part I; the English experience. *University of Cincinnati Law Review, 43*, 1–60.

Dershowitz, A. (1974b). The origins of preventive confinement in Anglo-American law—part II; the American experience. *University of Cincinnati Law Review, 43*, 781–846.

deVogel, V., deRuiter, C., vanBeek, D., & Mead, G. (2004). Predictive validity of the SVR-20 and Static-99 in a Dutch sample of treated sex offenders. *Law and Human Behavior, 28*, 235–251.

Diacu, F. (October 26, 2012). Is failure to predict a crime? *New York Times*. http://www.nytimes.com/2012/10/27/opinion/a-failed-earthquake-prediction-a-crime.html?_r=0.

Diamond, B. L. (1974). The psychiatric prediction of dangerousness. In J. Q. Quen (Ed.), *The psychiatrist in the courtroom: Selected papers of Bernard L. Diamond, M.D* (pp. 143–156). Hillsdale, NJ: The Analytic Press.

Dickey, R., Nussbaum, D., Chevolleau, K., & Davidson, D. L. (2002). Age as a differential characteristic of rapists, pedophiles, and sexual sadists. *Journal of Sex and Marital Therapy, 28*, 211–218.

DiFuria, G., & Mees, H. L. (1964). Legal and psychiatric problems in the care and treatment of sexual offenders (A national survey). *The American Journal of Psychiatry, 120*, 980–985.

Donaldson, T., & Wollert, R. (2008). A mathematical proof and example that Bayes's Theorem is fundamental to actuarial estimates of sexual recidivism risk. *Sexual Abuse, 20*, 206–217.

Doren, D. (2002). *Evaluating sex offenders: A manual for civil commitments and beyond*. Thousand Oaks, CA: Sage.

Doren, D. (2004a). Stability of the interpretative risk percentages for the RRASOR and Static-99. *Sexual Abuse: A Journal of Research and Treatment, 16*, 25–36.

Doren, D. (2004b). Toward a multidimensional model for sexual recidivism risk. *Journal of Interpersonal Violence, 19*, 835–856.

Downes, D., Rock, P., Chinkin, C., & Gearty, C. (2008). *Crime, social control and human rights. From moral panics to states of denial. Essays in honor of Stanley Cohen*. Portland, OR: Willan Publishing.

Doyle, M., Carter, S., Shaw, J., & Dolan, M. (2012). Predicting community violence from patients discharged from acute mental health units in England. *Social Psychiatry and Psychiatric Epidemiology, 47*, 627–637.

Dred Scott v. Sandford, 60 U.S. 393 (1857).

DuBois, W. E. B. (2008). *The Negro*. Radford, VA: A&D Publishing.

Ducro, C., & Pham, T. (2006a). Comparison of two risk assessment instruments for sexual offenders. *Sexual Abuse: A Journal of Research and Treatment, 18*, 193–206.

Ducro, C., & Pham, T. (2006b). Evaluation of the SORAG and the Static-99 on Belgian sex offenders committed to a forensic facility. *Sexual Abuse: A Journal of Research and Treatment, 18*, 15–25.

Dunning, D., Griffin, D. W., Milojkovic, J. D., & Ross, L. (1990). The overconfidence effect in social prediction. *Journal of Personality and Social Psychology, 58*, 568–581.

Duwe, G. (2013). To what extent does civil commitment reduce sexual recidivism? Estimating the selective incapacitation effects in Minnesota. *Journal of Criminal Justice, 42* (2), 193–202. doi: http://dx.doi.org/10.1016/j.jcrimjus.2013.06.009

Dvoskin, J., & Heilbrun, K. (2001). Risk assessment and release decision-making: Toward resolving the great debate. *The Journal of the American Academy of Psychiatry and the Law, 29*, 6–10.

Eck, J. E., & Weisburd, D. (1995). Crime places in crime theory. *Crime Prevention Studies, 4*, 1–33.

Eck, J. E., Clarke, R. V., & Guerette, R. T. (2007). Risky facilities: Crime concentration in homogeneous sets of establishments and facilities. *Crime Prevention Studies, 21*, 228. Retrieved from http://www.popcenter.org/tools/risky_faciliies/PDFs/Eck_etal_press.pdf.

Editorial: Effective against crime [Editorial]. (2006). *San Francisco Chronicle*. Retrieved from ccoso.org/ChronicleEditorial1-19-06.doc

Edwards, W. (1954). The theory of decision making. *Psychological Bulletin, 51*, 380–417. doi:10.1037/h0053870

Eher, R., Rettenberger, M., & Schilling, F. (2010). Psychiatrische Diagnosen von Sexualstraftätern—eine empirische Untersuchung von 807 inhaftierten Kindesmissbrauchstätern und Vergewaltigern (Psychiatric diagnoses in sexual offenders – an investigation of 807 incarcerated child molesters and rapists). *Zeitschrift für Sexualforschung, 23*, 23–35.

Eher, R., Matthes, A. S. F., Haubner-MacLean, T., & Rettenberger, M. (2012). Dynamic risk assessment in sexual offenders using STABLE-2000 and the STABLE-2007: An investigation of predictive and incremental validity. *Sexual Abuse: A Journal of Research and Treatment, 24*, 5–28.

Einhorn, H. G. (1982). Learning from experience and suboptimal rules in decision making. In D. Kahneman, P. Slovic, & A. Tversky (Eds.), *Judgment under uncertainty: Heuristics and biases* (pp. 268–283). New York: Cambridge University Press.

Eisenbarth, H., Osterheider, M., Nedopiln, N., & Stadtland, C. (2012). Recidivism in female offenders: PCL-R lifestyle factor and VRAG show predictive validity in a German sample. *Behavioral Sciences and the Law, 30*, 575–584.

Elliot, I. A., Beech, A. R., Mandeville-Norden, R., & Hayes, E. (2009). Psychological profiles of internet sexual offenders: Comparisons with contact sexual offenders. *Sexual Abuse: A Journal of Research and Treatment, 21*, 76–92. doi: 10.1177/1079063208326929

Elliot, I. A., Beech, A. R., & Mandeville-Norden, R. (2013). The psychological profiles of internet, contact, and mixed internet/contact sex offenders. *Sexual Abuse: A Journal of Research and Treatment, 25*, 3–20.

Endrass, J., Urbaniok, F., Held, L., Vetter, S., & Rossegger, A. (2009). The accuracy of the Static-99 in predicting recidivism in Switzerland. *International Journal of Offender Therapy and Comparative Criminology, 53*, 482–491.

Ennis, B. J., & Litwack, T. R. (1974). Psychiatry and the presumption of expertise: Flipping coins in the courtroom. *California Law Review, 62*, 693–732. Retrieved from http://scholarship.law.berkely.edu/californialawreview/vol62/iss3/2.

Epperson, D. L., Kaul, J. D., Huot, S. J., Hesselton, D., Alexander, W., & Goldman, R. (1998). *Minnesota Sex Offender Screening Tool-Revised (MnSOST-R)*. St. Paul, MN: Minnesota Department of Corrections.

Epstein, S. (1994). Integration of the cognitive and the psychodynamic unconscious. *American Psychologist, 49*, 709–724.

Erickson, W. D. (1995). Northern lights: Minnesota's experience with sex offender legislation. *American Academy of Psychiatry and Law Newsletter, 20* (1), 3–6.

Erickson, W. D. (undated). Critical analysis of the Psychopathic Personality Statute, unpublished manuscript, on file with author.

Esser, J. K., & Lindoerfer, J. S. (1989). Groupthink and the Space Shuttle Challenger accident: Toward a quantitative case analysis. *Journal of Behavioral Decision Making, 2*, 167–177.

Estrich, S. (1987). *Real rape: How the legal system victimizes women who say no.* Cambridge, MA: Harvard University Press.

Ewing, C. (1983). "Dr. Death" and the case for an ethical ban on psychiatric and psychological predictions of dangerousness in capital sentencing proceedings. *American Journal of Law and Medicine, 49*, 407–428.

Ewing, C. (1985). Schall v. Martin: Preventive detention and dangerousness through the looking glass. *Buffalo Law Review, 34*, 173–226.

Ewing, C. P. (2011). *Justice perverted. Sex offender law, psychology, and public policy.* Oxford: Oxford University Press.

Fabrigar, L. R., Wegener, D. T., MacCullum, R. C., & Strahan, E. J. (1999). Evaluating the use of exploratory factor analysis in psychological research. *Psychological Methods, 4*, 272–299.

Fagin; A. (1976). The policy implications of predictive decision-making: "Likelihood" and "dangerousness" in civil commitment proceedings. *Public Policy, 24*, 491–528.

Faigman, D. L., Saks, M. J., Sanders, J., & Cheng, E. K. (2000). How good is good enough?: Expert evidence under Daubert and Kumho. *Case Western Reserve Law Review, 50*, 645–667.

Falzer, P. R. (2013). Valuing structured professional judgment: Predictive validity, decision-making,and the clinical-actuarial conflict. *Behavioral Science and the Law, 31* (1), 40–54.

Family Research Council. (1999). APA admits error in publishing highly criticized "adult-child sex" study; FRC's Parshall applauds "good first step" as APA pledges "unprecedented" independent review. Retrieved from https://www.newgon.com/prd/science/FRC.html.

Farrington, D. P. (1981). The Cambridge study in delinquent development. In S.A. Mednick, & A. E. Baert (Eds.), *Prospective longitudinal research: An empirical basis for the primary prevention of psychosocial disorders* (pp. 137–145). Oxford: Oxford University Press.

Farrington, D. P. (1985). Stepping stones to adult criminal careers. In D. Olweus, J. Block, & M. R. Yarrow (Eds.), *Development of antisocial and prosocial behavior* (pp. 359–384). New York: Academic Press.

Fazel, S., Sjöstedt, G., Långström, N., & Grann, M. (2006). Risk factors for criminal recidivism in older sexual offenders. *Sexual Abuse: A Journal of Research and Treatment, 18*, 159–167.

Feeley, M., & Simon, J. (2008). Folk devils and moral panics: An appreciation from North America. In D. Downes, P. Rock, C. Chinkin, & C. Gearty (Eds.), *Crime, social control and human rights: From moral panics to states of denial* (pp. 39–52). Portland, OR: Willan Publishing.

Feelgood, S., Cortoni, F., & Thompson, A. (2005). Sexual coping, general coping and cognitive distortions in incarcerated rapists and child molesters. *Journal of Sexual Aggression, 11*, 157–170.

Felson, M. K. (1998). *Crime and everyday life.* Thousand Oaks, CA: Sage.

Ferguson, C. J. (2010). Blazing angels or resident evil? Can violent video games be a force for good? *Review of General Psychology, 14*, 68–81. doi:10.1037/a0018941

Ferguson, C. J. (2013). Violent video games and the Supreme Court. Lessons for the scientific community in the wake of Brown v. Entertainment Merchants Association. *American Psychologist, 68*, 57–74. doi:10.1037/a0030597

Festinger, L. (1957). *A theory of cognitive dissonance*. Palo Alto, CA: Stanford University Press.

Feynman, R. P. (1988). An outsider's inside view of the Challenger inquiry. *Physics Today*, 26–37.

Fiedler, K. (2011). Voodoo correlations are everywhere—not only in neuroscience. *Psychological Science, 6*, 163–171. doi:10.1177/1745691611400237

Finn, P. (1997). *Sex offender community notification* (NCJ 162364). Washington, DC: Office of Justice Programs. Retrieved from https//www.ncjrs.gov/txfiles/162364.pdf.

Finucane, M. L., Alhakami, A. S., Slovic, P., & Johnson, S. M. (2000). The affect heuristic in judgments of risks and benefits. *Journal of Behavioral Decision Making, 13*, 1–17.

Fischhoff, B. (1982). Debiasing. In D. Kahneman, P. Slovic, & A. Tversky (Eds.), *Judgment under uncertainty: Heuristics and biases* (pp. 422–444). Cambridge, UK: Cambridge University Press.

Fischhoff, B. (2012). *Risk analysis and human behavior*. New York: Earthscan Publications (Routledge).

Fischhoff, B., & Beyth-Maron, R. (1983). Hypothesis evaluation from a Bayesian perspective. *Psychological Review, 90*, 239–260.

Fischhoff, B., & Kadvany, J. (2011). *Risk: A very short introduction*. Oxford: Oxford University Press.

Fisher, A. (1991). Risk communication challenges. *Risk Analysis, 11*, 173–179.

Fiske, S. T., Cuddy, A. J. C., & Glick, P. (2007). Universal dimensions of social cognition: Warmth and competence. *Trends in Cognitive Sciences, 11*, 77–83. doi:10.1016/j.tics.2006.11.005

Fitch, W. L. (2003). Sexual offender commitment in the United States. In R. A. Prentky, E. Janus, & M. Seto (Eds.), *Sexually coercive behavior: Understanding and management* (pp. 489–501). New York: Annals of the New York Academy of Sciences.

Foucha v. Louisiana, 504 U.S. 71 (1992).

Francia, C. A., Coolidge, F. L., White, L. A., Segal, D. L., Cahill, B. S. et al. (2010). Personality disorder profiles in incarcerated male rapists and child molesters. *American Journal of Forensic Psychology, 28*, 1–14.

Franklin, K. (October 27, 2013). *In the News blog: Black swan crash lands on Florida SVP program. Audit finds low recidivism, critiques reliance on inflated Static-99 risk estimates*. Retrieved from http://forensicpsychologist.blogspot.com/2013/10/black-swan-crash-lands-on-florida-svp.html.

Freudenburg, W. (1988). Perceived risk, real risk: Social science and the art of probabilistic risk assessment. *Science, 242*, 44–49.

Freund, K. (1976). Diagnosis and treatment for forensically significant anomalous erotic preferences. *Canadian Journal of Criminology and Corrections, 18*, 181–189.

Frewer, L. J., Miles, S., & Marsh, R. (2002). The media and genetically modified foods: Evidence in support of social amplification of risk. *Risk Analysis, 22*, 701–711.

Friendship, C., Mann, R. E., & Beech, A. R. (2003). Evaluation of a national prison-based treatment program for sexual offenders in England and Wales. *Journal of Interpersonal Violence, 18*, 744–759.

Gail, M. H., & Pfeiffer, R. M. (2005). On criteria for evaluating models of absolute risk. *Biostatistics, 6*, 227–239. doi: 10.1093/biostatistics/kxi005

Galanter, M. (1974). Why the "haves" come out ahead: Speculation on the limits of the legal change. *Law and Society Review, 9*, 165–230.

Galliher, J. F., & Tyree, C. (1985). Edwin Sutherland's research on the origins of sexual psychopath laws: An early case study of the medicalization of deviance. *Social Problems, 33*, 100–113.

Gallup. (2013). Guns. *Gallup*. Retrieved from http://www.gallup.com/poll/1645/guns.aspx.

Galton, F. (1886). Regression towards mediocrity in hereditary stature. *Journal of the Anthropological Institute of Great Britain and Ireland, 15*, 246–263.

Garb, H. N. (1998). *Studying the clinician*. Washington, DC: American Psychological Association.

Gardner, W., Lidz, C. W., Mulvey, E. P., & Shaw, E. C. (1996). A comparison of actuarial methods for identifying repetitively violent patients with mental illnesses. *Law and Human Behavior, 20,* 35–47.

Gauntlett, D. (1995). *Moving experiences: Understanding television's influences and effects*. New Barnet, UK: John Libbey Media.

Gazzaniga, M. S., & Steven, M. S. (April, 2005). Neuroscience and the law. *Scientific American Mind*, 43–49.

Geer, T. M., Becker, J. V., Gray, S. R., & Krauss, D. (2001). Predictors of treatment completion in a correctional sex offender treatment program. *International Journal of Offender Therapy and Comparative Criminology, 45*, 302–313.

Geissenhainer, M. T. (2008). The $62 million question: Is Virginia's new center to house sexually violent predators money well spent? *University of Richmond Law Review,* 1301–1336.

Gendreau, P., Little, T., & Goggin, C. (1996). A meta-analysis of the predictors of adult offender recidivism: What works? *Criminology, 34*, 575–607.

Gerhardstein, A. G. (2012). A first episode standard for involuntary treatment. *University of St. Thomas Law Journal, 10*, 469–501.

Gibson, R. A. (1979). The Negro holocaust: Lynching and race riots in the United States 1880–1950, Curriculum Unit 79.02.04. *Yale—New Haven Teachers Institute*. Retrieved from http://www.yale.edu/ynhti/curriculum/units/1979/2/79.02.04.x.html.

Gigerenzer, G. (2002). *Reckoning with risk: Learning to live with uncertainty*. London: Penguin Press.

Gigerenzer, G. (2007). *Gut feelings: Short cuts to better decision making*. London: Penguin Books.

Gigerenzer, G. (2008a). *Rationality for mortals: How people cope with uncertainty*. Oxford: Oxford University Press.

Gigerenzer, G. (2008b). Why heuristics work. *Perspectives on Psychological Science, 3*, 20–29.

Gill, C. J., Sabin, L., & Schmidt, C. H. (2005). Why clinicians are natural Bayesians. *British Medical Journal*, 330. Retrieved from http://www.ncbi.nim.nih.gov/pmc/articles/PMC557240.

Girardot, F. C. (February 1, 2013). Author: Cadaver dog discovered Black Dahlia death scene at Hollywood home. *The Sun News*. http://www.sbsun.com/general-news/20130202/author-cadaver-dog-discovered-black-dahlia-death-scene-at-hollywood-home.

Gleick, J. (1987). *Chaos: Making a new science*. New York: Penguin Books.

Goffman, E. (1961). *Asylums: Essays on the social situation of mental patients and other inmates*. New York: Anchor Books.

Goldyne, A. J. (2007). Minimizing the influence of unconscious bias in evaluations: A practical guide. *Journal of the American Academy of Psychiatry and Law, 35*, 60–66.

Gomes-Schwartz, B. (1978). Effective ingredients in psychotherapy: Prediction of outcome from process variables. *Journal of Consulting and Clinical Psychology, 46*, 1023–1035.

Goode, E., & Ben-Yehuda, N. (1994). *Moral panics: The social construction of deviance*. Oxford: Blackwell.

Goode, E. (January 3, 2001). Arnold Hutschnecker, 102, therapist to Nixon. *New York Times*. http://www.nytimes.com/2001/01/03/us/arnold-hutschnecker-102-therapist-to-nixon.html.

Gookin, K. (2007). Comparison of state laws authorizing involuntary commitment of sexually violent predators: 2006 update, Revised. *Washington State Institute for Public Policy, Document No.07-08-1101*. Retrieved from http://www.wsipp.wa.gov/rptfiles/07-08-1101.

Graham, B., & Dodd, D. L. (1940). *Security analysis: Principles and technique* (2nd ed.). New York: Whittlesey House, McGraw-Hill.

Green, D. M., & Swets, J. A. (1966). *Signal detection theory and psychophysics*. New York: Wiley.

Griffin, T., & Stitt, B. G. (2010). Random activities theory: The case for "Black Swan" criminology. *Critical Criminology 18* (1), 57–72.

Grinberg, E. (October 31, 2009). Police try to monitor sex offenders at Halloween. *CNN Justice.com*. Retrieved from http://www.cnn.com/2009/CRIME/10/31/sex.offenders.halloween/index.html.

Grisso, T. (1987). The economic and scientific future of forensic psychological assessment. *American Psychologist, 42*, 831–839.

Grisso, T., & Appelbaum, P. (1992). Is it unethical to offer predictions of future violence? *Law and Human Behavior, 16*, 621–633.

Grisso, T., & Steinberg, L. (2005). Between a rock and a soft place: Developmental research and the child advocacy process. *Journal of Clinical Child and Adolescent Psychology, 34* (4), 619–627.

Grosinger v. M.B.K., 639 N.W.2d 473 (N.D. 2002).

Group for the Advancement of Psychiatry. (1950). *Psychiatrically deviated sex offenders*. New York: The Mental Health Materials Center.

Group for the Advancement of Psychiatry. (1977). *Psychiatry and sex psychopath legislation: The 30s to the 80s*. New York: The Mental Health Materials Center.

Grove, W. M., & Meehl, P. E. (1996). Comparative efficiency of informal (subjective, impressionistic) and formal (mechanical, algorithmic) prediction procedures: The clinical-statistical controversy. *Psychology, Public Policy, and Law, 2*, 293–323.

Grove, W. M., Zald, D. H., Lebow, B. S., Snitz, B. E., & Nelson, C. (2000). Clinical versus mechanical prediction: A meta-analysis. *Psychological Assessment, 12*, 19–30.

Gunn, J. (1976). Sexual offenders. *British Journal of Hospital Medicine, 15*, 57–65.

Gunzelmann, & Gluck, K. A. (2004). Knowledge tracing for complex training applications: Beyond Bayesian mastery estimates. *Air Force Research Laboratory Proceedings of the Thirteenth Conference on Behavior Representation in Modeling and Simulation* (pp. 383–384). http://act-r.psy.cmu.edu/wordpress/wp-content/uploads/2012/12/710gunzelmann_gluck-2004.pdf

Haegerich, T. M., & Dahlberg, L. L. (2011). Violence as a public health risk. *American Journal of Lifestyle Medicine, 5*, 392–406. doi:10.1177/1559827611409127

Hall, G. C. N. (1995). Sexual offender recidivism revisited: A meta-analysis of recent treatment studies. *Journal of Consulting and Clinical Psychology, 63*, 802–809.

Hamdi, N. R., & Knight, R. A. (2012). The relationship of perpetrator and victim substance use to the sexual aggression of rapists and child molesters. *Sexual Abuse: A Journal of Research and Treatment, 24*, 307–327.

Hanley, J. A., & McNeil, B. J. (1982). The meaning and use of the area under a receiver operating characteristic. *Radiology, 143*, 29–36.

Hanley, J. A., & McNeil, B. J. (1983). A method of comparing the area under receiver operating characteristic curves. *Radiology, 148*, 839–843.

Hanson, R. K. (1997). *The development of a brief actuarial risk scale for sexual offense recidivism* (1997–04). Ottawa: Department of the Solicitor General.

Hanson, R. K. (1998). What do we know about sex offender risk assessment? *Psychology, Public Policy, and Law, 4*, 50–72.

Hanson, R. K. (2002). Recidivism and age: Follow-up data from 4,673 sexual offenders. *Journal of Interpersonal Violence, 17*, 1046–1062.

Hanson, R. K. (2006). Does Static-99 predict recidivism among older sexual offenders? *Sexual Abuse: A Journal of Research and Treatment, 18*, 343–355.

Hanson, R. K., Babchishin, K. M., Helmus, L., & Thornton, D. (2012). Quantifying the relative risk of sex offenders: Risk ratios for Static-99R. *Sexual Abuse: A Journal of Research and Treatment, 25*, 482–515. doi:10.1177/1079063212469060

Hanson, R. K., Bourgon, G., Helmus, L., & Hodgson, S. (2009). The principles of effective correctional treatment also apply to sexual offenders: A meta-analysis. *Criminal Justice and Behavior, 36*, 865–891.

Hanson, R. K., & Bussiere, M. T. (1998). Predicting relapse: A meta-analysis of sexual offender recidivism studies. *Journal of Consulting and Clinical Psychology, 66*, 348–362.

Hanson, R. K., Gordon, A., Harris, A. J., Marques, J. K., Murphy, W., & Quinsey, V. L. (2002). First report of the collaborative outcome data project on the effectiveness of psychological treatment for sex offenders. *Sexual Abuse: A Journal of Research and Treatment, 14*, 169–194.

Hanson, R. K., & Harris, A. J. (2000). Where should we intervene? Dynamic predictors of sex offense recidivism. *Criminal Justice and Behavior, 27*, 6–35.

Hanson, R. K., & Harris, A. J. (2001). A structured approach to evaluating change among sexual offenders. *Sexual Abuse: A Journal of Research and Treatment, 16*, 105–122.

Hanson, R. K., Harris, A. J., Scott, T., & Helmus, L. (2007). *Assessing the risk of sexual offenders on community supervision: The dynamic supervision project.* [PS3-1/2007-5]. Ottawa: Public Safety Canada.

Hanson, R. K., Lloyd, C. D., Helmus, L., & Thornton, D. (2012). Developing non-arbitrary metrics for risk communication: Percentile ranks for the Static-99/R and Static-2002/R sex offender Risk Tools. *International Journal of Forensic Mental Health, 11*, 9–23.

Hanson, R. K., Morton, K., & Harris, A. J. (2003). Sex offender recidivism risk: What we know and what we need to know. In R. A. Prentky, E. Janus, & M. Seto (Eds.), *Sexually coercive behavior: Understanding and management* (pp. 154–166). New York: Annals of the New York Academy of Sciences.

Hanson, R. K., & Morton-Bourgon, K. E. (2004a). Predictors of sexual recidivism: An updated meta-analysis. *Journal of Consulting and Clinical Psychology, 66*, 348–362.

Hanson, R. K., & Morton-Bourgon, K. E. (2004b). *The accuracy of recidivism risk instruments for sexual offenders: A meta-analysis* (PS4-36/2007E). Ottawa: Public Safety and Emergency Preparedness Canada.

Hanson, R. K., & Morton-Bourgon, K. E. (2005). The characteristics of persistent sexual offenders: A meta-analysis of recidivism studies. *Journal of Consulting and Clinical Psychology, 73*, 1154–1163.

Hanson, R. K., & Morton-Bourgon, K. E. (2009). The accuracy of recidivism risk assessments for sexual offenders: A meta-analysis of 188 prediction studies. *Psychological Assessment, 21*, 1–21.

Hanson, R. K., Scott, H., & Steffy, R. A. (1995). A comparison of child molesters and non-sexual criminals: Risk predictors and long-term recidivism. *Journal of Research in Crime and Delinquency, 32*, 325–337.

Hanson, R. K., & Thornton, D. (1999). *Static-99: Improving actuarial risk assessments for sex offenders* (1999–02). Ottawa: Department of the Solicitor General of Canada.

Hanson, R. K., & Thornton, D. (2000). Improving risk assessments for sex offenders: A comparison of three actuarial scales. *Law and Human Behavior, 24*, 119–136.

Hanson, R. K., & Thornton, D. (2003). *Notes on the development of Static-2002* (2003–01). Ottawa: Department of the Solicitor General.

Harcourt, B. E. (2007). *Against prediction: Profiling policing, and punishing in an actuarial age.* Chicago: The University of Chicago Press.

Hare, R. D. (1991). *The Revised Psychopathy Checklist.* Toronto: Multi-Health Systems.

Hare, R. D. (2003). *Hare Psychopathy Checklist-Revised (PCL-R)* (2nd ed.). Toronto: Multi-Health Systems.

Hare, R. D., & Neumann, C. N. (2008). Psychopathy as a clinical and empirical construct. *Annual Review of Clinical Psychology, 4*, 217–246. doi: 10.1146/annurev.clinpsy.3.022806.091452

Harris, G. T., & Rice, M. E. (2003). Actuarial assessment of risk among sex offenders. In R. A. Prentky, E. Janus, & M. Seto (Eds.), *Sexually coercive behavior: Understanding and management* (pp. 198–210). New York: Annals of the New York Academy.

Harris, G. T., & Rice, M. E. (2007a). Adjusting actuarial violence risk assessments based on aging or the passage of time. *Criminal Justice and Behavior, 34*, 297–313.

Harris, G. T., & Rice, M. E. (2007b). Characterizing the value of actuarial violence risk assessments. *Criminal Justice and Behavior, 34*, 1638–1658.

Harris, G. T., & Rice, M. E. (2013). Bayes and base rates: What is an informative prior for actuarial violence risk assessment? *Behavioral Sciences and the Law, 31*, 103–124. doi:10.1002/bsl.2048

Harris, G. T., Rice, M. E., & Quinsey, V. L. (1993). Violent recidivism of mentally disordered offenders: The development of a statistical prediction instrument. *Criminal Justice and Behavior, 20*, 315–335.

Harris, G. T., Rice, M. E., Quinsey, V. L., Lalumiere, M. L., Boer, D., & Lang, C. (2003). A multi-site comparison of actuarial risk instruments for sex offenders. *Psychological Assessment, 15*, 413–425.

Harris, G. T., Skilling, T. A., & Rice, M. E. (2001). The construct of psychopathy. In M. Tonry & N. Morris (Eds.), *Crime and justice: An annual review of research* (pp. 197–264). Chicago: University of Chicago Press.

Harris, K. M. (2009). *The national longitudinal study of adolescent health (add health) waves I and II, Wave III 2001–2002; Wave IV, 2007–2009*. Chapel Hill, NC: Carolina Population Center, University of North Carolina at Chapel Hill.

Hart, S. D. (2009). Evidence-based assessment of risk for sexual violence. *Journal of Criminal Justice, 1*, 143–165.

Hart, S. D., Kropp, P. R., Laws, D. R., Klaver, J., Logan, C., & Watt, K. A. (2003). *The risk for sexual violence protocol (RSVP)*. Burnaby, BC: Simon Fraser University, Mental Health, Law, and Policy Institute.

Hart, S. D., Laws, D. R., & Kropp, P. R. (2003). The promise and the peril of sex offender risk assessment. In T. Ward, D. R. Laws, & S. M. Hudson (Eds.), *Sexual deviance: Issues and controversies* (pp. 207–225). Newbury Park, CA: Sage.

Hart, S. D., Michie, C., & Cooke, D. J. (2007). Precision of actuarial risk assessment instruments: Evaluating the "margins of error" of group versus individual predictions of violence. *British Journal of Psychiatry, 190*, 60–65.

Hart, S. D., & Boer, D. (2010). Structured professional judgment guidelines for sexual violence risk assessment: The Sexual Violence Risk-20 (SVR-20) and Risk for Sexual Violence Protocol (RSVP). In R. K. Otto & K. S. Douglas (Eds.), *Handbook of violence risk assessment tools* (pp. 269–294). Abingdon, UK: Routledge.

Hart, S. D., & Logan, C. (2011). Formulation of violence risk using evidence-based assessment: The structured professional judgment approach. In P. Sturmey & M. McMurran (Eds.), *Forensic case formulation* (pp. 83–106). New York: Wiley.

Hastie, R., & Pennington, N. (1996). The O.J. Simpson stories: Behavioral scientists look at The People v. O.J. Simpson trial. *University of Colorado Law Review, 67*, 957–976.

Hastie, R., & Dawes, R. M. (2010). *Rational choice in an uncertain world. The psychology of judgment and decision making*. Thousand Oaks, CA: Sage.

Hatcher, L. (1994). *A step-by-step approach to using the SAS system for factor analysis and structural equation modeling*. Cary, NC: SAS Institute.

Haul, M. W., & Muehleman, T. (1986). Informed consent: The effects of clarity and specificity on disclosure in a clinical interview. *Psychotherapy, 23* (1), 93–101.

Haynes, S. N., & Lench, H. C. (2003). Incremental validity of new clinical assessment measures. *Psychological Assessment, 15*, 456–466.

Hegarty, T. (2010). "Power law distribution and solving the crime problem." *The Police Chief,* 28, 36. Retrieved from http://www.nxtbook.com/nxtbooks/naylor/CPIM1210/#/28.

Heilbrun, K. (March, 1988). Third party information in forensic assessment: Much needed, sometimes collected, poorly guided. *Paper presented at the mid-winter meeting of the American Psychology-Law Society (Division 41)*. Miami, FL: American Psychology-Law Society.

Heilbrun, K. (1992). The role of psychological testing in forensic assessment. *Law and Human Behavior, 16* (3), 257–272.

Heilbrun, K. (1997). Prediction versus management models relevant to risk assessment: The importance of legal decision-making context. *Law and Human Behavior, 21* (4), 347–359.

Heilbrun, K. (2001). *Principles of forensic mental health assessment*. New York: Kluwer/Plenum.

Heilbrun, K., Douglas, K. S., & Yasuhara, K. (2009). Violence-risk assessment: Core controversies. In J. Skeem, K. S. Douglas, & S. Lilienfeld (Eds.), *Psychological science in the courtroom: Controversies and consensus* (pp. 333–357). New York: Guilford Press.

Heilbrun, K., Nezu, C. M., Keeney, M., Chung, S., & Wasserman, A. L. (1998). Sexual offending: Linking assessment, intervention, and decision-making. *Psychology, Public Policy and Law, 4*, 138–174.

Heilbrun, K., Lee, R. J., & Cottle, C. C. (2005). Risk factors and intervention outcomes: Meta-analyses of juvenile offending. In K. Heilbrun, N. E. Goldstein, & R. E. Redding (Eds.), *Juvenile delinquency: Prevention, assessment, and intervention* (pp. 111–113). New York: Oxford University Press.

Heilbrun, K., Yasuhara, K., & Shah, S. A. (2010). Approaches to violence risk assessment: Overview and critical analysis. In R. Otto & K. S. Douglas (Eds.), *Handbook of violence risk assessment* (pp. 1–17). New York: Routledge.

Held, L., & Bové, D. S. (2014). *Applied statistical inference: Likelihood and Bayes*. New York: Springer. doi: 10.1007/978-3-642-37887-4

Helmus, L., & Hanson, R. K. (2007). Predictive validity of the Static-99 and Static-2002 for sex offenders on community supervision. *Sexual Offender Treatment, 2* (2), 1–14. Retrieved from http://www.sexual-offender-treatment.org/60.html.

Helmus, L., Hanson, R. K., Thornton, D., Babchishin, K. M., & Harris, A. J. (2012). Absolute recidivism rates predicted by Static-99R and Static-2002R sex offender risk assessment tools vary across samples: A meta-analysis. *Criminal Justice and Behavior, 39*, 1148–1171. doi:10.1177/0093854812443648

Helmus, L., Thornton, D., Hanson, R. K., & Babchishin, K. M. (2012). Improving the predictive accuracy of Static-99 and Static-2002 with older sex offenders: Revised age weights. *Sexual Abuse: A Journal of Research and Treatment, 24*, 64–100. doi:10.1177/1079063211409951

Helmus, L., & Thornton, D. (2014). The MATS-I risk assessment scale: Summary of methodological concerns and an empirical validation. *Sexual Abuse: A Journal of Research and Treatment*. Advance Online Publication. doi:10.1177/107906214529801

Herbert, W. (2010). Heuristics revealed: Understanding our sometimes perilous mental shortcuts. *Observer, 23*, 10–13.

Hirschi, T., & Gottfredson, M. (1983). Age and the explanation of crime. *American Journal of Sociology, 89*, 552–584.

Hodgins, S. (1997). An overview of research on the prediction of dangerousness. *Nordic Journal of Psychiatry, 51*, 33–88.

Holmes, R. C. (1961). *Composition and size of flood losses.* (Research Paper No. 70). Chicago: University of Chicago Department of Geography.

Hosmer, D. W., & Lemeshow, S. (2000). *Applied logistic regression.* New York: Wiley.

Huff Post Crime. (August 17, 2014). *One in six sex offenders change names to avoid registration: Study.* Retrieved from http://www.huffingtonpost.com/2012/07/15/sex-offenders-change-identity-study_n_1703282.html.

Hughes, L. (1980). *Probability forecasting: Reasons, procedures, problems* (NWS FCST24). Washington, DC: US Department of Commerce.

Hume, D. (2001). *An inquiry concerning human understanding*, section 12, Part III. Retrieved from http://www.bartleby.com/37/3/19.html.

Hutschnecker, A. (July 4, 1973). The stigma of seeing a psychiatrist. *New York Times*, 39.

In re Civil Commitment of Lingl, A12–0738, 2012 WL 5188139 (Minn. Ct. App. October 22, 2012).

In re Civil Commitment of Spicer, A13–2120, 2014 WL 4056029 (Minn. Ct. App. August 18, 2014).

In re Det. of Campbell, 124 P.3d 670 (Wash. Ct. App. 2005).

In re Rodriguez, 506 N.W.2d 660 (Minn. Ct. App. 1993).

Iowa County Attorney's Association. (2007). *Iowa County Attorney's Association statement on sex offender residency restrictions in Iowa.* Retrieved from http://csgjusticecenter.org/nrrc/publications/iowa-county-attorneys-association-statement-on-sex-offender-residency-restrictions-in-iowa-2.

Iowa Department of Human Rights. (2000). *The Iowa sex offender and recidivism 19.* Retrieved from http://www.state.ia.us/dhr/cjjp/images/pdf/01_pub/SexOffenderReport.pdf.

Jackson, J. (2006). Introducing fear of crime to risk research. *Risk Analysis, 26*, 253–264. doi:10.1111/j.1539-6924.2006.00715.x

Jackson, R. L., Rogers, R., & Shuman, D. W. (2004). The adequacy and accuracy of sexually violent predator evaluations: Contextualized risk assessment. *International Journal of Forensic Mental Health, 3*, 115–129.

Jacobson v. Massachusetts, 197 U.S. 11 (1905).

Jaffe, E. (2006). Regression toward the mean: Debating the biological and social origins of human cruelty. *Observer, 19*, 21–24.

Janis, I. L. (1982). *Groupthink.* Boston, MA: Houghton Mifflin.

Janus, E. S. (1996). Preventing sexual violence: Setting principled constitutional boundaries on sex offender commitments. *Indiana Law Journal, 72* (1), 157–214.

Janus, E. S. (2000). Civil commitment as social control: Managing the risk of sexual violence. In M. Brown & J. Pratt (Eds.), *Dangerous offenders: Punishment and order* (pp. 71–90). New York: Routledge.

Janus, E. S. (2001). Sexual predators. In J. Dessler (Ed.), *Encyclopedia of Crime & Justice, Vol. 4* (2nd ed.) (pp. 1475–1483). New York: Macmillan Reference USA.

Janus, E. S. (2006). *Failure to protect: America's sexual predator laws and the rise of the preventive state.* Ithaca, NY: Cornell University Press.

Janus, E. S. (2007). Don't think of a predator: Changing frames for better sexual violence prevention. *Sex Offender Law Report 8* (6), 81–96.

Janus, E. S., & Prentky, R. A. (2003). Forensic use of actuarial risk assessment with sex offenders: Accuracy, admissibility and accountability. *American Criminal Law Review, 40* (4), 1443–1499.

Janus, E. S., & Prentky, R. A. (2008) Sexual predator laws: A two-decade retrospective. *Federal Sentencing Reporter, 21* (2), 90–97.

Janus, E. S. (2010). The preventive state: When is prevention of harm harmful? In M. Nash & A. Williams (Eds.), *Handbook of public protection* (pp. 316–334). Abingdon, NY: Willan Publishing.

Janus, E. S. (2011). Sexual violence, gender politics, and outsider jurisprudence: Lessons from the American experience in prevention. In B. McSherry & P. Keyzer (Eds.), *Dangerous people: Policy, prediction, and practice* (pp. 73–82). New York: Routledge.

Jenkin, C. M. (1998). *Moral panic: Changing concepts of the child molester in modern America.* New Haven, CT: Yale University Press.

Jenkin, C. M. (2006). Risk perception and terrorism: Applying the psychometric paradigm. *Homeland Security Affairs, II*, 2. Retrieved from http://hsaj.org/?fullarticla=2.2.6.

Jenkins, P. (1992). *Intimate enemies: Moral panics in contemporary Great Britain.* New York: Aldine de Gruyter.

Jenkins, P. (2000). *The outer edges: Horror and the media in the late 1940s.* Retrieved from http://www.personal.psu.edu/faculty/j/p/jpj1/edges.htm.

Jennings, D. L., Amabile, T. M., & Ross, L. (1982). Informal covariation assessment: Data-based versus theory-based judgments. In D. Kahneman, P. Slovic, & A. Tversky (Eds.), *Judgment under uncertainty: Heuristics and biases* (pp. 211–230). Cambridge, UK: Cambridge University Press.

Jessica's Law. (2006). Cal. Legis. Serv. Prop. 83.

Johannesson, M. (1995). The relationship between cost-effectiveness analysis and cost-benefit analysis. *Social Science and Medicine, 41* (4), 483–489. doi:10.1016/0277-9536(94)00353-U

Joslyn, S., & LeClerc, J. (2013). Decisions with uncertainty: The glass half full. *Current Directions in Psychological Science, 22* (4), 308–315. doi:10.1177/0963721413481473

Junger, S. (1997). *The perfect storm.* New York: W.W. Norton & Company.

Kahneman, D. (1991). Judgment and decision making: A personal view. *Psychological Science,* 2 (3), 142–145.

Kahneman, D. (2003a). A perspective on judgment and choice: Mapping bounded rationality. *American Psychologist, 58*, 697–720.

Kahneman, D. (2003b). Maps of bounded rationality: Psychology for behavioral economics. *The American Economic Review, 9*, 1449–1475.

Kahneman, D. (2011a). The surety of fools. *The New York Times Magazine,* 30–62.

Kahneman, D. (2011b). *Thinking, fast and slow.* New York: Farrar, Straus and Giroux.

Kahneman, D., & Tversky, A. (1972). Subjective probability: A judgment of representativeness. *Cognitive Psychology, 3*, 430–454.

Kahneman, D., & Tversky, A. (1982a). On the psychology of prediction. In D. Kahneman, P. Slovic, & A. Tversky (Eds.), *Judgment under uncertainty: Heuristics and biases* (pp. 48–68). New York: Cambridge University Press.

Kahneman, D., & Tversky, A. (1982b). Variants of uncertainty. In D. Kahneman, P. Slovic, & A. Tversky (Eds.), *Judgment under uncertainty: Heuristics and biases* (pp. 509–520). New York: Cambridge University Press.

Kahneman, D., & Tversky, A. (1982c). Preface. In D. Kahneman, P. Slovic, & A. Tversky (Eds.), *Judgment under uncertainty: Heuristics and biases* (pp. xi–xiii). New York: Cambridge University Press.

Kansas Sex Offender Policy Board. (2007). *2007 Report.* Retrieved from http://www.calcasa.org/wp-content/uploads/2007/11/sopbreport.pdf.

Kansas v. Hendricks, 521 U.S. 346 (1997).

Karpman, B. (1951). The sexual psychopath. *Journal of Criminal Law, Criminology, and Police Science, 42*, 184–198.

Kasperson, R. E., Jhaveri, N., & Kasperson, J. X. (2000). Stigma and the social amplification of risk. In J. Flynn, P. Slovic, & H. Kunreuther (Eds.), *Risk, media, and stigma: Understanding public challenges to modern science and technology* (pp. 9–27). London: Earthscan.

Kasperson, J. X, Kasperson, R. E., Pidgeon, N., & Slovic, P. (Eds.). (2003). The social amplication of risk: Assessing fifteen years of research and theory. In N. Pidgeon, R. E. Kasperson, & P. Slovic, *The social amplification of risk*, (pp. 13–46). Cambridge: Cambridge University Press.

Kasperson, R. E., & Kasperson, J. (2005a). *The social contours of risk: Volume I: Publics, risk communication, and the social amplification of risk.* New York: Earthscan Publications (Routledge).

Kasperson, R. E., & Kasperson, J. (2005b). *The social contours of risk: Volume II: Risk analysis, corporations, and the globalization of risk.* New York: Earthscan Publications (Routledge).

Kasperson, R. E., Renn, O., Slovic, P., Brown, H. S., Emel, J., Goble, R. et al. (1988). The social amplification of risk: A conceptual framework. *Risk Analysis, 8*, 177–187.

Keppel, G. (1982). *Design and analysis: A researcher's handbook* (2nd ed.). Englewood Cliffs, NJ: Prentice Hall.

Kestin, S., & Williams, D. (September 19, 2013). Head of Florida's sex predator program resigns. *Sun Sentinel.* http://articles.sun-sentinel.com/2013-09-19/news/fl-sex-predator-director-resigns-20130919_1_cherish-perrywinkle-central-florida.

Kestin, S., & Williams, D. (September 22, 2013). State to tighten rules for sex-offender screening. *Sun Sentinel.* http://articles.sun-sentinel.com/2013-09-22/news/fl-sex-predator-program-changes-20130922_1_sexually-violent-predator-program-dan-montaldi-automatic-psychological-evaluation.

Keyes, J. M. (2014). *There are many variations of this quote.* Retrieved from http://quoteinvestigator.com/2011/07/22keynes-change-mind.

Kim, J. O. (1978). *Introduction to factor analysis: What is it and how to do it.* Newbury Park, CA: Sage.

Kim, J. O., & Mueller, C. W. (1978). *Factor analysis: Statistical methods and practical issues.* Newbury Park, CA: Sage.

Kingston, D. A., Seto, M., Firestone, P., & Bradford, J. M. (2010). Comparing indicators of sexual sadism as predictors of recidivism among adult male sexual offenders. *Journal of Consulting and Clinical Psychology, 78*, 574–584.

Kirwin, J. (2005). *Civil commitment of sexual predators in Minnesota: Legal overview.* Retrieved from http://www.mcaa-mn.org/content.aspx?ContentID=401.

Klein, J. F. (1976). The dangerousness of dangerous offender legislation: Forensic folklore revisited. *Canadian Journal Criminology & Corrections, 18*, 109–122.

Kleinmuntz, B. (1968a). *Formal representation of human judgment.* New York: John Wiley & Sons Inc.

Kleinmuntz, B. (1968b). The processing of clinical information by man and machine. In B. Kleinmuntz (Ed.) *Formal representation of human judgment.* New York: John Wiley & Sons.

Klinke, A., & Renn, O. (2012). A new approach to risk evaluation and management: Risk-based, precaution-based, and discourse-based strategies. *Risk Analysis, 22* (4), 701–711.

Knight, R. A., & Prentky, R. A. (1990). Classifying sexual offenders: The development and corroboration of taxonomic models. In W. L. Marshall, R. Laws, & H. Barbaree (Eds.), *Handbook of sexual assault: Issues, theories and treatment of the offender* (pp. 23–52). New York: Plenum.

Knight, R. A., & Sims-Knight, J. E. (2003). The developmental antecedents of sexual coercion against women: Testing alternative hypotheses with structural equation modeling. In R. A. Prentky, E. Janus, & M. Seto (Eds.), *Sexually coercive behavior: Understanding and management* (pp. 72–85). New York: Annals of the New York Academy of Sciences.

Knighton, J. C., Murrie, D. C., Boccaccini, M. T., & Turner, D. B. (2014). How likely is "likely to reoffend" in sex offender civil commitment trials? *Law and Human Behavior, 38* (3) 293–304.

Kock, R. (1999). *80-20 principle: The secret to success by achieving more with less.* New York: Doubleday.

Koehler, J. J. (1996). The base rate fallacy reconsidered: Descriptive, normative, and methodological challenges. *Behavioral and Brain Sciences, 19*, 1–53.

Konnikova, M. (2013). *Mastermind. How to think like Sherlock Holmes.* New York: Viking.

Korematsu v. United States, 323 U.S. 214 (1944).

Kropp, P. R., Hart, S. D., Webster, C. D., & Eaves, D. (1995). *Manual for the spousal assault risk assessment guide.* Vancouver, BC: The British Columbia Institute on Family Violence.

Kruttschnitt, C., Uggen, C., & Shelton, K. (2000). Predictors of desistance among sex offenders: The interaction of formal and informal social controls. *Justice Quarterly, 17*, 61–87.

LaFond, J. Q. (1998). The costs of enacting a sexual predator law. *Psychology, Public Policy and Law, 4* (12), 468–504.

LaFond, J. Q. (2005). *Preventing sexual violence: How society should cope with sex offenders.* Washington, DC: American Psychological Association.

Lalumiere, M. L., Harris, G. T., Quinsey, V. L., & Rice, M. E. (2005). *The cause of rape: Understanding individual differences in male propensity for sexual aggression*. Washington, DC: American Psychological Association.

Lancaster, R. N. (2011). *Sex panic and the punitive state*. Berkeley, CA: University of California Press.

Landers, C. (December 10, 2008). Exiles on main street. *Baltimore City Pages*. Retrieved from http://www2.citypaper.com/music/story.asp?id=17180.

Laney, G. P. (2008). *Residence restrictions for released sex offenders: CRS Report for Congress Domestic Social Policy Division (RL34353)*. Retrieved from http://www.criminallawlibraryblog.com.

Langevin, R. (1983). *Sexual strands: Understanding and treatment of sexual anomalies in men*. Hillsdale, NJ: Lawrence Erlbaum.

Langevin, R. (2006). Acceptance and completion of treatment among sex offenders. *International Journal of Offender Therapy and Comparative Criminology, 50*, 402–417.

Langhan, P. A., Schmitt, E. L., & Durose, M. R. (2003) *Recidivism of sex offenders released from prison in 1994*. U.S. Department of Justice, Bureau of Justice Programs Bureau of Justice Statistics.

Långström, N. (2004). Accuracy of actuarial procedures for assessment of sexual offender recidivism risk may vary across ethnicity. *Sexual Abuse: A Journal of Research and Treatment, 16*, 107–120.

*Langton, C. M., Barbaree, H., Hansen, K. T., & Peacock, E. J. (2007). Reliability and validity of the Static-2002 among adult sexual offenders with reference to treatment status. *Criminal Justice and Behavior, 34*, 616–640.

*Langton, C. M., Barbaree, H. E., Harkins, L., Arenovich, T., McNamee, J., Peacock, E. J. et al. (2008). Denial and minimization among sex offenders: Post-treatment presentation and association with sexual recidivism. *Criminal Justice and Behavior, 35*, 69–98.

*Langton, C. M., Barbaree, H. E., Harkins, L., & Peacock, E. J. (2006). Sex offenders' response to treatment and its association with recidivism as a function of psychopathy. *Sexual Abuse: A Journal of Research and Treatment, 18*, 99–120.

*Langton, C. M., Barbaree, H., Harkins, L., Peacock, E. J., & Arenovich, T. (2008). Further investigation of findings reported for the Minnesota Sex Offender Screening Tool: Revised. *Journal of Interpersonal Violence, 23*, 1363–1379.

Langton, C. M., Harkins, L., Peacock, E. J., & Barbaree, H. (2003). *Core dimensions underlying risk assessment instruments for sexual offenders*. Toronto: 111th Annual Convention of the American Psychological Association.

*Langton, C. M., Barbaree, H. E., Seto, M., Peacock, E. J., Harkins, L., & Hansen, K. T. (2007). Actuarial assessment of risk for re-offense among adult sex offenders: Evaluating the predictive accuracy of the Static-2002 and five other instruments. *Criminal Justice and Behavior, 34*, 37–59.

Lasher, M. P., & McGrath, R. J. (2012). The impact of community notification on sex offender reintegration: A quantitative review of the research literature. *International Journal of Offender Therapy and Comparative Criminology, 56*, 6–28. doi:10.1177/0306624X10387524

Laws, D. R. (2000). Sexual offending as a public health problem: A North American perspective. *The Journal of Sexual Aggression, 5*, 30–44.

Laws, D. R., & O'Donohue, W. (1997). *Sexual deviance: Theory, assessment and treatment.* New York: Guilford Press.

Laws, D. R., & O'Donohue, W. (2008). *Sexual deviance: Theory, assessment and treatment* (2nd ed.). New York: Guilford Press.

Leon, C. (2011). *Sex fiends, perverts, and pedophiles: Understanding sex crime in America.* New York: New York University Press.

Levenson, J. S., & Cotter, L. P. (2005). 1000 feet from danger or one step from the absurd? *International Journal of Offender Therapy and Comparative Criminology, 49*, 168–178.

Levenson, J. S., & Harris, A. J. (2012). 100,000 sex offenders missing . . . or are they? Deconstruction of an urban legend. *Criminal Justice Policy Review, 23*, 375–386. doi:10.1177/0887403411415398

Lewis, J. G., & Weigert, A. (1985). Trust as a social reality. *Social Forces, 63*, 967–985.

Lezzoni, L. I. (1994). Risk and outcomes. In L. I. Lezzoni (Ed.), *Risk adjustment for measuring health care outcomes* (pp. 1–28). Ann Arbor, MI: Health Administration Press.

Lichtenstein, S., & Fischhoff, B. (1980). Training for calibration. *Organizational Behavior and Human Performance, 26*, 149–171.

Lichtenstein, S., & Slovic, P. (2006). *Construction of preference.* Cambridge: Cambridge University Press.

Lidz, C., Mulvey, E., & Gardner, W. (1993). The accuracy of predictions of violence to others. *Journal of the American Medical Association, 269*, 1007–1011.

Linden, L. L., & Rockoff, J. E. (2006). *There goes the neighborhood? Estimates of the impact of crime risk on property values from Megan's laws* (NBER working paper #12253). Cambridge, MA: National Bureau of Economic Research. Retrieved from http://nber.org/papers/w12253.

Lipsey, M. W., & Derzon, J. H. (1998). Predictors of violent or serious delinquency in adolescence and early childhood: A synthesis of longitudinal research. In R. Loeber & D. P. Farrington (Eds.), *Serious and violent juvenile offenders: Risk factors and successful intervention* (pp. 86–105). Thousand Oaks, CA: Sage.

Lipton, P. (2004). *Inference to the best explanation* (2nd ed.). London: Routledge.

Litwack, T. (1984). The moral foundations of the insanity defense. *Criminal Justice Ethics, 3*, 12–19.

Litwack, T. R. & Schlesinger, L. B. (1999). Dangerousness risk assessments: Research, legal, and clinical considerations. In A. Hess & I. Weiner (Eds.), *Handbook of forensic psychology* (2nd ed.) (pp. 205–207). New York: John Wiley and Sons.

Loeber, R., Farrington, D. P., Stouthamer-Loeber, M., Moffitt, T. E., & Caspi, A. (1998). The development of male offending: Key findings from the first decade of the Pittsburgh youth study. *Studies in Crime and Crime Prevention, 7*, 141–172.

Loewenstein, G. F., Weber, E. U., Hsee, C. K., & Welch, N. (2001). Risk as feelings. *Psychological Bulletin, 127* (2), 267–286.

Logan, W. A. (2003). Sex offender registration and community notification: Emerging legal and research issues. In R. A. Prentky, E. Janus, & M. Seto (Eds.),

Sexually coercive behavior: Understanding and management (pp. 337–351). New York: Annals of the New York Academy of Sciences.

Long, M. L., Alison, L. A., & McManus, M. A. (2012). Child pornography and likelihood of contact abuse: A comparison between contact child sexual offenders and noncontact offenders. *Sexual Abuse: A Journal of Research and Treatment, 25*, 370–395.

Looman, J. (2006). Comparison of two risk assessment instruments for sexual offenders. *Sexual Abuse: A Journal of Research and Treatment, 18*, 193–206.

Losel, F., & Schmucker, M. (2005). The effectiveness of treatment for sexual offenders: A comparative meta-analysis. *Journal of Experimental Criminology, 1*, 146.

Lussier, P., & Healey, J. (2009). Rediscovering Quetelet, again: The "aging" offender and the prediction of reoffending in a sample of adult sex offenders. *Justice Quarterly, 26*, 827–856.

Lussier, P., & Davies, G. (2011). A person-oriented perspective on sexual offenders, offending trajectories, and risk of recidivism: A new challenge for policymakers, risk assessors, and actuarial prediction? *Psychology, Public Policy and Law, 17*, 530–561.

Lussier, P., Tzoumakis, J. C., Cale, J., & Amirault, J. (2010). Criminal trajectories of adult sex offenders and the age effect: Examining the dynamic aspect of offending in adulthood. *International Criminal Justice Review, 20*, 147–168. doi:10.1177/1057567710368360

Machlis, G. E., & Rosa, E. A. (1990). Desired risk: Broadening the social amplification of risk framework. *Risk Analysis, 10* (1), 161–168. doi:10.1111/j.1539-6924.1990.tb01030.x

Magee, B. (1975). *Popper*. Glasgow, UK: Fontana/Collins.

Maksimovic, V., Weber, E. U., Hsee, C. K., & Welch, E. S. (2001). Risk as feelings. *Psychological Bulletin, 127*, 267–286.

Malamuth, N. M. (2003). Criminal and non-criminal sexual aggressors: Integrating psychopathy in a hierarchical-mediational confluence model. In R. A. Prentky, E. Janus, & M. Seto (Eds.), *Sexually coercive behavior: Understanding and management* (pp. 33–58). New York: Annals of the New York Academy of Sciences.

Mann, R. E., Hanson, R. K., & Thornton, D. (2010). Assessing risk for sexual recidivism: Some proposals on the nature of psychologically meaningful risk factors. *Sexual Abuse: A Journal of Research and Treatment, 22*, 191–217.

Mannes, A. E., & Moore, D. A. (2013). A behavioral demonstration of overconfidence in judgment. *Psychological Science, 24*(7), 1190–1197. doi:10.1177/0956797612470700

Marchese, M. C. (1992). Clinical versus actuarial prediction: A review of the literature. *Perceptual and Motor Skills, 75*, 583–594.

Mariner, W. K., Annas, G. J., & Glantz, L. H. (2005). Jacobson v. Massachusetts: It's not your great-great grandfather's public health law. *American Journal of Public Health, 95* (4), 581–590. doi: 10.2105/AJPH.2004.055160

Marques, J. K., Day, D. M., Nelson, C., & West, M. A. (1993). Findings and recommendations from California's experimental treatment program. In G. C. Nagayama, R. Hirschman, J. R. Graham, & M. S. Zaragoza (Eds.), *Sexual aggression: Issues in etiology, assessment, and treatment* (pp. 197–214). London: Taylor & Francis.

Marques, J. K., Nelson, C., Alarcon, J. M., & Day, D. M. (2000). Preventing relapse in sex offenders: What we have learned from SOTEP's experimental treatment program. In D. R. Laws, S. M. Hudson, & T. Ward (Eds.), *Remaking relapse prevention with sex offenders: A sourcebook* (pp. 321–340). Thousand Oaks, CA: Sage.

Marques, J. K., Wiederanders, M., Day, D. M., Nelson, C., & van Ommeren, A. (2005). Effects of a relapse prevention program on sexual recidivism: Final results from California's sex offender treatment and evaluation project (SOTEP). *Sexual Abuse: A Journal of Research and Treatment, 17* (1), 79–107.

Marsh, J. E. (2003). Empirical support for the United States Supreme Court's protection of the psychotherapist-patient privilege. *Ethics and Behavior, 13*(4), 385–400.

Marshall, W. L., & Barbaree, H. E. (1984). A behavioral view of rape. *International Journal of Law and Psychiatry, 7*, 51–77.

Marshall, W. L., & Barbaree, H. E. (1990). An integrated theory of the etiology of sexual offending. In W. L. Marshall, R. Laws, & H. E. Barbaree (Eds.), *Handbook of sexual assault: Issues, theories, and treatment of the offender* (pp. 257–275). New York: Plenum.

Marshall, W. L., & Marshall, L. E. (2007). The utility of the random controlled trial for evaluating sexual offender treatment: The gold standard or an inappropriate strategy? *Sexual Abuse: A Journal of Research and Treatment, 19*, 175–191.

Marshall, W. L., & Marshall, L. E. (2008). Good clinical practice and the evaluation of treatment: A response to Seto et al. *Sexual Abuse: A Journal of Research and Treatment, 20*, 256–260.

Matson, S. (2001). *Community notification and education*. Silver Spring, MD: Center for Sex Offender Management.

Mausner, B., & Mausner, J. (1955). A study of the anti-scientific attitude. *Scientific American, 192*, 35–39.

Maynard, R. (April 1970). Doctor would test children to curb crime. *The Los Angeles Times*, p. 9.

Mayr, E. (1988). *Toward a new philosophy of biology*. Cambridge, MA: Harvard University Press.

Mazur, A. (2004). *True warnings and false alarms: Evaluating fears about the health risks of technology, 1948–1971*. Washington, DC: RFF Press.

McAlinden, A. M. (2006). Managing risk: From regulation to the reintegration of sexual offenders. *Criminology and Criminal Justice, 6*, 197–218. doi:10.1177/1748895806062981

McCammon, I. (2004). Heuristic traps in recreational avalanche accidents: Evidence and implications. *Avalanche News, 67*, 1–10.

McCann, K., & Lussier, P. (2008). Antisociality, sexual deviance, and sexual reoffending in juvenile sex offenders: A meta-analytical investigation. *Youth Violence and Juvenile Justice, 6*, 363–385.

McGrath, R. J., & Cumming, G. F. (2003). *Sex offender treatment needs and progress scale manual*. Centre for Sex Offender Management (CSOM). Retrieved from http://www.csom.org/ref/assesment.html.

McGrath, R. J., Cumming, G. F., Burchard, B., Zeoli, B., & Ellerby, L. (2010). *Current practices and emerging trends in sexual abuser management: The safer society 2009*. Brandon, VT: Safer Society Press.

McGrath, R. J., Cumming, G. F., & Livingston, J. A. (2005). *Predictive validity of the sex offender treatment needs and progress scale (TPS)*. Salt Lake City, UT: Annual Research and Treatment Conference of the Association for the Treatment of Sexual Abusers.

McGrath, R. J., Hoke, S. E., Livingston, J. A., & Cumming, G. F. (2001). *The Vermont Assessment of Sex Offender Risk (VASOR): An initial reliability and validity study*. San Antonio, TX: Annual Research and Treatment Conference of the Association for the Treatment of Sexual Abusers.

McGrath, R. J., Lasher, M. P., & Cumming, G. F. (2012). The Sex Offender Treatment Intervention and Progress Scale (SOTIPS) psychometric properties and incremental predictive validity with Static-99R. *Sexual Abuse: A Journal of Research and Treatment, 24*(5), 431–458. doi: 10.1177/1079063211432475

McKillop, N., Smallbone, S., Wortley, R., & Andjic, I. (2012). Offender's attachment and sexual abuse onset: A test of theoretical propositions. *Sexual Abuse: A Journal of Research and Treatment, 24*, 591–610.

McMahon, P. M. (2000). The public health approach to the prevention of sexual violence. *Sexual Abuse: A Journal of Research and Treatment, 12*, 27–36.

McMahon, P. M., & Puett, R. C. (1999). Child sexual abuse as a public health issue: Recommendations of an expert panel. *Sexual Abuse: A Journal of Research and Treatment, 11*, 257–266.

Meehl, P. E. (1954). *Clinical versus statistical prediction: A theoretical analysis and review of the evidence*. Minneapolis, MN: University of Minneapolis Press.

Meehl, P. E. (1978). Theoretical risks and tabular asterisks: Sir Karl, Sir Ronald, and the slow progress of soft psychology. *Journal of Consulting and Clinical Psychology, 46*, 806–834.

Meehl, P. E. (1996). *Clinical versus statistical prediction: A theoretical analysis and a review of the evidence*. Minneapolis, MN: University of Minnesota Press.

Meehl, P. E. (1998). *The power of quantitative thinking*. Chicago: Association for Psychological Science.

Meehl, P. E., & Rosen, L. (1955). Antecedent probability and the efficiency of psychometric signs, patterns, or cutting scores. *Psychological Bulletin, 52*, 194–216.

Megargee, E. (1981). Methodological problems in the prediction of violence. In J. Hays, T. Roberts, & K. Solway (Eds.), *Violence and the violent individual* (pp. 179–191). New York: Spectrum.

Melton, G. B., Petrila, J., Poythress, N. G., & Slobogin, C. (2007). *Psychological evaluations for the courts: A handbook for mental health professionals and attorneys*. New York: Guilford Press.

Menzies, R., Webster, C. D., McMain, S., Staley, S., & Scaglione, R. (1994). The dimensions of dangerousness revisited. *Law and Human Behavior, 18*, 1–28.

Mercado, C. C., & Ogloff, J. R. (2006). Risk and preventive detention of sex offenders in Australia and the United States. *International Journal of Law and Psychiatry, 30*, 49–59.

Mercy, J. A., & O'Carroll, P. W. (1988). New directions in violence prediction: The public health arena. *Violence and Victims, 3*, 285–301.

Mercy, J. A. (1999). Having new eyes: Viewing child sexual abuse as a public health problem. *Sexual Abuse: A Journal of Research and Treatment, 11*, 317–325.

Merluzzi, A. (February 2014). Cognition colored by emotion. *Observer, 27* (2), 9–10.

Millard v. Harris, 406 F.2d 964 (D.C. Cir. 1968).

Miller, T. R., Cohen, M. A., & Wiersema, B. (1996). *Victim costs and consequences: A new look* (NCJ 155282). Washington, DC: Office of Justice Programs, Department of Justice. Retrieved from https://www.ncjrs.gov/pdfffiles/viccost.pdf.

Mills, J. F., Kroner, D. G., & Morgan, R. D. (2011). *Clinician's guide to violence risk assessment*. New York: Guilford Publications.

Miner, M., & Dwyer, M. (1995). Analysis of dropouts from outpatient sex offender treatment. *Journal of Psychology and Human Sexuality, 7* (3), 77–94.

Minnesota Department of Corrections. (2003). *Level three sex offenders: Residential placement issues*. Retrieved from http://www.leg.state.mn.us/docs/2003/mandated/030175.pdf.

Moffitt, T. E. (1991). *Juvenile delinquency: Seed of a career in violent crime, just sowing wild oats—or both?* Washington, DC: Science and Public Policy Seminars of the Federation of Behavioral, Psychological, and Cognitive Sciences.

Moffitt, T. E. (1993). Adolescence-limited and life-course persistent antisocial behavior: A developmental taxonomy. *Psychological Review, 100*, 674–701.

Moffitt, T. E., Arseneaultb, L., Belsky, D., Dickson, N., Hancox, R. J., Harrington, H. et al. (2011). A gradient of childhood self-control predicts health, wealth, and public safety. *Vol. 108. National Academy of Sciences* (pp. 2693–2698). http://dx.doi.org/10.1073/pnas.1010076108.

Moffitt, T. E., Poulton, R., & Caspi, A. (2013). Lifelong impact of early self-control: Childhood self-discipline predicts adult quality of life. *American Scientist, 101*, 352. doi:10.1511/2013.104.352

Mokros, A., Dombert, B., Osterheider, M., Zappalà, A., & Santtila, P. (2010). Assessment of pedophilic sexual interest with an attentional choice reaction time task. *Archives of Sexual Behavior, 39*, 1081–1090. doi: 10.1007/s10508-009-953

Monahan, J. (1975). The prediction of violence. In D. Chappell & J. Monahan (Eds.), *Violence and criminal justice* (pp. 15–31). Lexington, MA: Lexington Books.

Monahan, J. (1976). The prevention of violence. In J. Monahan (Ed.), *Community mental health and the criminal justice system* (pp. 13–34). New York: Pergamon Press.

Monahan, J. (1981). *Predicting violent behavior: An assessment of clinical techniques*. Beverly Hills, CA: Sage.

Monahan, J. (1984). The prediction of violent behavior: Toward a second generation of theory and policy. *American Journal of Psychiatry, 141* (1), 10–15.

Monahan, J. (1985). Evaluating potentially violent persons. In C. P. Ewing (Ed.), *Psychology, psychiatry and the law: A clinical forensic handbook* (pp. 9–39). Sarasota, FL: Professional Resource Exchange Inc.

Monahan, J. (1996). Violence prediction: The past twenty and the next twenty years. *Criminal Justice and Behavior, 23*, 107–120.

Monahan, J. (2003). Judicial decision thresholds for violence risk management. *International Journal of Forensic Mental Health, 2*, 1–6.

Monahan, J. (2008). Statistical literacy: A prerequisite for evidence-based medicine. *Psychological Science in the Public Interest, 21*, 15–17. doi:10.1111/j.1539-6053.2008.00033_1.x

Monahan, J., & Appelbaum, P. (2000). Reducing violence risk: Diagnostically based clues from the MacArthur Violence Risk Assessment Study. In S. Hodgins (Ed.), *Violence among the mentally ill: Effective treatments and management strategies* (pp. 19–34). Boston, MA: Kluwer Academic Publishers.

Monahan, J., & Cummings, L. (1975). Social policy implications of the inability to predict violence. *Journal of Social Issues, 31*, 153–163.

Monahan, J., Heilbrun, K., Silver, E., Nabors, E., Bone, J., & Slovic, P. (2002). Communicating violence risk: Frequency formats, vivid outcomes, and forensic settings. *International Journal of Forensic Mental Health, 1*, 121–126.

Monahan, J., & Silver, E. (2003). Judicial decision thresholds for violence risk management. *International Journal of Forensic Mental Health,* 2 (1), 1–6.

Monahan, J., & Steadman, H. (1994a). *Violence and mental disorder: Developments in risk assessment.* Chicago: University of Chicago Press.

Monahan, J., & Steadman, H. (1994b). Toward a rejuvenation of risk assessment research. In J. Monahan & H. Steadman (Eds.), *Violence and mental disorder: Developments in risk assessment* (pp. 1–17). Chicago: University of Chicago Press.

Monahan, J., & Steadman, H. (1996). Violent storms and violent people. How meteorology can inform risk communication in mental health law. *American Psychologist, 51*, 931–938.

Monahan, J., & Wexler, D. (1978). A definite maybe: Proof and probability in civil commitment. *Law and Human Behavior,* 2 (1), 37–42.

Monahan, J., Steadman, H., Silver, E., Appelbaum, P., Robbins, P., Mulvey, E. et al. (2001). *Rethinking risk assessment: The MacArthur study of mental disorder and violence.* New York: Oxford University Press.

Moor, A., Ben-Meir, E., Golan-Shapira, D., & Farchi, M. (2013). Rape: A trauma of paralyzing dehumanization. *Journal of Aggression, Maltreatment and Trauma, 22*, 1051–1069.

Moore, D. A., & Healy, P. J. (2008). The trouble with overconfidence. *Psychological Review, 115*, 502–517. doi:10.1037/0033-295X.115.2.502

Mossman, D. (1994a). Assessing predictions of violence: Being accurate about accuracy. *Journal of Consulting and Clinical Psychology, 62*, 783–792.

Mossman, D. (1994b). Is expert psychiatric testimony fundamentally immoral? *International Journal of Law and Psychiatry, 17*, 347–368.

Mossman, D. (2006). Another look at interpreting risk categories. *Sexual Abuse: A Journal of Research and Treatment, 18*, 41–63.

Mossman, D. (2013). Evaluating risk assessments using receiver operating characteristics analysis: Rationale, advantages, insights, and limitations. *Behavioral Sciences and the Law, 31*, 23–39.

Mossman, D., & Hart, K. J. (1996). Presenting evidence of malingering to courts: Insights from decision theory. *Behavioral Sciences and the Law, 14* (3), 271–291.

Mulvey, E., & Lidz, C. W. (1984). Clinical considerations in the prediction of dangerousness in mental patients. *Clinical Psychology Review, 4*, 379–401.

Mulvey, E., & Lidz, C. W. (1985). Back to basics: A critical analysis of dangerousness research in a new legal environment. *Law and Human Behavior, 9*, 209–219.

Mulvey, E., & Lidz, C. W. (1995). Conditional prediction: A model for research on dangerousness to others in a new era. *International Journal of Law and Psychiatry, 18*, 129–143.

Murano, G. (2013). *Most curious anti-rape interventions.* Retrieved from http://www.oddee.com/item_98705.aspx.

Murrie, D. C., Boccaccini, M. T., Guarnera, L. A., & Rufino, K. A. (2013). Are forensic experts biased by the side that retained them? *Psychological Science, 24*, 1889–1897. doi:10.1177/0956797613481812

Myers, D. G., & Lamm, H. (1975). The polarizing effect of group discussion. *American Scientist, 63*, 297–303.

Myers, D. G., & Lamm, H. (1976). The group polarization phenomenon. *Psychological Bulletin, 83* (4), 602–627.

Myers, D. G., & Kaplan, M. F. (1976). Group-induced polarization in simulated juries. *Personality and Social Psychology Bulletin, 2*, 63–66.

Myers, R. (2002). *U.S. Supreme court holds that mandatory prison treatment program requiring admission of guilt does not violate convicted sex offender's constitutional rights. Sex Offender Law Report, 3* (5), 67–68(2). ISSN 1529-0697.

Naqvi, N., Shiv, B., & Bechara, A. (2006). The role of emotion in decision making: A cognitive neuroscience perspective. *Current Directions in Psychological Science, 15*, 260–264.

National Research Council. (1989). *Improving risk communication.* Washington, DC: National Academy Press.

Netter, B. (2007). Using group statistics to sentence individual criminals: An ethical and statistical critique of the Virginia risk assessment program. *Journal of Criminal Law & Criminology, 97*, 699–730.

Nezu, A. M., & Nezu, C. M. (Eds.). (1989). *Clinical decision-making in behavior therapy: A problem-solving perspective.* Champaign, IL: Research Press.

Nicholaichuk, T., Gordon, A., Gu, D., & Wong, S. (2000). Outcome of an institutional sexual offender treatment program: A comparison between treated and matched untreated offenders. *Sexual Abuse: A Journal of Research and Treatment, 12*, 139–153.

Nisbett, R. E., & Ross, L. (1980). *Human inference: Strategies and shortcomings of social judgment.* Englewood Cliffs, NJ: Prentice Hall.

Norusis, M. J. (2005). *SPSS 13.0. Statistical procedures companion.* Chicago: SPSS.

Nowell, D., & Spruill, J. (1993). If it's not absolutely confidential, will information be disclosed? *Professional Psychology: Research and Practice, 24*, 367–369.

Nuffield, J. (1982). *Parole decision-making in Canada: Research towards decision guidelines.* Ottawa, ON: Solicitor General of Canada.

Nunes, K. L., Firestone, P., Bradford, J. M., Greenberg, D. M., & Broom, I. (2002). A comparison of modified versions of the Static-99 and the Sex Offender Risk Appraisal Guide (SORAG). *Sexual Abuse: A Journal of Research and Treatment, 14*, 253–269.

N. Y Mental Hyg. Law § 10.01(e), (2010).

O'Connor v. Donaldson, 422 U.S. 563 (1975).

Olver, M. E., Beggs-Christofferson, S. M., Grace, R. C., & Wong, S. C. P. (2013). Incorporating change information into sexual offender risk assessments using the Violence Risk Scale–Sexual Offender Version. *Sexual Abuse: A Journal of Research and Treatment.* Advance online publication. doi: 10.1177/1079063213502679

O'Malley, S. S., Suh, C. S., & Strupp, H. H. (1983). The Vanderbilt Psychotherapy Process Scale: A report on the scale development and a process-outcome study. *Journal of Consulting and Clinical Psychology, 51*, 581–586.

O'Meara, K. P. (2009). Innocence lost? *Insight on the News, 15* (22).

Oskamp, S. (1982). Overconfidence in case-study judgments. In D. Kahneman, P. Slovic, & A. Tversky (Eds.), *Judgment under uncertainty: Heuristics and biases*. Cambridge: Cambridge University Press.

Otto, R., & Heilbrun, K. (2002). The practice of forensic psychology. A look toward the future in light of the past. *American Psychologist, 57*, 5–18. doi:10.1037//0003-066x.57.1.5

Otway, H., & Wynne, B. (1989). Risk communication: Paradigm and paradox. *Risk Analysis, 9*, 141–145.

Papachristou v. City of Jacksonville, 405 U.S. 156 (1972).

Parent, G., Guay, J., & Knight, R. A. (2011). An assessment of long-term risk of recidivism by adult sex offenders. *Criminal Justice and Behavior, 38*, 188–209.

Patrick, C. J. (2006). *Handbook of psychopathy*. New York: Guilford Press.

Pealer, J. A., & Latessa, E. J. (2004). Applying the principles of effective interventions to juvenile corrections. *Corrections Today*, 26–29.

People v. Ward, 952 N.E.2d 601 (1999).

Perilloux, C., Duntley, J. D., & Buss, D. M. (2012). The costs of rape. *Archives of Sexual Behavior, 41*, 1099–1106. doi:10.1007/s10508-011-9863-9

Peters, J. W. (October 9, 2014). Cry of G.O.P. in campaign: All is dismal. *New York Times*. Retrieved from http://www.nytimes.com/2014/10/10/us/politics/republican-strategy-midterm-elections.html?_r=0.

Peterson, W. W., Birdsall, T. G., & Fox, W. C. (1954). The theory of signal detectability. *IRE Professional Group on Information Theory, 4*, 171–212.

Petrila, J. P. (2009). Finding common ground between scientific psychology and the law. In J. L. Skeem, K. S. Douglas, & S. O. Lilienfeld, (Eds.), *Psychological science in the courtroom: Consensus and controversy* (pp. 387–407). New York, NY: The Guilford Press.

Petrunik, M. (1994). *Models of dangerousness: A cross jurisdictional review of dangerousness legislation and practice, public safety and emergency preparedness*. Canada. Retrieved from http://www.securitepublique.gc.ca/cnt/rsrcs/lbrr/ctlg/shwttls-eng.aspx?d=PS&i=2961626.

Phillips, L. D., & Edwards, W. (1966). Conservatism in a simple probability inference task. *Journal of Experimental Psychology, 72*, 346–354.

Phillips, V. L., Saks, M. J., & Peterson, J. L. (2001). The application of signal detection theory to decision-making in forensic science. *Journal of Forensic Science, 46*, 294–308.

Pidgeon, N., Kasperson, J., & Slovic, P. (2003). *The social amplification of risk*. Cambridge: Cambridge University Press.

Piquero, A. R. (2000). Assessing the relationships between gender, chronicity, seriousness, and offense skewness in criminal offending. *Journal of Criminal Justice, 28*, 103–116. doi:10.1016/S0047-2352(99)00040-9

Pittman, N., & Nugent, Q. (2011). *A snapshot of juvenile sex offender registration and notification laws: A survey of the United States*. Defender Association of Philadelphia. Retrieved from http://www.google.com/#q=a+snapshot+of+juvenile+sex+offender%27%27.

Pittman, N. (2014). Personal communication. July 24, 2014.

Plous, S. (1993). *The psychology of judgment and decision-making*. New York: McGraw-Hill.

Polanyi, M. (1958). *Personal knowledge*. Chicago: The University of Chicago Press.

Polanyi, M. (1964). *Science, faith and society*. Chicago: The University of Chicago Press.

Pope, J. C. (2008). Fear of crime and housing prices: Household reactions to sex offender registries. *Journal of Urban Economics, 64*, 601–614.

Popper, K. R. (1975). *The logic of scientific discovery*. London: Hutchinson & Co. Ltd.

Posner, K. A. (2010). *Stalking the black swan: Research and decision making in a world of extreme volatility*. New York: Columbia University Press.

Post, L. A., Mezey, N. J., Maxwell, C., & Wibert, W. N. (2002). The rape tax: Tangible and intangible costs of sexual violence. *Journal of Interpersonal Violence, 17*, 773–782.

Prentky, R. A. (2003). A 15-year retrospective on sexual coercion: Advances and projections. In R. A. Prentky, E. Janus, & M. Seto (Eds.), *Sexually coercive behavior: Understanding and management, Vol. 989* (pp. 13–32). New York: Annals of the New York Academy of Sciences.

Prentky, R. A., & Burgess, A. W. (1990). Rehabilitation of child molesters: A cost-benefit analysis. *American Journal of Orthopsychiatry, 60*, 108–117.

Prentky, R. A., & Burgess, A. W. (2000). *Forensic management of sexual offenders*. New York: Kluwer Academic/Plenum Publishers.

Prentky, R. A., Gabriel, A., & Coward, A. (2011). Treatment for perpetrators of sexual violence. In G. F. White, M. P. Koss, & A. E. Kazdin (Eds.), *Violence against women and children: Navigating solutions* (pp. 115–135). Washington, DC: American Psychological Association.

Prentky, R. A., Janus, E., Barbaree, H., Schwartz, B., & Kafka, K. (2006). Sexually violent predators in the courtroom: Science on trial. *Psychology, Public Policy, and Law, 12*, 357–393. doi: 10.1037/1076-8971.12.4.357

Prentky, R. A., Knight, R. A., & Lee, A. F. (1997). Risk factors associated with recidivism among extrafamilial child molesters. *Journal of Consulting and Clinical Psychology, 65*, 141–149.

Prentky, R. A., Knight, R. A., Lee, A. F., & Cerce, D. (1995). Predictive validity of lifestyle impulsivity for rapists. *Criminal Justice and Behavior, 22*, 106–128.

Prentky, R. A., & Lee, A. F. (2007). Effect of age-at-release on long term sexual re-offense rates in civilly committed sexual offenders. *Sexual Abuse: A Journal of Research and Treatment, 19*, 43–59.

Prentky, R. A., Lee, A. F., Knight, R. A., & Cerce, D. (1997). Recidivism rates among child molesters and rapists. *Law and Human Behavior, 21*, 635–659.

Prentky, R. A., Li, N. C., Righthand, S., Schuler, A., Cavanaugh, D., & Lee, A. F. (2010). Assessing risk of sexually abusive behavior among youth in a child welfare sample. *Behavioral Sciences and the Law, 28*, 24–45.

Prentky, R. A., Pimental, A., & Cavanaugh, D. (2009). Predicting risk of sexual recidivism in juveniles: Predictive validity of the J-SOAP-II. In A. R. Beech, L. A. Craig, & K. D. Browne (Eds.), *Assessment and treatment of sexual offenders: A handbook* (pp. 265–292). Chichester, UK: John Wiley & Sons.

Prentky, R. A., & Schwartz, B. (2006). *Invited VAWnet applied research forum document on treatment of adult sex offenders.* Retrieved from www.vawnet.org.

Prescott, J. J., & Rockoff, J. E. (2008, February). *Do sex offender registration and notification laws affect criminal behavior?* Retrieved from http://www.nber.org/papers/w13803.

President's Commission on Law Enforcement and Administration of Justice. (1967). *The challenge of crime in a free society.* Washington, DC: United States Government Printing Office.

Price, R. (1997). On the risks of risk prediction. *The Journal of Forensic Psychiatry, 8* (1), 1–4.

Quillian, L., & Pager, D. (2010). Estimating risk: Stereotype amplification and the perceived risk of criminal victimization. *Social Psychology Quarterly, 73* (1), 79–104.

Quinsey, V. L. (1980). The baserate problem and the prediction of dangerousness: A reappraisal. *The Journal of Psychiatry & Law, 8*, 329–340.

Quinsey, V. L., Coleman, G., Jones, B., & Altrows, I. F. (1997). Proximal antecedents of eloping and reoffending among supervised mentally-disordered offenders. *Journal of Interpersonal Violence, 12*, 794–813.

Quinsey, V. L., Harris, G. T., Rice, M. E., & Cormier, C. A. (1998). *Violent offenders: Appraising and managing risk.* Washington, DC: American Psychological Association.

Quinsey, V. L., Harris, G. T., Rice, M. E., & Cormier, C. A. (2006). *Violent offenders: Appraising and managing risk* (2nd ed.). Washington, DC: American Psychological Association.

Quinsey, V. L., & Maguire, A. (1986). Maximum security psychiatric patients: Actuarial and clinical prediction of dangerousness. *Journal of Interpersonal Violence, 1*, 143–171.

Radelet, M. L., Bedau, H. A., & Putnam, C. E. (1992). *In spite of innocence.* Boston: Northeastern University Press.

Rancan, A. (2013). Modigliani's and Simon's early contributions to uncertainty (1952–61). *History of Political Economy, 45*, 1–38. doi:10.1215/00182702-1965177

Rayner, S. (1988). Muddling through metaphors to maturity: A commentary on Kasperson et al. "The social amplification of risk". *Risk Analysis, 8*, 201–204.

Reitzel, L. R., & Carbonell, J. L. (2006). The effectiveness of sexual offender treatment for juveniles as measured by recidivism: A meta-analysis. *Sexual Abuse: A Journal of Research and Treatment, 18*, 401–421.

Renn, O., Burns, W. J., Kasperson, J., Kasperson, R. E., & Slovic, P. (1992). The social amplification of risk: Theoretical foundations and empirical applications. *Journal of Social Issues, 48*, 137–160. doi:10.1111/j.1540-4560.1992.tb01949.x

Rettenberger, M., & Eher, R. (2006). Actuarial assessment of sex offender recidivism risk: A validation of the German version of the Static-99. *Sexual Offender Treatment, 1*, 1–11.

Rettenberger, M., & Eher, R. (2007). Predicting reoffence in sexual offender subtypes: A prospective validation study of the German version of the Sex Offender Risk Appraisal Guide (SORAG). *Sexual Offender Treatment, 2*, 12.

Rettenberger, M., Matthes, A., Boer, D., & Eher, R. (2010). Prospective actuarial risk assessment: A comparison of five risk assessment instruments in different sexual offender subtypes. *International Journal of Offender Therapy and Comparative Criminology, 54*, 169–186.

Reyes, R. M., Thompson, W. C., & Bower, G. H. (1980). Judgmental biases resulting from differing availabilities of arguments. *Journal of Personality and Social Psychology, 39*, 2–12.

Reyna, V. F., & Zayas, V. (2014). *The neuroscience of risky decision-making*. Washington, DC: American Psychological Association Press.

Rice, M. E. (1997). Violent offender research and implications for the criminal justice system. *American Psychologist, 52*, 414–423.

Rice, M. E., & Harris, G. T. (1995). Violent recidivism: Assessing predictive validity. *Journal of Consulting and Clinical Psychology, 63*, 737–748.

Rice, M. E., & Harris, G. T. (1997). Cross validation and extension of the Violence Risk Appraisal Guide for child molesters and rapists. *Law and Human Behavior, 21*, 231–241.

Rice, M. E., & Harris, G. (2002). Men who molest their sexually immature daughters: Is a special explanation required? *Journal of Abnormal Psychology, 111*, 329–339.

Rice, M. E., & Harris, G. T. (2005). Comparing effect sizes in follow-up studies: ROC area, Cohen's d, and r. *Law and Human Behavior, 29*, 615–620.

Rice, M. E., Harris, G. T., & Quinsey, V. L. (1990). A follow-up of rapists assessed in a maximum-security psychiatric facility. *Journal of Interpersonal Violence, 5*, 435–448.

Rice, M. E., Quinsey, V. L., & Harris, G. T. (1991). Sexual recidivism among child molesters released from a maximum security institution. *Journal of Consulting and Clinical Psychology, 59*, 381–386.

Rice, M. E., Harris, G. T., Lang, C., & Cormier, C. A. (2006). Violent sex offenses: How are they best measured from official records. *Law and Human Behavior, 30*, 525–541.

Rind, B., Tromoich, P., & Bauserman, R. (1998). A meta-analytic examination of assumed properties of child sexual abuse college samples. *Psychological Bulletin, 124*, 22–53.

Rip, A. (1988). Should social amplification of risk be counteracted? *Risk Analysis, 8*, 193–197.

Robb, D. L. (2012). *The gumshoe and the shrink: Guenther Reinhardt, Dr. Arnold Hutschnecker, and the Secret History of the 1960 Kennedy/Nixon Election*. Solana Beach, CA: Santa Monica Press LLC.

Roberts, C. F., Doren, D., & Thornton, D. (2002). Dimensions associated with assessments of sex offender recidivism risk. *Criminal Justice and Behavior, 29*, 569–589.

Robinson, L. O. (2003). Sex offender management. The public policy challenges. In R. A. Prentky, E. Janus, & M. Seto (Eds.), *Sexually coercive behavior: Understanding and management* (pp. 1–7). New York: Annals of the New York Academy of Sciences.

Robinson v. California, 370 U.S. 660 (1962).

Rodriguez-Srednicki, O., & Twaite, J. A. (2004). Understanding and reporting child abuse: Legal and psychological perspectives. Part one: Physical abuse, sexual abuse, and neglect. *The Journal of Psychiatry and Law, 32*, 315–359.

Roeser, S. (2010). *Emotions and risky technologies*. Dordrecht: Springer.

Rogers, R. (1986). *Conducting insanity evaluations*. New York: Van Nostrand Reinhold.

Rogers, R., & Jackson, R. L. (2005). Sexually violent predators: The risky enterprise of risk assessment. *Journal of the American Academy Psychiatry and the Law, 33*, 528.

Roman, J. K., Dunworth, T., & Marsh, K. (Eds.). (2010). *Cost-benefit analysis and crime control*. Washington, DC: The Urban Institute Press. Retrieved from http://www.ncjrs.gov/app/publications/abstract.aspx?ID=254880.

Rosa, E. A. (2003). The logical structure of the social amplification of risk framework (SARF): Metatheoretical foundations and policy implications. In N. Pidgeon, J. Kasperson, & P. Slovic (Eds.), *The social amplification of risk* (pp. 47–79). Cambridge: Cambridge University Press.

Rose, N. (2002). At risk of madness. In T. Baker & J. Simon (Eds.), *Embracing risk: The changing culture of insurance and responsibility* (pp. 209–237). Chicago: The University of Chicago Press.

Ross, L. (1977). The intuitive psychologist and his shortcomings: Distortions in the attribution process. In L. Berkowitz (Ed.), *Advances in experimental social psychology, Vol. 10* (pp. 173–220). Orlando, FL: Academic Press.

Rossegger, A., Gerth, J., Singh, J. P., & Endrass, J. (2013). Examining the predictive validity of the SORAG in Switzerland. *Sexual Offender Treatment, 8*, 2.

Rowland, J. M., Greenleaf, L. J., Dorfman, W. J., & Davidson, D. L. (1993). Aging and sexual function in men. *Archives of Sexual Behavior, 22*, 545–557.

Rutherford, A. (2008). Sexual offenders and the path to a purified domain. In D. Downes, P. Rock, C. Chinkin, & C. Gearty (Eds.), *Crime, social control and human rights* (pp. 66–79). Portland, OR: Willan Publishing.

Rylsky, M. (1986). A town born of the atom. *Soviet Life, 7* (8), 13.

Sadoff, R. L. (1964). Psychiatric views of the sexual psychopath statutes. *Corrective Psychiatry and Journal of Social Therapy, 10*, 242–255.

Saks, M. J., & Neufeld, S. L. (2011). Convergent evolution in law and science: The structure of decision-making under uncertainty. *Law, Probability and Risk, 10*, 133–148. doi:10.1093/lpr/mgr005

Salerno, J. M., & Peter-Hagene, L. C. (2013). Interactive effect of anger and disgust on moral outrage and judgments. *Psychological Science, 24*, 2069–2078.

Saltzman, L. E., Green, Y. T., Marks, J. S., & Thacker, S. B. (2000). Violence against women as a public health issue: Comments from the CDC. *American Journal of Preventive Medicine, 19*, 325–329.

Sampson, R. J., & Laub, J. H. (2003). Life course desisters? Trajectories of crime among delinquent boys followed to age 70. *Criminology, 41*, 301–339.

Sampson, R. J., & Laub, J. H. (2005). A life-course view of the development of crime. *The Annals of the American Academy of Political and Social Science, 602*, 12–45. doi:10.1177/0002716205280075

Sandman, P. (1989). Hazard versus outrage in the public perception of risk. In V. T. Covello, D. B. McCallum, & M. T. Pavlova (Eds.), *Effective risk communication: The role and responsibility of government and nongovernmental organizations* (pp. 45–49). New York: Plenum Press.

San Francisco Chronicle. (2006). Effective against crime. *San Francisco Chronicle*.

Sarbin, T. R. (1943). A contribution to the study of actuarial and individual methods of prediction. *American Journal of Sociology, 48*, 593–602.
Sarbin, T. R. (1944). The logic of prediction in psychology. *Psychological Review, 51*, 210–228.
Sawyer, J. (1966). Measurement and prediction, clinical and statistical. *Psychological Bulletin, 66*, 178–200.
Schlesinger, S. E. (1979). Therapy on a treadmill: The role of the prison psychotherapist. *Professional Psychology, 10*, 307–317.
Schmidt, A. F., Gykiere, K., Vanhoeck, K., Mann, R., & Banse, R. (2014). Direct and indirect measures of sexual maturity preferences differentiate subtypes of child sexual abusers. *Sexual Abuse: A Journal of Research and Treatment, 26*, 107–128. doi: 10.1177/1079063213480817
Schopp, R. F. (1996). Communicating risk assessments: Accuracy, efficacy, and responsibility. *American Psychologist, 51*, 939–944.
Schrag, C. (1973). *Crime and justice: American style.* Washington, DC: National Institute of Mental Health.
Schroeder, M. (1991). *Fractals, chaos, power laws: Minutes from an infinite universe.* New York: Freeman.
Scurich, N., & John, R. S. (2011). The effect of framing actuarial risk probabilities on involuntary civil commitment decisions. *Law and Human Behavior, 35*, 83–91. doi:10.1007/s10979-010-9218-4
Scurich, N., & John, R. S. (2012a). Prescriptive approaches to communicating the risk of violence in actuarial risk assessment. *Psychology, Public Policy, and Law, 18*, 50–78. doi:10.1037/a0024592
Scurich, N., & John, R. S. (2012b). A Bayesian approach to the group versus individual prediction controversy in actuarial risk assessment. *Law and Human Behavior, 36*, 246. doi:10.1037/h0093973
Scurich, N., Monahan, J., & John, R. S. (2012). Innumeracy and unpacking: Bridging the nomothetic/idiographic divide in violence risk assessment. *Law and Human Behavior, 36*, 548–554.
Selvog, H. H. (2001). Social state to penal state: Moral panic and sex offenders: Megan's Law as a result of moral panic. *Justice Policy Journal, 1*, 72–93.
*Seto, M. C. (2005). Is more better? Combining actuarial risk scales to predict recidivism among adult sex offenders. *Psychological Assessment, 17*, 156–167. doi:10.1037/1040-3590.17.2.156
Seto, M. C., Harris, G. T., Rice, M. E., & Barbaree, H. E. (2004). The screening scale for pedophilic interests predicts recidivism among adult sex offenders with child victims. *Archives of Sexual Behavior, 33*, 455–466.
Seto, M. C., & Lalumiere, M. L. (2001). A brief screening scale to identify pedophilic interests among child molesters. *Sexual Abuse: A Journal of Research and Treatment, 13*, 15–25.
Seto, M. C., Marques, J. K., Harris, G. T., Chaffin, M., Lalumiere, M. L., Miner, M. L. et al. (2008). Good science and progress in sex offender treatment are intertwined: A response to Marshall and Marshall (2007). *Sexual Abuse: A Journal of Research and Treatment, 20*, 247–255.
Shah, S. A. (1975). Dangerousness and civil commitment of the mentally ill: Some public policy considerations. *American Journal of Psychiatry, 132* (5), 501–505.

Shah, S. A. (February, 1977). Editorial. *American Psychological Association Monitor, 8*, 2.

Shah, S. A. (1978). Dangerousness: A paradigm for exploring some issues in law and psychology. *American Psychologist, 33*, 224–238. doi:10.1037/0003-066X.33.3.224

Shapiro, D. L. (1984). *Psychological evaluation and expert testimony: A practical guide to forensic work*. New York: Van Nostrand Reinhold.

Shapiro, D. L. (1991). *Forensic psychological assessment: An integrative approach*. Boston: Allyn & Bacon.

Sheppes, G., Scheibe, S., Suri, G., & Gross, J. J. (2011). Emotion-regulation choice. *Psychological Science, 22*, 1391–1396. doi:10.1177/0956797611418350

Sherman, L. W., Gartin, P. R., & Buerger, M. E. (1989). Hot spots of predatory crime: Routine activities and the criminology of place. *Criminology, 27*, 27–55.

Shrader-Frechette, K. S. (1991). *Risk and rationality*. Berkeley, CA: University of California Press.

Shuman, D. W., & Zervopoulos, J. A. (2010). Empathy or objectivity: The forensic examiner's dilemma? *Behavioral Sciences and the Law, 28*, 585–602.

Siegel, M. (February, 1977). Editorial. *American Psychological Association Monitor, 8*, 5.

Silver, N. (2012). *The signal and the noise: Why so many predictions fail—but some don't*. New York: Penguin Press.

Simon, H. A. (1955). A behavioral model of rational choice. *The Quarterly Journal of Economics, 69*, 99–118. doi:10.2307/1884852

Singh, J. P., Desmarais, S. L., & VanDorn, R. A. (2013). Measurement of predictive validity in violence risk assessment studies: A second-order systematic review. *Behavioral Sciences and the Law, 31* (1), 55–73. doi:10.1002/bsl.2053

Singh, J. P., Grann, M., & Fazel, S. (2011). A comparative study of violence risk assessment tools: A systematic review and metaregression analysis of 68 studies involving 25,980 participants. *Clinical Psychology Review, 31*, 449–513.

Sjöstedt, G., & Långström, N. (2001). Actuarial assessment of sex offender recidivism risk: A cross-validation of the RRASOR and the Static-99 in Sweden. *Law and Human Behavior, 25*, 629–645.

Sjöstedt, G., & Långström, N. (2002). Assessment of risk for criminal recidivism among rapists: A comparison of four different measures. *Psychology, Crime and the Law, 8*, 25–40.

Skeem, J., & Monahan, J. (2011). Current directions in violence risk assessment. *Current Directions in Psychological Science, 20* (1), 38–42. doi:10.1177/0963721410397271

Skeem, J., Polaschek, D. L. L., Patrick, C. J., & Lilienfeld, S. O. (2011). Psychopathic personality: Bridging the gap between scientific evidence and public policy. *Psychological Science in the Public Interest, 12*, 95–162.

Skelton, A., & Vess, J. (2008). Risk of sexual recidivism as a function of age and actuarial risk. *Journal of Sexual Aggression, 14*, 199–209.

Skelton, A., Riley, D., Wales, D., & Vess, J. (2006). Assessing risk for sexual offenders in New Zealand: Development and validation of a computer-scored risk measure. *Journal of Sexual Aggression, 12*, 277–286.

Slobogin, C. (2010). The right to voice reprised. *Seton Hall Law Review, 40* (4), 1647–1662.

Sloman, S. A. (1996). The empirical case for two systems of reasoning. *Psychological Bulletin, 119*, 3–22.

Slovic, P. (1987). Perception of risk. *Science, 236*, 280–285.

Slovic, P. (1992). Perception of risk: Reflections on the psychometric paradigm. In S. Krimsky & D. Golding (Eds.), *Social theories of risk* (pp. 117–152). New York: Praeger.

Slovic, P. (2000). The perception of risk. In P. Slovic (Ed.), *The perception of risk* (pp. 220–231). London: Earthscan Publications.

Slovic, P. (2010). *The feeling of risk: New perspectives on risk perception.* New York: Earthscan Publications.

Slovic, P., Finucane, M. L., Peters, E., & MacGregor, D. G. (2002). Rational actors or rational fools: Implications of the affect heuristic for behavioral economics. *Journal of Socio-Economics, 31*, 329–342.

Slovic, P., Finucane, M. L., Peters, E., & MacGregor, D. G. (2004). Risk as analysis and risk as feelings: Some thoughts about affect, reason, risk, and rationality. *Risk Analysis, 24*, 311–322.

Slovic, P., Fischhoff, B., & Lichtenstein, S. (1982). Facts versus fears: Understanding perceived risk. In D. Kahneman, P. Slovic, & A. Tversky (Eds.), *Judgment under uncertainty: Heuristics and biases* (pp. 463–489). Cambridge: Cambridge University Press.

Slovic, P., Fischhoff, B., & Lichtenstein, S. (2000). Cognitive processes and societal risk taking. In P. Slovic (Ed.), *The perception of risk* (pp. 32–50). London: Earthscan Publications.

Slovic, P., Kunreuther, H., & White, G. F. (2000). Decision processes, rationality and adjustment to natural hazards. In P. Slovic (Ed.), *The perception of risk* (pp. 1–31). London: Earthscan Publications.

Slovic, P., Monahan, J., & MacGregor, D. G. (2000). Violence risk assessment and risk communication: The effects of using actual cases, providing instruction, and employing probability versus frequency formats. *Law and Human Behavior, 24*, 271–296.

Slovic, P., & Peters, E. (2006). Risk perception and affect. *Current Directions in Psychological Science, 15* (6), 322–325.

Slovic, P., Peters, E., Finucane, M. L., & MacGregor, D. G. (2005). Affect, risk, and decision making. *Health Psychology, 24* (4 Suppl), S35–S40.

Smid, W. J., Kamphuis, J. H., Wever, E. C., & Van Beek, D. J. A comparison of the predictive properties of nine sex offender risk assessment instruments. *Psychological Assessment, 26* (3), 691–703. doi:10.1037/a0036616

Solomon, M. (1978). Jimmy Carter and playboy: A sociolinguistic perspective on style. *Quarterly Journal of Speech, 64*, 173–182. doi:10.1080/00335637809383423

Spaeth, E. G. (1988). A judge's three worlds: Proof, philosophy, and the prison. *Bulletin of the American Academy of Psychiatry and the Law, 16*, 123–130.

Stadtland, C., Hollweg, M., Kleindienst, N., Dietl, J., Reich, U., & Nedopil, N. (2005). Risk assessment and prediction of violent and sexual recidivism in sex offenders: Long-term predictive validity of four risk assessment instruments. *Journal of Forensic Psychiatry and Psychology, 16*, 92–108.

Stanislaw, H., & Todorov, N. (1999). Calculation of signal detection theory measures. *Behavior Research Methods, Instruments, and Computers, 31*, 137–149.

State of Minnesota ex rel. Pearson v. Probate Court 309 U.S. 270 (60 S.Ct. 523, 84 L.Ed. 744).

Steenbarger, B. N. (2002). *The psychology of trading: Tools and techniques for minding the markets.* Hoboken, NJ: Wiley.

Steinberg, L., Cauffman, E., Woolard, J., Graham, S., & Banich, M. (2014). Reconciling the complexity of human development with the reality of legal policy. *American Psychologist, 64*, 601–604.

Sunstein, C. R. (2002). Probability neglect: Emotions, worst cases, and law. *The Yale Law Journal, 112*, 61–107.

Sunstein, C. R. (2003). Terrorism and probability neglect. *The Journal of Risk and Uncertainty, 26*, 121–136.

Sunstein, C. R. (2005). *Laws of fear.* Cambridge: Cambridge University Press.

Sutherland, E. H. (1950a). The diffusion of sexual psychopath laws. *American Journal of Sociology, 56*, 142–148.

Sutherland, E. H. (1950b). The sexual psychopath laws. *Journal of Criminal Law and Criminology, 40*, 543–554.

Swets, J. A. (1973). The relative operating characteristic in psychology. *Science, 182*, 990–1000.

Swets, J. A. (1986). Forms of empirical ROCs in discrimination and diagnostic tasks: Implications for theory and measurement performance. *Psychological Bulletin, 99*, 181–198.

Swets, J. A. (1992). The science of choosing the right decision threshold in high-stakes diagnostics. *American Psychologist, 47*, 522–532.

Swets, J. A., Dawes, R. M., & Monahan, J. (2000). Psychological science can improve diagnostic decisions. *Psychological Science in the Public Interest, 1*, 1–26.

Szczurek, L., Monin, B., & Gross, J. J. (2012). The stranger effect: The rejection of affective deviants. *Psychological Science, 23*, 1105–1111.

Szmukler, G., & Rose, N. (2013). Risk assessment in mental health care: Values and costs. *Behavioral Sciences and the Law, 31*, 125–140. doi:10.1002/bsl.2046

Taleb, N. N. (1978). *Antifragile: Things that gain from disorder.* New York: Random House.

Taleb, N. N. (2005). *Fooled by randomness: The hidden role of chance in life and in the markets.* New York: Random House.

Taleb, N. N. (2007). *The black swan: The impact of the highly improbable.* New York: Random House.

Tanner Jr, W. P., & Swets, J. A. (1954). A decision-making theory of visual detection. *Psychological Review, 61*, 401–409. doi:10.1037/h0058700

Taube, D. O., & Elwork, A. (1990). Researching the effects of confidentiality law on patients' self-disclosures. *Professional Psychology: Research and Practice, 21*, 72–75.

Taylor, S. E., & Fiske, S. T. (1978). Salience, attention, and attribution: Top of the head phenomena. In L. Berkowitz (Ed.), *Advances in Experimental Social Psychology* (pp. 249–288). New York: Academic Press.

Tetlock, P. E. (2005). *Expert political judgment: How good is it? How can we know?* Princeton, NJ: Princeton University Press.

Thomas, E. A. C., & Hogue, A. (1976). Apparent weight of evidence, decision criteria, and confidence ratings in juror decision making. *Psychological Review, 83*, 442–465.

Thompson, K. (1998). *Moral panics*. London: Routledge.

Thornton, D. (2002). Constructing and testing a framework for dynamic risk assessment. *Sexual Abuse: A Journal of Research and Treatment, 14*, 139–153.

Thornton, D. (2006). Age and sexual recidivism: A variable connection. *Sexual Abuse: A Journal of Research and Treatment, 18*, 123–135.

Thornton, D., & Hanson, R. K. (2003). *Models of real re-offence rates: Clinical implications*. St. Louis, MO: Annual Meeting of the Association for the Treatment of Sexual Abusers.

Thornton, D., & Knight, R. A. (2013). Construction and validation of SRA-FV Need Assessment. *Sexual Abuse: A Journal of Research and Treatment*. doi:10.1177/1079063213511120

Tjaden, P., & Thoennes, N. (November 1988). Prevalence, Incidence, and Consequences of Violence Against Women: Findings From the National Violence Against Women Survey. National Institute of Justice. Centers for Disease Control and Prevention. Research in Brief. https://www.ncjrs.gov/pdffiles/172837.pdf.

Turchik, J. A., & Edwards, K. M. (2012). Myths about male rape: A literature review. *Psychology of Men and Masculinity, 13*, 211–226.

Tversky, A., & Kahneman, D. (1971). The belief in the law of small numbers. *Psychological Bulletin, 76*, 105–110.

Tversky, A., & Kahneman, D. (1972). *Availability as a determinant of frequency and probability judgments* (Oregon Research Institute Technical Report 12 (1)). Oregon Research Institute.

Tversky, A., & Kahneman, D. (1973). Availability: A heuristic for judging frequency and probability. *Cognitive Psychology, 5*, 207–232.

Tversky, A., & Kahneman, D. (1974). Judgment under uncertainty: Heuristics and biases. *Science, 185*, 1124–1130.

Tversky, A., & Kahneman, D. (1982). Judgment under uncertainty: Heuristics and biases. In D. Kahneman, P. Slovic, & A. Tversky (Eds.), *Judgment under uncertainty: Heuristics and biases* (pp. 3–20). New York: Cambridge University Press.

Tyler, T. R. (2001). Trust and law-abidingness: A proactive model of social regulation. *Boston University Law Review, 81*, 361–406.

United States v. Salerno, 481 U.S. 739 (1987).

Urbaniok, F., Noll, T., Grunewald, S., Steinbach, J., & Endrass, J. (2006). Prediction of violent and sexual offences: A replication study of the VRAG in Switzerland. *Journal of Forensic Psychiatry and Psychology, 17*, 23–31.

Vars, F. E. (2011). Rethinking the indefinite detention of sex offenders. *Connecticut Law Review, 44* (1), 161–194.

Vaughan, K. (October 10, 2014). *James Winston rape investigation hampered by police, FSU*. Retrieved from http://nypost.com/2014/10/10/jameis-winston-investigation-hammpered-by-police-fsu.

Viljoen, J. L., Mordell, S., & Benetau, J. L. (2012). Prediction of adolescent sexual reoffending: A meta-analysis of the J-SOAP-II, ERASOR, J-SORRAT-II and Static-00. *Law and Human Behavior, 36*, 423–438. doi:10.1037/h0093938

Vitacco, M. J., Gonsalves, V., Tomony, J., Smith, B., & Lishner, D. A. (2012). Can standardized measures of risk predict inpatient violence? *Social Psychiatry and Psychiatric Epidemiology, 47*, 627–637.

von Bertalanffy, L. (1968). *General system theory*. New York: Braziller.

Vrieze, S. I., & Grove, W. M. (2010). Multidimensional assessment of criminal recidivism: Problems, pitfalls, and proposed solutions. *Psychological Assessment, 22*, 382–395.

Vygotsky, L. (1992). An analysis of closing arguments to a jury. *New York Law School Review, 37*, 55–122.

Vygotsky, L. (1997). Ethical behavior. In *Educational Psychology* (pp. 227). Boca Raton, FL: St. Lucie Press.

Wald, A. (1950). *Statistical decision functions*. New York: John Wiley & Sons.

Warr, M. (2000). Fear of crime in the United States: Avenues for research and policy. Measurement and analysis of crime and justice. *Criminal Justice, 4*, 450–489. Retrieved from http://www.crime-reg.com/police/warr fear of crime.pdf.

Warren, S. D., & Brandeis, L. D. (1890). The right to privacy. *Harvard Law Review, 4*, 193–196.

Webster's New Universal Unabridged Dictionary. (1983). New York, NY: Simon & Schuster/ Dorset & Barber.

Webster, C. D., Douglas, K. S., Eaves, D., & Hart, S. D. (1997). *HCR-20: Assessing risk for violence, version* 2. Burnaby, BC: Mental Health, Law, and Policy Institute, Simon Fraser University. Retrieved from sfu.ca/psychology/groups/mhlpi/hcr-20.htm.

Weisberg, J. (2009). Locating IBE in the Bayesian framework. *Synthese, 167*, 125–143.

Weiss, J. W., & Weiss, D. J. (2009). *A science of decision making: The legacy of Ward Edwards*. Oxford: Oxford University Press.

Welch, M. (2000). *Flag burning: Moral panic and the criminalization of protest*. New York: Aldine de Gruyter.

White, P. (July 5, 2012). *Rapists in the ranks*. Boulder Weekly. Retrieved from http://wwwboulderweekly.com/article-9090-rapists-in-the-ranks.html.

White, W. F. (1929). *Rope and faggot: A biography of Judge Lynch*. New York: Knopf.

Whitting, L., Day, A., & Powell, M. (2014). The impact of community notification on the management of sex offenders in the community: An Australian perspective. *Australian and New Zealand Journal of Criminology, 47*, 240–258.

Wildavsky, A. (1979). No risk is the highest risk of all. *American Scientist, 67*, 32–37.

Wilkens, J. (May 6, 2010). Predators' paradise: Coalinga mental hospital. *Union Tribune*. http://www.utsandiego.com/news/2010/may/16/predators-paradise-coalinga-mental-hospital/.

Williamson, R. M. (2008). "A little neglect may breed great mischief". Retrieved from http://swspitcrew.com/articles/For%20the%20want%20of%20a%20nail%201108.pdf.

Wilson, R. J., Looman, J., Abracen, J., & Pake, D. K. (2013). Comparing sexual offenders at the Regional Treatment Centre (Ontario) and the Florida Civil Commitment Center. *International Journal of Offender Therapy and Comparative Criminology, 57*, 377–395.

Wilson, R. J., Picheca, J., & Prinzo, M. (2007). Evaluating the effectiveness of professionally-facilitated volunteerism in the community-based management of high-risk sexual offenders: Part two—a comparison of recidivism rates. *The Howard Journal, 46*, 327–337.

Windholz, M. J., & Silberschatz, G. (1988). Vanderbilt Psychotherapy Process Scale: A replication with adult outpatients. *Journal of Consulting and Clinical Psychology, 56*, 56–60.

Witt, P. H., Dattilio, F. M., & Bradford, J. M. (2011). Sex offender evaluations. In E. Y. Drogin, F. M. Dattilio, R. L. Sadoff, & T. G. Gutheil (Eds.), *Handbook of forensic assessment: Psychological and psychiatric perspectives* (pp. 97–120). New York: Wiley.

Wolfgang, M. E., Figlio, R. M., & Sellin, T. (1972). *Delinquency in a birth cohort.* Chicago: University of Chicago Press.

Wolfgang, M. E. (1988). The medical model versus the just deserts model. *Bulletin of the American Academy of Psychiatry and the Law, 16*, 111–121.

Wollert, R. (2001). Adversarial forum: An analysis of the argument that clinicians under-predict sexual violence in civil commitment cases. *Behavioral Sciences and the Law, 19*, 171–184.

Wollert, R. (2006). Low base rates limit expert certainty when current actuarials are used to identify sexually-violent predators: An application of Bayes's Theorem. *Psychology, Public Policy and Law, 12*, 56–85.

Wollert, R., Cramer, E., Waggoner, J., Skelton, A., & Vess, J. (2010). Recent research (N=9,305) underscores the importance of using age-stratified actuarial tables in sex offender risk assessments. *Sexual Abuse: A Journal of Research and Treatment, 22*, 490. doi:10.1177/1079063210384633.

Woods, K. M., & McNamara, J. R. (1980). Confidentiality: Its effect on interviewee behavior. *Professional Psychology, 11*, 714–721.

Woodworth, G. G., & Kadane, J. B. (2004). Expert testimony supports post-sentence civil incarceration of violent sexual offenders. *Law, Probability and Risk, 3*, 241.

Yoon, S. O., Suk, K., Goo, J. K., Lee, J., & Lee, S. M. (2013). The devil is in the specificity: The negative effect of prediction specificity on prediction accuracy. *Psychological Science, 27*, 1164–1170.

Zajonc, R. (1980). Feeling and thinking: Preferences need no inferences. *American Psychologist, 35*, 151–175.

Zajonc, R. (1984). On the primacy of effect. *American Psychologist, 39*, 117–123.

Zevitz, R. G., & Farkas, M. A. (2000a). *Sex offender community notification: Assessing the impact in Wisconsin* (NCJ179992). Washington, DC: United States Department of Justice.

Zevitz, R. G., & Farkas, M. A. (2000b). Impact of sex-offender community notification on probation/parole in Wisconsin. *International Journal of Offender Therapy and Comparative Criminology, 44*, 8–21.

Zevitz, R. G., & Farkas, M. A. (2000c). Sex offender notification: Managing high risk criminals or exacting further vengeance. *Behavioral Sciences and the Law, 18*, 375–391.

AUTHOR INDEX

SUBJECT INDEX